The Melody of Time

The Melody of Time

Music and Temporality in the Romantic Era

BENEDICT TAYLOR

OXFORD
UNIVERSITY PRESS

OXFORD

UNIVERSITY PRESS

Oxford University Press is a department of the University of
Oxford. It furthers the University's objective of excellence in research,
scholarship, and education by publishing worldwide.
Oxford is a registered trade mark of Oxford University Press
in the UK and in certain other countries.

Published in the United States of America by
Oxford University Press
198 Madison Avenue, New York, NY 10016

This volume is published with generous support of the John Daverio
Endowment of the American Musicological Society, funded in part by the
National Endowment for the Humanities and the Andrew W. Mellon Foundation.

Library of Congress Cataloging-in-Publication Data
Taylor, Benedict, 1981–
The melody of time: music and temporality in the romantic era / Benedict Taylor.
pages cm
Includes bibliographical references and index.
ISBN 978-0-19-020605-5 (hardback: alk. paper)   1. Time in music.   2. Music—19th century—
Philosophy and aesthetics.   3. Music—19th century—History and criticism.   I. Title.
ML3845.T37 2015
780.9′034—dc23
2015010445

1 3 5 7 9 8 6 4 2
Printed in the United States of America
on acid-free paper

CONTENTS

ACKNOWLEDGEMENTS

This book is the result of several years' work but even longer musing about the problematics of music and temporality. It probably started at Princeton, where, having just completed my PhD on time and memory in Mendelssohn's instrumental music, Scott Burnham's casual remark that 'somebody ought to write a study of temporality in Beethoven's last three piano sonatas' slowly set off a chain of events that led rather improvidently to my current undertaking. From this period stems the conception of chapters one and four, and I would especially like to thank Scott for his generous support and advice throughout this project and Simon Morrison for his input into what became chapter four. Later at Oxford, long discussions with Eric Clarke, generous critical comments on drafts from Daniel Grimley, Susan Wollenberg, and Kofi Agawu, and conversations with Martin Pickup and Tim Williamson over coffee or tea at New College all greatly contributed to the development of various chapters. Numerous students at Magdalen and New College and the graduates attending my 'Music and Temporality' Master's course in the Faculty of Music also shared my puzzlement concerning the nature of music and time and helped focus my inchoate thoughts through their curiosity and readiness to venture suggestions.

Halfway through writing, attending the Music and Philosophy Conference on 'Time Theories and Music' at the Ionian University of Corfu in April 2012 proved an invaluable stimulus to completing the remaining chapters, and I would like to thank Robin Le Poidevin, Jeremy Shapiro, Magdaleni Tsevreni, and Panos Vlagopoulos for their willingness to share ideas and listen to my often unformed ruminations. Several parts of the book have been presented at other conferences across Europe and America, and I gratefully acknowledge all those who have proffered comments and questions (especially Andreas Dorschel, Lydia Goehr, Clemens Risi, and Aidan Thomson), alongside the advice, support, and welcome doses of sanity offered throughout by Michael Burden, Hermann Danuser, Rachel Moore, Adeline Mueller, Michael Philips, and Dean

Sutcliffe. Nathaniel once again helped with the formatting of the musical examples while Damian saved the manuscript from several errors that had eluded me. At Oxford University Press Suzanne Ryan has been a wonderfully supportive editor, and the final manuscript has greatly benefited from the comments of the anonymous readers. Finally I would like to express my gratitude to the Proctor Fellowship Trustees, the Alexander von Humboldt Stiftung, the Andrew W. Mellon Foundation, Magdalen College, and New College Oxford, for the generous opportunities and financial support they have provided along the way.

Permission to reproduce the cover illustration, *Phantasie über die Musik* after Carl Gustav Carus, was kindly granted by the Stiftung Weimarer Klassik, and the image for Carus's *Die Musik*, reproduced in the introductory chapter, was provided by AKG Images. The copy of Nicolas Poussin's *A Dance to the Music of Time* also found in the introduction is taken from the public domain image on Wikimedia Commons: http://commons.wikimedia.org/wiki/File%3AThe_ dance_to_the_music_of_time_c._1640.jpg. A small section from chapter two is used in revised form as the introduction to a much longer discussion in 'The Triumph of Time in the Eighteenth Century: Handel's *Il trionfo del Tempo* and historical conceptions of musical temporality', *Eighteenth-Century Music*, 11/2 (September 2014), 257–81, © Cambridge University Press, and different versions of chapters three and four have appeared, respectively, as 'Schubert and the Construction of Memory: The Quartet in A minor, D. 804 ('Rosamunde')', *Journal of the Royal Musical Association*, 139/1 (Spring 2014), 41–88, © Taylor & Francis, and 'Temporality in Russian Music and the Notion of Development', *Music & Letters*, 94/1 (February 2013), 78–118, published by Oxford University Press.

ἐξ ὧν δὲ ἡ γένεσίς ἐστι τοῖς οὖσι, καὶ τὴν φθορὰν εἰς ταῦτα γίνεσθαι κατὰ τὸ χρεών· διδόναι γὰρ αὐτὰ δίκην καὶ τίσιν ἀλλήλοις τῆς ἀδικίας κατὰ τὴν τοῦ χρόνου τάξιν.

(All things that are created of necessity also perish; for they must pay the penalty and make atonement to one another for their injustice according to Time's decree.)

—Anaximander, Fragment DK12 B1

The Melody of Time

Introduction

Before the earliest surviving words of Western philosophy, before even history, there was myth. The one that I would like to relate here is that of Cronus, swallowing up his children. Hegel, in common with many of his contemporaries, found the urge to identify the child-devouring titan Cronus with the Orphic deity Chronos, symbolising time, altogether irresistible. 'Cronus, this chief Titan. . .obviously signifies time: he swallows all his children just as time annihilates everything it has brought to birth. This myth is not lacking in symbolical meaning', thought Hegel. 'For natural life is in fact subjected to time and brings into existence only the ephemeral'.[1]

That these reflections are made in the *Lectures on Aesthetics* is no coincidence. For 'the muse', Hegel adds, 'gives duration and consolidation to everything which as natural life and actual action is only ephemeral, and in the course of time has passed away'. 'Art liberates the true content of phenomena from the pure appearance and deception of this bad, transitory world, and gives them a higher actuality, born of the spirit'. 'The individual living thing in nature is transient, vanishing, changeable in outward appearance, while the work of art persists'.[2]

Of all the arts music is seemingly the most temporal and most transient. This attribute had helped lead Kant, infamously, to relegate it to the lowest position within the fine arts. Yet somehow by Hegel's generation music had gained a higher foothold on the philosophers' Parnassus. How had it overcome its temporal limitations? Might its apparent physical incorporeally and transience in fact have become a virtue? Could it even have suggested the overcoming of time? After all, Zeus escaped and overthrew Cronus and the reign of the titans. And from the union of Zeus and Mnemosyne (Memory) came the nine Muses, as similarly from Zeus and Leto arose Apollo, the god of music and diviner of the future.[3] Just as Orpheus had triumphed over Hades, so would music in a

---

[1] Georg Wilhelm Friedrich Hegel, *Aesthetics: Lectures on Fine Art*, trans. T.M. Knox, 2 vols. (Oxford: Clarendon Press, 1975), vol. II, p. 459.

[2] Ibid., pp. 459, 9, 29.

[3] Hesiod, *Theogony*, 40–43; 916–18.

1

manner triumph over time. Or perhaps Hegel's identification of Chronos with the child-eating Cronus was merely inaccurate—like, for its many critics, the overwrought claims and false identities symptomatic of idealist philosophy.

Such sentiments on time's fugitive nature are contained in an otherwise unremarkable poem entitled 'Die Zeit' (Time) from 1813, written at much the same time as Hegel was developing his philosophical thought. The poem connects a group of themes that had long been associated—time as transience, irreversibility, and mortality; time as breath (and implicitly therefore as spirit and consciousness); time as sound or music—and connects all these to moral virtue in a somewhat conventional way.

Unaufhaltsam rollt sie hin	Rolling unrelenting on
Nicht mehr kehrt die Holde wieder	The fair one returns no more again
Stät im Lebenslauf Begleiterin	Companion through the course of life
Senkt sie sich mit uns ins Grab hernieder.	She descends with us into the grave below.
Nur ein Hauch!—und er ist Zeit	But a breath!—for such is time
Hauch! schwind' würdig ihr dort nieder	Breath! pass ye worthily away
Hin zum Stuhle der Gerechtigkeit	Towards the throne of justice
Bringe deines Mundes Tugendlieder!	Voicing your songs of virtue!
Nur ein Schall! und er ist Zeit	But a sound!—for such is time
Schall! schwind' würdig ihr dort nieder	Sound! pass ye worthily away
Hin zum Sitze der Barmherzigkeit	Towards the seat of mercy
Schütte reuig Flehen vor ihm nieder!	Pouring out penitence before it!
Unaufhaltsam rollt sie hin	Rolling unrelenting on
Nicht mehr kehrt die Holde wieder	The fair one returns no more again
Stät im Lebenslauf Begleiterin	Companion through the course of life
Senkt sie sich mit uns ins Grab hernieder.	She descends with us into the grave below.[4]

---

[4] Schubert, 'Die Zeit', May 1813, in Otto Erich Deutsch, *Schubert: Die Dokumente seines Lebens* (Kassel: Bärenreiter, 1964), p. 25; a rather freer translation is given in Deutsch, *Schubert: A Documentary Biography*, trans. Eric Blom (London: Dent, 1947), pp. 31–2.

Introduction 3

Taken by itself the poem would barely be worthy of note were it not for the fact that it was penned by the sixteen-year-old Franz Schubert. Though the poem speaks of the transience equally of time and sound, Schubert's own compositional efforts within a year of its creation would seem to point in at least one sense to the persistence of music within history.

A third and final example here of the relation perceived between music and time in the early nineteenth century is given by the painter, physician, and natural scientist Carl Gustav Carus in two paintings styled after music. How music, this most temporal and least visual of the arts, might be depicted in this most spatial of art forms already suggests the presence of a paradox. Both of Carus's works are saturated with Romantic tropes to an extent that might seem overblown for a present-day audience but would have fitted perfectly into some *Frühromantik* panegyric to music's ineffable powers.[5] In the 1823 *Phantasie über die Musik* (reproduced as the cover of this book) and *Die Musik* from 1826 (illustrated below in Fig. 0.1), Carus focuses on Romantic images suggestive of incorporeity, ethereality, and ephemerality to express the uncertain ontology of music. The angelic harp stands on the gothic balcony, bathed in a moonlight whose intangibility and secretive, silver beauty seem a perfect match for the ungraspable being and mystery of music. In the background to each picture the dim outline of a Gothic cathedral is also seen; the implication appears to be that music is a form of divine worship as found in the tenets of Romantic art-religion and echoed in the young Schubert's poem.

Most evident in both paintings is the absence of any performer. Human agency seems lacking for this music; instead a natural or even supernatural cause is posited. In the 1823 painting the shroud enfolds, wraith-like, the presumed body of the player, a body which is entirely invisible to the observer. This lack of materiality, a fitting complement to the use of moonlight as source of illumination, forms a clear correlate to the incorporeal and invisible substance of music. Music transcends the representational. In accordance with the strictures of the early Romantics, Carus's painting calls attention again to the limits of what can be denoted within its medium. That all this occurs at night only further suggests the denial of traditional Enlightenment values of visuality and rational observation.

In the 1826 version, a translucent angelic shape materialises out of the harp as if giving shape to the musical sounds that are presumed to be produced. Yet

[5] The writings of Wackenroder spring to mind (discussed here in chapter two). The original oil version of the 1823 picture is missing, the image surviving in an 1827 gouache copy that was presented to Goethe (by no means a supporter of Romantic excess), who pronounced it highly Romantic and declared himself very satisfied with the gift. See Stefan Grosche, *'Zarten Seelen ist gar viel gegönnt': Naturwissenschaft und Kunst im Briefwechsel zwischen C.G. Carus und Goethe* (Göttingen: Wallstein, 2001), pp. 149–50.

Fig. 0.1 Carl Gustav Carus, *Die Musik* (1826). (Galerie Neue Meister, Staatliche Kunstsammlungen Dresden)

its apparent materiality is illusive. The angel, like music, 'casts no shadow'. Music may possess form and shape without having physical substance. The angel also points to an unexpected though fitting link with time. In Aquinas's *Summa Theologica*, angels are claimed to exist in aeviternity, a middle point between the imperfection of human time and the perfection of God's eternity: partaking of elements of both, they are temporal and yet transcend time.[6]

[6] St Thomas Aquinas, *Summa Theologica*, I, 10.5. The musicologist Barbara Barry, in her book dealing with this very question of music and time, similarly describes musical time as something special, as with Aquinas's angelic aeviternity a state existing between time and eternity (*Musical Time: The Sense of Order* [Stuyvesant, NY: Pendragon Press, 1990], pp. 266–73).

Fig. 0.2 Nicholas Poussin, *The Dance to the Music of Time* (1634–6). (The Wallace Collection, London)

The use of the harp, the most evident symbol for music in the picture, is traditional in painterly depictions of this art form, bringing with it further angelic and beatific connotations. The lack of bodily presence of any performer might be thought to connect to the Romantic infatuation with the natural and untutored, such as was provided by the Aeolian harp on which the wind's breath created its natural and mysterious melodies. Music is thus depicted as a natural or divine language, in contrast to those of human artifice. Yet it is surely noteworthy that a similar harp-like instrument (apparently a lyre) is also that held by Chronos in Poussin's famous *Dance to the Music of Time* painted almost two centuries before (Fig. 0.2).

The bodily incarnation of time in Poussin has now been replaced in Carus by a disembodied, invisible spirit. Classical ontic certainty gives way to Romantic spiritual mystery. Above the round-dance of the seasons in Poussin's allegory, Apollo speeds with his chariot across the diurnal race of the day, a moving image of the divine eternity, and standing on the left-hand side Janus simultaneously looks back into the past and towards into the future. Rather than any god being present above in the clouds, however, Carus's musical spirit, reflecting the modern epistemic uncertainty of humanity, dissolves into the ether and starry heavens above, whether ultimately to meet its heavenly maker no one knows. Like beings in time (and like Klee's famous *Angelus Novus* a century later), the angel is simply looking backward from whence it came: the past is visible but the future unknown.

The connection between music and time that has been gradually teased out of Carus's examples is hardly coincidental. In fact, nearly all of these elusive qualities that Carus faced in depicting music can be said to apply to time—'colourless, inapprehensible Time' as Proust memorably remarks—itself.[7] Much of music's apparent resistance to visual representation is a property shared by time, shared because they are properties that music possesses as a consequence of its irreducibly temporal nature. They are the problems inevitably encountered trying to represent the temporal and immaterial in the spatial and material.

So far this introduction has presented an assortment of thoughts on time and music from the decades around 1820—a philosopher speaking of myth and its symbolic meaning in art, a composer trying his hand at poetry, a trained medical doctor painting musical allegories. None of these examples is actually music, even though all implicate music, to a greater or lesser degree. Accounts of time created in visually or linguistically representative media have almost invariably felt the disparity between (almost tautologically put) time's temporal nature and their own spatial and seemingly fixed, stable categories. But what of our understanding of time that is created through a temporal medium such as music?

This present book explores the connection between music and time in Romantic music from late Beethoven to Elgar. Its survey spans the century that stretches from 1815 to 1914, from the final defeat of Napoleon at Waterloo and the Congress of Vienna to the outbreak of the First World War. This specific historical period is hardly accidental to the argument I shall be making. The distinguished physicist and historian of time G.J. Whitrow notes that 'in the nineteenth century the idea of temporal succession came to assume greater importance in human life and thought than ever before', and it is widely accepted that since the middle of the preceding century Western Europe witnessed what may be termed an increasing 'temporalisation' of experience.[8] The historical rise in significance accorded to time during this period is crucially interlinked with that of two other cultural phenomena. First is the role of subjectivity within nineteenth-century philosophy, art, and culture, the importance of the self in modern thought and society. Second is the establishment of instrumental music as an art form capable of serious aesthetic claims, indeed as perhaps constituting

[7] Marcel Proust, *Time Regained*, in *Remembrance of Things Past*, trans. C.K. Scott Moncrieff and Terence Kilmartin, 3 vols. (Harmondsworth: Penguin, 1981), vol. III, p. 1087.

[8] G.J. Whitrow, *Time in History: Views of Time from Prehistory to the Present Day* (Oxford: Oxford University Press, 1988), p. 171; see further the first section of chapter two in the present book, 'Musical Time in History'.

the highest type of art that exists (or so many people would claim). For all three of these issues are closely bound up with one another.

As the most quintessentially temporal of the arts, music has been seen from the Romantic era onwards as having a privileged ability to invoke the human experience of time. Obviously all art forms require time for their apprehension, but there is something peculiar to music—its apparent absence of materiality, the relative insignificance of any visual or spatial dimension, the uncertain ontological status of the work—that focuses on this dimension even more than the other arts.[9] Through its play of themes and recurrence of events music has the ability to stylise in multiple ways our temporal relation to the world, with far-reaching implications for modern conceptions of memory and subjectivity. Such qualities have important consequences for the role music could play in creating modern notions of personal and national identity, cultural memory, and history. Music's relation to its surrounding culture and history is hence reciprocal: music constructs cultural meaning just as much as cultural meaning is in turn reflected and propagated by music. In fact a central idea in this book is to take seriously the notion that music since 1800 was, and may still be, understood as disclosing aspects of human temporality that are incapable of being expressed in the same way through verbal formulations (and by extension, philosophy). For when all words were found wanting, repeatedly we find music coming to the rescue. If this age understood time, it was almost invariably through the metaphor of a melody.

It should be emphasised from the start that this study is not an attempt at a grand, unified theory of musical time. As has already been made apparent, time is a puzzling, polyvalent, and contradictory creature, one that for millennia has proved notoriously hard to define for thinkers across all disciplines. A multitude of different, often conflicting understandings exist, none of which appears to be adequate alone as a theory. One might say that the very nature of the topic precludes ultimate answers. It would seem to follow that if time is a subject to which no one seems able to offer a single, definitive answer, it would therefore be foolhardy to insist on one, comprehensive understanding of musical time. As Lewis Rowell nearly two decades ago cautioned,

> If what we have been seeking is a 'grand solution', an intellectual breakthrough that enables us to understand the temporality of music in fundamentally new and satisfying ways, I fear we are not much nearer than

---

[9] It should be emphasised here that this claim is historical rather than universal, being rooted in a Romantic aesthetics of music and its work concept, and the distinction between music and other temporal arts is probably more a matter of degree than kind. Again, these issues are discussed at greater length in chapter two.

we were in 1960 . . . Perhaps we ought rather to adjust our expectations [and] dampen some of our scholarly hybris . . .[10]

I fear in turn that we are no closer to tracking down this chronic chimera now than Rowell was in 1996; neither are we ever likely to be. Instead, it may be more prudent to see the relation between music and time as one admitting of multiple realisations. Since time, as thinkers from Aristoxenus to Kant have argued, cannot be perceived in itself, our understanding of this abstract, mysterious entity is largely a human construct, and hence invariably reflects different cultural and methodological constructions—ones which themselves have changed through time.[11] There is not, therefore, *a* theory of musical time, but a plurality of approaches to understanding how time may be manifested in music as an object of human activity.

Thus this book examines the multiple ways in which nineteenth-century music—primarily instrumental music—relates to, and may provide insight into, the problematics of human time.[12] On the most basic level the book is formed from a series of case-studies exploring a theme in the philosophy of time in relation to a specific musical repertory—Beethoven with ideas of temporal transcendence and timelessness, Schubert with memory and nostalgia, the late-nineteenth-century Russian symphonic tradition in connection to cultural conceptions of history, the French cyclic sonata concerning time's various possible structures, and Elgar with the sense of a guiding spirit behind time. While the progression is chronological, no attempt has been made to give a comprehensive survey of nineteenth-century music from the perspective of its temporality (surely an unfeasible undertaking), but instead a constellation of notable

---

[10] Lewis Rowell, 'The Study of Time in Music: A Quarter-Century Perspective', *Indiana Theory Review*, 17 (1996), 88.

[11] In a similar vein, Rowell continues 'We grasp [time] only by means of the events and processes that pass through our experience, and the ways in which we observe, store, manipulate, and retrieve these events and processes. . . . *Time* is such a convenient, all-encompassing term for such a variety of concepts and percepts that it seduces us into believing it to be a single thing. It is not. The idea of time must surely be among the grandest and most persistent contradictions in intellectual history.' Ibid., 88.

[12] A historical disclaimer should nonetheless be issued here: while nineteenth- and early twentieth-century thinkers clearly predominate in these pages, the discussion of time is not confined simply to philosophical sources dating from the time of the music under consideration. In many cases contemporaneous views on time and its relation to music are crucial to the discussion, creating a picture of the understanding of time and music's potential meaning for this at a particular stage in history. But in seeking to articulate the philosophical problems that music, in the nineteenth century, was heard to respond to, we must also look on occasion to the wider history of time. The temporal conundrums that the era grappled with were in many cases those which had perplexed thinkers millennia earlier and even to this day remain a source of intense debate.

examples is presented through a series of studies dealing with a specific temporal issue. The one reversal of this format is the second chapter, itself consisting of three, interlinked sections, an extended account of the historical relationship between music, time, and philosophy in this period which forms the philosophical heart of the book. Rather than asking what philosophy can do for the understanding of musical time, this part turns the question round to enquire why music has proved so significant for the philosophical understanding of time.[13]

Despite the complementarity of the chapters' approaches, though, common threads run underneath them which emerge repeatedly throughout the book. Forming a prologue to the ensuing discussion, the opening chapter on Beethoven's late sonatas provides a rich musical starting point, an accessible introduction to the book's subject matter that will be given greater theoretical weight in subsequent chapters. Alongside the first section of the second chapter, 'Musical Time in History', this opening part sets out the historical situation that gave rise to music's new-found capacity for expressing such a powerful sense of temporality by 1820—the development in compositional techniques and aesthetic changes in musical reception. Deeper philosophical and theoretical questions left provisionally at the end of this account are reengaged in the remaining two parts of chapter two through an explication of just why music was considered uniquely capable of uncovering the aporias of temporality, setting up the philosophical terms for the remaining four chapters and working towards a full statement of the methodological concerns attendant on the entire study.

Complementing the focus of the opening chapter on Beethoven and timelessness, the third chapter turns to the topic of Schubert and memory. Questions of pastness and tense critiqued here will be subsequently taken up as part of the argument in chapter five, which, continuing from the concerns of chapter two, addresses a philosophical problem in our understanding of time, namely its topology or structure, and the role music may hold in its explication. Taking quite a different approach, chapter four examines a culture's historical understanding of time as reflected within music, continuing from the brief account laid out in the first part of chapter two and foreshadowing the concluding chapter on the spirit of history. And the final chapter, a type of epilogue to the concerns of the book, returns to the questions of temporal transcendence raised in the opening two chapters, the separation of music into distinct temporal layers witnessed in the third, the notion of music as the expression of history seen in the fourth, and the cyclic thematic structures considered in the fifth, whilst itself thematicising this very idea of a unifying musical theme behind time. The final

---

[13] To this extent, this section forms a musicologically centred response to the fascinating avenue of inquiry opened up from a philosophical perspective by Andrew Bowie in his numerous writings from the last two decades on music's role within modernity.

section offers a parting summing up of the questions of both the chapter and book as a whole, returning to my admission of the limits of this enterprise at the close of chapter two yet nonetheless affirming music's continued importance for understanding the complexities of time and human subjectivity.

In this way, I think one may best view the book as forming a *constellation*. The chapters belong together and make most sense in conjunction, although each shines as a separate point, illuminating a perspective on the elusive entity that is time. This conception reflects the fact that time, like the imaginary figure of the constellation, cannot be grasped in itself, but rather our understanding of it derives from the distinct though partial illuminating points provided by its tangible elements. Yet each individual part would not have the same meaning taken on its own: numerous issues discussed in one chapter rely on ideas exposited in others. It is only when these separate spots of temporal luminescence are taken in their entirety that we may perceive the intended outline of the constellation (one we could call 'Chronos'). This structure draws out of the design of the very first chapter, which, in its apparently discrete series of mobiles that nonetheless build up unobtrusively to a cumulative argument, reflects in form the notions of non-linear time and parenthetical enclosure treated in the subject matter, alongside a sense of each part being a variation on the same, sometimes hidden, theme.

In the interests both of space and of tackling a variety of philosophical issues, some significant figures have found themselves left out of the current volume. Both Schumann and Mahler, for instance, would seem obvious candidates for inclusion in a book-length account of time, memory, and subjectivity in Romantic music. The reason for their neglect has nothing to do with personal regard for their music (quite the contrary in fact) but relates to the desire not to repeat arguments offered elsewhere, either by other scholars or as part of the exploration of particular themes within this present book. I have also resisted the urge to speak of Mendelssohn again, since he has already been covered by me in an earlier monograph. Bruckner, too, would have formed a valuable figure for inclusion, while from the early twentieth century the music of such a figure as Charles Ives would have similarly made a fascinating case-study. In the case of the first four composers named, a further motivating reason has been the need I have felt not to extend the emphasis on the music of Austro-German composers more than already is the case. Though a certain initial basis is formed from the examples of Beethoven and Schubert, the provenances of the music discussed does range over a wider selection of nationalities, moving out from Germany and Austria to Russia, France, and England. Indeed the relation to national identities vis-à-vis perceived Germanocentric historiography and values will come to the fore in later stages of the book.

The concentration on instrumental music, meanwhile, has good justification. Apart from the final example from Elgar—and this given by a work originally described by the composer as a 'symphony', in which the music can be justifiably held to transcend its text as part of its very message—all the major examples given are from instrumental works. My interest in how music may convey a unique understanding of time supports the focus on music emancipated from the design given by a text, which as a consequence has to structure its material to create a temporal form without dependence on an external framework, rather than types of music for which questions of temporal signification rely primarily on linguistic denotation. In opera, for instance, for which there exists an already considerable discourse on the complex temporal relationships that may be found within, the relationship to text and plot introduces key differences in approach. This is one reason for the apparent lacuna of Italian music in these pages, since there is little instrumental music from this country of a comparable significance to its operatic repertoire in the nineteenth century. Overt issues of narrative or represented time arise in dramatic media that simply are less present or at any rate less significant within instrumental music.

In historical scope, the present book neatly fills out the period between the music covered by Karol Berger's recent consideration of musical time *c*.1720–1820 and the plentiful work on temporality in twentieth-century music (such as that found in the pioneering writings of Jonathan Kramer).[14] Thus the not-inconsiderable discourse on time up to and including Beethoven's music forms the starting context, and I leave off on the cusp of the First World War, with the immanent destruction of an older social order and technological changes that would shake the world and its concomitant sense of time. It is indeed arguable that by the early decades of the new century the spread of recording technology was decisively altering the conception not only of musical time but of time in general, and thus it seems prudent to break off the discussion before the entire terms of this debate were to change.[15] Moreover, by this stage the question of musical temporality and the theoretical debates surrounding it become considerably more varied, and my selection would become unrepresentative of the variety and richness of twentieth-century music.

---

[14] Karol Berger, *Bach's Cycle, Mozart's Arrow: An Essay on the Origins of Musical Modernity* (Berkeley and Los Angeles: University of California Press, 2007); Jonathan D. Kramer, *The Time of Music: New Meanings, New Temporalities, New Listening Strategies* (New York: Schirmer, 1988), and a number of related articles. Kramer certainly does consider eighteenth- and nineteenth-century music in his writings and has many insightful points to make, though his primary focus is on the post-war avant-garde. David B. Greene has also left two valuable accounts of musical temporality that straddle the outer edges of my historical period, namely *Temporal Processes in Beethoven's Music* (New York: Gordon and Breach, 1982) and *Mahler, Consciousness and Temporality* (New York: Gordon and Breach, 1984).

[15] See Jonathan D. Kramer, 'New Temporalities in Music', *Critical Inquiry*, 7 (1981), 543–4.

In many ways this study can be viewed as a successor and continuation of the line of research found in my earlier *Mendelssohn, Time and Memory*, broadening the scope of investigation out from Mendelssohn to extend across the long nineteenth century from Beethoven to Elgar.[16] I have also written elsewhere on several related though tangential topics: on Handel's *Il trionfo del tempo* and eighteenth-century conceptions of time, about temporality in late nineteenth-century English opera and musical constructions of national identity, on nostalgia and cultural memory in post-war America, and concerning Olivier Messiaen's theories of time.[17] However, this new book goes beyond the hermeneutic methodology of the earlier monograph to place greater emphasis on music's meaning as articulated through its historical reception and a more sustained emphasis on the philosophy of time. I am interested here in creating a philosophical account of music and temporality that, while possessing significance for our present understanding of these two problematic though endlessly fascinating topics, is nevertheless embedded within the culture and thought of its age. Investigating music from the standpoint of its temporality offers one of the most rewarding perspectives on music's role within society and human experience.

[16] *Mendelssohn, Time and Memory: The Romantic Conception of Cyclic Form* (Cambridge: Cambridge University Press, 2011).

[17] 'The Triumph of Time in the Eighteenth Century: Handel's *Il trionfo del tempo* and historical conceptions of musical temporality', *Eighteenth-Century Music*, 11 (2014), 257–81 (which grows out of the discussion in the first section of chapter two in the present volume); 'Sullivan, Scott, and *Ivanhoe*: Constructing Historical Time and National Identity in Victorian Opera', *Nineteenth-Century Music Review*, 9 (2012), 295–321; 'Nostalgia and Cultural Memory in Barber's *Knoxville: Summer of 1915*', *Journal of Musicology*, 25 (2008), 211–29; 'On Time and Eternity in Messiaen', chapter in Judith Crispin (ed.), *Messiaen: The Centenary Papers* (Cambridge: Cambridge Scholars Publishing, 2010), pp. 222–43.

1

Time and Transcendence
in Beethoven's Late Piano Sonatas

Time, they say, *exists not at all with* GOD
— Sir William Jones, 'On the Chronology of the Hindus',
copied out by Beethoven in 1816[1]

The most significant phenomenon that the world can show is
not the conqueror of the world, but the overcomer of the world
— Schopenhauer, *The World as Will and Representation,*
vol. I (1818), §86[2]

We begin near the end of Beethoven's Op. 109. Following the contrapuntal intricacy of the preceding *allegro* section the finale's sixth and final variation returns to the tempo and *cantabile* marking of the movement's opening (*Tempo I del tema*), along with an evident return to the simplicity of the variations' underlying theme. Now the rhythm has been largely smoothed out into simple crotchets with repeated dominant Bs in treble and tenor voices forming a type of slow but constantly pulsating pedal (Ex. 1.1).[3] By the third bar these Bs have unobtrusively doubled in speed to quavers; two bars later their frequency increases further to the equivalent of quaver triplets (the time signature changing from $\frac{3}{4}$ to $\frac{9}{8}$); a bar later to sextuplets (measured in semiquavers). What was a slight hint of the chromatic lower neighbour a♯ at b. 157 has turned into a full-scale

---

[1] Beethoven, *Tagebuch* 1816 (94d): 'Zeit findet durchaus bey Gott nicht statt', cited by Maynard Solomon, *Late Beethoven: Music, Thought, Imagination* (Berkeley and Los Angeles: University of California Press, 2003), p. 207. Original from Sir William Jones, 'Dissertation on the Chronology of the Hindus' (1788), in *Dissertations and Miscellaneous Pieces Relating to the History and Antiquities, the Arts, Sciences, and Literature of Asia,* 2 vols. (London: G. Nicol, 1792), vol. I, p. 285.

[2] Arthur Schopenhauer, *The World as Will and Representation,* trans. E.F.J. Payne, 2 vols. (New York: Dover, 1969), vol. I, pp. 385–6.

[3] Yet the bass here has been subtly altered by the intervening journey of five variations; rising as if in mirror image to the treble, it reflects the canonic inversion of the preceding fifth variation.

trill-like oscillation. Soon this pulsation has reached the level of demisemi-quavers (b. 160): the pedal's oscillating frequency has intensified in eight bars from one to eight vibrations per underlying crotchet beat. With this constant rhythmic acceleration pushing at the boundaries of the quantifiable in execu-tion, where is there to go other than to an unmeasured trill in both voices? But Beethoven is far from finished. The melody and bassline find themselves drawn into this overpowering drive: having already increased from crotchets to quavers at b. 161, with the arrival of the double trill in alto and tenor in b. 164 the outer voices trace a melodic diminution of the theme in triplets.

The texture abruptly alters for the second half of the binary theme, yet such is the accumulated momentum of the music that this change passes the listener by almost without notice. Cascading demisemiquavers in the right-hand over the low B trill now in the bass distinctly call to mind the *Adagio espressivo* passage inter-polated into the first movement's exposition (bb. 12–13), along with a cadential bar from the finale's fourth variation (b. 104) that had seemed to allude to this earlier passage. Finally, as the peak of this giddy process of rhythmic acceleration, the trill, now in the treble, forms the support for running demisemiquavers in the bass (alluding quite possibly to the bass of variation three) and a high right-hand line that picks out the notes of the theme's second half in offbeat quavers.

This is the climax of the finale's six variations. Three different degrees of rhythmic movement are superimposed on each other—the crotchet pulse of the upper voice corresponding to the original theme (albeit now syncopated), the demisemiquavers in the bass, and the even more rapid unmeasured trill at the centre, flickering out rhythmic energy at the level at least of hemidemisemiqua-vers. We are presented with a snapshot of multiple levels of motion, a synoptic view of different measures of time ongoing simultaneously. The sixth variation has encapsulated the accelerating course of the movement's first four variations in microcosm, culminating in the overlaying of these as a simultaneity.

At the movement's close the theme returns in its original limpid simplicity. Its recall imparts a circular frame to the music, imbuing it with a profound calm as we are borne back to this earlier time, a past that had been left behind by the six intervening variations. Yet an attentive listener may well hear beyond the bare phenomena of this recalled melody the preceding music still humming in the background, a celestial whirl most are deaf to, a secret music for those alone who know for what to listen. We are back again, but everything is new, fresh, redis-covered. The theme now contains a lifetime worth of experience.[4] Every rise and fall, every corner rings.

---

[4] It 'may . . . be compared to the old man who utters the same creed as the child, but for whom it is pregnant with the significance of a lifetime' (Hegel, *Logic* [*Encyclopaedia*, Part I], *Zusatz* to §237, trans. William Wallace [Oxford: Clarendon Press, 1975], p. 293).

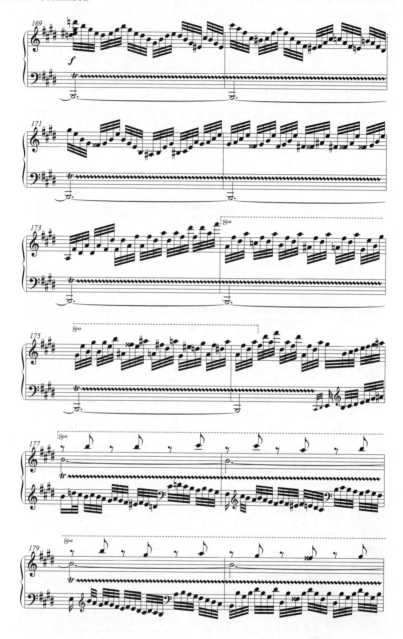

This variation is an invitation to meditate upon the nature of time in music.

Beethoven has long been celebrated in music historiography for his command over the dimension of time. Charles Rosen calls him simply 'the greatest master of musical time' while Carl Dahlhaus states quite openly that 'it has always been acknowledged that the temporal quality of music is at its most pronounced in Beethoven's symphonic style'.[5] Jonathan Kramer, similarly, claims that 'Beethoven's time-sense . . . is unsurpassed'. 'Beethoven's music, perhaps more than any other pre-contemporary music, deals with subtle and often profound structuring of the listener's time-experience'.[6] Several German critics have gone even further. In Ernst Bloch's opinion the Beethovenian sonata 'compresses time like a special material and lets us actually hear this mysterious facet of the work'. In the hands of 'this tremendous strategist of time' the existence of time, 'previously so wraith-like, spontaneously raises its head'.[7] For Theodor W. Adorno, Beethoven's middle-period works provide the paradigm of the 'intensive' symphonic type of time in which time is contracted and subjugated through the composer's utter musical mastery. And 'in the strict sense', Adorno concludes (without even the slightest dialectical hesitation), 'symphonic time belongs to Beethoven alone'.[8] Time structures are also a recurring theme in Dahlhaus's writings on Beethoven; such is Beethoven's mastery over time that music is heard not in time but rather, time is now in the music.[9]

[5] Charles Rosen, *The Classical Style* (London: Faber & Faber, 1971), p. 445; Carl Dahlhaus, *Ludwig van Beethoven: Approaches to His Music*, trans. Mary Whittall (Oxford: Clarendon Press, 1991), p. 84.

[6] Jonathan D. Kramer, 'Multiple and Non-Linear Time in Beethoven's opus 135', *Perspectives on New Music*, 11 (1973), 123, 122–3.

[7] Ernst Bloch, *Essays on the Philosophy of Music*, trans. Peter Palmer (Cambridge: Cambridge University Press, 1985), p. 102.

[8] Theodor W. Adorno, *Beethoven: The Philosophy of Music*, ed. Rolf Tiedemann, trans. E. Jephcott (Cambridge: Polity Press, 1998), pp. 89–91, 228. Haydn is also (not unreasonably) mentioned by Adorno in connection with the creation of this intensive symphonic time, but mysteriously drops out in order to provide greater space for his laudation of Beethoven's genius. Beethoven's model is indeed so overwhelming for this critic that it is arguable his consideration of musical time is skewed towards the normative paradigm provided by the works of Beethoven's middle period; see Robert Adlington, 'Musical Temporality: Perspectives from Adorno and de Man', *Repercussions*, 6 (1997), 5–28, or Richard Klein, 'Thesen zum Verhältnis von Musik und Zeit', in Richard Klein, Eckehard Kiem, and Wolfram Ette (eds.), *Musik in der Zeit: Zeit in der Musik* (Göttingen: Velbrück Wissenschaft, 2000), pp. 102–3.

[9] Music 'not only proceeds in the medium of time, but it is also, in an emphatic sense, "composed time"'. Beethoven's allegro movements represent time 'so emphatically that it seems that it [time] would not exist if the music did not make it' (Dahlhaus, *Ludwig van Beethoven*, 84, 87). A sceptical critique of Dahlhaus's claims may be found in Heinz von Loesche, 'Final gerichtete Zeit oder final gerichtete Musik?', in Diether de la Motte (ed.), *Zeit in der Musik—Musik in der Zeit* (Frankfurt: Peter Lang, 1997), pp. 69–76.

Despite this formidable array of critical might, one could reasonably question quite what such claims actually signify on a practical level. Is Beethoven's music and its relation to time really so different from that of his predecessors and successors, and even if so, does the Beethovenian way with time surpass that of all other music, however different these approaches may be? What does it mean, practically, to state that Beethoven controls time (after all, notwithstanding the impact of his music on the listener, the man still grew old and died in the very medium he is alleged to have mastered—as, presumably, will the listener)? Given that no one—physicist, philosopher, psychologist, least of all musicologist—can agree on what time actually is, can it really be demonstrated that time is *in* music—and this if and only if that music has the name Beethoven affixed to it—or is this mere critical hyperbole, a consequence of the adulation accorded to Beethoven in musicological discourse across the last two centuries?

I have no wish to contribute further to the well-established beatification of Beethoven by offering support here to the more extravagant claims on his behalf—to suggest that his music is both radically different from and furthermore unequivocally better than that of all other composers. Many of the ways in which Beethoven's music may be heard to play with notions of time and temporality are not simply unique to his music, and what other composers do in their own way may be every bit as interesting as what Beethoven accomplishes in his. But Beethoven's music is surely the most apt starting point for any consideration of the idea of music and temporality in the nineteenth century. Not only does Beethoven generally occupy a pivotal position in music history and his work form a touchstone of musicological criticism, but his music has furthermore been consistently received as demonstrating a new relationship to temporality, reflecting a radical broader shift in contemporary conceptions of time and history. There are few, if any, better places to start.

Theorising Musical Time and Movement

In the last variation of Op. 109's finale we witnessed the simultaneous presentation of different speeds of rhythmic movement—the running demisemiquavers in the bass, trills in the treble, the quaver notes of the theme above them. The same type of procedure is also seen in the Sonata in A♭, Op. 110 following the recurrence of the *Klagender Gesang* in the finale. First the fugue theme enters in inversion (b. 137), 'nach und nach wieder auflebend'. After four fugal entries the prime form is once again introduced, but this time in augmentation and syncopated across the bar (b. 152); the fugal countersubject in quavers is now suspiciously similar in contour to the fugal subject played in rhythmic diminution. In fact the rising fourths of the fugue have simply been modified into thirds; to all

Ex. 1.2 Beethoven: Piano Sonata in A♭, Op. 110 (1821), finale, bb. 137–78, return of fugue subject

intents and purposes we are experiencing the fugue simultaneously at half and at three times its original speed.

At b. 168 the acceleration is further increased to semiquavers (six times quicker), although the *meno allegro* tempo indication smoothes the transition. The opening tempo gradually re-establishes itself until at b. 174 the original form of the fugue in dotted crotchets is finally heard against an even semiquaver

Ex. 1.1 Continued

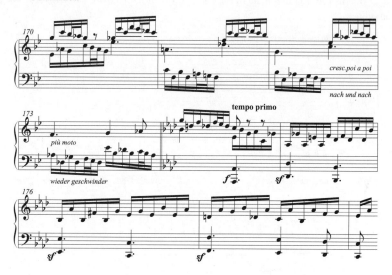

figuration clearly drawn from the diminuted fugue subject, a texture which drives the piece to its final cadence (Ex. 1.2). Op. 111's *Arietta*, too, presents a cornucopia of superimposed layers of rhythmic movement. As with the finale of Op. 109, the concluding C major movement is formed as an 'acceleration' type of variation set, charting a successive diminution of rhythmic values that culminates again in an extended trill following the fourth variation. Charles Rosen has described the incremental acceleration of rhythmic values well in his analysis of this sonata. In the last variation, 'the rhythm is a synthesis of all that went before: the rhythmic accompaniment of Variation IV (the fastest measured motion) and the theme in its original form (the slowest) are both suspended under the unmeasured stillness of the trill'.[10]

It is tempting to speak here in these climactic passages of the last three sonatas of the superimposition of different 'times', such is the effect of Beethoven's overlayering of different, seemingly independent levels of motion, the simultaneity of what had originally been heard temporally separated across the movement. After all, in Beethoven's own day philosophers and thinkers were beginning to voice the notion that rather than there being only one, monolithic universal

[10] Charles Rosen, *The Classical Style*, p. 448. As the above examples demonstrate, there is an apparent connection between Beethoven's increased use of contrapuntal and combinatorial techniques typical of pre-Classical music (the simultaneous overlayering of different levels of movement in Op. 109's finale or the fugal techniques of Op. 110) and the absence of a clear sense of teleological drive, a feature that some scholars have seen as characteristic of renaissance and Baroque music. To this extent the purported 'timeless' temporal quality of Beethoven's late music is neither unique nor especially new; its effect is just set into greater relief by the contrast with the expectation and partial retention of the more dynamised, goal-directed style typifying his earlier music.

time, invariant and absolute as in Newton's influential formulation, it might instead be more apt to envisage the intrinsic plurality of time, the simultaneous coexistence of the individual times inherent in every living creature.[11] Two decades before the composition of Beethoven's last sonatas Johann Gottlieb Herder had claimed that as 'every mutable thing has the measure of its own time within itself' there must be 'at any one time in the universe innumerably many times'.[12] In a similar manner, the Romantic poet and thinker Novalis contended that 'every temporal individual has its own sphere, its own scale' of time, and Friedrich Schelling could hold 'no thing has an external time, but rather each has only one, inner, individual time, inborn and intrinsic to it'.[13]

To this extent Beethoven's conception is strikingly reminiscent of Schopenhauer's near contemporaneous description of music as reflecting the different gradations of Will embodied in nature, their different speeds of motion and respective times—from the rude inorganic matter of the planets in the slow-moving bass, through the middle voices of plant life and the inchoate consciousness of animals to the highest spiritual level of mankind in the upper melodic voice (long associated with determinate consciousness).[14] Such spatial and optical metaphors spring readily to mind from this music. The last variations of Opp. 109 and 111 and the close of Op. 110 might present the receptive listener with an image of cosmic order—the teeming multiplicity of the universe, each level moving with its own pace, like the vision described by the archangels in Goethe's prologue to *Faust*. It is as if we are granted a panoptic view of our globe from some higher, supermundane perspective, the different temporal layers moving concentrically, the great circle of the equator spinning faster than lesser circles, engirdling the stillness of the trill at the pole. In Beethoven's examples, however, the details are partially inverted—the motion is quicker in the bass than in the upper voice, as if the lower hemisphere is somehow spinning twice as fast as the upper.[15] The synoptic fusion of the spatial and temporal here is akin to that conceived in Borges's Aleph—the point where all points

[11] Isaac Newton, *The Mathematical Principles of Natural Philosophy*, trans. Andrew Motte, rev. Florian Cajori, 2 vols. (Berkeley: University of California Press, 1934), vol. I, p. 7.

[12] Johann Gottlieb Herder, 'Genese des Begriffs der Zeit, nach Datis der menschlichen Natur und Sprache', from *Eine Metakritik zur Kritik der reinen Vernunft* (1799), ed. Friedrich Bassenger (Berlin: Aufbau Verlag, 1955), p. 68.

[13] Novalis, *Das Allgemeine Brouillon*, Fragment 474, in *Schriften: Die Werke Friedrich von Hardenbergs*, eds. Paul Kluckhohn, Richard Samuel, Gerhard Schulz, and Hans-Joachim Mähl, 6 vols. (Stuttgart: Kohlhammer, 1960–2006), vol. III, p. 340; Friedrich Wilhelm Joseph Schelling, *Die Weltalter: Fragmente, in den Urfassungen von 1811 und 1813*, ed. Manfred Schröter, *Schellings Werke* (Nachlaßband) (Munich: C.H. Beck, 1946), p. 78.

[14] Schopenhauer, *The World as Will and Representation*, vol. I, §52. A similar conception would later be taken up by Messiaen and in Gilles Deleuze's philosophy of music.

[15] I confess to stealing this image from Scott Burnham.

converge, where all may be seen without distortion or reduction simultaneously from every perspective—Blake's 'To see a World in a Grain of Sand, /
And a heaven in a wild flower, / Hold Infinity in the palm of your hand, / And
Eternity in an hour'—Hölderlin's belief that 'all the sacred places of the earth
are together in one place'.[16]

A more sober assessment, however, might read these passages as simply overlayering different levels of movement, albeit in a complex and highly expressive
manner, which does not warrant being taken as really constituting different times.
What is the connection, one might ask then, between movement—rhythmic
activity—and time in music? Multiple ways of understanding this relationship are
possible, some of which may well appear to support the rather extravagant interpretation offered above, though these are not without their potential pitfalls. To take
an Aristotelian perspective, for instance, one might wish to propose that if 'time is
the measure of movement', different measures of movement could thus be thought
of as constituting different times.[17] However, the analogy, thus expressed, is rather
superficial. For a start, quavers, crochets, demisemiquavers, are all measured
by the same temporal scale, being merely subdivisions of a common measure.
To believe that this results in different times is tantamount to suggesting that
a child who when walking must take two steps for every one of an adult is living twice as quickly as its parents (experience would teach us, if anything, the
contrary may be the case).[18] What exactly does the temporal-spatial category
of 'movement' mean in music anyway? A sound-wave has an amplitude and
wavelength, but these matters of pitch have nothing to do with the length of
duration of an individual note. The equating of rhythmic pulse and movement
looks purely metaphorical.[19] Secondly, the question of who is perceiving these
times has not yet been raised. If each living creature has its own time inside itself
(following the Kantian resubjectification of time), then for the listener there is

[16] Jorge Luis Borges, 'The Aleph' (1945); William Blake, *Auguries of Innocence*, ll. 1–4, in *Complete Writings* (London: Oxford University Press, 1966), p. 431; Friedrich Hölderlin, letter to Casimir Ulrich Böhlendorff, 2 December 1802, in *Sämtliche Werke (Große Stuttgarter Ausgabe)*, eds. Friedrich Beißner and Adolf Beck, 8 vols. (Stuttgart: Cotta, 1943–85), vol. VI, p. 433, letter No. 240. (Hölderlin is implicitly drawing on the Ancient Greek idea of Delphi as forming the navel of the world.)

[17] Aristotle, *Physics*, IV, 11 (200ª34), *The Complete Works of Aristotle*, ed. Jonathan Barnes, 2 vols. (Princeton: Princeton University Press, 1984), vol. I, p. 374.

[18] In Einsteinian relativity, of course, time does go slower for a body moving at a faster speed relative to another; however, the quicker the music would move the more mass it would gain, and it is not quite clear how sound could begin to approach the speed of light. The analogy is obviously metaphorical, and on being taken to this extreme becomes nonsensical.

[19] Note the claim made by Mark L. Johnson and Steve Larson in ' "Something in the Way She Moves"—Metaphors of Musical Motion', *Metaphor and Symbol*, 18 (2003), 63–84; also, for a wider reconsideration of music and motion, Robert Adlington, 'Moving Beyond Motion: Metaphors for Changing Sound', *Journal of the Royal Music Association*, 128 (2003), 297–318.

just one time, his or her own, in which different types of movement are perceived (which would only constitute times if each musical voice anthropomorphised into a separate consciousness, and this only for an omnipresent being or at the abstract, theoretical level of the totality). The question here hinges on the notion of whether time is an internal part of our consciousness (as Augustine, Kant, and Schopenhauer would believe and Aristotle may imply) or a pre-existing external reality, a medium into which we are thrown (like Plato or Newton in their different ways).

There appears to be no single way of understanding the relationship between time and music, since there is no single, uncontested theory of time to draw upon. Furthermore, many of the approaches that are possible are problematic in various ways—some admittedly more so than others. Clearly the interpretations just offered are largely metaphorical. (Then again more recent philosophies of language tend towards arguing that all meaning is more-or-less metaphorical.[20] The extent to which our understanding of time is merely metaphorical, at least when put into words, is also contentious.) Having said this, it is nevertheless possible that a descriptive analogy might still suggest something to a listener or performer that chimes with his or her understanding of the work, that deepens or enriches the musical experience. Handled sensitively such temporal metaphors may provide an intriguing interpretation of Beethoven's music, a way of imparting a new or richer meaning to familiar passages.

These issues are all being raised here as necessary methodological questions prior to any future consideration of music and temporality. Though this matter requires further and deeper examination later in this book, perhaps we just have to admit at this stage that there are different, mutually incompatible theories of time, that no one theory is going to be fully satisfactory either as an explanation of time or of musical time, and that the relationship between musical experience and linguistic meaning is a slippery one constantly being re-mediated through praxis.

Parenthetical Enclosure and Non-Linear Time

The first movement of Op. 109 presents an intriguing instance of the alternation or even interruption of different 'types' of time. After eight and a half bars of the opening *Vivace ma non troppo*'s invention-like texture a rhapsodical *Adagio espressivo* breaks in just where the move to the dominant intimated at b. 6 seems about to be confirmed. The *Vivace*'s constant semiquaver movement is actually

---

[20] See particularly the (not uncontroversial) claim in George Lakoff and Mark Johnson's *Metaphors We Live By* (Chicago: University of Chicago Press, 1980), and their numerous subsequent writings.

sustained across the first bars of the *Adagio*, but the abrupt change in tempo and apparent improvisatory freedom of the new section entirely negates the previous sense of orderly progression through time and introduces a new, more introspective sense of temporality. If the *Vivace*'s even motoric course suggested the filling out of an external temporal framework (albeit one complicated by the persistent Lombardic rhythm and subtle play between polyphonic voices),[21] the *Adagio* in contrast results in an inwardising or subjectification of temporal experience. Having swerved the music towards the relative minor the new *Adagio* section resumes the tonicisation of B through cadenza-like passagework, thus fully effecting a modulation to the secondary key which is confirmed by the re-entry of the *Vivace* material in the function of closing theme (b. 16). The effect is of the resumption or continuation of this opening material from where it had left off eight bars earlier. One could almost join the two *Vivace* sections together over the intervening music. While the bass's F♯-f♯ of b. 8 is somewhat lower than the d♯^{1}-f♯^{1} that picks up at b. 16 (Beethoven probably taking the tessitura down for the second half of bar 8 in order to strengthen the rhetorical effect of the following arpeggiated diminished seventh that initiates the *Adagio*), the treble's b^2 clearly resolves the a♯^{2} that was left hanging at b. 8.[22] The shortest route between the two *Vivace* statements is not necessarily that heard in performance time.

William Kinderman has aptly labelled this procedure 'parenthetical enclosure', a technique 'whereby contrasting passages are heard as an interruption within the larger context'. In Kinderman's view this type of design 'enriches the temporality' of Beethoven's musical forms, opening up 'narrative possibilities rare in instrumental music'. 'The entire *Adagio* section is thus positioned at the moment of the interrupted cadence, and the resulting parenthetical structure gives the effect of a suspension of time in the contrasting section, or the enclosure of one time within another'.[23] At a broader level Jonathan Kramer has written perceptively on the apparently non-linear succession of musical events in some of Beethoven's later music and the implications for a non-linear or even multiple conception of temporality these procedures may suggest.[24] In a work

[21] See Glenn Stanley, 'Voices and their Rhythms in the First Movement of Beethoven's Piano Sonata Op. 109: Some Thoughts on the Performance and Analysis of a Late-Style Work', in Scott Burnham and Michael Steinberg (eds.), *Beethoven and his World* (Princeton: Princeton University Press, 2000), pp. 88–123.

[22] Having said this, the modulation to the dominant would be drastically under-articulated had b. 8 led directly to b. 16; the intervening passage could certainly be argued to be necessary harmonically, even if rhetorically and texturally it seems out of place, a disruption of the preceding music.

[23] William Kinderman, *Beethoven* (Oxford: Oxford University Press, 1995), pp. 12, 220. Also see the same author's 'Thematic Contrast and Parenthetical Enclosure in the Piano Sonatas, Op. 109 and 111', in Harry Goldschmidt and Georg Knepler (eds.), *Zu Beethoven: Aufsätze und Dokumente* (Berlin: Neue Musik, 1988), pp. 43–59.

[24] Kramer, 'Multiple and Non-Linear Time in Beethoven's opus 135', 125–6.

such as the first movement of Op. 135, a passage strongly suggesting closure may be heard at the beginning, giving the effect that Beethoven has reordered an otherwise more conventional musical layout; this same point in the movement's [narrative] time may be revisited later, even multiple times.[25] Speaking of the difference between the implicit ('semantic') temporality of musical gestures (generic opening or closing figures, various levels of cadential definition) and their variable syntactical placement, Kramer continues 'Music frees us from the tyranny of the linear-time of the physical world and of daily life: it allows a future event to be earlier than a past event, a past event to be later than a present event'. In short, 'Music makes the past-present-future exist on a plane other than that of the earlier-simultaneous-later'.[26]

In Op. 109 the *Vivace* and *Adagio* themes in fact stem originally from different pieces: the *Vivace* seems to have its origins in an independent Bagatelle that Beethoven had been writing at this time, into which he inserted the parenthetical *Adagio* to make an unusual and temporally intriguing sonata movement.[27] Their different temporal profiles are a consequence of the nature of the two dissimilar materials used and the differing types of time they respectively suggest. Barry Cooper has aptly described the two as differing in almost every conceivable way—'a contrast between $\frac{2}{4}$ and $\frac{3}{4}$, dynamism and stasis, regular and irregular rhythm—suggesting images of action set against thought ... time against timelessness'.[28] Michael Spitzer similarly reads the movement as opposing two kinds of temporality—'a rushing *molto perpetuo*, and "cadenza time"'.[29] A comparable juxtaposition of insistent movement and subjective introspection may be witnessed in the second subject of Op. 111, a transient moment of calm amidst the otherwise unrelenting drive of the opening movement, while the recurrence

[25] This technique of course has a veritable history before Beethoven: Haydn's Quartet Op. 33 No 5, like the finale of Op. 76 No. 5, begins with a 'final' sounding cadence that is subsequently reused in a more proper syntactical position as the first theme's cadential close, while the finale of Op. 33 No. 2 ('The Joke') plays repeatedly with the idea of ending; effectively this piece has not just one, but multiple ends.

[26] Ibid., 134. This point will be developed in chapter 5. Kramer is drawing on models of time formulated by the philosopher D.S. Mackay derived from the famous 'A and B series' devised by John McTaggart in his seminal article 'The Unreality of Time', *Mind*, 68 (1908), 457–74. On the difference between 'syntactical' and 'semantic' types of musical time see Raymond Monelle, *The Sense of Music: Semiotic Essays* (Princeton: Princeton University Press, 2000), pp. 82–4.

[27] William Meredith, 'The Origins of Beethoven's Op. 109', *The Musical Times*, 126 (1985), 713–16; Nicholas Marston, *Beethoven's Piano Sonata in E, Op. 109* (Oxford: Clarendon Press, 1995), pp. 15–31.

[28] Barry Cooper, *Beethoven (The Master Musicians)* (Oxford: Oxford University Press, 2008), p. 301.

[29] Michael Spitzer, *Music as Philosophy: Adorno and Beethoven's Late Style* (Bloomington, IN: Indiana University Press, 2006), p. 126.

of the *Klagender Gesang* in the finale of Op. 110 alternates the backward-looking memory of the *arioso* with the forward-looking time of the fugue.

A related type of procedure to the superimposition of rhythmic times seen in the finales of Opp. 109 and 111 and the alternation of temporalities in Op. 109's opening movement may be glimpsed in the first movement of Op. 110. The sonata's opening page consists of a loose succession of phrases—a gentle opening figure of descending thirds and ascending fourths (theme 1.1, bb. 1–4), a song-like rising melody over a self-consciously simple chordal bass (1.2, bb. 5–11), followed by glistening arpeggio passagework (1.3→Tr, bb. 12ff) functioning as a transition on to a secondary area that, in common with those second subjects of Opp. 109 and 111, seems to provide a tranquil pool of inward reflection operating outside the main time of the opening movement. These three ideas are subject to functional redefinition across the course of Beethoven's movement. The exceptionally concise development simply consists of the laconic eight-fold repetition of the first idea's characteristic opening two-bar rhythmic unit through changing harmonic contexts over the repeated chordal accompaniment of the second idea, for its latter half changing to the sinuous semiquavers familiar from the exposition's codetta. The recapitulation, unassumingly reached, then proceeds to fuse the first theme with the shimmering demisemiquavers of the transition, which all along had held out the promise of forming a counterpart to something similar, an unfulfilled texture that awaited a theme.

The limpid grace of this passage is astounding—what Tovey memorably described as 'the locus classicus of those Greek simplicities of Beethoven's later style'.[30] In place of gritty motivic working-out and fragmenting his themes through developmental strife Beethoven simply successively fuses their accompanimental textures, a superimposing of different times or types of movement. In fact all three ideas can be shown to be closely related, though topically and gesturally they appear to have little in common. The first theme (fragment of a theme would perhaps describe it better) imparts the suggestion of an underlying sarabande rhythm in the second bar's emphasis on the second crotchet beat of the $\frac{3}{4}$ metre, though the first bar's mild syncopation of this second beat implies a possible compound duple time instead. This rhythmic template is closely followed for the second theme that starts at b. 5, despite the dissimilar melodic profiles of the two:

1.1, bb. 1–2 | ♩. ♪♩♪♫ | ♩ ♩ |

1.2, bb. 5–6 | ♩. ♩ ♪ | ♩ ♩ |

<hr />

[30] Donald Tovey, *A Companion to Beethoven's Pianoforte Sonatas* (London: The Associated Board of the Royal Schools of Music, 1931), p. 231.

Ex. 1.3 Beethoven: Piano Sonata in A♭, Op. 110, first movement, bb. 1–15, harmonic reduction of opening themes (1.1, 1.2, 1.3)

Yet the rising arpeggiac contour of the second theme may still be glimpsed in embryo in the tenor voice of b. 3, whose line rises up through the A♭ triad (E♭–A♭–c) foreshadowing the distinctive treble theme of b. 5 (c^1–$e♭^1$–$a♭^1$). The third idea (1.3) shares its bar-by-bar harmonic progression with the first (1.1), even mirroring its underlying bass progression for the opening bars. In fact all three themes are based around a similar harmonic template (Ex. 1.3).

This movement supplies a paradigm in Beethoven's music of Carl Dahlhaus's concept of 'subthematicism'—a network or constellation of affinities providing a deeper unity to a fractured or seemingly disparate musical surface by an underlying thematic idea that need not be heard in essential form, a Platonic conception rather akin to Schoenberg's *Grundgestalt*.[31] Connections do exist between the diverse elements of the exposition, but their relationship is not linear or organically composed out in the style of thematic working typifying Haydn and Beethoven's first two periods. Instead, a complex network of associations spread across the movement (and even work) suggests the essential underlying simultaneity of time.

> The actual formal process—the guarantee of coherence and continuity in instrumental music—withdraws, so to speak, from the surface of the music . . . into its interior: into a 'subthematic' realm in which threads are tied criss-cross at random, instead of the musical logic manifesting itself as the commanding, goal-orientated course of events—as in the works of the middle period.[32]

This re-working of sonata form in late Beethoven gives rise to a more fragmented quality vis-à-vis the goal-orientated middle style and its more transparent motivic logic, while still proving capable of supporting a distinctive lyricism. The older Beethoven—or at least Dahlhaus and many later critics—no doubt

---

[31] Dahlhaus, *Ludwig van Beethoven*, pp. 215–18.
[32] Ibid., p. 204.

approved of the obscure Ephesian axiom that unseen harmony is better than the apparent.[33]

Beethoven's Temporalities: 'Heroic' and 'Late' Time

The distinction between a contemplative, internalised time and the forward-directed time observed in the first movements of Opp. 109 and 111 and finale of Op. 110 calls to mind the analysis of Karol Berger of what he labels 'Beethoven dreamer'. As Berger notes in relation to the late piano sonatas, 'This is a music that assumes the existence of two distinct ontological levels, the real and the imagined or remembered worlds of the protagonist, and that makes palpable a shifting of attention between these two levels'.[34] The 'most fundamental feature' of the 'other world' to which the protagonist is drawn

> is that in it the normal laws governing the musical time and space are suspended or at least drastically slowed down in relation to the surrounding 'real world'. The alternative world is not the world of action, but of contemplation. What gets contemplated during the suspension of the normal flow of time is either the interiority of the individual mind or God, either the world within or the world beyond.[35]

Such a suspension of time may be related, in Berger's opinion, to the nature of aesthetic experience as conceived by Kant, and thus in turn to the musical theories of E.T.A. Hoffmann and Schopenhauer. The result is both a sense of musical self-reflexivity (Beethoven's music, he contends, is 'music about music', about the act of aesthetic experience itself) and links to the sense of noumenal or transcendent, that which lies outside experiential categories in time and space. 'The traditional image of Beethoven as the tone poet of the heroic Napoleonic history, while not false, is one-sided', Berger concludes. 'The Beethovenian abstraction out of time is the obverse side of the Beethovenian heroic quest and its temporal teleology . . . At the beginning of the modern age, side by side with Beethoven hero stands Beethoven dreamer'.[36]

[33] Heraclitus, Fragment B. 54 (G.S. Kirk, J.E. Raven, and M. Schofield, *The Presocratic Philosophers* [Cambridge: Cambridge University Press, 1983], p. 192).

[34] Karol Berger, 'Beethoven and the Aesthetic State', *Beethoven Forum VII* (1999), 31 (rephrased in *Bach's Cycle, Mozart's Arrow*, pp. 329–30).

[35] Ibid., 35 (rephrased in *Bach's Cycle, Mozart's Arrow*, pp. 332–3).

[36] Ibid., 43 (rephrased in *Bach's Cycle, Mozart's Arrrow*, p. 340).

This dichotomy Berger schematises may be present within a single piece of music, especially in the early and late piano sonatas, though such a distinction between a forward-driving temporality and more static, even temporally suspended conception also overlaps in a wider chronological sense with a shift from the composer's middle period to the late works, at least as evinced in Beethoven historiography. Using the same hero versus dreamer schema, A.B. Marx had already contrasted over a century before the 'dream phantasmagoria' of Beethoven's late style with the now departed 'time of the heroic symphony with its world-historical battle scenes'.[37] It is one of the most persistent truisms of music history that the works of Beethoven's middle period embody a revolutionary new approach to musical time, a heroic, forward striving and insatiable orientation towards the future. This model is epitomised in the first movement of the *Eroica* Symphony with its seemingly inevitable orientation towards the massive coda, in which previously incomplete ideas find their full realisation and consummation, or at a wider level, the entire course of the Fifth Symphony, a monumental composing out of a *per aspera ad astra* narrative plot-archetype into music that would imprint itself indelibly onto Western consciousness for the next two centuries. As if in direct opposition to over two millennia of covert Platonism in Western thought and values, Beethoven's music seems to celebrate and revel in the temporal Becoming, still emerging, over eternal Being, the fully-formed.[38]

This shift in musical temporality has been contextualised by Reinhold Brinkmann with radically changing contemporary conceptions of time and historical progress. Beethoven's works after 1800 'mirror a shift in consciousness. They mirror the emphatic embrace of the new, of a new time', marked by the acceleration of temporal experience and the orientation towards an emphatically new future. 'And in the temporal art of music', through Beethoven's ability to temporalise musical form 'the experience of time, of a new . . . revolutionary structural use of time, assumed a central role'.[39] David Greene explains this idea of 'revolutionary' time well: 'Beethoven's sonata-allegro movements

[37] A.B. Marx, *Ludwig van Beethoven: Leben und Schaffen*, 2 vols. (Berlin: Janke, 1863), vol. II, p. 311.

[38] It is not necessarily the case, though, that even the most iconic of Beethoven's 'heroic works' are entirely linear in the concept of temporality they seem to convey. Scott Burnham makes the important point that the future-orientation of such works culminate in endings that appear to summarise and re-present the foregoing course of the music from some transcendent (Utopian?) perspective; the temporality suggested by a Beethovenian coda is thus a mixture of linear and cyclical time, standing outside the immanent course of the preceding music while nonetheless being the result of it. Scott Burnham, *Beethoven Hero* (Princeton: Princeton University Press, 1995), pp. 123–45.

[39] Reinhold Brinkmann, 'In the Times(s) of the "Eroica"', in Scott Burnham and Michael Steinberg (eds.), *Beethoven and his World* (Princeton: Princeton University Press, 2000), pp. 15–16.

resemble those of Haydn and Mozart in that they mirror the temporal process of a free agent shaping a future which responds both to the self and to the past'. However,

> Beethoven's temporal processes differ from those of his predecessors in the degree to which he rejected the prevailing concepts of continuity, that is . . . what could follow a given past without falling into chaos . . . a temporal process in which change can be profound and surprising. . . . The temporal processes in much of Beethoven's music are ones in which revolution is possible if 'revolution' means actualising a future that is not mechanically determined by the past and does not flow easily from human decisions, but that can be summoned only through a momentuous struggle, yet is nevertheless profoundly related to the past.[40]

This 'revolutionary' time, then, may be said to be a more extreme outcome of the temporalisation of experience attested to by historians from the late eighteenth century onwards, where the future may not have been predictable before it occurred but can notwithstanding be retrospectively understood as a necessary consequence, even if this was not the only possible outcome.[41] The temporality of much of Beethoven's middle-period work thus continues the temporalisation of the musical process and dynamic orientation towards the future that is already present in the music of Haydn and Mozart, but extends these qualities still further, as if to breaking point.

Almost as prevalent is the idea that Beethoven's later music retreats from this overwhelming sense of teleological drive and negates or at least frequently undercuts it by suggesting a more fractured or static temporal state. The first signs of this change may be witnessed, according to its proponents, as early as the final Violin Sonata Op. 96, the 'Archduke' Trio Op. 97, or Piano Sonata Op. 101, with their renewed emphasis on lyricism and expansivity—possibly even as far back as the 'Pastoral' Symphony. Theodor Adorno contrasts the 'intensive' temporality of the middle period with the more 'extensive' time of these 'late-middle' works, while Dahlhaus has written perceptively of the new lyrical quality of the works from c.1812–16 and their importance for the formation of the Romantic lyrical style of Schubert and Mendelssohn.[42] It is the works after 1818, though,

[40] Greene, *Temporal Processes in Beethoven's Music*, pp. 52–3.

[41] See Reinhard Koselleck, *Futures Past: On the Semantics of Historical Time*, trans. Keith Tribe (Cambridge, MA: MIT Press, 1985); *Zeitschichten: Studien zur Historik* (Frankfurt: Suhrkamp, 2003).

[42] Adorno, *Beethoven*, pp. 88–92, Dahlhaus, *Ludwig van Beethoven*, pp. 202–3. See also Elaine Sisman, 'Memory and Invention at the Threshold of Beethoven's Late Style', in Burnham and Steinberg, *Beethoven and his World*, pp. 51–87; Richard Will, 'Time, Morality, and Humanity in Beethoven's *Pastoral* Symphony', *Journal of the American Musicological Society*, 50 (1997), 271–329.

that provide the central locus for this 'late' sense of temporality—the final four Piano Sonatas (Opp. 106 and 109–111), the last five Quartets (Opp. 127, 132, 130, 131, and 135, with the *Grosse Fuge* for good measure), the 'Diabelli' Variations, *Missa Solemnis*, and (possibly) Ninth Symphony, besides a handful of Bagatelles. Eckehard Kiem, following Adorno's diagnosis, contends that the sense of progressive, subjective time of Beethoven's middle period is pushed to the very extremes of comprehensibility in his late style.[43] For Wolfgang Rathert, similarly, the radicalised temporal conception of Beethoven's late works erode the teleological conception and formal closure of his earlier classical aesthetic, supplanting a linear model of time with a circular one.[44] Typically these qualities may be related to a wider cultural context by aligning Beethoven with the political climate of Restoration Vienna, the influence or common affinity with Romantic thought in this period of broader social and intellectual change, or a cluster of autobiographical reasons (such as Beethoven's now almost total deafness, the composer's struggles with his sister-in-law over his nephew Karl, his coming to terms with approaching death or purported turn inward to a more spiritual realm, a notion especially beloved in nineteenth-century hagiography).[45]

Something of this new, anti-heroic approach to time may be read in the Sonata Op. 111. The first movement is one of the most craggy and unremitting in Beethoven's oeuvre. David Greene reads it as 'a continuous search for events that will genuinely satisfy the past' and give their strivings 'a satisfactory completion'. 'Again and again', however, 'we hear failure'.[46] The sonata's *Maestoso* introduction imposes on the listener a single-minded working-out of diminished seventh complexes in the archaic dotted style of the French overture. Deriving its outline from the material of this jagged introduction the principal thematic material of the *Allegro con brio* consists of a brusque, clearly defined motive spanning a diminished fourth (c–e♭–b), but rather than proving susceptible to organic-sounding development in the manner of Beethoven's heroic middle period its continuation is laboured, repetitive, coming in fits and starts, a rage over a penny that is well and truly lost. The first theme-group is a series of trial attempts at eliciting an adequate continuation of the motivic material;

---

[43] Eckehard Kiem, 'Der Blick in Abgrund: Zeitstruktur beim späten Beethoven', in Richard Klein, Eckehard Kiem, and Wolfram Ette (eds.), *Musik in der Zeit: Zeit in der Musik* (Göttingen: Velbrück Wissenschaft, 2000), pp. 216–18.

[44] Wolfgang Rathert, 'Ende, Abschied und Fragment: Zu ästhetik und Geschichte einer musikalischen Problemstellung', in Otto Kolleritsch (ed.), *Abschied in die Gegenwart: Teleologie und Zuständlichkeit in der Musik* (Vienna and Graz: Universal Edition, 1998), pp. 214–16.

[45] On Beethoven and Romanticism see the general thrust of Maynard Solomon, *Late Beethoven*, and Stephen Rumph, *Beethoven After Napoleon: Political Romanticism in the Late Works* (Berkeley and Los Angeles: University of California Press, 2004).

[46] Greene, *Temporal Processes in Beethoven's Music*, p. 33; also see Rumph's insightful analysis of this movement, *Beethoven After Napoleon*, pp. 127–30.

old-fashioned *Fortspinnung* boils over into empty motoric movement, to be succeeded by an antiquated-sounding two-part contrapuntal invention functioning as a sonata transition. As if in frustration born of this inability to progress
through the smooth development of its material towards something more satisfying, the keyboard writing is pushed to the extremes of register (bb. 48–50).
A parenthetically inserted second-subject theme in the submediant (what Susan
McClary once memorably described as the nineteenth-century's 'Never-never
land')[47] provides the only respite, and even this is short-lived, the omnipresent
diminished-fourth motive returning as the exposition's closing theme (b. 58).
The development wrenches the allegro motive back into the gestures of the
exposition's opening, before finding itself party to the fugal treatment that all
along seemed a fitting adjunct to this somewhat recherché material.

All this sound and fury mysteriously vanishes away into thin air in the coda.
'The ending of the movement provides a strange, relaxed benediction, strange,
because it does not seem to have been earned'. For Greene, here, Beethoven
'does not retreat from temporality and seek fulfilment in some atemporal reality' but instead, 'struggle itself' becomes the only victory. Yet at a higher level,
the succeeding of this movement by the C major *Arietta* arguably forms at least
some type of withdrawal from the intractable temporal striving of the first movement following the uneasy truce of its coda (as we shall see, this final movement
has conveyed notions of timelessness and transcendence to generations of critics and listeners).[48]

Variation and the Eternal

As epitomised in the final movements of Op. 109 and Op. 111 the idea of variation structure informs a considerable extent of Beethoven's late music.[49] This
design, one might say, already contains a certain inherent Platonism in the contrast it fashions between an underlying theme and its varied manifestations—a
quasi-supertemporal essence and its temporally changing surface phenomena.
In both of Beethoven's examples here this contrast is underscored by the circular recall of the opening theme at the movement's close, thus explicitly returning to the unchanging source which had all along lain behind the variations and

[47] Susan McClary, *Conventional Wisdom: The Content of Musical Form* (Berkeley and Los
Angeles: University of California Press, 2000), p. 123.

[48] Greene, *Temporal Processes in Beethoven's Music*, pp. 33–4.

[49] See Dahlhaus, *Ludwig van Beethoven*, p. 222. Other notable examples are to be found in the slow
movements of the Quartets Opp. 127, 131, and 135 and 'Diabelli' Variations, alongside hybrid types
such as the double variations of Op. 132 and the slow movement and finale of the Ninth Symphony.

forming a circle (the shape long associated with the eternal, without beginning or end). And as we saw at the start of this chapter, in both these sonatas the final variation before the return of the theme seems furthermore highly suggestive of the synthesis of all the foregoing variations, the overlaying of what was heard temporally consecutive into a simultaneity. Quite how this may appear to be the case is worth examining further.

Implicit within the concept of the variation set is the sense in which each variation forms a unit that is equivalent to and may therefore map onto any of the others: in terms of the phenomenology of this design's form, the listener readily relates the individual variation to its surrounding variations or theme, a conceptual spatialising of temporal experience. While each variation obviously occurs in time, nevertheless there is a sense in which the musically trained listener assumes that each variation may be understood from a higher formal perspective as a distinct unit, a whole, rounded and self-enclosed. Moreover, in the finale of Op. 109 especially, the actual theme seems itself designed to be internally circular and symmetrical at several layers—the arch-shaped progression of the bass's contour in the first half, the motivic repetition within the theme's melodic line, and the cadence back onto degree $\hat{3}$ at its close, the point from which it had started. Thus each variation may be conceived of as a 'moment'—a perfect whole, complete and temporally indivisible—a type of 'eternity'.

The type of temporal process resulting from the accumulation of these units would appear at first sight to be additive; the very idea of the variation set is an inherently paratactic one. Nicholas Marston notes that 'compared to sonata form, Classical variation form might seem largely antithetical to the creation of goal-directed structures', threatening to produce circularity, even stasis.[50] At the same time, Beethoven seeks to overcome this potential stasis by the larger-scale directionality and closure provided by the increasing diminution of note-values and the reprise of the theme at the movement's end. The result is an interplay between the variations' inherent parataxis and a composed-in teleology that gives rise to a sense that the succession of these variations in time is not simply additive (one variation replacing another) but accumulative (each variation is added to the former, but in such a way as to occupy the same point in time). Like the historical progression of Hegel's contemporaneous World-Spirit, it forms 'a circle of progressive embodiments, which looked at in one aspect still exist beside each other, and only as looked at from another point of view appear as past'.[51]

[50] Nicholas Marston, '"The sense of an ending": Goal-directedness in Beethoven's music', in Glenn Stanley (ed.), *The Cambridge Companion to Beethoven* (Cambridge: Cambridge University Press, 2000), p. 89.

[51] Hegel, Introduction to the *Lectures on The Philosophy of History*, trans. J. Sibree (New York: Dover, 1956), p. 79.

This attribute is something inherent in variation structure, but enormously intensified in Beethoven's particular design in Op. 109, where Variation 6 forms a microcosm of the rhythmic acceleration of Variations 1 to 3, followed by their superimposition, alongside a further reference back to Variation 4. With the return of the simple cantabile variation theme we still hear the plenitude of Variation 6 and the earlier course of the movement ringing in our ears. The latent equivalence of each variation to another suggests their presence at the same time on different levels—rather than linear temporal telesis it implies an increasing 'depth' of vision, a summary and simultaneity of the preceding, the sense of pan-opticism already characteristic of the coda to the *Eroica*.[52] The variation principle of Op. 109 demonstrates that what is separated in time may be overlaid, superimposed, 'embracing the whole of everlasting life in one simultaneous present'.[53] In Berger's words, 'It makes simultaneous what should be successive—abolishing the succession of past, present, and future in favour of the simultaneity of the present and thus neutralising the flow of time in favour of the eternal Now'.[54]

The variations echo Martin Cooper's wider assertion that Beethoven's late works orientate themselves around the search for a 'unity lying behind the diversity of the phenomena of human existence'.[55] The implication of the process seen in these variations is that temporal separation does not exist, just as for God apparently 'time does not exist'. This theme connects to a long tradition of mystic thought, found both in the Hindu and Buddhist religions that Beethoven, as his journals attest, had been delving into around this time, and in the West from Plato and Neoplatonism. The circular journey charted here is indeed reminiscent of an entry in Beethoven's *Tagebuch* from his readings in Indian philosophy that several scholars have drawn attention to: 'All things flowed clear and pure from God. If afterwards I became darkened through passion for evil, I returned after manifold repentance and purification, to the elevated and pure source, to the Godhead'.[56] In comparable manner, calling upon Plotinus to be our guide,

[52] See especially Burnham, *Beethoven Hero*, pp. 52–6. Also see Lewis Lockwood, '"Eroica" Perspectives: Strategy and Design in the First Movement', in Alan Tyson (ed.), *Beethoven Studies*, vol. 3 (Cambridge: Cambridge University Press, 1982), pp. 98–101; Robert G. Hopkins, 'When a coda is more than a coda: Reflections on Beethoven', in Eugene Narmour and Ruth Solie (eds.), *Explorations in Music, the Arts, and Ideas: Essays in Honor of Leonard B. Meyer* (Stuyvesant, NY: Pendragon, 1988), pp. 403–4.

[53] Boethius, *The Consolation of Philosophy*, V/6.

[54] The formulation is taken from Karol Berger's reading of the *St Matthew Passion*'s opening chorus, *Bach's Cycle, Mozart's Arrow*, p. 13. The religious or mystical sense of time Berger perceives in Bach's music seems if anything more appropriate for Beethoven's work.

[55] Martin Cooper, *Beethoven: The Last Decade 1817–1827* (London: Oxford University Press, 1970), p. 420.

[56] Beethoven, *Tagebuch* Entry of 1815 (63a), reproduced in Maynard Solomon, *Beethoven Essays* (Cambridge, MA: Harvard University Press, 1988), p. 267.

the music's underlying theme—'that which neither has been nor will be, but simply possesses being, what which enjoys stable existence as neither in process of change nor having ever changed—that is Eternity'. The variations, like 'things and beings in the Time order . . . are still bound to sequence; they are deficient'. But 'if, then, the Soul withdrew, sinking itself again into its primal unity, Time would disappear'.[57] Through mystical communion with the One or God, the soul may glimpse for brief moments this higher unity, a state of timelessness, the *nunc stans* in which everything that ever has happened or ever will happen appears at once as a simultaneity.

We recall that for Berger's 'Beethoven dreamer', what gets contemplated during these moments of apparent timelessness is either the interiority of the mind or God, which Berger connects to the Kantian ideality of time and from there to Schopenhauer's formulation of the aesthetic experience. In the fourth book of the second volume of *The World as Will and Representation* Schopenhauer offers an extended discussion of the timeless *nunc stans*, only conceivable through the stilling of the will and the realisation of the irreality of all transitory phenomena—a state attainable through philosophical insight or aesthetic contemplation:

> what is really essential in things, in man, in the world, lies permanently and enduringly in the *Nunc stans*, firm and immovable; and that the change of phenomena and of events is a mere consequence of our apprehension of it by means of our perception of time[.]
>
> There is only *one present*, and this always exists: for it is the sole form of actual existence. We must arrive at the insight that the *past* is not *in itself* different from the present, but is so only in our apprehension. This has *time* as its form, by virtue of which alone the present shows itself as different from the past. To make this insight easier, let us imagine all the events and scenes of human life, good and bad, fortunate and unfortunate, delightful and dreadful, which are presented to us successively in the course of time and variety of places, in the most motley multifariousness and succession, as existing *all at once and simultaneously* and for ever, in the *Nunc stans*[.][58]

It would be hard to find an more apt analogy for the effect of Op. 109's finale and of its final variation.

---

[57] Plotinus, *The Enneads*, III.7.3, trans. Stephen MacKenna (Harmondsworth: Penguin, 1991), p. 216; III.7.6, p. 220; III.7.12, p. 229.

[58] Schopenhauer, *The World as Will and Representation*, vol. II ch. 41 ('On Death and its Relation to the Indestructibility of Our Inner Nature'), pp. 489–90, 480.

Intermovement Links and the Sonata Trilogy

In Op. 109's finale it is not only the opening *Andante* theme that returns at the end but a wider network of allusions back to the first movement that are incorporated across the course of the movement. Most clearly of all the texture of the second variation—fleet-footed semiquavers split between the two hands—brings to mind the opening *Vivace* of the first movement, while (as noted earlier) in the fourth variation the binary theme's first half cadence (b. 104) manages to call the listener's consciousness back to the interpolated *Adagio* parenthesis in the first movement, a passage further alluded to at the corresponding moment of the final variation (b. 169). The andante variation theme itself may also be read as possessing deeper links with the material of the first movement.[59] Thus behind the finale's variations the opening theme forms a persistent underlying thread, and behind the movement as a whole we may also sense intermittently the presence of the first movement.[60] Though this might sound familiar from the thematic principle of cyclic form found with increasing frequency throughout the nineteenth century, the material relation between the two movements is not transparent in the manner that would soon after become typical of the Romantic cyclic style. As with Dahlhaus's reading of subthematicism in the first movement of Op. 110, these moments of inter-section are only passing hints, little windows or 'wormholes' from different points in performance time onto each other, not a full-bodied system of inter-connections (as exemplified, say, in the work of Franck or d'Indy). The prin-ciple is thus much the same as that of Kinderman's 'parenthetical enclosure' or Jonathan Kramer's 'non-linear time' we noted earlier, though manifested

---

[59] See Philip Barford, 'The Piano Music—II', in Denis Arnold and Nigel Fortune (eds.), *The Beethoven Companion* (London: Faber & Faber, 1971), p. 172. Nicholas Marston gives a detailed Schenkerian account of structural parallelisms and continuities between the outer movements in 'Schenker and Forte Reconsidered: Beethoven's Sketches for the Piano Sonata in E, Op. 109', *19th-Century Music*, 10 (1986), 24–42.

[60] Commentators have also been keen to emphasise the sense of unity they have felt between the different movements of Beethoven's sonatas. Wilhelm von Lenz claimed that the whole work 'con-sists of a single movement [*Satz*], in several parts or tempi [*Bewegungen*]—one and the same idea is posed in the Adagio recitative and becomes beatified in the variations' (*Beethoven: Eine Kunst-Studie*, 5 vols. [Hamburg: Hoffmann und Campe, 1860], vol. V, p. 56). Wilfrid Mellers makes a similarly bold claim for the sonata as a whole to be the emergence of the 'Song' of the finale that had lain latent in the first two movements (*Beethoven and the Voice of God* [London: Faber & Faber, 1983], p. 221). Edward T. Cone sees the sixth variation as exposing 'a hidden unity of structure' beneath the division of the sonata into separate movements, based on the reflection of first movement's first and second subjects in the two halves of the finale's theme (*The Composer's Voice* [Berkeley: University of California Press, 1974], pp. 150–1).

here at a higher level.[61] As Dahlhaus explains concerning the resulting musical temporality:

> When a thematic—or 'subthematic'—connection reaches across from one movement to another, as in Op. 109, that is one of the traits of a musical logic that is less a goal-directed process than a network, the strands of which can radiate in all directions. Associations that take this form are . . . the corollary of a lyricism that beckons us to linger in contemplation, and eschews the drama of determining the present from the vantage point of the future.[62]

In the sonata Op. 110, similarly, passing intermovement relationships may be perceived. For Kinderman, the A♭ major Sonata incorporates 'a network of forecasts and reminiscences of themes'; Charles Rosen claims 'no sonata of Beethoven's is more tightly unified by the recurrence of the same or similar motifs throughout the work, and by the clear desire . . . that the movements succeed each other without pause', while Michael Spitzer calls Op. 110 the most unified of the 32 sonatas.[63] Most evidently the sequence of arpeggios at its final cadence echoes the transitional theme of the first movement's exposition, the whole work, in Lewis Lockwood's view, suggesting 'a circular time-space by its closing reference back to the cascading tonic arpeggios of the first movement'.[64] Further potential motivic connections may be observed between the second movement *Allegro molto* and *Arioso dolente* (the minor-key descending $\hat{5}$–$\hat{4}$–$\hat{3}$–$\hat{2}$–$\hat{1}$–$\hat{7}$ figure), and first movement and fugue (in the alternating sequence of descending thirds and rising fourths). Links between the two movements

---

[61] Besides this interest in techniques of parenthetical enclosure, Kinderman has claimed that 'Beethoven's complex use of thematic foreshadowing and reminiscence contributes a dimension to his music that transcends a linear temporal unfolding' (*Beethoven*, p. 12). The connection between the bass's linear descent of the *Prestissimo* second movement and the bassline of the first movement recapitulation (and additionally perhaps the new theme appearing in that movement's coda, bb. 78ff, added almost as an afterthought in the manner of Schumann), is a reasonable example of such thematic foreshadowing.

[62] Dahlhaus, *Ludwig van Beethoven*, p. 217.

[63] Kinderman, 'Integration and Narrative Design in Beethoven's Piano Sonata in A-flat Major, Opus 110', *Beethoven Forum I* (1992), 111; Charles Rosen, *Beethoven's Piano Sonatas: A Short Companion* (New Haven: Yale University Press, 2002), p. 235; Spitzer, *Music as Philosophy*, p. 154. For historic interest one may sample Armin Knab's 'Die Einheit der Beethovenschen Klaviersonate in As-Dur, op. 110', *Zeitschrift für Musikwissenschaft*, 1 (1919), 388–99.

[64] Lewis Lockwood, *Beethoven: The Music and the Life* (New York: Oxford University Press, 2003), p. 388.

of Op. 111, on the other hand, are less easy to observe; one might say that the stark opposition between the two is the most notable feature of their relationship. Lawrence Kramer has expressed their complementary association as one of 'expressive doubling': the relationship 'is all but subliminal. It does not depend on the recurrence of musical textures . . . but on underlying affinities between textures as different as Beethoven can make them'.[65] Going one stage further, on continued exposure all three sonatas slowly begin to reveal suggestive similarities between themselves. Most obviously the variation finales of Opp. 109 and 111 appear to contain some undefined point of intersection, a distinct quality of likeness. This affinity comes not just from the larger structural similarity the two evince but also seems surely to lie in the very nature of the opening themes. The general tone is similar, and the thematic constituents of the two do admittedly possess some general affinity—the prominent descending intervals in the theme and the element of upward movement in the bass—but these are hardly convincing in analytical demonstration. What is surely closer to the crux of the matter is the common rhythmic profile of the two. On the page the relation is not so apparent, but if we rebar the Arietta theme of Op. 111 so as to shift the present anacrusis to the start of each $\frac{9}{16}$ bar the distinct sarabande quality this melody shares with Op. 109's *Andante* theme is clear to see. The initial repeated harmonies in the first two bars suggest a

$$|---\smile|---\smile|$$

stress pattern that comes across quite clearly in performance, before the notated barring asserts itself from b. 2^3 onwards with a minuet- or Ländler-like

$$|-\smile\smile|-\smile\smile|.$$

(The ambiguity between notation, harmonic rhythm, and hypermeter in this opening theme has long been a source of scholarly fascination.) But as suggested earlier, the start of Op. 110 also embodies elements of the sarabande, prominent especially in the second bar of each two-bar unit, which then begins to feel like it is cut from the same Beethovenian cloth as the other two works. Indeed, in the context of these last three sonatas the opening bars of the *Moderato Cantabile* sounds like the beginning of a variation theme. Perhaps the perceived similarity

---

[65] Lawrence Kramer, *Music as Cultural Practice, 1800–1900* (Berkeley and Los Angeles: University of California Press, 1992), p. 49. Wilfrid Mellers purports to find motivic links between Op. 111's two movements (*Beethoven and the Voice of God*, p. 244), though his demonstration is not particularly convincing. More plausible is the similarity between the contour of the Arietta's opening (C . . . E . . . B) and the head motive of the prior Allegro (C–E♭–B). See Rudolph Réti, *The Thematic Process in Music* (New York: Macmillan, 1951), p. 94.

is formed simply by virtue of all three sonatas containing prominent slow-to-moderate tempo major-key movements in triple time using soft dynamics, with a mild emphasis often placed on the second beat of each three-beat grouping.

Earlier commentators have not been slow to pick up on these resemblances between the material of the three sonatas. The affinity of Op. 110's opening to the concluding variation theme of Op. 109 has often been noted. Alfred Brendel sees all three sonatas interfused by an alternating pattern of thirds and fourths.[66] Additionally, Martin Cooper believes that the rhythm of the descending octaves in the second subject of Op. 110's first movement 'clearly recalls' the opening of the recapitulation of Op. 109, Richard Kramer points to the similarity in the use of widely spaced parallel tenths in both these sonatas' second subjects, and Hugo Riemann claims that Op. 111's 'consolatory second theme is so clearly reminiscent of the Arioso dolente of Op. 110'.[67] Having observed such connections between individual movements within a given sonata, the next logical step up is positing the possibility of all three sonatas Opp. 109–111 forming some type of 'meta-work'. These sonatas have, after all, often been claimed as forming a trilogy.[68] The idea is attractive, though more extreme examples from Beethoven reception might warn us against reading too much into such inter-opus connections; the very nature of these works' fractured surfaces might suggest paradigms of overt unity and coherence are inappropriate to describe them.[69] Again, as with the ideas of subthematicism and non-linear time we explored earlier, it might be better to suggest a looser network of affinities between the sonatas rather than insisting on their forming a definite three-part metawork. A more fitting way of viewing these sonatas' relationship is perhaps to view them, as Michael Spitzer proposes, as belonging together in the form of Walter Benjamin's concept of 'constellation'.[70]

Yet to the extent that the three may be heard as a coherent group, one might wonder what type of 'metanarrative' may be traced across the sonatas. What are

[66] Alfred Brendel, 'Schubert's Last Sonatas', in *On Music: Collected Essays* (London: Robson, 2007), pp. 172–3.

[67] Cooper, *Beethoven: The Last Decade*, p. 188; Richard Kramer, '*Adagio espressivo*: Opus 109 as Radical Dialectic', in *Unfinished Music* (New York: Oxford University Press, 2008), p. 276; Hugo Riemann, *Ludwig van Beethovens sämtliche Klavier-Solosonaten*, 3 vols. (Berlin: Max Hesses Verlag, 1919), vol. III, p. 455.

[68] See Denis Matthews, *Beethoven Piano Sonatas (BBC Music Guides)* (London: BBC Publications, 1967), p. 51; Lockwood, *Beethoven*, p. 384; Barry Cooper, *Beethoven*, pp. 310–11; Mellers, *Beethoven and the Voice of God*, p. 199: 'it is valid to regard them as three components of one work'. Often, however, this terminology appears to be used by commentators merely in a loose sense, denoting the sonatas as forming a chronologically discrete set.

[69] The most prominent example of this urge for finding inter-opus unity may be found in Deryck Cooke, 'The Unity of Beethoven's Late Quartets', *The Musical Review*, 24 (1963), 30–49.

[70] Spitzer, *Music as Philosophy*, pp. 124–5.

the possible differences in overall temporal 'plot' between the pieces? Do they form some progressive exploration of musical temporality? The first of the group, Op. 109, is clearly the most circular, rounded, beautiful in the third movement's tranquil return to the variation theme at its close; even the vehemence of the central *Prestissimo* helps profile the wider circularity suggested by similarities between the outer movements. There is a sense of perfection and spiritual grace to the temporal journey of this sonata present only fitfully in the succeeding two. Although starting out from a point of Arcadian grace and apparent simplicity (though perhaps a mediated one, a 'second nature'), Op. 110 suggests in contra-distinction a path through conflict with the rude brusqueness of the scherzo, the hyper-expressivity of the *Arioso dolente*'s lament and its disruptive return within the forward striving of the fugue. The overall course of the A♭ major Sonata is that of overcoming through struggle, thus the most akin to the 'Heroic' paradigm of Beethoven's middle years (despite the otherwise considerable expressive distance of parts of it). Finally the first movement of Op. 111 presents the most fragmented, jagged conception of temporality (the heroic paradigm gone sour?), withdrawing into an otherworldly interiority in the *Arietta*. The close of the Arietta's variations attempt the same return to their opening as that glimpsed in the final page of Op. 109. Now, however, this naïve desire appears impossible: the theme, on its recall, is something broken, gone. We can no longer return to Arcadia; the gates of Paradise are barred, and the cherub stands behind us. The Op. 109 sonata is the beautiful to Op. 111's sublime, 'the still point of the turning world' opposed to 'Things fall apart; the centre cannot hold'.[71] If the passage at the end of Op. 109, where the ringing multiplicity of movement of the sixth variation returns back to the stillness of the underling theme, is akin to a genie going back into a bottle,[72] then the variations of Op. 111's *Arietta* open Pandora's jar, renouncing any possi-bility of closure. And (as Thomas Mann's Wendell Kretzschmar might contend of that 'pathetically consoling' c♯ in the final variation),[73] all that remains—the last, most jesting gift of the gods to mankind—is hope.

Such a plot-archetype fits rather neatly into familiar tripartite schemas. Mytho-poetically, one might trace a 'Paradise Lost–Paradise Regained' trope with a Romantic, pessimistic twist at its end. The three sonatas thus chart a uni-versal history from an initial Golden Age, through the Fall and a heroic striving to regain this lost Eden, to a final acceptance of the irrecoverableness of the former Arcadian state. Such an underlying narrative is, after all, an all-pervasive theme within German thought of the late-eighteenth and early nineteenth centuries

[71] T.S. Eliot, 'Burnt Norton', from *Four Quartets*; Yeats, 'The Second Coming'.

[72] I am again indebted to Scott Burnham for this wonderfully apt analogy.

[73] Thomas Mann, *Doktor Faustus: Das Leben des deutschen Tonsetzers Adrian Leverkühn, erzählt von einem Freunde* (Frankfurt: Fischer Verlag, 1947), p. 73.

(Schiller is probably its most prominent theorist).[74] Historically, the succession of musical temporalities furthermore parallels the theories of the historian Reinhold Koselleck concerning the chronological development of temporal conceptions up to Beethoven's day. We start with a circular pre-modern Religious time in which the future is wedded to the past, progress through the humanistic forward striving of the late 18th-century with its accelerated time sense, and, disappointed by the failure of humanity to obtain an earthy Utopia in the aftermath of the revolutionary and Napoleonic periods, end with a Romantic withdrawal into the self, a continual, internalised aesthetic state of revolution.[75] Pushing this hermeneutic approach to its extremes (one might say *ad absurdum*), the progression of these three sonatas might even be analogised with the customary division of Beethoven's oeuvre into three 'style periods'. Though there is little commonality between the E major Sonata and Beethoven's early style, the central sonata of this series, Op. 110, is certainly most akin in musical temporality to those works of the heroic middle period, and Op. 111, like a typical 'late work', is the most fractured, sublime of the three in the temporal vicissitudes it opens up.

Beethoven as Voice of God: On Timelessness and Transcendence

Beethoven's late style has been heard to evoke a sense of timelessness, the numinous and transcendental. Recent reception of the late music has emphasised the special sense of time felt to be present in these pieces. This ranges from musings on Beethoven's time in history (such as Carl Dahlhaus, who speaks of timelessness in various ways including the late works' *untimeliness*) to consideration of individual pieces (such as Joseph Kerman's and Daniel Chua's reading of timelessness on the *Heiliger Dankgesang* movement of Op. 132).[76] These three late

[74] See for instance Hans Joachim Mähl, *Die Idee des goldenen Zeitalters im Werk des Novalis* (Heidelberg: Carl Winter, 1965), Constantin Behler, *Nostalgic Teleology: Friedrich Schiller and the Schemata of Aesthetic Humanism* (Berne: Peter Lang, 1995), and generally M.H. Abrams, *Natural Supernaturalism: Tradition and Revolution in Romantic Literature* (New York: Norton, 1971). I discuss this idea further in *Mendelssohn, Time and Memory*, pp. 18–24 and 104–5.

[75] See here M.H. Abrams's notion of 'revolution through imagination' (*Natural Supernaturalism*, pp. 335–47).

[76] Dahlhaus, *Ludwig van Beethoven*, pp. 219–20; Joseph Kerman, *The Beethoven Quartets* (New York: Norton, 1966), p. 257, Daniel K.L. Chua, *The 'Galitzin' Quartets of Beethoven* (Princeton: Princeton University Press, 1995), pp. 138–51. Also see Birgit Lodes's reading of a circular, mythic time in the first movement of Op. 127: '"So träumte mir, ich reiste . . . nach Indien": Temporality and Mythology in Op. 127/I', in William Kinderman (ed.), *The String Quartets of Beethoven* (Urbana and Chicago: University of Illinois Press, 2006), pp. 168–212.

sonatas are particularly prevalent in such discussions. The language used by commentators frequently emphasises timeless, celestial and transcendent attributes, abounding in metaphors of height, weightlessness, and light. Concerning the sixth variation of Op. 109 Martin Cooper speaks of the 'transfiguration of the theme in an atmosphere so rarefied', 'the impression of a music that hovers at a great height above the world of everyday experience', and the 'ethereal quality' of Op. 110's first movement.[77] Wilfrid Mellers considers the finale of Op. 109 a 'rejection of time' in which the counterpoint of variation 4 'destroys time' and the climactic variation 6 effaces it, while the close of Op. 110 offers a 'celestial vision', a 'moment outside time'.[78] Similarly for Kinderman, in the final variation of Op. 109 'an urgent will to overcome the inevitable passing of time and sound seems to fill up the spaces of the slow theme with a virtually unprecedented density of material', while 'transcendental and even religious characteristics' surface in the finale of Op. 110.[79]

Above all, the *Arietta* of Op. 111 forms a focal point for the impression of timelessness and transcendence in Beethoven's late music. Wilhelm von Lenz calls upon Dante's *Paradiso* to capture the 'heavenly peace' and 'cosmic universality' he sees in Beethoven's movement, just as Denis Matthews almost a century later, in a mixture of Dantean and Winckelmannesque language, uses words such as 'celestial', 'transfiguration', 'ascending into upper reaches', 'noblest simplicity'.[80] Hans von Bülow reads the sonata's two movements from the perspective of Buddhist thought as *samskara* (purification) and *nirvana* (the extinction of the individual and subsumption into the supreme spirit, a timeless state of beatitude). One of the most poetic accounts is given by Paul Bekker in his 1911 biography: in Beethoven's final variation 'the accompanimental rhythm dissolves into rippling harp arpeggios, high above sparkle the stars in glimmering trills. And between the two floats the melody like a silver thread, the yearning of a great man which stretches from earth to heaven'.[81] For Edwin Fischer, the *Arietta* simply represents the transcendental, the Beyond, just as Philip Barford later perceives a 'heavenly atmosphere' to its 'transcendent meditation'.[82] Martin Cooper writes of the 'simplicity and static quality of the Arietta', whose 'ethereal, floating' end breathes the 'air of the heights', whilst his patronymic namesake, Barry, senses 'an extraordinary visionary quality'.[83] Lewis Lockwood meanwhile

[77] Martin Cooper, *Beethoven*, pp. 185–6, 188–9.
[78] Mellers, *Beethoven and the Voice of God*, pp. 213, 216, 220, 238, 239.
[79] Kinderman, *Beethoven*, pp. 224–5, 227.
[80] Lenz, *Beethoven*, vol. V, pp. 92–3, 95; Matthews, *Beethoven Piano Sonatas*, p. 56.
[81] Paul Bekker, *Beethoven* (Berlin: Schuster and Loeffler, 1912), p. 191.
[82] Edwin Fischer, *Ludwig van Beethovens Klaviersonaten: Ein Begleiter für Studierende und Liebhaber* (Wiesbaden: Insel-Verlag, 1956), p. 134, Barford, 'The Piano Music—II', pp. 191, 180.
[83] Martin Cooper, *Beethoven*, pp. 200, 204, Barry Cooper, *Beethoven*, p. 312.

presents the variations as a heroic quest *ad astra*, if now internalised through Kantian categories: 'this spirit, of the mortal, vulnerable human being striving against the odds to hold his moral being steady in order to gather strength as an artist to strive toward the heavens'.[84] Even the usually sober Tovey indulges in what is for him a purple passage ('static and ecstatic visions'), while Heinrich Schenker resorts to cosmic analogy (a 'milky way of tones').[85]

The movement's specific 'timelessness' or its momentary annulment of time figures especially in accounts from the mid twentieth century onwards. Thus 'the slow movement of op. 111 succeeds as almost no other work in suspending the passage of time at its climax' writes Charles Rosen in 1971.[86] Mellers, again, claims that 'the Arietta effaces time'; for Beethoven in this final movement, 'time was no longer relevant'. In the fourth variation 'time stops', while later in the modulating passage starting at b. 106 'it is as though the endless trills were released by that moment outside Time at the end of the [fourth] variation; the vast distance between treble and bass seems to separate soul from body'. Finally, in the very last variation 'it is as though Beethoven is looking back at the world from a great height, floating in a crepuscular haze'.[87] For Stephen Rumph, 'the sonata aspires to timelessness'. 'If the first movement "falls" into horizontal time, the second movement finds redemption in a timeless verticality'.[88] Johannes Forner hears the loss of all temporal sense in the passage beginning at b. 106; for Rosen soon after, 'all forward motion is suspended', and Robert Taub finds the very close 'a moment of transcendence; after nearly thirty minutes of music time seems to stand still, even to reverse itself'.[89]

Though a common factor throughout these pieces' historical reception seems to be the alignment with the transcendent and spiritual, the explicit pur-ported 'timelessness' of Beethoven's late music thus seems to be more a feature of the later twentieth century. As we saw, 'Time exists not at all with God'. An implication of this might be that timeless is to this extent identifiable with the numinous. One might be tempted to make the whimsical analogy that just as in Scott Burnham's famous formulation for the middle-period 'Beethoven's Hero' became 'Beethoven Hero', so in these late works 'Beethoven as voice

---

[84] Lockwood, *Beethoven*, p. 391.

[85] Tovey, *A Companion to Beethoven's Pianoforte Sonatas*, p. 278; Heinrich Schenker, *Beethoven: Die letzten Sonaten. Kritische Ausgabe mit Einführung und Erlauterung*, ed. Oswald Jonas (Vienna: Universal Edition, 1971–2), Op. 111, p. 61.

[86] Rosen, *The Classical Style*, p. 446.

[87] Mellers, *Beethoven and the Voice of God*, pp. 273, 263, 265, 267.

[88] Rumph, *Beethoven After Napoleon*, pp. 131, 130.

[89] Johannes Forner, *Ludwig van Beethoven—Die Klaviersonaten: Betrachtung zu Werk und Gestalt* (Altenburg: Kamprad, 2011), p. 173; Rosen, *Beethoven's Piano Sonatas*, p. 248; Robert Taub, *Playing the Beethoven Piano Sonatas* (Portland, OR: Amadeus Press, 2002), p. 248.

of God' became something akin to 'Beethoven as God', Beethoven himself becoming virtually deified for a secular age. After all, one of the earliest divisions of Beethoven's oeuvre is Liszt's three part division of Beethoven's creative periods—'the adolescent–the man–the god'.[90]

More specifically, one might ask *how* may the music suggest timelessness and transcendence (we have already seen some reasons in the discussion of variation form earlier). I will focus here on the *Arietta* of Op. 111. Obviously certain types of musical parameters are more suited to giving the impression of calmness, purity, depth, or height, such as a high or widely spaced tessitura, a slow underlying tempo, and major key. In many of these the connection with transcendence is through a perceived structural commonality or just symbolic, that is to say a mapping established by cultural convention. For instance, Robert Hatten, coming from the perspective of topic theory, considers the move to a high tessitura as signifying the 'transcendent', and relating specifically to the *Arietta* theme speaks of the use of a solemn, monumental texture and 'primitive effect of chord repetition across the barline to create a stasis that might be interpreted as timelessness'. Hatten also notes that formally 'the additive nature of variation form . . . supports the more static quality of serene contemplation'.[91] The juxtaposition of the troubled C minor first movement and translucent C major of the *Arietta* also points up the latter's qualities through their emphatic contrast with the preceding music. Kinderman reasonably suggests that the 'uplifting and visionary quality' of the *Arietta* stems 'not only from the transformation of the theme and from the culminating effect of synthesis and recapitulation, but also from the role of this movement as a transcendence of the turbulent Allegro movement', and the reception history of this sonata is indeed full of binary oppositions between the two.[92]

Certainly there is something in the theme itself that lends itself towards these interpretations. The opening presentation conveys solemnity through the subdued tessitura and solid chordal writing, just as the upper regions of the keyboard attained by the later variations in turn suggest height and weightlessness in their filigree melodic diminutions. Lawrence Kramer also notes that the theme's lack of chromaticism results in a 'sonority of crystalline purity and peacefulness'.[93] And to a large extent the putative sense of 'timelessness' is surely due to the sheer

---

[90] Cited by Fischer, *Ludwig van Beethovens Klaviersonaten*, p. 10.

[91] Robert S. Hatten, *Musical Meaning in Beethoven: Markedness, Correlation, and Interpretation* (Bloomington, IN: Indiana University Press, 1994), pp. 14, 88–9.

[92] Kinderman, *Beethoven*, p. 235. On the two movements as forming a complementary pair— 'expressive doublings' in Lawrence Kramer's reading noted earlier—we find such antonymic pairings as Resistance and Acquiescence (Lenz), Samskara and Nirvana (Bülow), Darkness and Light (Bekker), and Here and Beyond (Fischer).

[93] Kramer, *Music as Cultural Practice*, p. 58.

slowness of the music. One of the best explanations of this feature is given by Barbara Barry in her book on musical time. In the *Arietta*

> the phenomenal present is 'stretched' across the still, empty spaces from one harmony to another, and where there is the minimum of melodic and rhythmic activity over a slow, sustained harmonic rate, often of the purest diatonicism . . . . It is in the spaces and stillness between the notes . . . that eternity and its infinite depth may be glimpsed behind time.[94]

At a larger level, too, the constant tempo of the movement alongside its escalating surface rhythmic diminutions gives rise to the sense of increasing excitement explicable as a type of ritualistic or mystical ecstasy. The fourth variation especially may be aptly conceived as 'trancelike', a quality apparent in the passage of hypnotically repeated Es (b. 89ff) in the theme's second half which has long perplexed and fascinated listeners. Eckehard Kiem pertinently remarks here on the 'resulting amorphous and empty temporal drive, in which the music takes on the aspect of a succession of nows drained of any individual quality'. 'This passage brings us to the limits of what we are able to perceive as a meaningful shaping of time'.[95] Additionally, the blurring of tonic and dominant harmony implied by this passage (a feature found earlier in the transition back from the final variation to the returning theme at the close of Op. 109) creates a wash of sound effectively dissolving the forward-leading sense of functional harmonic progression and disorientating the listener's experience of musical time.

As with Op. 109's concluding *Andante cantabile*, though, what is probably the most persistent and idiosyncratic feature of the *Arietta* that contributes to this sense of otherworldliness and temporal annulment is Beethoven's use of the trill. The prevalence of this marked feature seemingly calls out for hermeneutic explanation. As John Harley puts it, such trills dissolve reality (or a previous, more mundane level of it) under their touch, revealing 'another and truer level of reality', where Beethoven 'passes into a higher state of mind, and is free'.[96] Rosen explains 'a long trill creates an insistent tension while remaining completely static; it helped Beethoven both to accept the static form of the variation set and to transcend it'. Rosen goes on to speak of Beethoven's 'power to suspend motion, seeming to stop the movement of time'.[97] If, as Burnham notes on the 'presence' of the heroic style, 'the present moment is thus alive with both an assessment of the immediate past and an expectancy of the immediate future',

---

[94] Barry, *Musical Time*, p. 272.

[95] Kiem, 'Der Blick in Abgrund', p. 229. Also see Forner, *Ludwig van Beethoven*, p. 171.

[96] John Harley, 'The Trill in Beethoven's Later Music', *The Musical Times*, 95 (1954), 70.

[97] Rosen, *The Classical Style*, pp. 447, 448.

in Op. 111, in contradistinction, the utter slowness of the music's opening with its concomitant focus on the experienced present, the repetitive nature of both the larger-scale form and such passages as seen in variation 4, and the ethereal textures created by the multiple trills towards the close all still this sense of temporal purposiveness and growth, 'freezing' our time-experience into detached moments.[98]

We have seen how generations of listeners and critics have perceived these late works of Beethoven to be imbued with a special relationship to time, in more recent decades even suggesting that they might represent, evoke, or instantiate an experience of timelessness. Though analytically and philosophically the attempt to substantiate these claims is not always straightforward or easy—indeed the very nature of the topic seems to resist comprehensive explanation or proof—it is nevertheless the case that such interpretations chime with something that seems an important part of our understanding and aesthetic experience of this music. Even if no definitive answers are forthcoming, we may at least return to these pieces both aesthetically richer and a little wiser for having made the journey. This relation between music and time will be extended and deepened across the ensuing chapters of this book, starting with a fuller philosophical exploration of the two and their importance within this era.

[98] Burnham, *Beethoven Hero*, p. 33.

2

Music, Time, and Philosophy

The central problematic of all ontology is rooted in the phenomenon of time.

Temporality 'is' not at all an *entity*. It is not; rather, it *temporalises* [*zeitigt*] itself.

Temporality can temporalise itself in different possibilities and different ways [*Weise*].

—Martin Heidegger, *Sein und Zeit*[1]

Metaphysicians are musicians without musical ability.

—Rudolf Carnap, 'Überwindung der Metaphysik durch logische Analyse der Sprache'[2]

In the Fifth Walk from his *Reveries of a Solitary Walker*, Jean-Jacques Rousseau sets out a theme that would become an *idée fixe* of later eighteenth- and nineteenth-century thought:

> Everything is in constant flux on this earth. Nothing keeps the same unchanging shape, and our affections, being attached to things outside us, necessarily change and pass away as they do. Always out ahead of us or lagging behind, they recall a past which is gone or anticipate a future which may never come into being; there is nothing solid there for the heart to attach itself to. Thus our earthy joys are almost without exception the creatures of a moment; I doubt whether any of us knows the meaning of lasting happiness. Even in our keenest pleasures there is scarcely a single moment of which the heart could truthfully

---

[1] Martin Heidegger, *Sein und Zeit* (Tübingen: Max Niemeyer, 1967), §§5, 65, 61, translation slightly altered from *Being and Time*, trans. John Macquarrie and Edward Robinson (New York: Harper and Row, 1962), pp. 40, 377, 351. It is noteworthy—and extremely apposite—that 'Weise' can also mean 'melodies', although it seems unlikely that Heidegger was intending a musical allusion here.

[2] Rudolf Carnap, 'Überwindung der Metaphysik durch logische Analyse der Sprache', *Erkenntnis*, 2 (1932), 240.

say: 'Would that this moment could last for ever!' And how can we give the name of happiness to a fleeting state which leaves our hearts still empty and anxious, either regretting something that is past or desiring something that is yet to come?

But if there is a state where the soul can find a resting-place secure enough to establish itself and concentrate its entire being there, with no need to remember the past or reach into the future, where time is nothing to it, where the present runs on indefinitely but this duration goes unnoticed, with no sign of the passing of time, and no other feeling of deprivation or enjoyment, pleasure or pain, desire or fear than the simple feeling of existence, a feeling that fills our soul entirely, as long as this state lasts, we can call ourselves happy, not with a poor, incomplete and relative happiness such as we find in the pleasures of life, but with a sufficient, complete and perfect happiness which leaves no emptiness to be filled in the soul. Such is the state which I often experienced on the Island of Saint-Pierre in my solitary reveries, whether I lay in a boat and drifted where the water carried me, or sat by the shores of the stormy lake, or elsewhere, on the banks of a lovely river or a stream murmuring over the stones.

What is the source of our happiness in such a state? Nothing external to us, nothing apart from ourselves and our own existence; as long as this state lasts we are self-sufficient like God.[3]

The similarities with the dilemma of Goethe's Faust are evident, as are the differences in proposed solution. Rather than embracing the continual flux of life, pressing ahead to seize each new moment, Rousseau laments time's transience and seeks something approaching stasis, a quasi-timeless state. By negating the sense of before and after, the operation of memory and expectation, Rousseau's solitary wayfarer is able to concentrate solely on the sensation of the present, taken out of any temporal continuum, stretched out as pure subjective duration without change. He seeks nothing less than to annul time.

What Rousseau is searching for here, one might say, is pure Being (understood with both its Platonic and Existential overtones): for permanence, something enduring unchanging without a before and after, a surrogate eternity. Yet this temporal suspension can only ever be a temporary state. We inhabit a world of flux, of time and becoming, and such moments offer at best fleeting respite.

[3] Jean-Jacques Rousseau, *Reveries of the Solitary Walker*, trans. Peter France (Harmondsworth: Penguin, 1979), pp. 88–9. Several later passages of Schopenhauer, for instance, directly echo Rousseau's complaint (e.g., *The World as Will and Representation*, vol. I, p. 196 [§38]; *Parerga and Paralipomena*, trans. E.F.J. Payne, 2 vols. (Oxford: Clarendon Press, 1974), vol. II, p. 284 [§144]).

Happiness endures merely for as long as this state can last, and Rousseau's wanderer will soon be plunged back from his momentary oneness with nature, his concentration on *aesthesis* in and of itself, into the course of the world.

The distinction outlined here between eternal being and temporal change and mutability, the desire for persistence amidst time's passing and the consequent transience of human existence, is among the oldest of all philosophical problems. It essentially reduces to the familiar antitheses of Being versus Becoming, persistence contrasted with change, identity opposed to flux, Parmenides and the Eleatics against Heraclitus, of which Platonism is perhaps the earliest philosophical attempt at resolving.[4] Manifestations of this theme extend throughout the course of Western history. In Hellenic and Hebraic traditions we read, respectively, that 'as is the life of the leaves, so is that of men' and 'as for man, his days are as grass'.[5] Indeed, Goethe is hardly the first or most impassioned expositor of the Faust theme. Long before, Marlowe's Doctor had already pleaded 'Stand still, you ever-moving spheres of heaven / That time may cease and midnight never come!'[6] But the problem of time and change unquestionably becomes an ever-more prominent concern in Western culture from the latter eighteenth century onwards, an obsession that persists without abatement to the present day. With the rise and acceleration of technological and social change, the decline of former religious certitudes and fixed points of reference, comes an ever greater awareness of the lack of immutability of everything contained within our world of experience. The problem of time is thus one of the central issues of the modern age.

As is also exemplified in the passage above, solace is found by Rousseau in an awareness of the self, in pure self-consciousness—the ego that served as the epistemological ground of Western thought since Descartes and would become the central issue in subsequent idealist philosophy, the existing 'I' which would form the bedrock of existentialism from Kierkegaard to Heidegger and beyond. For at this time we also see in philosophy the rise of epistemology, a new importance attached to subjectivity and the self in philosophical systems, alongside a related concern for the discipline of aesthetics. In fact, the interest in subjectivity in this period is closely connected to the problematisation of time as being something intrinsically related to the self,

---

[4] By Platonism I am meaning the ideas stemming from a handful of influential dialogues conventionally dated to the middle period of Plato's creative life, such as the *Republic, Phaedo, Phaedrus, Symposium, Timaeus, Meno*, emphasising timeless forms and the doctrine of knowledge as recollection (*anamnesis*).

[5] Homer, *The Iliad*, VI, 171–2 (trans. from H.D.F. Kitto, *The Greeks* (Harmondsworth: Penguin, 1951), p. 61); Psalms 103:15 (King James Version).

[6] Christopher Marlowe, *The Tragical History of Doctor Faustus*, 5.2, ll. 60–1 (A) 135–6 (B).

that which is in post-Kantian philosophy the a priori condition of the subject's very possibility for perception.

And last but by no means least, the figure of Rousseau also holds one final key in this discussion: he was a composer.[7] One further, crucial strand of modern thought which forms the central thread to this chapter is the new significance attached to instrumental music, its aesthetic claims and importance within philosophy. All three issues above are closely interwoven as 'modern' concerns (just as we saw that Rousseau was a composer as well as philosopher and one of the most influential proponents of subjectivity—some might say egotist—in the eighteenth century). Music was perceived by many figures in the nineteenth century as offering some form of commentary on this search for unity in diversity and permanence within change, if not a form of solution. By offering an example of temporally separated events that nevertheless are perceived to belong together and fit into an indivisible whole, music provides an actualisation of identity amidst flux that so vexed attempts at theorising. 'Since a sequence of successive moments is always itself a kind of eternity', wrote Goethe to his friend the composer Carl Friedrich Zelter, 'it was given to you to be ever constant in that which passes'.[8] (Had Faust only been a composer rather than philosopher he evidently might have had a better time.) Music's ability to model a living flow of temporal becoming was utilised by philosophers as an invaluable exemplification of how subjective time might be constituted, its ability to suggest a duration that endures even while it perishes being seen as the perfect instantiation of the paradox of human self-consciousness.

Music thus became a vital tool for philosophers to articulate and try to understand problems of time, be it merely as a metaphor, an instantiation, or even a potential solution. Indeed, for many Romantic thinkers, music had a distinct advantage over language, enabling the disclosure of some deeper truth that verbal concepts were unable to articulate. Might not music be able to cast light on the essential nature of time, human temporality and consciousness, hold forth the promise of something enduring, permanent, in this world of flux, even (as some believed) contain the key to solving seemingly intractable philosophical aporias? Though such claims might appear hyperbolic for a modern-day audience, these problems are still our problems. At the very least, confronting them once again

---

[7] Albeit that Rousseau, the editor who passed along Fontenelle's quip against wordless music 'Sonate, que me veux-tu?' in his *Dictionaire de la Musique*, was a proponent of operatic, not instrumental music, whose aesthetic dominance dates from the decades following Rousseau's death.

[8] Goethe to Zelter, 11 March 1832; *Briefwechsel zwischen Goethe und Zelter*, ed. Max Hecker, 3 vols. (Frankfurt: Insel Verlag, 1987), vol. III: 1828–32, p. 639. The discussion pursued in this chapter takes up several themes exposited in the discussion of Goethe, *Faust*, and music in *Mendelssohn, Time and Memory*, ch. 2, where I previously cited this passage.

enables us to reengage with that oldest and obscurest of enigmas, the question of time; to understand historically how this endeavour was once conceived; and to appreciate more fully the central constitutive role of music in the modern era.

MUSICAL TIME IN HISTORY

That music has often been understood as uniquely capable of articulating certain aspects of existence in time is evidently closely related to the fact that it has long been considered 'the temporal art *par excellence*'.[9] 'The field of music is time' claimed Rousseau in the *Essay on the Origins of Language*.[10] Music, after all, is an art that is primarily of the ear, not the eye, and ever since Augustine, time has been considered more susceptible to aural than to visual sense.[11] Such a distinction between spatial and temporal arts is a prominent feature of aesthetic discourse in the later eighteenth and early nineteenth centuries, finding classic formulations in Rousseau's *Essay*, Lessing's *Laocoon*, and Herder's own *Essay on the Origins of Language*.[12] Romantic thinkers such as Friedrich Schlegel, Jean Paul, Novalis, and Wordsworth concurred with Augustine that whereas the eye is spatial, other senses, above all the ear, are temporal, contributing to a reversal of what Coleridge called the 'despotism of the eye' so firmly entrenched within neoclassical aesthetics.[13] In contrast to

---

[9] Gisèle Brelet, *Le temps musical: Essai d'une esthétique nouvelle de la Musique*, 2 vols. (Paris: Presses Universitaires de France, 1949), vol. I, p. 25.

[10] Rousseau, *Essai sur l'origine des langues*, ch. 16: 'Le champ de la musique est le temps, celui de la peinture est l'espace'. *Œuvres complètes de J. J. Rousseau*, ed. Victor-Donatien Musset-Pathay, 22 vols. in 8 parts (Paris: Dupont, 1824), *Philosophie*, vol. II, p. 483.

[11] Augustine, *Confessions*, XI. One further reason for Augustine's concentration on aurality might be to avoid problems of the rather intimate connection with motion besetting visually based accounts of time (as in Aristotle).

[12] See Gotthold Ephraim Lessing, *Laokoon, oder über die Grenzen der Malerei und Poesie* (1766), §XVI, in *Werke*, ed. Herbert G. Göpfert et al., 8 vols. (Munich: Winkler, 1970–9), vol. VI, pp. 102–3 (although Lessing himself is concerned only to distinguish between the spatial nature of visual art and the temporal nature of poetry); Johann Gottfried Herder, *Abhandlung über den Ursprung der Sprache* (1770), who argues significantly for the primacy of sound over sight in the historical development of language.

[13] Samuel Taylor Coleridge, *Biographia Literaria; or, Biographical Sketches of My Literary Life and Opinions*, ed. John Shawcross, 2 vols. (Oxford: Clarendon Press, 1907), vol. I, p. 64. For example Aristotle, after whom much in pre-Romantic aesthetics bases its values, famously opens the *Metaphysics* with a tribute to the eye as the primary organ of intellectual scrutiny. On this reversal of neoclassical visuality in Romantic aesthetics see M.H. Abrams, *The Mirror and the Lamp: Romantic Theory and the Critical Tradition* (Oxford: Oxford University Press, 1953).

the eighteenth-century visually oriented mimesis of the external world, by the early nineteenth century the ear becomes hallowed as the organ of subjectivity.[14] Furthermore (as explored presently), music's immaterial manifestation seems most akin to the abstract, intangible nature of time, bound up with a mutual sense of flow, passing away, and corresponding reliance on memory for its constitution. Thus it becomes a commonplace assertion in the early nineteenth century that music is the quintessential temporal art, an aesthetic medium bound up with time in a manner more pronounced and intimate than any other of the muses' gifts. Time is the 'universal element in music' claims Hegel in his *Aesthetics*, while his antipode Schopenhauer similarly observed that 'perceptions through *hearing* are exclusively in *time*; hence the whole nature of music consists in the measure of time'.[15]

One of the least disputed claims routinely made about music and temporality is the contention that music is in a privileged position to reflect a particular historical consciousness of time and human temporality. As the *New Grove* entry on 'Time' states, music 'reflects the temporal sensibilities of its cultural milieu'. More eloquently, music might well be taken, in Melanie Wald's words, as 'the most sensitive seismograph' for the relationship with temporality developed by a culture.[16] Music allows the historian to explore 'the cultural construction of time' claims Dean Sutcliffe. 'Surely no other art could reveal more about how composing and listening subjects might have experienced the temporal succession of their lives'.[17] In such a vein Theodor W. Adorno, perhaps the most prominent spokesperson of music's historicity, argues that the 'temporal consciousness' transmitted by a Palestrina choral piece, a Bach fugue, a Beethoven symphony, a Debussy prelude,

[14] Hegel's definition of sound in the *Encyclopaedia* is a typical example: in his view, sound is the manifestation of an organism's inwardness, 'subjectivity in process of liberation'. 'In sight, the physical self manifests itself spatially, and in hearing, temporally' (*Philosophy of Nature* [*Encyclopaedia*, Pt II], §301 and Zusatz to §358, trans. A.V. Miller [Oxford: Oxford University Press, 1970], pp. 140, 383).

[15] Hegel, *Aesthetics*, vol. II, p. 907; Schopenhauer, *The World as Will and Representation*, vol. II, p. 28.

[16] Justin London, 'Time', (3), *The New Grove Dictionary of Music and Musicians*, 29 vols. (London: Macmillan, 2001), vol. XXV, p. 479; Melanie Wald, 'Moment Musical: Die wahrnehmbarkeit der Zeit durch Musik', *Das achtzehnte Jahrhundert*, 30 (2006), 207.

[17] W. Dean Sutcliffe, 'Temporality in Domenico Scarlatti', in Massimiliano Sala and W. Dean Sutcliffe (eds.), *Domenico Scarlatti Adventures: Essays to Commemorate the 250th Anniversary of His Death* (Bologna: Ut Orpheus, 2008), pp. 370, 371. Examples are legion: see Andres Briner, *Der Wandel der Musik als Zeit-Kunst* (Vienna: Universal Edition, 1955); Walter Wiora, 'Musik als Zeitkunst', *Die Musikforschung*, 10 (1957), 27–8; Lewis Rowell, 'The Subconscious Language of Musical Time', *Music Theory Spectrum*, 1 (1979), 96–106; Jonathan Kramer, 'New Temporalities in Music', 539–56; Helga de la Motte-Haber, 'Historische Wandlungen musikalischer Zeitvorstellungen', in Diether de la Motte (ed.), *Neue Musik—Quo vadis? 17 Perspektiven* (Mainz: Schott, 1988), pp. 53–66; Richard Klein, 'Thesen zum Verhältnis von Musik und Zeit', pp. 62 and 66; Susan McClary, 'Temp Work: Music and the Cultural Shaping of Time', *Musicology Australia*, 23 (2000), 160–61.

or an aphoristic Webern quartet movement is 'endlessly different', an 'experience of time that is specifically unique to it'. 'Just as the temporal form of every music, its inner historicity, varies historically, so this inner historicity also always reflects real, external time. . . . the time that is immanent in every music, its inner historicity, *is* real historical time, reflected as appearance'.[18]

Yet this notion—that musical time is historical through and through—is surely itself historical: it reflects the 'temporalisation of time', the awareness of time (and those arts bound to it) as something that is mutable in conception, a temporal self-consciousness which has arguably only been possible since the mid-eighteenth century. For as the examples just cited from Rousseau to the nineteenth century bring to light, why was music heard as capable of articulating time particularly *at this historical time*? The answer rests on two related features: how the notion of time becomes more problematised in Western Europe by the end of the eighteenth century, and how music by this time had become more capable of articulating this newly sensed complexity about temporal experience.

The Historical Temporalisation of Time

As was mentioned in the previous chapter, it has been axiomatic within recent scholarship in the humanities that the eighteenth century witnessed a decisive shift in the conception of time throughout much of Western Europe—a profoundly new awareness of time as a force of change, a temporalisation of history and experience. This idea of 'temporalisation' was introduced back in the 1930s by the historian and philosopher Arthur Lovejoy in order to describe the growth in the eighteenth century of the idea of progress, but the notion received its most influential articulation from the 1970s onwards in the work of the German conceptual historian Reinhart Koselleck.[19] For Koselleck, at some stage between 1700 and 1800 the idea of history took on a new dynamic aspect. In the premodern age, the ancient wisdom that there was essentially 'nothing new under the sun' still held true: life followed the cyclical agrarian and religious calendars of medieval world, unchanging through the generations, a static conception in

---

[18] T.W. Adorno, 'On the Contemporary Relationship of Philosophy and Music', in *Essays on Music*, ed. Richard Leppert, trans. Susan H. Gillespie (Berkeley and Los Angeles: University of California Press, 2002), pp. 143–4. For an overview of Adorno's many writings on musical time see the chronological survey in Nikolaus Bacht, 'Music and Time in Theodor W. Adorno' (PhD diss., King's College London, 2002).

[19] Arthur O. Lovejoy, *The Great Chain of Being: A Study of the History of an Idea* (Cambridge, MA: Harvard University Press, 1936), p. 244: 'one of the principal happenings in eighteenth-century thought was the temporalizing of the Chain of Being'; Koselleck, *Futures Past, Zeitschichten*.

which time was barely cognised as an entity. Time belonged to God; one occupied it for one's allotted share, to be succeeded by the next generation. Since
history was essentially unchanging and the past to this extent continuously
present, its lessons were ever reapplicable (*historia magna vita*). Yet by the end
of the century all this had been swept away. History did not follow the cyclical
recurrence of the past but constantly changed, in ways unforeseeable; the present's implicit wedding to the past was replaced by an explicit orientation towards
the unknown future. The world one experienced then was unrecognisable from
that of one's parents, soon (following the widespread symptoms of acceleration)
even from what it had been a decade before. Rather than time being an empty
medium in which events happened, it became an insatiable driving force.

Despite some later criticisms directed at specific details of Koselleck's outline, his position still holds as a generalisation of a broader cultural trend. His
reading of a movement from a premodern static conception to a dynamic,
forward-moving time is attested to in the work of a number of other scholars,
arising from the conjunction of many social, intellectual, and scientific changes
during this period.[20] Ever since Leibniz declared 'we must recognise a certain
constant and unbounded progress of the whole universe such that it always
proceeds to greater development' the idea of progress took increasing hold on
the European imagination.[21] Following the trend started earlier by Copernicus,
Galileo, and Newton, such scientific advancement as the redating of the age
of the earth by the geological sciences and speculations on the origins of the
universe encouraged a new scepticism towards earlier religious dogma, and
technological developments resulted in the ability to measure time more accurately.[22] Allied to the gradual secularisation of history, the ideology of progress

[20] Wolf Lepenies, for instance, argues that the turn of the nineteenth century marks the temporalisation and end of natural history: the circular tradition of natural models gives way to the idea
of history as process (*Das Ende der Naturgeschichte: Wandel kutureller Selbstverständlichkeiten in den
Wissenschaften des 18. und 19. Jahrhunderts* [Munich and Vienna: Hanser, 1976]). A range of scholarly accounts can be found in Mircea Eliade, *The Myth of the Eternal Return* (New York: Pantheon
Books, 1954), focusing on the decline in the modern era of earlier cyclic conceptions of time;
Georges Poulet, *Studies in Human Time*, trans. Elliott Coleman (Baltimore: Johns Hopkins Press,
1956); Marcel Gauchet, *The Disenchantment of the World: A Political History of Religion*, trans. Oscar
Burge (Princeton: Princeton University Press, 1997), concerning the dissipation of a cyclical, anti-
historical religious time conception around 1700; Rudolf Wendorff, *Zeit und Kultur: Geschichte des
Zeitbewußtseins in Europa* (Opladen: Westdeutscher Verlag, 1983), pp. 253–337, with particular reference to this process of temporalisation as reflected within art and culture.

[21] Gottfried Wilhelm Leibniz, 'On the Ultimate Origination of Things' (1697), in *Die philosophischen Schriften*, ed. C.I. Gerhardt, 7 vols. (Berlin: Weidmann, 1875–90), vol. VII, p. 308.

[22] See G.J. Whitrow, *Time in History*, pp. 139–51, 177–86, and *The Natural Philosophy of Time*
(Oxford: Clarendon Press, 1980); David S. Landes, *Revolution in Time: Clocks and the Making of
the Modern World* (Cambridge: Belknap Press, 1983); John Bender and David E. Wellbery (eds.),
Chronotypes: The Construction of Time (Stanford: Stanford University Press, 1991).

resulted in the growth of the idea of Universal History, as found in Turgot, Kant, or Condorcet, while in reciprocity to this belief in progress came a relativising of historical time—historicism—from the newly conscious awareness of the qualitative difference in historical periods (such as is seen most prominently in Herder).[23]

Clearly it is dangerous to narrow down an entire era and culture to one viewpoint (even supposing Western Europe can be treated as a collective entity). Just as we may find within the long eighteenth century such quintessential Enlightenment formulations as Newton's absolute time and causality, so we encounter equally 'modern' objections to both by Locke, Berkeley, and Hume. Leibniz's belief in human progress famously finds an ironic echo in Voltaire's *Candide*; linear history meets its counterpart in Vico's cyclic *Principi di scienza nuova*. Most pointedly, the wilfully fractured temporal narrative and sense of subjectivity in Laurence Sterne's *Tristram Shandy* (1759–67) stands as a reaction against a larger belief in linear development and the ultimate reality of objective time. Perhaps it is more accurate to say that for a multitude of reasons time became more of an issue in the eighteenth century.[24] Time becomes both temporalised and increasingly problematised: thus it may seem hard to give one, unitary definition for the age. But all this supports the view that time was a fundamental concern in this period precisely because it was so diversified, problematic, and therefore all the more apparent. Just as all philosophising is said to begin with wonder, so the concept of time becomes more discussed, disputed, the more keenly its impact is felt.

The Historical Temporalisation of Musical Time

Correlatively, time seems to become far more an issue in music during this period. The same general claim—of the temporalisation, or at least problematisation, of time as a medium—holds for music as for history. As numerous scholars have proposed, by the late eighteenth century, and from there continuing until at least the early twentieth century, music's sensitivity to temporal

---

[23] Similarly Michel Foucault sees a decisive break in historical episteme at the beginning of the nineteenth century, whereby 'a profound historicity penetrates into the heart of things, isolates and defines them in their own coherence, imposes upon them the forms of order implied by the continuity of time'. *The Order of Things: An Archaeology of the Human Sciences*, trans. A.M. Sheridan Smith (London: Tavistock, 1970), p. xiii.

[24] See the special issue of *Das achtzehnte Jahrhundert*, 30 (2006), dedicated to 'Zeitkonzepte: Zur Pluralisierung des Zeitdiskurses im langen 18. Jahrhundert', especially Stefanie Stockhorst, 'Zur Einführung: Von der Verzeitlichungsthese zur temporalen Diversität', 157–64.

placement becomes fundamental to its construction and cognition.[25] For David Greene, Baroque temporality is an image of time as supposed in Newtonian physics. Time is an indifferent, external, homogenous medium. One time is identical to another: each has the same measure, the same laws apply throughout. Music inhabits an orderly and predictable universe, where the future is in essence no different from the past. Given complete information about the current state one could almost predict the subsequent course of the movement (just as J.S. Bach is said by his son Carl Philipp Emanuel to have worked out on first hearing all the possible paradigmatic permutations in a contrapuntal piece at its start).[26] But ever since the latter eighteenth century music more readily suggests a process, an onward-moving stream—not static Being but a dynamic Becoming. Music, as Wilhelm Seidel has put it, becomes a *Zeitkunst* instead of *Tonkunst*.[27]

More recently this narrative has been given renewed exposure by Karol Berger in his division between cyclical Baroque and linear Classical conceptions of musical time—symbolised by the circle and the arrow respectively. Berger's central claim is a familiar one: that

> in the later eighteenth century European art music began to take seriously the flow of time from past to future. Until then music was simply 'in time'; it 'took time'—events had somehow to be arranged successively, but the distinction between past and future, 'earlier' and 'later', mattered little to the way the music was experienced and understood.

But 'at some point between the early and late eighteenth century, between Bach and Mozart, musical form became primarily temporal and the attention of musicians—composers, performers, and listeners alike—shifted toward the temporal disposition of events'. 'From that point on music added the experience of linear time . . . to its essential subject matter. Music could no longer be experienced with understanding unless one recognised the temporal ordering of events'.[28] Berger's ideal types have been reproached in some quarters for their

[25] See for instance Kurt von Fischer, 'Das Zeitproblem in der Musik', in Rudolf W. Meyer (ed.), *Das Zeitproblem im 20. Jahrhundert* (Bern: Francke, 1964), pp. 304–5; Greene, *Temporal Processes in Beethoven's Music*, pp. 7–27; Monelle, 'The Temporal Image', in *The Sense of Music*, pp. 81–114; Wald, 'Moment Musical'; Berger, *Bach's Cycle, Mozart's Arrow*.

[26] Greene, *Temporal Processes in Beethoven's Music*, pp. 7–17; the last example is given by Berger in *Bach's Cycle, Mozart's Arrow*, p. 96.

[27] Wilhelm Seidel, 'Division und Progression: Der Begriff der musikalischen Zeit im 18. Jahrhundert', *Il Saggiatore Musicale*, 2 (1995), 47–65.

[28] Berger, *Bach's Cycle, Mozart's Arrow*, pp. 9, 179, 9.

evident overschematisation, but the basic point—that musical time in this era becomes temporalised—has long been uncontroversial.[29]

Reasons for this change are plentiful. Most fundamentally, the growth of music's capacity for conveying a distinctively temporal character owes to the rise of a genre—that of instrumental music—and its connotations for musical syntax and attendant modes of listening. Instrumental music is not derivative upon a text's pre-given structure: its temporal unfolding has to be moulded into a satisfying design unaided by such external factors, hence being conceivable as a more unmediated shaping of time. As such, it is 'surely no exaggeration to designate the development of a genuine musical formal syntax . . . and the musical aesthetic of autonomy that goes with this, as one of the most important events in music history of the eighteenth century'.[30] With this development, too, comes the rise of the work concept and new ideologies concerning how music should be perceived: not passively heard in the ever-fleeing present, but actively cognised, focussing the listener's attention onto the music's temporal flow and its necessary retention in memory.[31]

Matching Seidel's view of the metamorphosis of music from an art of tones to one of time, verbal descriptions of musical structure shifted from spatial to temporal metaphors across this period. The governing paradigms change from the static Baroque allegory of music as painting to the Classical comparison of music to punctuated, syntactic language, and finally in the Romantic era to music as organic life.[32] Thus in the understanding of its historical contemporaries, music became both increasingly temporalised and subjectivised. And in terms of musical structure, across the eighteenth century there is correspondingly a reduction in more literally repetitive forms in favour of newly dynamic designs, resulting in a 'temporalisation of form'. The ritornello and da capo aria give way to the sonata and through-composed operatic number, in which any recall is significantly modified (for example tonally, as in the sonata's recapitulation, rather than in the surface ornamentation of the da capo reprise).[33] A sense of musical time

---

[29] See John Butt, *Bach's Dialogue with Modernity* (Cambridge: Cambridge University Press, 2010), p. 109; Bettina Varwig, 'Metaphors of Time and Modernity in Bach', *Journal of Musicology*, 29 (2012), 154–90.

[30] Wald, 'Moment Musical', 212.

[31] See Mark Evan Bonds, *Music as Thought: Listening to the Symphony in the Age of Beethoven* (Princeton: Princeton University Press, 2006).

[32] Michael Spitzer, *Metaphor and Musical Thought* (Chicago: University of Chicago Press, 2004), p. 60.

[33] Admittedly expositions—and initially second halves—of sonatas are still repeated, but even this gradually disappears in the nineteenth century. Wald suggests that in opera, too, the decline in da capo aria format and levelling of sharp distinctions between recitative and aria in Gluck's reform operas stem from the desire to achieve a more realistic balance between represented time and the time of representation ('Moment Musical', 216).

governed by the constant restitution of the past as the present is replaced by irreversible, cumulative movement towards an altered future. At a smaller level too, the widespread use of paradigmatic construction in Baroque music—a model 'invention' and its possible permutations—relates to a relative indifference to linear ordering, whereas by the end of the century syntactic position has become significantly marked.[34] Likewise in thematic working, a *Fortspinnung*-based technique of motivic elaboration through sequential repetition secedes to thematic development (as found in Haydn and Beethoven), with significant implications for the sense of growth and temporal progression.

At the level of harmonic language there is also general agreement that the rise of tonality gave rise to a greater sense of musical directionality, whether this is located in the seventeenth-century movement from modality to tonality itself, or later in the eighteenth century, as tonality becomes ever more powerfully conceived. One sees a development across this period from the Baroque centripetal arrangement of keys around the tonic (still harking back to its harmonic origins in modal practice) to a more pronounced tonic-dominant polarity. Rather than the free return of the tonic in a style where dominant, subdominant, and relative key areas carry virtual equivalence, different keys now carry different weightings in tonal hierarchy and temporal order. A subdominant may not appear at the stage reserved for the dominant within a sonata-form movement: the two are temporally determined in placement. In turn, stemming from this increased power perceived in tonal motion is a greater sense of 'causality' between successive events: one note leads necessarily to another. Alongside the greater differentiation of levels of cadential closure this will give rise to a stronger sense of punctuation, of logical syntax.[35] Thus a texture is created in which the interaction of harmony and motivic process appears to drive the music forward in a logical and predominantly linear manner.

Most evidently the nature of a style's use of musical tempo has implications for the sense of time communicated to the listener. Baroque music not only

[34] See Christopher Wintle, 'Corelli's Tonal Models: The Trio Sonata op. 3, no. 1', in Sergio Durante and Pierluigi Petrobelli (eds.), *Nuovissimi Studi Corelliani: Atti del Terzo Congresso Internazionale Fusignano, 1980* (Florence: Olschki, 1982), pp. 29–69; Laurence Dreyfus, *Bach and the Patterns of Invention* (Cambridge, MA: Harvard University Press, 1996); V. Kofi Agawu, *Playing with Signs: A Semiotic Interpretation of Classic Music* (Princeton: Princeton University Press, 1991), pp. 26–50, and Berger, *Bach's Cycle, Mozart's Arrow*, p. 96. The rhetorical models called upon by earlier eighteenth-century theory presuppose some notion of appropriate beginning and ending gestures, but this is certainly less syntagmatically determined than is found later in the century; see Mark Evan Bonds, *Wordless Rhetoric: Musical Form and the Metaphor of the Oration* (Cambridge, MA: Harvard University Press, 1991).

[35] William E. Caplin, 'The Classical Cadence: Conceptions and Misconceptions', *Journal of the American Musicological Society*, 57 (2004), 51–117.

exhibits a unity of affect but also a unity of rhythmic intensity. A regular unit of rhythmic movement usually runs throughout earlier Baroque movements (seen particularly clearly in fugues), thus leaving tempo as a neutral backdrop for musical events.[36] Later music, in contradistinction, tolerates far greater discontinuities. Already in Scarlatti, and especially in C.P.E. Bach, abrupt contrasts can manifest themselves, calling attention to time as more than just an empty vessel for material. The Viennese Classical Style in particular is highly differentiated in its rhythmic aspects: harmonic rhythm and movement are variable, and can be carefully organised in order to build up and dissipate tension.[37] Unsurprisingly, accounts of music controlling or subduing time, of containing time within it rather than being itself in time, have their historical focus on the music of this triumvirate, especially that of Beethoven. And at larger metrical level, whereas earlier polyphonic styles are less symmetrical and more fluid, seldom being formed from hierarchical units more than a few bars in length, there is a greater sense of hypermeter in Galant and Classical music. The latter possesses a greater 'projective potential', enabling a stronger sense of articulation of musical time, projecting a hypothetical phrasing beyond the here-and-now of the perceptual present into the musical future.[38]

Such observations are supported by historical theories of musical metre. Mattheson's Baroque conception of rhythm and metre is based on the principle of the subdivision of the equal measure, a spatialised conception proceeding from a view of the whole, an extra-temporal view of time from a synoptic, God-like perspective. Within this framework, each bar is equivalent to the next. 'In the return of the measure (*Zeitmaß*) as ever-present it is possible to conceive of static being and to conceive of passage, transition, and becoming as illusory.'[39] 'Music, while it is going on, leads to a forgetting of time', sums up Seidel. 'Time is not music's object; music neither grasps, alters, nor interprets time. It has time only as a space for observation.'[40] In other words, time is merely an unstated

[36] This point, admittedly, depends to a significant degree on performance style, modern observance of *notes inégales* creating a quite different effect from the constant pulse of mid-twentieth-century practice.

[37] Rosen, *The Classical Style*, pp. 60–2; a classic example is given in Rosen's analysis of the first movement of Mozart's K. 466 (pp. 229–33).

[38] See Christopher Hasty, *Meter as Rhythm* (New York: Oxford University Press, 1997), pp. 218–20. Hasty has shown how in a work like Beethoven's First Symphony this sense of metre may be constituted more as a *process*, creating a continual redefinition of a projected future. Greene, in *Temporal Processes in Beethoven's Music*, analyses at a larger level the temporal implications of varied phrase-weightings.

[39] Hasty, *Meter as Rhythm*, p. 24.

[40] Wilhelm Seidel, *Über Rhythmustheorien der Neuzeit* (Bern: Franke, 1975), pp. 56–7, quoted by Hasty, *Meter as Rhythm*, p. 25.

THE MELODY OF TIME

precondition in Baroque music, not a problematised medium or explicit prod-
uct of a process as happens later (an understanding similar to how scholars have
regarded the early stages of the development of human time-perception).[41]
Conversely, the isochronous pulse of later eighteenth-century theories suggests an indefinitely extended time—a more modern temporal conception,
contingent upon the finite human perspective. Thrasybulos Georgiades speaks
on the novel nature and uniqueness of Classical metre, its concentration on
'here and now'. In previous music, past, present, and future 'form an unbroken
whole. Time was not realised as an independent element . . . The Viennese classical technique consists in our becoming conscious of time. Temporality forces
its way in'.[42]

Thus across the eighteenth century, European music becomes newly temporalised and problematised. This characteristic is found within different periods and styles and should not simply be reduced to the Viennese Classical
Style (let alone to Beethoven). Sutcliffe has spoken of a 'present tenseness' in
Domenico Scarlatti's music, which through its obstinate repetitions, unpre-
dictability, and unruly disruptions of projected order 'makes us aware of the
contingent nature of musical time'.[43] C.P.E. Bach's seemingly wilful temporal
discontinuities suggest the extreme subjectivisation of musical time, a fitting
corollary to the aesthetics of *Empfindsamkeit*.[44] Haydn, meanwhile, is a master at
problematising musical succession and the corresponding sense of temporality.
Reinhard Kapp describes him as 'the first composer to have written fully articulated, seamlessly formed movements, in which virtually every note possesses
an inherent temporal index'.[45] For Haydn, the fact that music may be so clearly
heard to project a temporal position enables the playing with continuity and
discontinuity that so distinguishes his instrumental writing. Hans-Ulrich Fuß,
taking up the long-standing analogy with Laurence Sterne, argues persuasively
that Haydn's music similarly plays with 'multiple possibilities, openness, chance,
indetermination and deviation from the predetermined path, the interleaving of

[41] In primitive man, Mircea Eliade argues, 'an object or an act becomes real only insofar as it imi-
tates or repeats an archetype' (*The Myth of the Eternal Return*, p. 34).

[42] Thrasybulos Georgiades, *Music and Language*, trans. Marie Louise Göllner (Cambridge:
Cambridge University Press, 1982), p. 113.

[43] Sutcliffe, *The Keyboard Sonatas of Domenico Scarlatti and Eighteenth-Century Musical Style*
(Cambridge: Cambridge University Press, 2004), p. 147.

[44] See Laurenz Lütteken, *Das Monologische als Denkform in der Musik zwischen 1760 und 1785*
(Tübingen: Niemeyer, 1998).

[45] Reinhard Kapp, 'Haydns Persönliche Zeiterfahrung', in Marie-Agnes Dittrich, Marin Eybl, and
Reinhard Kapp (eds.), *Zyklus und Prozess: Joseph Haydn und die Zeit* (Vienna: Böhlau Verlag, 2012),
pp. 67–8. Kapp sees the 'new style' heralded by Haydn in the Op. 33 set as closely related to this temporalised (and temporally problematised) style.

multiple temporal tendencies'.[46] With Mozart on the other hand, there is often a sense of the composer seeking to create continuity from the most disparate, heterogeneous materials.[47] Beethoven and the nineteenth century were by no means the inventors of a dynamic time-sense in music, but rather the inheritors of a musical idiom already capable of great flexibility and subtlety in the articulation of musical time.

TIME AND MUSICAL TIME

In accounts of time one frequently encounters the despairing metaphor that time is hydra-headed, like the mythical polycephalic beast each of whose heads, on further analysis, separated into yet more. Chronos was, in fact, not so arrayed, although it is sometimes said that he possessed three—presumably one to see the past, another the future, and one the present. It remains to be asked how, more precisely, music relates to time. We have briefly explored musical style at a specific historical stage, which has provided some historical grounding to the question of musical temporality (indeed, to the very possibility of posing the question itself), but have not yet really inquired as to what time might be.

Time is notoriously tricky to define. Philosophers have long found it satisfying to admit the difficulty of their task, even if they fully intend subsequently to attempt an answer.[48] One might indeed be better advised to respond by posing a riddle,[49] asserting gnomically time's eternal impenetrability,[50] or simply by playing music (presumably Beethoven's, as we saw). It is probably intractable as

---

[46] Hans-Ulrich Fuß, 'Ein Laurence Sterne der Musik: Zur Kunst der Parenthesen im Instrumentalwerk Haydns', in Marie-Agnes Dittrich, Marin Eybl, and Reinhard Kapp (eds.), *Zyklus und Prozess: Joseph Haydn und die Zeit* (Vienna: Böhlau Verlag, 2012), p. 236. As suggested in chapter 1, such a reading plausibly locates a problematised attitude to musical time and multiple temporality long before Jonathan Kramer's dating of this notion to late Beethoven.

[47] Most particularly, as seen in the opening movements of many of the mature piano concerti (e.g., K. 467). The famous topical interplay of the F major Sonata, K. 332, is a case where the sheer variety almost threatens to overwhelm the musical thread and sense of temporal continuity.

[48] For instance Plotinus, *The Enneads*, 3.7.1; Augustine, *Confessions*, XI.xiv (17), Berkeley, *Principles of Human Knowledge*, §97.

[49] For example that posed by Voltaire: 'What is the longest and shortest thing in the world, the quickest and the slowest, the most easily divisible and the most extensive, the most neglected and the most regretted, without which nothing can be done, which consumes everything small and revives everything large?' (*Zadig* [1747], quoted by Sutcliffe, 'Temporality in Domenico Scarlatti', p. 369).

[50] Such as the famous inscription at Sais: 'I am that which was, which is, and will come. No man has ever lifted my veil'.

to how precisely music relates to time, because it is not clear what time is, or if there are not, rather, multiple valid, though apparently exclusive, conceptions. I am assuming here, given the still unresolved debates on the nature of time both within and across disciplinary boundaries, that it would be ill-advised to insist on a unitary definition of time. There is simply too little consensus, the variables are too numerous and themselves variable. Still, in order to clarify the limits of the ensuing discussion it would be helpful to outline here some common philosophical distinctions.[51]

- The most prevalent distinction in categorising time is the binary opposition formed between *internal* and *external* time conceptions, or expressed in a related (though not necessarily equivalent) pairing, *subjective* and *objective*. Is time a pregiven part of the universe, or something intrinsically bound-up with human consciousness? Does our own temporal sense merely reflect sensitivity to an outer reality, the time of the world, or does it alone constitute time, the notion of an external universal time being an intellectual abstraction?
- Is there one time or many? A pluralistic perspective is more readily found in conjunction with a subjective/internal time conception, but need not be so.[52]
- Does time itself 'flow' or is it merely events in time that do? A different dualism is formed between what is known as *Relational* and *Absolutist* conceptions. Relational or Reductionist theories posit time as inextricably bound up with events in time, as reliant on change or movement. Under this understanding, without change there can be no time. An Absolutist perspective, conversely, sees time as independent of what happens within time—an empty container, envelope or 'manifold' for events. (This then raises the tricky question that if time itself flows, what does it move in relation to?)
- Standing above this discussion is another opposition that time itself forms with eternity, and eternity moreover has two forms: the sempiternal—an infinite duration of time—and the eternal per se—that existing outside time, without division into a before and after.

These are the most pertinent distinctions for considering musical time, though there are obviously many other points of contention and grey areas

---

[51] For a good overview of different time conceptions see Ned Markosian, 'Time', *The Stanford Encyclopedia of Philosophy* (rev. 2010), ed. Edward N. Zalta, <http://plato.stanford.edu/archives/win2010/entries/time/>. Also, for a range of accounts, Robin Le Poidevin and Murray MacBeath (eds.), *The Philosophy of Time* (Oxford: Oxford University Press, 1993).

[52] See for instance Murray MacBeath, 'Time's Square', in Robin Le Poidevin and Murray MacBeath (eds.), *The Philosophy of Time* (Oxford: Oxford University Press, 1993), pp. 183–202.

between those categories enunciated above.[53] For instance, certain pairs will often be associated (such as objective time with an absolutist conception) but still irreducible to each other; one might posit middle terms (such as an inter-subjective time of everyday life between universal time and that of subjective experience); or view certain definitions as collapsing these distinctions (Kant's analysis of time is in a manner both subjective and objective; Einstein's relativity neither purely absolute in the sense of Newton's, nor relational). Even from this brief overview it is apparent that each conceptual branch of time seems to bifurcate at will. The hydra metaphor is evidently not ill-chosen.

Secondly, albeit at the risk of predetermining the conception of time being assumed, what terminology best describes music's relation with time? We read variously that music mirrors, models, captures, transforms time, and so on. But the implications of these terms seem to be quite different. Some writers, for example, understand music as an 'expression' of time.[54] Yet the notion of expression implies attributing subjective agency to music (a metaphor that, although often attractive, is already quite loaded). Even to say that music can be 'heard as' expressing time might imply that time is something that can potentially be expressed as if it were a content. 'Suggests' is a more neutral term but needlessly weak, for surely the main point of music is that it *is* an instance of time in an important sense. Formative or constructive metaphors meanwhile—forms, moulds, constructs—even if given in dynamic verbal forms, impute a physical tangibility and architectural solidity seemingly inconsistent with music's temporal intangibility.[55]

One of the most popular conceptions is provided by Susanne Langer in describing music as 'an image of time': 'Music spreads out time for our direct and complete apprehension . . . [it] *makes time audible, and its form and continuity sensible*'.[56] Victor Zuckerkandl likewise conceives of 'tone as the image of time', as David Greene in turn argues that music 'offers us aural images of temporality'[57] Though the term 'image' need not connote something visual

---

[53] A selection of other debates include: whether time is bounded or unbounded; whether it has only one direction; whether it is discrete or continuous and infinitely divisible; whether it is branching or non-branching; if past and future are real properties or only perspectival (A- and B-Theorist arguments).

[54] See Wiora, 'Musik als Zeitkunst', 26–7.

[55] For instance, Hans Heinrich Eggebrecht claims that music instigates, founds or builds [*stiftet*] time (*Musik als Zeit* [Wilhelmshaven: Florian Noetzel, 2001], pp. 21–5).

[56] Susanne K. Langer, 'The Image of Time', in *Feeling and Form: A Theory of Art* (New York: Scribner, 1953), p. 110.

[57] Victor Zuckerkandl, *Sound and Symbol: Music and the External World*, trans. Willard R. Trask (London: Routledge & Kegan Paul, 1956), pp. 248–64; Greene, *Temporal Processes in Beethoven's Music*, p. vii. Also see Monelle, 'The Temporal Image'.

and static, it is nonetheless highly suggestive of such spatial connotations, however, and therefore not ideal.[58] An alternative, not far away but seemingly more neutral, is 'represents'. Thus, for the philosopher Georg Picht, music is a representation of time.[59] Though seemingly spatial and visual in implication, the term need not entail such attributes: 're-presents' might suggest presentification, bringing a time into the present. But again, this expression, though not perhaps incorrect, is slightly misleading. Time seems not to be replicable. What music does through its use of time cannot be wholly separated from time, however this is conceived; it is not a copy in this sense, does not stand in for or substitute for time, cannot be placed somewhere else 'there' (Da[r]-stellen).

To be more precise, I would like to say that music represents time *by* time, 'homomorphically', through a particular instance: it *instantiates* time.[60] This conception of instantiation is more neutral, applicable to most understandings of time. It contains the possibility that music in a manner creates its own time but is nonetheless *in* this time; that musical time may transform time while still being time; that musical time cannot in the first instance be wholly separate from other, non-musical time.[61]

Larger claims for music's relation to time predominantly concern the idea of internal, subjective time. Susanne Langer, for instance, comes down firmly on this side of the debate: 'Musical duration is an image of what might be termed 'lived' or 'experienced' time . . . it has not merely a different measure, but an

[58] Slightly pre-empting the grounds of the argument, in the context of her exploration of subjective, experienced time the metaphor of the image also runs counter to Langer's Bergsonian affiliations (cf. Henri Bergson: 'The inner life . . . cannot be represented by images', 'Introduction to Metaphysics', in *The Creative Mind: An Introduction to Metaphysics*, trans. Mabelle L. Andison [New York: Philosophical Society, 1946], p. 165). A more nuanced defence of the image terminology is given by Zuckerkandl, *Sound and Symbol*, pp. 254–64.

[59] Georg Picht, 'Grundlinien einer Philosophie der Musik', in *Wahrheit—Vernunft—Verantwortung: Philosophische Studien* (Stuttgart: Ernst Klett, 1969), pp. 408–26.

[60] On the former point see Robin Le Poidevin, *The Images of Time: An Essay in Temporal Representation* (Oxford: Oxford University Press, 2007), p. 134: the term 'homomorphic' is taken from Gregory Currie, *Image and Mind: Film, Philosophy and Cognitive Science* (Cambridge: Cambridge University Press, 1995). I would like to thank Le Poidevin for suggesting the term 'instantiation' in conversation.

[61] A further nuance that might be added which takes up the transformative potential of music is the conception of mimesis found in Harper-Scott's claim that 'Music is a mimesis of human temporality'. Mimesis is here understood as not merely derivative imitation but a reflection or representation which enables the disclosure of an aspect of time otherwise concealed. Thus a 'work of music is a mimesis of humankind's lived temporality, and lights up for us the structures of our own existence' (J.P.E. Harper-Scott, *Edward Elgar, Modernist* [Cambridge: Cambridge University Press, 2007], pp. 10, 12). In other words, as Andrew Bowie argues, 'music is world-disclosive' (*Music, Philosophy, and Modernity* [Cambridge: Cambridge University Press, 2007], p. 27).

altogether different structure from practical or scientific time'. Barbara Barry concurs, in that 'by reflecting the continuity and dynamic of emotion, experiential musical time is the most sensitive outward re-presentation of subjective "lived time".[62] Although played music may equally be said to exist in external or objective time, and much of music's interest may in fact arise from its ability to mediate between these subjective and objective conceptions, subjective time nonetheless forms the most fitting starting point for consideration of music's temporality.

Music and Subjective Time: Continuity and Consciousness

The perceived connection between temporality, consciousness, and music goes back a long way. The relationship between consciousness and time—at least internal time—is comparatively straightforward (the more problematic interaction between internal and external time conceptions can be left to one side for the moment). From Aristotle onwards philosophers have questioned whether if there were no soul there could still be time.[63] The first significant formulation of an internal, subjective time is given by Augustine in book XI of the *Confessions*, but it is really in the modern era, following the resubjectification of time introduced in Kant's *Critique of Pure Reason* that the idea becomes omnipresent within philosophical thought.[64] Schelling argues that 'Time is not something that flows independently of the self; the *self itself* is time conceived of in activity', as Hegel will similarly conclude that 'time is the same principle as the I = I of pure self-consciousness'. 'The self is in time, and time is the being of the subject himself'.[65] And just as in idealist thought, so the equating of subjective time with the being of the self is found later in the contrasting phenomenological investigations of Henri Bergson and Edmund Husserl, for whom the temporal flux of consciousness is nothing other than 'absolute subjectivity'.[66] This line of thought culminates in the early Heidegger's near tautological attempts at formulating this

---

[62] Langer, 'The Image of Time', p. 109 (as her discussion later suggests, however, even musical time is difficult to pin down); Barry, *Musical Time*, p. 242.

[63] Aristotle, *Physics*, IV.14, 223ª22–8.

[64] Although Kant in fact implies that the self (or at least the transcendental ground for the self) is metaphysically prior to or 'outside' time.

[65] F.W.J. Schelling, *System of Transcendental Idealism* (1800), trans. Peter Heath (Charlottesville, University Press of Virginia, 1978), p. 103; Hegel, *Philosophy of Nature*, §258, p. 35, and *Aesthetics*, p. 908.

[66] Edmund Husserl, *The Phenomenology of Internal Time Consciousness*, trans. James Churchill (The Hague: Martinus Nijhoff, 1964), §36.

relationship between self and time: '*Each Dasein is itself time* . . . The genuine being [*eigentliche Sein*] of Dasein is temporalness [*Zeitlichsein*]'. 'In what way "time" *exists* and how it *is* temporal, we can understand only by looking at the true being [*eigentlichen Sein*] of "time"'. Or in Maurice Merleau-Ponty's rather more succinct formulation, 'I am myself time'.[67]

Secondly, we may turn to the connection posited between consciousness, time, and *music*. 'How is it that rhythms and melodies, although only sound, resemble states of the soul?' asks Aristotle.[68] Again, the idea has an ancient lineage. We read of this connection between a melody and the soul earlier in Plato, just as Augustine later found that souls were more moved when sacred words were sung: all the diverse emotions of our spirit 'are stirred by a mysterious inner kinship' with music.[69] What differs in the modern examples is the absence of the Pythagorean underpinning provided by the music of the spheres, the soul mirroring in microcosm the macrocosm of the universe's consonant movements.[70] Instead, befitting the new, modern sense of the individual subject and subjective turn present in philosophy since Descartes, the perceived link between music and consciousness is conceived in terms of their common grounding in internal time.

Around 1800 the analogy between music and the temporal being of the self becomes all-pervasive. One might credit not only the emergence of subjectivity as, in Andrew Bowie's words, the preeminent philosophical concern,[71] new aesthetics of listening and the metaphorical understanding of music as an organic process, but also the fact that, as noted earlier, music now possessed a remarkable flexibility and capacity to convey more complex temporal states (which in turn fed into the perceived ability to convey a greater sense of musical subjectivity). 'The mind of man is fashioned and built / Even as a strain of music'

---

[67] Martin Heidegger, *The Concept of Time*, trans. Ingo Farin (London: Continuum, 2011), pp. 47, 51; Maurice Merleau-Ponty, *The Phenomenology of Perception*, trans. Colin Smith (London: Routledge, 2002), p. 489.

[68] Aristotle, *Problems*, XIX.29, 920ª3.

[69] Plato, *Laws*, VII (812c); Augustine, *Confessions*, X.xxxiii (49), trans. Henry Chadwick (Oxford: Oxford University Press, 1998), pp. 207–8.

[70] See especially Plato's *Timaeus* on this connection between musical ratios and the cosmic soul.

[71] Bowie, *Aesthetics and Subjectivity: From Kant to Nietzsche* (Manchester: Manchester University Press, 2003), p. 2. On the important notion of musical subjectivity in the nineteenth century see Julian M. Johnson, 'The Subjects of Music: A Theoretical and Analytical Enquiry into the Construction of Subjectivity in the Musical Structuring of Time' (DPhil diss., University of Sussex, 1994), pp. 25–72; Michael P. Steinberg, *Listening to Reason: Culture, Subjectivity, and Nineteenth-Century Music* (Princeton: Princeton University Press, 2004), esp. pp. 4–11; and, for a brief overview, my earlier account in *Mendelssohn, Time and Memory*, pp. 26–31. A broader and theoretically rich account of musical subjectivity is also given by Naomi Cumming, *The Sonic Self: Musical Subjectivity and Signification* (Bloomington and Indianapolis: Indiana University Press, 2000).

claimed Wordsworth early in his autobiographical account of the artist's coming to self-consciousness, *The Prelude*.[72] According to his contemporary Schelling, since 'the principle of time within the subject is self-consciousness' we may understand 'the close relationship between the sense of hearing in general and music and speech in particular with self-consciousness', for 'music on the whole is the art of reflection or of self-consciousness'.[73] In Hegel's opinion, 'every melody, although it has harmony as its basis, has a higher and more free subjectivity in itself'. 'Music', as he is fond of saying, 'takes as its subject-matter the subjective inner life itself'.

> Music's . . . own proper element is the inner life as such, explicitly shapeless feeling which cannot manifest itself in the outer world and its reality but only through an external medium which quickly vanishes and is cancelled at the very moment of expression

—in other words, through time. 'Here there is also in evidence the connection between subjective feeling and time' he holds, for time 'is the universal element in music'.[74] In Friedrich Schleiermacher's *Aesthetics*, music makes us 'conscious of the mobility of human self-consciousness'.[75] Even for Schopenhauer, whose metaphysics in many ways are quite the reverse of the subjectivity of his contemporaries, some statements on music nevertheless imply this idea of self-consciousness, albeit that of the universal Will rather than individual subject. In the melodies of music

> we again recognize the universally expressed, innermost story of the will conscious of itself. Melody is always a deviation from the keynote through a thousand crotchety wanderings up to the most painful discord. After this, it at last finds the keynote again, which expresses the satisfaction and composure of the will, but which nothing more can then be done, and the continuation of which would be only a wearisome and meaningless monotony corresponding to boredom.[76]

---

[72] Wordsworth, *The Prelude* (1799), I, ll. 67–8. The line is slightly altered in later versions: 'The mind of man is framed even like the breath / And harmony of music' (1805, I, ll. 351–2).

[73] Schelling, *Philosophy of Art*, trans. Douglas W. Stott (Minneapolis: University of Minnesota Press, 1989), §77, p. 109, and §105, p. 162.

[74] Hegel, *Aesthetics*, pp. 141, 907, 626, 909.

[75] Schleiermacher, *Ästhetik*, ed. Rudolf Odebrecht (Berlin: de Gruyter, 1931), p. 395, quoted by Bowie, *Aesthetics and Subjectivity*, p. 211.

[76] Schopenhauer, *The World as Will and Representation*, vol. I, p. 321. Evidently the close of Beethoven's Fifth must have driven Schopenhauer to distraction.

This must, however, be understood as the opposite of subjectivity—rather, the deepest objectivity.[77]

Moving into the twentieth century, the same understanding is still present with Bergson: 'A melody to which we listen with our eyes closed, heeding it alone, comes close to coinciding with this time which is the very fluidity of our inner life'.[78] Even in the present day philosophers and psychologists call upon music in trying to explain time. Laird Addis, building on the work of Susanne Langer, argues for an 'ontological affinity' of music and consciousness. 'States of consciousness and sounds alone are such that, while they require time for their existence, they do not require change', he contends. This leads Addis to the conclusion that music 'represents' or is 'isomorphic' to 'possible states of consciousness'.[79]

Music and the Problem of Time: Augustine to Kierkegaard

Why do philosophers and thinkers speak of music so often in considering time? Is it simply the case that they have an abiding love of music and thus turn to it in preference to other art forms? If so, many are strangely silent about the actual music they are describing. It is clear from this customary absence of detail that it is usually not a particular piece, composer, or repertoire that is being referred to, but rather the characteristics of music in general during this period. The context of many nineteenth- and early twentieth-century accounts would seem to imply a general common-practice style—tonal, homophonic, melodically driven—but this can range from Kierkegaard's love of Mozart, Coleridge's tribute to Cimarosa, Tieck's regard for Reichardt, and the affection for Rossini (about the only thing) shared by Hegel and Schopenhauer to Sartre's use of an old gramophone record of a popular song in *Nausea*.[80]

[77] In will-less aesthetic experience, time, the individual subject, and correspondingly subjectivity, are irrelevant ('Time, place, the individual that knows, and the individual that is known, have no meaning', ibid., vol. I, p. 179). Art stops the wheel of time: the genius is characterised by absolute objectivity, *not* subjectivity.

[78] Although, Bergson notes, a melody 'still has too many qualities, too much definition, and we must first effect the difference among the sounds, then do away with the distinctive features of sound itself, retaining of it only the continuation of what precedes into what follows'. *Duration and Simultaneity*, trans. Leon Jacobson (New York: Library of Liberal Arts, 1922), p. 44.

[79] Laird Addis, *Of Mind and Music* (Ithaca, NY: Cornell University Press, 1999), p. 69. Addis's argument has not inspired universal consent. Aaron Ridley suggests that lack of extension might be better grounds for suggesting this relationship (review, *Mind*, 110 [2001], 425)—thus bringing the discussion closer to Langer's Bergsonian heritage.

[80] The words Sartre quotes in his novel are in fact from two popular songs: 'Some of These Days' and Gershwin's 'The Man I Love'. Bonds notes that this lack of specificity as to what music

The reason lies in the fact that music proved an ideal aid for explaining the nature of time and offering solutions to apparent aporias in the conception of temporality. Time is a philosophical problem, in that the past and future do not, in a straightforward sense, exist (that is, they exist *no longer*, and *not yet*), and neither does the present, if understood as merely the instant dividing past and future. The same, of course, is true of music. Music, just as speech, 'is vanishing existence . . . like Time, no longer immediately present in the very moment of its being present'.[81] So, if all existence is necessarily in time, and no part of time truly exists, does nothing exist? Clearly music points to the fact that a temporal entity must be believed to exist in some form, however unclear its ontology. Despite Kant's objection to music's lack of persistence, few would seriously doubt the sensuous reality that we experience listening to music. One may intellectually doubt time, argue for its unreality or illusory nature, but music, surely, is something more than a phantom. It is this almost tangible sense of presence—a presence, as Langer notes, made up entirely out of apparent absence—that provides the key for philosophers attempting to ground the concept of time in phenomenal reality.

This problem receives its classic formulation much earlier in Augustine, in the Eleventh Book of his *Confessions*. Take the past and future:

> How can they 'be' when the past is not now present and the future is not yet present? Yet if the present were always present, it would not pass into the past: it would not be time but eternity. If then, in order to be time at all, the present is so made that it passes into the past, how can we say that this present also 'is'? The cause of its being is that it will cease to be. So indeed we cannot truly say that time exists except in the sense that it tends towards non-existence.[82]

Just as music, time appears to be a perpetual perishing. Indeed, examining the present itself leads to an infinite vanishing: 'not even one day is entirely present. . . . One hour is itself constituted of fugitive moments'.

> If we can think of some bit of time which cannot be divided into even the smallest instantaneous moments, that alone is what we can call 'present'. And this time . . . is an interval with no duration. If it has duration, it is divisible into past and future.[83]

such writers were thinking of reflects earlier philosophical concerns (*Music as Thought*, p. 11); one might similarly claim that it suggests a desire to speak of music in general and not just a particular genius-composer singled out for their music's unique properties.

[81] Hegel, *Phenomenology of Spirit*, trans. A.V. Miller (Oxford: Oxford University Press, 1979), p. 432.

[82] Augustine, *Confessions*, XI.xiv (17), p. 231.

[83] Ibid., XI.xv (20), p. 232.

In order to solve this impasse, Augustine famously points to the necessity of memory in constituting time: time only 'exists' in the conscious mind, in the present, as it considers what is past, or passing, or to come. Though customarily we speak of the past, present, and future,

> it would be more exact to say: there are three times, a present of things past, a present of things present, a present of things to come. In the soul there are these three aspects of time, and I do not see them anywhere else. The present considering the past is the memory, the present considering the present is immediate awareness, the present considering the future is expectation.[84]

But how, then, do we measure time if all is contained in the present of consciousness? Rejecting the Aristotelian cosmological measurement of time from external motion as insufficient, Augustine instead turns his attention to sound, whose temporality does not possess a clear physical correlate, specifically to the sound of the human voice. It is here that the discussion of the recitation of a Psalm offers Augustine his ideal illustration of the temporal flow of events from the future through the present and into the past.

> Before I begin, my expectation is directed towards the whole. But when I have begun, the verses from it which I take into the past become the object of my memory. . . . by that the future is transferred to become the past. As the action advances further, the shorter the expectation, the longer the memory . . . until the entire action is finished, and it has passed into the memory.

By this, too, 'the life of this act of mine is stretched two ways, into my memory . . . and into my expectation'. This process is analogous for Augustine of 'the entire life of a single person . . . and the total history of the "sons of men" where all human lives are but parts'.[85]

Hence although the temporal being of time, like music, is a problem, it is one that can be addressed by the use of music itself.[86] Still, it is not clear that all the problems here have been fully resolved. Even if the present moment does contain past and future, if it is nonetheless in itself only a durationless instant how does

---

[84] Ibid., XI.xx (26), p. 235.

[85] Ibid., XI.xxviii (38), p. 243.

[86] Augustine uses the musical recitation of a poetic text, but his argument is based on the musicality and rhythm of the sounds rather than the semantic signification of the words.

it belong to time? A memory, as the past *in the present*, must have duration too, otherwise it in turn does not exist. (To ground this in a further memory just leads to an infinite regress.) And duration, as Augustine has already noted, implies the potential to be divided into a past and a future, thus bringing us back to the original problem. How could time be constituted from a series of atemporal points, and consequently what would connect these vanishing instants, giving continuity to the perpetually moving present? Through the example of a hymn, Augustine has certainly provided a practical refutation of the atomistic viewpoint—a demonstration of the presence of time in the soul, the movement of projected future events through the present and into the past, the consequent distension of the soul into expectation and remembrance, and its ability to measure time by long and short values. But by the end of his discussion the specific question of the durationless present has been left to the side, its aporetic quality overcome through the immediacy of poetic instantiation rather than dismantled through intellectual analysis.

Since Aristotle philosophers have rejected the idea of time as consisting of a succession of instants, at the risk of falling into Zeno-like paradoxes, an Eleatic world without motion or individuation. To most people it seems nonsensical to suggest that not only does the present not exist, but neither does duration, and therefore that change cannot either. Even one-and-a-half millennia later the conundrum was still being raised by Kierkegaard. 'The present . . . is not a concept of time, except precisely as something infinitely contentless, which again is the infinite vanishing'. 'Time is, then, infinite succession; the life that is in time and is only of time has no present'.[87] From this aesthetic we are led irresistibly to Kierkegaard's famous account of music in *Either/Or*, which sees *Don Giovanni* as the quintessential topic for music because of the latter's perpetual vanishing of the present and need for its continual replacement, a procedure which mirrors the serial amorous proclivities of Mozart's protagonist.[88] Philosophically Kierkegaard will solve this aporia by introducing eternity as the only possible grounding of time, as Augustine, too, had grounded the fallen distension of human time within

---

[87] Søren Kierkegaard (writing as 'Vigilius Haufniensis'), *The Concept of Anxiety: A Simple Psychological Orienting Deliberation on the Dogmatic Issue of Hereditary Sin*, trans. Reidar Thomte and Albert B. Anderson (Princeton: Princeton University Press, 1981), p. 86.

[88] 'Love from the soul is a continuation in time, sensual love a disappearance in time, but the medium which expresses this is precisely music'. Don Giovanni's life has no substance but 'hurries on in a perpetual vanishing, just like music, of which it is true that it is over as soon as it stops playing and only comes back into existence when it starts again'. Kierkegaard (writing as 'A'), 'The Immediate Erotic Stages, *or* the Musical Erotic', in *Either/Or: A Fragment of Life*, trans. Alastair Hannay (Harmondsworth: Penguin, 1992), pp. 101, 107–8.

a discussion of God's eternity.[89] But what do we do without calling upon a *deus ex tempore*?

The more mundane solution is to distinguish between the abstractions of objective time (which supports the notion of a durationless present) and the evident real existence of the present for psychological time, and to give the latter a duration by introducing into it temporal distention—i.e., a 'thick' present that retains the immediate past shading into the present consciousness.[90] This solution is arguably present in embryo in Augustine's doctrine of the *distentio animi*, but it is fully developed only in the philosophical and psychological examination of internal time consciousness which came to prominence at the end of the nineteenth century. Once again, the three most significant theorists in this field all rely, to a greater or lesser extent, on the example of music to underpin their theories.[91]

Music and the Phenomenology of Time: James, Bergson, Husserl

One of the first and most influential proponents of this understanding of time and consciousness was the American philosopher William James. In his monumental *The Principles of Psychology* James argues for what he terms the 'stream of thought', the continuous flux of mental activity across time: 'Consciousness, then, does not appear to itself chopped up in bits ... It is nothing jointed, it flows. A "river" or a "stream" are the metaphors by which it is most naturally described.'[92] In chapter 15, 'The Perception of Time', James popularises the idea of the 'specious present' after this term's introduction in an earlier work

---

[89] Kierkegaard, *The Concept of Anxiety*, pp. 87–9: 'The moment signifies the present as that which has no past and no future, and precisely in this lies the imperfection of the sensuous life. The eternal also signifies the present as that which has no past and no future, and this is the perfection of the eternal. . . . Thus understood, the moment is not properly an atom of time but an atom of eternity. It is the first reflection of eternity in time, its first attempt, as it were, at stopping time. . . . The moment is that ambiguity in which time and eternity touch each other, and with this the concept of *temporality* is posited whereby time constantly intersects eternity and eternity constantly pervades time'.

[90] It should also be noted that psychological research shows a minimum durational threshold for auditory perception—it seems that anything under about 0.002 seconds cannot be perceived by the human mind. The example of music also clearly demonstrates that the perceptual present cannot be instantaneous, for a sound has a specific, non-zero wavelength.

[91] On the prehistory of these ideas see Holly K. Andersen and Rick Grush, 'A Brief History of Time-Consciousness: Historical Precursors to James and Husserl', *Journal of the History of Philosophy*, 47 (2009), 277–307.

[92] William James, *The Principles of Psychology*, 2 vols. (New York: Holt, 1890), vol. I, p. 239.

by E.R. Clay: the experienced present has a duration (about six seconds, certainly no more than twelve James concludes), in which the immediate past is still felt to be present as a diminishing echo.[93] 'The practically cognized present is no knife-edge, but a saddle-back, with a certain breadth of its own, on which we sit perched, and from which we look in two directions into time'.[94]

As with his predecessors, James finds that hearing is the sense best suited to the perception of duration, and again musical examples are in evidence to support the conception of a continuous experienced time in which the immediate past is still heard as dynamically contributing towards the present. In Clay's formulation (cited by James), 'All the notes of a bar of a song seem to the listener to be contained in the present'.[95] That a melody appears as a melody and not merely as a collection of notes presented successively across time indicates that the listener must be able to sense succession *qua* succession. '*A succession of feelings, in and of itself, is not a feeling of succession*'. Therefore 'what is past . . . must be known with what is present, and *during* the "present" spot of time'.[96] This permeation of the past within the present is a vital part of subjective time experience but something unnecessary for the concept of an objective, impersonal time, and the apparent temporal wholeness of a musical phrase (a constructed unity, not present in the notes themselves) appears the best example of this perception.

Yet greater is the importance of music for the philosophy of Henri Bergson. Musical analogies and metaphors abound throughout Bergson's writings. Like James (whom he greatly admired), Bergson clearly recognises the inherent problem if time is conceived of as consisting of instants. 'What exactly is the present?' he asks. 'If it is a question of a mathematical instant . . . it is clear that such an instant is a pure abstraction . . . it cannot have real existence'. 'Our consciousness tells us that when we speak of our present we are thinking of a

---

[93] Coincidentally or otherwise, in medieval times the term 'moment' was actually used as a unit of time, corresponding to a period of one-and-a-half minutes. This intuitive feeling for an enduring present over the abstract philosophical positing of the durationless instant might also be given as significant anthropological evidence for the perceptual reality of the distended 'specious present'.

[94] Ibid., vol. I, p. 609.

[95] [Edmund R. Clay], *The Alternative: A Study in Psychology* (London: Macmillan, 1882), p. 167, quoted by James, *The Principles of Psychology*, vol. I, p. 609 (the book was published anonymously but James names the author). James's later conclusion, 'with the fading of the present thing there must at all times mingle the fading echo of all those other things which the previous few seconds have supplied' (ibid., p. 635) concurs with Clay in both content and metaphor used. It is evident that James at least is speaking figuratively; as later writers have pointed out, practically speaking this is implausible, in that we do not hear previous notes prolonged, however faintly, as if the sostenuto pedal had been held down on a piano (see Husserl, *The Phenomenology of Internal Time Consciousness*, pp. 30, 41); the example of music actually shows this apparent solution to have been premature.

[96] James, *The Principles of Psychology*, vol. I, pp. 628–9, emphasis in original.

certain interval of duration.'[97] 'Without the survival of the past in the present
there would be no duration but only instantaneity.'[98] 'For our duration is not
merely one instant replacing another; if there were there would be nothing but
the present—no prolonging of the past into the actual, no evolution, no concrete duration.'[99] Bergson argues against what he will famously call in *Creative
Evolution* the cinematographic model of reality, as something formed from discrete points in time. Such misconceptions arise from the natural (but falsifying)
need to derive becoming from being, movement from rest, to pin down existence to stable moorings which will guarantee truth claims about the world. In
fact, 'reality is mobility.'[100]

Instead, real time (*temps réel*) or duration (*durée*) is quite different from the
space it is usually reduced to (*temps espace*)—a continuous, non-homogenous,
intensive medium, in which the past accumulates within the present. Music
is used by Bergson as means for explaining this intuition, which is habitually
obscured by the spatial concepts sedimented inside language. The *Essai sur les
données immédiates de la conscience* (1889), his doctoral thesis, sets out the kernel
of his idea of duration, its equivalence to the self in time, and its intimate link
with the effect of music. Two of many possible instances may serve to illustrate
the central role of music for Bergson's attempts at explicating this true sense
of time:

> Pure duration ... forms both the past and the present states into an
> organic whole, *as happens when we recall the notes of a tune, melting, so to
> speak, into one another*. Might it not be said that, even if these notes suc-
> ceed one another, yet we perceive them in one another, and that their
> totality may be compared to a living being[?] We can thus conceive of
> succession without distinction, and think of it as a mutual penetration,
> and interconnexion and organisation of elements, each one of which
> represent the whole, and cannot be distinguished or isolated from it
> except by abstract thought.[101]

This analogy will become omnipresent throughout Bergson's career. In
'Philosophical Intuition' (1911), for instance, the author speaks of the 'continuous fluidity of real time which flows along indivisible ... *as in a melody*

[97] Henri Bergson, 'The Perception of Change', in *The Creative Mind*, p. 151.

[98] Bergson, 'Introduction to Metaphysics', p. 179.

[99] Bergson, *Creative Evolution*, trans. Arthur Mitchell (New York: Henry Holt, 1911), p. 4.

[100] Bergson, 'Introduction to Metaphysics', p. 188.

[101] Bergson, *Time and Free Will: An Essay on the Immediate Data of Consciousness*, trans. F.L.
Pogson (London: George Allen and Co., 1910), pp. 100, 101, my emphasis.

where everything is becoming'.[102] Or, formulated in 'The Perception of Change', 'when we listen to a *melody* we have the purest impression of succession we could possibly have ... and yet it is the very continuity of the melody and the impossibility of breaking it up which make that impression upon us'. Bergson concludes that since for *durée* the present is filled with the past, it is possible hypothetically to include in the present one's entire conscious past—'not as instantaneity, not like a cluster of simultaneous parts, but as something continually present which would also be something continually moving: such ... is the *melody*'.[103] Any lacunae in the logical argument of Bergson's conception of time are explained by the fact that he insists on the impossibility of language and concepts to do justice to duration. In order to resolve the problem of time, Bergson maintains, the would-be philosopher needs intuition—or it seems, more often a melody. Music saves us from the aporias arising from language.

One final, notable example of music's use in phenomenological investigations of subjective time is provided by Edmund Husserl in his 1905 lectures *On the Phenomenology of Internal Time Consciousness*. This is a thorough (and, in comparison with Bergson, somewhat longwinded) examination of our internal time sense as it manifests itself through the phenomena of our perception. The 'temporal object' Husserl most often uses to explicate the phenomenological content of this lived experience of time proves to be sound, characteristically a melody. In this, Husserl is following the lead not just of Clay, James, and Bergson, but also of his German predecessors Brentano and Stern, whose melodious examples are cited by Husserl as part of his critique of these earlier theories. A few examples out of the innumerable instances in Husserl's work will suffice for illustrating the all-pervading presence of music in his account.

Forming the very starting point of his investigation, Husserl 'brackets' external or objective time and concerns himself solely with our conscious experience of time.[104] (Rather like Bergson before and his pupil Heidegger after, he implies later that objective time is an intellectual abstraction from the perceptual reality of subjective time, a lesser, derivative species as it were.) Concerning the reality of this inner time Husserl finds no further need for justification: 'We assume an existing time; this, however, is not the time of the world of experience but the *immanent time* of the flow of consciousness. The evidence that consciousness of a tonal process, a melody, exhibits a succession even as I hear it is such as to make every doubt or denial appear senseless'.[105] The presupposition of this

---

[102] Bergson, 'Philosophical Intuition', in *The Creative Mind*, p. 127, my emphasis.

[103] Bergson, 'The Perception of Change', pp. 149, 152, my emphasis.

[104] Husserl, *The Phenomenology of Internal Time Consciousness*, §1.

[105] Ibid., p. 23.

presuppositionless phenomenological enterprise is evidently given by music. Apodictic certainty is grounded in the fleeting notes of a tune.

At the most critical stage in the unfolding of Husserl's argument, an example of the perception of the successive notes of a melody serves to critique earlier, inadequate theories of time perception (§7), introducing the celebrated notion of 'retention' or primary memory (§§8–13).[106] Here, rather than each successive note merely replacing the previous one (in which no sense of continuity, of temporality, would be present), the former sound sinks back into the past but is yet held fast by consciousness in 'retention', whereby we are still conscious of it for a while as 'having been', before gradually 'running off' as the phenomenal present moves forward. 'The retentional sound is not actually present but "primarily remembered" precisely in the now . . . it is consciousness of *what has just been.* . . . Retentional consciousness includes real consciousness of the past of sound, primary remembrance of sound, and is not to be resolved into [either] sensed sound [or] apprehension as memory'.[107] Melody is used again in distinguishing this retentive primary memory from what Husserl calls secondary memory or recollection (§14), when he asks his audience to remember a melody, 'let us say, which in our youth we heard during a concert. Then it is obvious that the entire phenomenon of memory has, *mutatis mutandis*, exactly the same constitution as the perception of the melody'.[108] This in turn introduces the corollary of retention, 'protention', 'the expectation of the sound to come'.[109]

A clarification of perception, retention, and recollection brings music to the fore; that the distinctions Husserl introduces seem to derive from the difference between the tones of music and mere succession of sounds only further emphasises music's privileged role:

> In the 'perception of a melody', we distinguish the tone *given now*, which we term the 'perceived', from those which *have gone by*, which we say are 'not perceived'. On the other hand, we call the *whole melody* one that is *perceived*, although only the now-point actually is. We follow this procedure because not only is the extension of the melody given point for point in an extension of the act of perception but also the unity of retentional consciousness still 'holds' the expired tones themselves in consciousness and continuously establishes the unity of

---

[106] This idea of retention is implicit in James, *Principles of Psychology*, pp. 629–30, but Husserl certainly offers the most comprehensive and finished formulation of the concept.

[107] Husserl, *The Phenomenology of Internal Time Consciousness*, §12, pp. 53–4.

[108] Ibid., §14, p. 57.

[109] Ibid., p. 58.

consciousness with reference to the homogenous temporal object, i.e., the melody.

The whole melody . . . appears as present so long as it still sounds, so long as the notes *belonging to it*, intended in the *one* nexus of apprehensions, still sound. The melody is past only after the last note has gone.[110]

Husserl uses music throughout his deliberations as the quintessential temporal object revealing the flux that constitutes internal time. Although unconcerned with musical particulars (such as the ways in which different musical styles might alter perceptions of continuity or the importance of secondary memory in the constitution of musical form as intentional object),[111] Husserl's example illustrates how the broad attributes of Western common-practice music have been readily utilised by philosophers to help elucidate problematic concepts of time and consciousness, a tendency that holds to the present day. Even from a more recent perspective informed by contemporary cognitive psychology, the editors of a recent book on music and consciousness note that while consciousness is a problematic, disputed, multifaceted concept, 'paying due attention to the structured temporality of music . . . might help bring a much needed focus to the key dimension of time in the constitution of consciousness'.[112]

To this extent, one could justly claim that music is as important for philosophy as philosophy is for understanding music.[113] Although Friedrich Schlegel had claimed that 'there is a certain tendency of all pure instrumental music towards philosophy', it would appear that there is a converse tendency of much nineteenth- and twentieth-century philosophy towards music.[114] Even Schlegel would admit 'Every art has musical principles and when completed becomes itself music. This is true even of philosophy and thus probably of literature too, perhaps also of life'.[115]

[110] Ibid., §16, pp. 60–1.

[111] See David Clarke's consideration in 'Music, phenomenology, time consciousness: meditations after Husserl', in David Clarke and Eric Clarke (eds.), *Music and Consciousness: Philosophical, Psychological, and Cultural Perspectives* (Oxford: Oxford University Press, 2011), pp. 1–28; also, for a post-Husserlian phenomenological account of music touching on many of these deeper issues, his pupil Roman Ingarden's *The Musical Work and the Problem of its Identity*, trans. Adam Czerniawski (London: Macmillan, 1986).

[112] David Clarke and Eric Clarke (eds.), *Music and Consciousness: Philosophical, Psychological, and Cultural Perspectives* (Oxford: Oxford University Press, 2011), p. xix.

[113] As David Greene states, 'The idea that music matters to us because of its images of temporality matter to us may suggest to philosophers that they may learn from music' (*Temporal Processes in Beethoven's Music*, p. viii).

[114] Friedrich Schlegel, *Athenaeum Fragmente*, No. 444, in *Kritische Friedrich-Schlegel-Ausgabe*, ed. Ernst Behler et al, 35 vols. (Paderborn, Munich, Vienna: Schöningh, 1958–2002), vol. II, p. 254.

[115] Schlegel, *Vermischte nachgelassene Fragmente*, No. 120, in *Kritische Friedrich-Schlegel-Ausgabe*, vol. XVI, p. 213.

Music and Subjectivity: From Locke to Hegel

What gives rise to this perceived association between music and consciousness
(or more precisely, self-consciousness—the self's awareness of the self or 'apperception' as it is sometimes termed)? At a fundamental level, the connection
appears to lie in the sense of identity within transitoriness common to both: as
Schlegel again discerned, the temporal, incorporeal nature of the self is pro-
foundly akin to music in its ability to suggest persistence amidst constant passing.[116] Indeed the affinity between the two was widely recognised by thinkers
during this period: in his detailed study of temporal consciousness in German
Romantic thought, Manfred Frank concludes that for figures such as Novalis
music was not only the temporal art par excellence but through this very temporal nature became seen as the most adequate expression of self-consciousness.[117]

The rise of self-consciousness as a philosophical theme is historically connected with the changing sense of time we saw occurring in the modern
period—the acceleration of change and temporalisation of experience. G.J.
Whitrow argues for instance that a strong sense of self-consciousness became
developed in Western history only around the eighteenth century, through the
cessation of living in a continual present and the consequent reliance on memory.[118] At the same time, however, the ability of philosophy to demonstrate the
unity of the self had become problematic. Locke had argued for the central constitutive role of memory in creating personal identity, in its ability to connect
dispersed temporal states into one consciousness: 'personal identity consists,
not in the identity of substance, but . . . in the identity of consciousness'.

> Consciousness always accompanies thinking and . . . makes every one
> to be, what he calls *self*; and thereby distinguishes himself from all other
> thinking things, in this alone consists *personal identity, i.e.* the sameness

---

[116] Schlegel, *Die Entwicklung der Philosophie*, bk VII, in *Kritische Friedrich-Schlegel-Ausgabe*, vol.
XIII, pp. 57–8. The same association is made earlier in the fourth *Kritische Wäldchen* of Herder (writ-
ten in 1769 but not published until 1846)—a significant precursor of Romantic views on music: 'die
Wollust der Tonkunst liegt tief in uns verborgen; sie würkt in der Berauschung: sie verschwindet und
läßt eine so kurze Spur nach, als das Schiff im Meer und der Pfeil in der Luft, und der Gedanke in der
Seele. Kannst du also, o Philosoph, dein Inneres Gefühl außen vor dich setzen, und den unteilbaren
Ton wie eine Farbe zergliedern: kannst du fühlen und zugleich denken, und das vorüberfliegende
Moment erhaschen und zur Ewigkeit fixieren[?]' (*Werke*, ed. Martin Bollacher, 10 vols. (Frankfurt:
Deutscher Klassiker Verlag, 1985–2000), vol. II, p. 336).

[117] Manfred Frank, *Das Problem 'Zeit' in der deutschen Romantik: Zeitbewußtsein und Bewußtsein
von Zeitlichkeit in der frühromantischen Philosophie und in Tiecks Dichtung* (Munich: Winkler, 1972),
p. 229.

[118] Whitrow, *The Natural Philosophy of Time*, p. 114.

of a rational being. And as far as this consciousness can be extended back-wards to any past action or thought, so far reaches the identity of that person . . .

If there be any part of its existence, which I cannot upon recollection join with that present consciousness whereby I am now my *self*, it is in that part of its existence no more my *self* than any other immaterial being.[119]

The fragility of the grounds on which personal identity rests implicit in Locke's account was taken further by Hume. Humans 'are nothing but a bundle or col-lection of different perceptions, which succeed each other with an inconceiv-able rapidity, and are in a perpetual flux and movement' Hume argues. 'I never catch myself *without* a perception, and never observe anything *but* the percep-tion'. 'The mind is a kind of theatre, where several perceptions successively make their appearance; pass, re-pass, glide away, and mingle in an infinite variety of postures and situations'. We perceive merely a succession of impressions, and given that causality between events, in Hume's analysis, is merely a customary association without necessary connection, it follows that 'the identity, which we ascribe to the mind of man, is only a fictitious one'.[120] Responding to such utter scepticism, Kant, though purporting to salvage causality from Hume's devastat-ing attack through his a priori cognitive preconditions of time and space, was still unable to answer what the self, the 'transcendental unity of apperception', was. Hence the unity of the self became 'transcendental'—i.e., a necessary pre-condition for a given reality, the fact that we do remember previous cognitions and that there therefore must be something persisting across time which does this, a self which cannot itself be known directly but only deduced as existing from what it accomplishes.

While Kant had let such questions rest as beyond the limits of pure reason, his successors were less modest. As Andrew Bowie has demonstrated, the solu-tions proffered by post-Kantian Idealist and Romantic thinkers exhibited a radical temporalisation of self-consciousness. It is here that the connection with music becomes most apparent. Following on the heels of the *Critique of Pure Reason*, Fichte turns self-consciousness into a process, which provides the basis for an entire philosophy: '*self* and *self-reverting act* are perfectly identical con-cepts'; 'philosophy starts out from . . . an Act'.[121] Fichte does not bring music into his analysis, but his successors do.

---

[119] John Locke, *An Essay Concerning Human Understanding* (Oxford: Clarendon Press, 1979), II/27 'Of Identity and Diversity', §§19, 9, 24, pp. 342, 335, 345, punctuation slightly modernised.

[120] David Hume, *A Treatise of Human Nature*, ed. L.A. Selby-Bigge (Oxford: Clarendon Press, 1951), I/IV/6, 'Of Personal Identity', §§3, 4, 15, pp. 252, 253, 259.

[121] Johann Gottlieb Fichte, *Science of Knowledge*, trans. Peter Heath and John Lachs (Cambridge: Cambridge University Press, 1982), pp. 37, 42. A further useful account of the link

The temporalisation of the search for the unity of self-consciousness may be found soon after in Schelling, in his early *System of Transcendental Idealism* (1800). As with Hegel afterwards, Schelling reads 'the whole of philosophy' as 'progressive history of self-consciousness'.[122] Self-consciousness is 'not a kind of being, but a kind of knowing'—an activity, like self-identity—and like music (as Schelling will suggest elsewhere in the *Philosophy of Art*).[123] 'The self is pure act, a pure doing': 'what the self is' is undemonstrable; 'one can only describe the action whereby it comes about'.[124] Thus (as with Hume) the identity of the self is a mediated one, created by the subject itself, not a given; but it is one whose solution can be ever more realised, and this is achieved above all through art.[125] For within Schelling's philosophical system art holds an extraordinarily privileged role, and music is implicitly the most perfectly suited medium to carry out this task (though the full implications of this feature are left undeveloped in Schelling's thought).

Somewhat outside this stream of philosophy stands Schopenhauer, who vehemently rejected the idealist thought of Fichte, Schelling, and Hegel. Yet Schopenhauer still finds use for music as the only fitting analogy to describe the real transcendental unity of apperception (which for him is the primordial Will). In discussing what keeps consciousness together, what gives it 'unity and consequence', the 'simple thread on which everything is arranged', Schopenhauer rejects memory as insufficient along with Kant's transcendental I, and asserts it is 'the will that gives [consciousness] unity and holds all its representations and ideas together, accompanying them, as it were, like a continuous ground-bass'. Or again, 'the course of life itself retains throughout the same *fundamental tone*; in fact, its manifold events and scene are at bottom like variations on one and the same theme'.[126]

Most famous of the post-Kantian Idealists is Hegel, whose thought is permeated throughout by the concept of subjectivity—of the subject knowing itself as self, a reflection of the self equivalent to self-consciousness, or 'the subjective inner life' as he often describes it. It is in terms of this notion of subjectivity that music is explicitly and almost invariably described. Hegel's account of music in the *Aesthetics*, while undoubtedly partial, flawed and superficial in many of its aspects,

---

between music and self-consciousness at this time, relating specifically to Novalis, Schelling, and Schleiermacher, is given in Bowie's *Music, Philosophy, and Modernity*, pp. 145–65 and 411–12. On the issue of time and self-consciousness in early German Romanticism see also Frank, *Das Problem 'Zeit' in der deutschen Romantik*, and relating specifcally to music, James H. Donelan, *Poetry and the Romantic Musical Aesthetic* (Cambridge: Cambridge University Press, 2008).

[122] Schelling, *System of Transcendental Idealism*, p. 2.

[123] Ibid., p. 17; cf. p. 25.

[124] Ibid., pp. 27, 29.

[125] Ibid., p. 45, also cf. p. 102.

[126] Schopenhauer, *The World as Will and Representation*, vol. II, pp. 139, 140, 35.

is also of enormous insight for understanding the projected connection between music, self-consciousness, and temporality in his era, and still has valuable observations even now for attempts at comprehending their intimate relationship.

As we saw, for Hegel, music's 'own proper element is the inner life'.[127]

> If the inner life . . . is in fact to be manifested as a subjective inwardness, the genuinely correspondent material cannot be of such a kind that it persists on its own account. . . . we need a material which for our apprehension is without stability and even as it arises and exists vanishes once more. . . . this complete withdrawal, of both the inner life and its expression, into subjectivity, brings completely into being the second romantic art—music.[128]

Music is the most subjective of the arts, corresponding most nearly with the inner movements of our consciousness. The fleeting, transient presence of sound is closely akin to subjective self-consciousness, the inner stage upon which the content of our consciousness glides in and out as Hume would have it. Our inner subjectivity corresponds to the resounding of music, since 'sound, is an externality which in its coming-to-be is annihilated again by its very existence, and it vanishes of itself'.[129]

This connection is explained by means of a consideration of rhythm and metre, following Schelling's earlier example (though departing from his erstwhile friend by emphasising music's subjective character).

> Things together in space can comfortably be seen at a glance; but in time one moment has gone already when the next is there, and in this disappearance and reappearance the moments of time go on into infinity. This indeterminacy has to be given shape by the regularity of the musical beat which produces a determinateness and continuously recurring pattern and thereby checks the march to infinity.

'The beat of music has a magical power to which we are so susceptible that often, in hearing music, we beat time to it without being aware of the fact' claims Hegel.

> This recurrence of equal time intervals is not something belonging objectively to the notes and their duration. To the note as such, and

[127] Hegel, *Aesthetics*, p. 626.
[128] Ibid., p. 889.
[129] Ibid., p. 890.

to time, to be divided and repeated in this regular way is a matter of indifference. The beat therefore appears as something purely created by the subject, so that now in listening we acquire the immediate certainty of having in this regularization of time something purely subjective and *indeed the basis of the pure self-identity which the subject inherently possesses as his self-identity and unity and their recurrence in all the difference and most varied many-sidedness of experience.* Therefore the beat resounds in the depths of our soul and takes hold of us in virtue of this inner subjectivity, a subjectivity at first abstractly self-identical. From this point of view it is not the spiritual content, not the concrete soul of feeling, which speaks to us in the musical notes; neither is it the note as note that moves us in our inmost being; on the contrary, *it is this abstract unity, introduced into time by the subject, which echoes the like unity of the subject.*[130]

This is enabled through memory: Music's expression

does not produce an object persisting in space but shows through its free unstable soaring that it is a communication which, instead of having stability on its own account, is carried by the inner subjective life, and is to exist for that life alone [i.e., memory]; the notes re-echo only in the depths of the soul which is gripped and moved in its subjective consciousness.[131]

'Here there is also in evidence', Hegel continues, 'the connection between (a) *subjective feeling* and (b) *time* as such which is the universal element in music'. For

the actual self itself belongs to time, with which . . . it coincides. . . . The self is in time, and time is the being of the subject himself. Now since time, and not space as such, provides the essential element in which sound gains existence in respect of its musical value, and since the time of the sound is that of the subject too, sound on this principle penetrates the self, grips it in its simplest being, and by means of the temporal movement and its rhythm sets the self in motion.[132]

In Hegel's view, then, music not only possesses an emotive, expressive impact on the passions but reveals a deeper physiological sympathy with the temporal

[130] Ibid., p. 249, emphasis mine.
[131] Ibid., pp. 891–2.
[132] Ibid., pp. 907–8, emphasis mine.

nature of the self arising from the identity constructed across temporal distention common to both. Both the self and music exist only as a *process*. And, with
a superb sense of dramatic timing, Hegel then rounds off his discussion with the
lapidary one-line paragraph 'This is what can be advanced as the essential reason
for the elemental might of music'.[133]

As the examples just given have demonstrated, music has been able to provide for philosophers an example of identity within temporal diversity—the
positing of a supertemporal unity that is constituted out of the temporal, what
could in a manner be understood as an ontological overcoming of time's apparent transience. The question was posed as to whether this ability of music might
eventually point the way to the solution or at least aesthetic transfiguration of
philosophical problems relating to this attribute of time. In working towards
addressing this question the following section examines in turn how the musical parameters of rhythm and metre, form, harmony, and polyphony have
been used in philosophical attempts at explaining the potential transcendence
of time.

Unifying Time: Rhythm and Metre in Schelling and Wackenroder

Our first port of call is the role metre and rhythm play in the construction of musical time, an issue already raised in Hegel's consideration, and it is to his one-time
roommate and colleague, Schelling, that we turn our attention. Schelling leaves
some pregnant remarks in his *Philosophy of Art* concerning music's link with
self-consciousness, its mediation between subjective and objective time and its
rhythm's potential for overcoming external time.[134] His account of music is in
many ways old-fashioned and derivative, but throws out some intriguing ideas
which could be taken further. The current discussion will consider the importance of Schelling's theory of rhythm for the philosophy of time; larger questions that arise from his speculations will be taken up towards the close of this
chapter.

It is noteworthy that music appears to be the most *objective* of the arts for
Schelling, rather than the most subjective as with Hegel and for many others
in this period. Early in the *Philosophy of Art* Schelling lays down the tenet that
'Music . . . is nothing other than the primal rhythm of nature and of the universe
itself'.[135] Here we reencounter the idea of objective or cosmic time, long absent

---

[133] Ibid., p. 908 (possibly due to Hotho, the compiler of the text).
[134] Schelling, *Philosophy of Art*, §§77–83.
[135] Ibid., p. 17.

from this discussion of musical temporality. This objective nature is underscored in Schelling's aesthetic system by his placing of music as the first of the 'real' or formative arts—as the most objective of the objective artistic media, prior to painting, architecture, and sculpture—not within the 'ideal' verbal arts.

Yet it is also clear that for Schelling, just as with so many of his philosophic brethren, music is deeply connected with self-consciousness ('music on the whole is the art of reflection or of self-consciousness'), and hence with subjective or internal time.[136] This connection is created, as with Hegel, through the subjective perception of metre:

> The necessary form of music is succession, for time is the universal form of the informing [einbilden: imagining] of the infinite into the finite and to that extent is intuited as form, abstracted from the real. The principle of time within the subject is self-consciousness, which is precisely the informing, within the ideal, of the unity of consciousness and multiplicity.[137]

Thus the essential being of music appears to be analogous to the subjective constitution of time through self-consciousness, only that it is given by an objective entity and thus implicates a cosmic, external time. Given this fact, and the corresponding similarity with speech later brought up by the author, one could equally claim from Schelling's account that music is at the same time the most subjective of the arts, just as Hegel was to posit soon after.[138] What is also implicit here is that music somehow appears to be a link between the cosmic rhythms of the universe and subjective time consciousness. Indeed, music suggests the potential to bridge this long-standing dichotomy between these two conceptions of time. Standing behind Schelling's 'objective' reading of musical time appears to be the Pythagorean heritage of the music of the spheres, *harmonia kosmou*, familiar from the later accounts of Plato and Boethius. This is not merely the case of a Romantic love of a vague Platonic mysticism (though there is certainly something of this in Schelling, as with Novalis and his Romantic contemporaries), but links to a primary solution (however improbable it may now seem) to a long-standing philosophical aporia.

---

[136] Ibid., p. 162.

[137] Ibid., p. 109.

[138] It thus seems that music is placed within the formative arts for the sake of the architecture of Schelling's aesthetic system as well as his desire—to this extent followed in Hegel—ultimately to privilege word over sound.

According to Plutarch, Pythagoras had held that time was the 'soul of the universe', the procreative element that brings all into being.[139] By fusing the cosmos with the soul Pythagoras had at one stroke overcome the division that would beset later accounts of time, that constituted it either out of consciousness or as an external, objectively given property of the universe, but rarely found an adequate explanation for how exactly these two quite distinct conceptions matched. Platonic thought continues this line of analogy, the two realms being bridged by the mirroring of the macrocosm in the microcosm, the universe in the soul. Thus we understand from the *Timaeus* that the soul is deeply moved by music because of its resonance with the music of the spheres. Plotinus, too, speaks of the cosmic soul through which time is able to subsist.[140] But for thinkers unwilling to anthropomorphise the cosmos, a division between self and nature, between subjective and objective time, opened up. Already, as we saw, Aristotle doubted whether, despite its apparent objective basis in the universe, time could be said exist without the soul to measure it, and after Augustine's subjective solution to the problem of time's being the chasm between the two was fully set (Newton's assertion of an absolute, objective time ignored rather than resolved the problem). In fact, putting together an argument that is only implicit in Schelling's early philosophical system, one could argue that music could be construed as the best piece of evidence for the interconnection of subjective and objective time—a connection that, though posited, is weakly supported by the logic of Schelling's own philosophy.

The theoretical background to Schelling's conception of time is supplied in the earlier *System of Transcendental Idealism*. Here he argues after Kant that although time is given primordially in consciousness as the subject's a priori condition for perception, this subjective time connects to an intuition of a single, external, objective time through the schema imposed by this same consciousness. Recall that time, for Schelling, arises from the self, in fact *is* the self's own activity: 'Time is not something that flows independently of the self; the *self itself* is time conceived of in activity'. Time is 'nothing else but objectified inner sense', that is 'inner sense becoming an object to itself'.[141] Implicitly this begins afresh for every subjective consciousness.[142] But if each consciousness constitutes time from and for itself, how can we ever get to the notion of an objective time?

[139] Plutarch, *Platonic Questions*, No. VIII ('What Means Timaeus when he says [42d] that Souls are Dispersed into the Earth, the Moon, and into Other Instruments of Time?'): 'Pythagoras also, when he was asked what time was, answered, it was the soul of the universe' (trans. R. Brown in Plutarch, *Essays and Miscellanies*, ed. William W. Goodwin, 5 vols. [Boston and New York: Little, Brown and Co., 1909], vol. V, p. 440).

[140] Plotinus, *The Enneads*, III.7.11.

[141] Schelling, *System of Transcendental Idealism*, pp. 103, 104, 106.

[142] Ibid., p. 118.

Schelling agrees with Kant there is only one time—but this is intuited from the inner, 'pure', or 'absolute' time through its combination with space. Time is the one common factor between inner and outer sense, imposed onto the latter through the Kantian schema ('the sensorily intuited rule for the bringing forth of an empirical object').[143] Schelling objects via the principle of Ockham's razor to the idea that the time of the conscious self and that of the outer world are simply two separate clocks, which just happen to coincide.[144] The 'outside me' is an intuition, he concludes.[145] Yet, as in Kant, this identifying of the self's time with a unitary objective time merely because the two appear to coincide seems distinctly weak support for philosophically grounding the real existence of this external time (as opposed to viewing external time as merely an intellectual abstraction created for pragmatic purposes).[146] The terminology ('real') for the subjective conception already suggests the derivative nature of objective time (as later with Bergson and Heidegger). Revealingly, later in his unfinished magnum opus *Die Weltalter*, Schelling will disagree with this Kantian argument, coming down more radically on the purely subjective (and irreducibly pluralistic) side of time.[147]

Hence, when the account of music in the *Philosophy of Art* is placed within the context of Schelling's early struggles to define the relationship between internal and external time, we may see that music offers the philosopher an 'objective' instance of this interaction between consciousness and external time, one that his own philosophical explanation has left under-supported. It is not clear whether the philosophical problem has been entirely solved—the assertion that music's beat belongs to the real, to objective time, already presupposes the existence of such objective time (one of the points in contention)—but at least music affords an ideal example of a conduit between the two conceptions in a manner more convincing than that given by Schelling earlier in his *System*.

For Schelling, the means by which music connects objective and subjective time is provided through its use of rhythm. This 'particular informing [imagining] of unity into multiplicity . . . is rhythm'.[148] The distinction between metre and rhythm is not ideally clear here—indeed, as Christopher Hasty has argued, is rarely clear and is moreover subject to historical variation—and hence the significance of Schelling's formulation is best understood when placed within

---

[143] Ibid., p. 138. Cf. Kant, *Critique of Pure Reason*, A140/B180.

[144] Schelling, *System of Transcendental Idealism*, p. 154.

[145] Ibid., p. 173.

[146] See the good summary by Paul Ricoeur here on this problem in Kant's account of time (*Time and Narrative*, trans. Kathleen Blamey and David Pellauer, 3 vols. [Chicago: University of Chicago Press, 1984–8], vol. III, pp. 44–59). I will return to this point towards the end of this chapter.

[147] See Schelling, *Die Weltalter*, p. 78 (cited in chapter 1).

[148] Schelling, *Philosophy of Art*, p. 111.

the context of preceding metrical theories. By the end of the eighteenth century, a theory of musical metre began to be established, 'based on the notion of a constant train of isochronous pulses'—one which 'with relatively little alteration has been carried into present-day metrical theory'.[149] While metre is invariant in this understanding, rhythm, in contradistinction, 'flows' (as its apparent etymology would suggest). For the theorist and aesthetician Johann Georg Sulzer, 'metre turns time into spatial concepts . . . Through uniformity, an infinite succession of events can be surveyed at a glance and held in the mind', while rhythm is nothing other 'than a periodic arrangement of a series of homogenous things whereby the uniformity of these same things is united with diversity'.[150] It is this Sulzerian viewpoint that Schelling readily adopts (despite preceding his account of music with a needless jibe against his predecessor).[151]

Thus, as is implicit in Schelling's account, metre can be conceived as an abstract, objective pulsed framework (hence the connection posited with objective, universal time) and rhythm a subjective grouping of these pulses introduced by consciousness—'the transformation of an essentially meaningless succession into a meaningful one'. But Schelling goes further. Elaborating upon this interaction of rhythm and time, he moves the terms of discussion from the idea of music merely being in time to that of time being *in* music. 'The transformation of the accidental nature of a sequence into necessity = rhythm, whereby the whole is no longer subjected to time but rather possesses time *within itself*'.[152] This same idea is returned to in Schelling's later discussion of poetry: 'Since both music and speech are characterised by movement in time, their works would not be self-contained wholes if they were subject to time, and if they did not rather subject time to themselves and possess it internally. This control and subjugation of time = rhythm'.[153] Given the fact that his claim seems to amount to little more than describing one temporal object (music) as incorporating two opposing time conceptions at the same time but nevertheless in different ways, one might accuse Schelling of overstatement here. (Indeed, one could think as with Hegel that the conception of pulsed metre is itself introduced by the perceiving subject

---

[149] Hasty, *Meter as Rhythm*, p. 26; on the historical and national contingency of this now-widely accepted understanding of the distinction see also William Rothstein, 'National metrical types in music of the eighteenth and early nineteenth centuries', in Danuta Mirka and Kofi Agawu (eds.), *Communication in Eighteenth-Century Music* (Cambridge: Cambridge University Press, 2008), pp. 112–59.

[150] Johann Georg Sulzer, *Allgemeine Theorie der schönen Künste* (Leipzig: In der Weidmannschen Buchhandlung, 1792), vol. II, pp. 21, 96, cited by Spitzer, *Metaphor and Musical Thought*, p. 238, and Hasty, *Meter as Rhythm*, p. 26, from Seidel, *Über Rhythmustheorien der Neuzeit*, p. 92.

[151] Schelling, *Philosophy of Art*, p. 103.

[152] Ibid., p. 111.

[153] Ibid., p. 205.

upon the indifferent raw sonic data.) This charge may be just, but yet—especially given the mutability of the concept of time—there are possible interpretations that could support Schelling's reading.

From the relational view of time described earlier, the nature of the events contained in a piece of music will inevitably affect the perception of musical time (an idea proposed in the previous chapter on Beethoven). This need not be understood in a crude sense that quicker note values indicate the quicker passing of time (quicker in relation to what?) but that the complex interaction of melodic succession, rhythm, harmony, harmonic rhythm, phrase structure, and even texture, dynamics, and tessitura, with their implicated sense of logical causality, is able to create and structure divergent subjective time-senses. After all, simpler psychological studies have unequivocally verified the commonly perceived phenomenon that the perception of time can be significantly altered by the type of events in time.[154] More nuanced still is thus the idea, suggested by Schelling, that the way in which a seemingly objective pulsed metre may be heard by the listening subject as interacting with and conditioned by the rhythmic grouping of musical events might affect our perception of time, especially if time is assumed to be primordially subjective in constitution.[155] In other words, the commonplace idea that we earlier saw circulated in Bloch, Adorno, and Dahlhaus of music controlling time, while tending towards the hyperbolic in expression, might have some potential foundation in philosophic plausibility. Schelling's discussion provides the necessary background to Adorno's in fact far-from-radical claim, 'musical time is really musical—in other words not just the measurable time of the duration of a piece—only as time that is dependent on the musical content and in turn determines that content, the concrete means of transmission of the successive'.[156] By the same token, Gilles Deleuze and Félix Guatarri have spoken of how for music 'time is not an a priori form; rather, the refrain [*ritournelle*] is the a priori form of time, which in each case fabricates different times'.[157]

An extended imaginative literary treatment of this claim of Schelling's is given in a contemporaneous Romantic story by Wilhelm Heinrich Wackenroder,

[154] See Barry, *Musical Time*, pp. 132 and 165–230, on what she terms the 'axiom of density information'. As Barry suggests, objective time is relatively neutral as a medium: it acquires qualities through what occurs in it (p. 81).

[155] This distinction is familiar in later music theory: compare for instance David Epstein's division between 'chronometric' and 'integral' time (*Shaping Time: Music, the Brain, and Performance* [New York: Schirmer, 1995]).

[156] Adorno, 'The Relationship of Philosophy and Music', p. 143.

[157] Gilles Deleuze and Félix Guattari, '1837: Of the Refrain', in *A Thousand Plateaus*, trans. Brian Massumi (London: Continuum, 2004), p. 385.

'Ein wunderbares morgenländisches Mährchen von einem nackten Heiligen'
('A Wondrous Eastern Tale of a Naked Saint') from the posthumously published
Phantasien über die Kunst.[158] Hans Heinrich Eggebrecht finds Wackenroder's
allegory so insightful that he even reprints the entire tale in a chapter dedicated
to music's relation to time.[159] Wackenroder's story tells of an eastern holy man,
living as a hermit, driven to despair by the ceaseless whirring of the wheel of time,
which only he seems able to perceive. 'Forever and ever, without a momentary
standstill, without a second's rest, so it sounded in his ears'.[160] Unable to rest, he
was seen day and night in the most strenuous activity, like a man who is striving
to turn a gigantic wheel. From his wild, broken utterances onlookers gathered
that he believed he was being dragged along by the wheel; yet at the same time
he appeared to want to exert all his strength assisting in its violent revolutions
in order to ensure there was no danger of time even for a moment standing still.
If asked what he was doing, he would cry back 'You wretched ones! Do you not
hear the roaring wheel of time?' and just continue in his exertions. The hermit's
only occasional moments of respite were on beautiful nights when a moonbeam
shone directly in front of his dark cave, when he would be overcome by a longing for unknown beautiful things and wailed like a child to be rescued from the
wheel of time.[161]

For a long time this continued, until one wondrously beautiful summer
night, two lovers came floating down the river that ran by the hermit's cave in a
little boat. A moonbeam 'illuminated the pair to the innermost depths of their
souls, releasing their most tender feelings which flowed forth united in boundless streams. From the boat there welled an ethereal music up to the heavens
above, sweet horns and I know not what other magical instruments created a
swimming world of tones', within whose undulations a song could be perceived (Wackenroder, or his editor Tieck who published the story, provides a
three-verse poem within the text here).[162]

> With the first note of music and song the whirring wheel of time van-
> ished for the saint. They were the first sounds that fell upon this wilder-
> ness; the unknown longing was stilled, the spell broken, his erring spirit
> freed from its earthly husk. The shape of the saint had disappeared; an

[158] Wilhelm Heinrich Wackenroder, 'Ein wunderbares morgenländisches Mährchen von einem
nackten Heiligen' (pub. 1799), in *Phantasien über die Kunst für Freunde der Kunst*, Part II: I, ed.
Ludwig Tieck, in Wackenroder, *Sämtliche Werke und Briefe: Historisch-kritische Ausgabe*, ed. Silvio
Vietta and Richard Littlejohns, 2 vols. (Heidelberg: Carl Winter, 1991), vol. I, pp. 201–4.

[159] Hans Heinrich Eggebrecht, 'Das Rad der Zeit', in *Musik als Zeit*, pp. 47–62.

[160] Wackenroder, 'Ein wunderbares morgenländisches Märchen', p. 201.

[161] Ibid., pp. 202–3.

[162] Ibid., p. 203. Silvio Vietta suggests the poem is an addition of Tieck's (p. 390).

angelically beautiful spirit, woven from light fragrance, floated out of
the cave, stretched its slim arms longingly to the heavens above, and
lifted itself after the tones of music in dancelike motion.[163]

Ever higher and higher the luminous shape floats up into the sky, dancing round
the stars, before finally dissipating within the firmament. People in travelling
caravans who saw this wondrous apparition were astounded, and the lovers
believed they were witnessing the spirit of love and music.

Wackenroder's tale is clearly packed with symbolic meaning and allusions: the Platonic allegories of the cave and related Romantic reversals of sunlight and moonlight (with their implicit critique of Enlightenment rationality),
the music of the spheres and its connection with the soul, the link between
beauty, love, and music, and the apt use of images for music's ineffability and
temporal transience such as the incorporeal moonlight, the angel-like spirit
and the Heraclitean river.[164] The two Carus paintings entitled 'Music' given
earlier in this book are distinctly called to mind by the common themes of
music, moonlight and disembodiment, the angel rising up to the starry heavens (Carus's designation 'Phantasie über die Musik' expressly seems to call
attention to its allegiance with this most musical of Wackenroder's *Phantasien
über die Kunst*). Most significant in the present context, however, are the
opposed understandings of time in Wackenroder's text, and their crucial interaction within music.

Time is initially perceived by the hermitic protagonist as an objective, impersonal medium: the never-ending succession of the same; a grey, monotonous
procession of nows that continually pass away into yesterdays that mark time's
thievish progress to eternity. The individual subject is in thrall to this time, not
daring to stop but instead pursuing his senseless activity with manic zeal, as if
by this he might dupe himself into believing the cart is pushing the horse. Such
diagnoses of the modern condition of humanity, our fallenness and separation
from wholeness, are endemic at this time in Germany: as Schiller put it in his
slightly earlier *Aesthetic Education of Man*, 'everlastingly chained to a single little fragment of the Whole, man himself develops into nothing but a fragment;
everlastingly in his ear the monotonous sound of the wheel that he turns, he
never develops the harmony of his being'. Not long after Schopenhauer will
likewise use the symbol of the Wheel of Ixion to describe the senseless striving
of the Will in a humanity separated in time and space through the *principium*

---

[163] Wackenroder, 'Ein wunderbares morgenländisches Märchen', p. 204.

[164] In a later *Phantasie* (Part II: V 'Das eigentümliche innere Wesen der Tonkunst, und die
Seelenlehre der heutigen Instrumentalmusik') Wackenroder will explicitly compare music with a
stream.

individuationis.[165] Yet in Wackenroder's story, 'with the first note of music . . . the whirring wheel of time vanished'. Romantic paeans to the power of music, its divine provenance, and its capacity to unite that formerly dispersed and divided are of course hardly unusual at this time—think of the *Märchen* of Novalis (for instance 'Arion' in *Heinrich von Ofterdingen*) or Heinrich von Kleist's 'St Cecilia'. But Wackenroder's allegory, more than all these other homilies, is especially revealing for elucidating the discussion of music's interaction between objective and subjective time given in Schelling.

Music possesses the power to organise and aestheticise the empty passing of time, even here to subjugate it. As with the isochronous pulses of abstract metre, the wheel of time presents an objective, unyielding framework of an external time that consists solely of successive moments empty of any content or worth: yet music fills out these beats' vacant potential, connecting them organically together and introducing a meaningful subjective grouping to them. This procedure is even instantiated in the Wackenroder/Tieck story by the very incorporation of the lovers' song within the text, the conventional prose broken up by poetic lines that organise time through their varied metric structure and use of rhyme. False, objective time becomes subjectified. As Heidegger might have expressed it, the self is rescued from its fallen existence within the monotony of inauthentic within-time-ness and returned to authentic temporality through the *Augenblick* given by the moonlit conjunction of love and music. (In his own unique language, 'Dasein is fetched back from the "One" [*Man*] and enters the unique thisness and one-time-ness of its thereness'.[166]) Through music, the empty passing of time is transformed into a meaningful succession in which past and future become part of an ecstatic present, and humanity united once again with nature and the heavens.[167]

Form, Harmony, Polyphony

Building on the interaction between metre and rhythmic grouping seen in Schelling's formulation, the implications of such interplay between objective points of temporal articulation and their subjective synthesis may be extended

---

[165] Friedrich Schiller, *On the Aesthetic Education of Man*, Letter VI, trans. E.M. Wilkinson and L.A. Willoughby (Oxford: Clarendon Press, 1967), p. 35; Schopenhauer, *The World as Will and Representation*, vol. I, p. 195.

[166] Heidegger, *The Concept of Time*, p. 70; see also pp. 64–5.

[167] Such sentiments are closely echoed by Novalis in the same period: music enables the mind to be 'for short moments in its earthly home. . . . all love and goodness, future and past are aroused within it'. *Das Allgemeine Brouillon*, fragment 245, in *Schriften*, vol. III, p. 283.

further to encompass larger spans of music—the idea of rhythm writ large. Any salient event within the course of the music possesses the potential to serve as an objective point of formal articulation, and the reiteration of such events may be synthesised by the schematism of the perceiving mind into an ideal unity, thus impressing the same unity onto a pre-given temporal multiplicity encountered earlier. Schelling's line of thought indeed provides the underlying historical context for the notion of 'structural listening' made famous over a century later by Adorno. Thus, claims Adorno, through the fusion of temporal unfolding (created through the thematic process) and accent structure (higher points of articulation), a movement by Beethoven both mimics time and compresses it. As such, 'time is abolished and, as it were, suspended and concentrated in space'—the whole movement seen in an instant.[168]

What Adorno's point is on to is a particularly dynamic understanding of the creation of musical form: how, in Carl Dahlhaus's words, 'a timeless, reversible structure is realised and made aesthetically present in a temporal, goal-directed process'.[169] Versions of this idea may be found in twentieth-century writers in the phenomenological and Gestalt traditions, such as Roman Ingarden and Victor Zuckerkandl, and even in the work of anthropologists such as Claude Lévi-Strauss in his famous description of music as an instrument 'for the obliteration of time'. Music, for Lévi-Strauss, is a type of language which 'transcend[s] articulate expression while at the same time—like articulate speech, but unlike painting—requiring a temporal dimension in which to unfold'.[170] Exactly the same dualism is encapsulated in Iannis Xenakis's statement that 'music is everywhere steeped in time: time in the form of impalpable flux or time in its frozen form, outside time, made possible by memory'.[171] The origins of this notion of form as intentional object date from some time earlier, however. It is arguable that one can find its traces as far back as René Descartes, whose early *Compendium Musicae* of 1618 speaks of this same unification of music into a synchronic totality through the hypermetric groupings of bars introduced by the listener's

---

[168] Adorno, 'Stravinsky: A Dialectical Portrait', in *Quasi una Fantasia: Essays on Modern Music*, trans. Rodney Livingstone (London: Verso, 1998), pp. 165–6. On this idea of structural listening see for example 'The Radio Symphony' (1941), in *Essays on Music*, pp. 251–70.

[169] Carl Dahlhaus, 'Musik und Zeit', in Carl Dahlhaus and Hans Heinrich Eggebrecht, *Was ist Musik?* (Wilhelmshaven: Florian Noetzel, 1985), p. 176. The discussion of musical form here is a complement to my earlier account in *Mendelssohn, Time and Memory*, pp. 154–7.

[170] Claude Lévi-Strauss, *The Raw and the Cooked*, trans. John and Doreen Weightman (Chicago: University of Chicago Press, 1983), pp. 15–16. 'Lévi-Strauss's entire scientific enterprise is about snatching a universal, achronic structure from the unfolding of time' notes Jean-Jacques Nattiez (*The Battle of Chronos and Orpheus*, trans. Jonathan Dunsby [Oxford: Oxford University Press, 2004], p. 59).

[171] Iannis Xenakis, 'Concerning Time', *Perspectives of New Music*, 27 (1989), 91.

memory: 'when we hear the end', claims Descartes, 'we recall to ourselves in this instant what there was at the beginning and in the rest of the song'.[172]

One of the best accounts along these lines of how musical form is constructed is provided by Barbara Barry, drawing on a wide range of musicological, theoretical, cognitive, and philosophical approaches. Paraphrasing her account here, Barry argues that the notion of musical form must contradict the ephemerality of passing time by creating the illusion of substance. In order to see music as an object, its temporal dimension with its continually disappearing parts has to be frozen so that the work can be expressed as a simultaneity—in other words, become spatialised. The objective basis for this process of spatialisation in music is created by the principle of repetition. As the construction of defined shape in time, repetition constitutes the foundation of musical form. Repetition can thus be considered the prime form-building agent and the most fundamental construction principle of musical form. Memory is the essential subjective element in this procedure, for without memory the slippage of time would mean a succession of momentary presents without pasts. By establishing musical objects, which consolidate groups of these momentary presents by recognisable characteristics, and patterning them by repetition into an overall design, memory creates the form of the work as a layout through time of distinct musical features. Our understanding of time is always organised through the search for points of reference and articulation, and durational spans are created by the shaping of information between those points: it is through points of articulation that time can be structured into durational spans, and through defined characteristics design can be understood and remembered.[173]

Expressed poetically, all this is succinctly encapsulated by Eliot's lines in *Four Quartets*:

> *Words move, music moves*
> *Only in time; but that which is only living*
> *Can only die. . . .*
> *. . . Only by the form, the pattern,*
> *Can words or music reach*
> *The stillness . . .*

---

[172] Descartes, *Compendium Musicae*, in *Oeuvres*, ed. Charles Adam and Paul Tannery, 13 vols. (Paris: L. Cerf, 1897–1913), vol. X, p. 93: 'Haec autem proportio talis servatur saepissime in membris cantilenae, vt possit apprehensionem nostram ita juvare, vt dum vltimum audimus, adhuc temporis, quod in primo fuit et quod in reliquâ cantilenâ, recordemur; quod fit, si tota cantilena vel 8, vel 16, vel 32, vel 64, et caetera, membris constet, vt scilicet omnes divisiones a proportione duplâ procedant'. See further Wilhelm Seidel, 'Descartes' Bemerkungen zur musikalischen Zeit', *Archiv für Musikwissenschaft*, 27 (1975), 288–303.

[173] Barry, *Musical Time*, pp. 58, 65–7, 69, 262.

> . . . *that the end precedes the beginning,*
> *And the end and the beginning were always there*
> *Before the beginning and after the end.*
> *And all is always now.*[174]

In other words, as implied in Adorno's claim for structural listening, form perception is equivalent to the perception of rhythm at the largest scale. Thus we
move from multiplicity to unity, from music as a distended succession of physical sounds to an ideal simultaneity created in the conscious mind.

It has furthermore proved appealing for some writers to see even the individual musical note, taken within the context of a tonal phrase, as endowed with
the properties of past, present, and future, and thus to this extent as constituting
a type of eternity. We have seen the basis for this idea in Augustine's threefold
present as well as in Husserl's analysis of cognitive retention and protention,
where such properties belong to the perceiving subject, but other thinkers project these temporal qualities onto the being of music itself.

The perception of a type of eternity intuited into the present moment has a
veritable heritage behind it. In Leibniz's *Monadology*, the interconnection of all
within space and time ensures that every moment reflects all that has happened
or will happen in the past and future, although only God may fully grasp this:

> every body feels the effect of all that takes place in the universe, so
> that he who sees all might read in each what is happening everywhere,
> and even what has happened or shall happen, observing in the pres-
> ent that which is far off as well in time as in place: *sympnoia panta*, as
> Hippocrates said.[175]

By hypostasising such qualities to become actual objective properties of
time and gently sidelining God, we arrive at Hegel's discussion of time in the
Encyclopaedia, where the spectre of eternity is explicitly raised: 'in the positive
meaning of time, it can be said that only the Present *is*, that Before and After are
not. But the concrete Present is the result of the Past and is pregnant with the
Future. The true Present, therefore, is eternity'.[176] The final step is to combine this
perceived unity of time's three modalities with the sense of necessary causal connection between successive temporal events that a musical phrase (especially in

[174] T.S. Eliot, *Burnt Norton*, V.

[175] Leibniz, *The Monadology*, §61, trans. by Robert Latta, *The Monadology and Other Philosophical
Writings* (London: Oxford University Press, 1925), p. 251. This idea is common throughout Leibniz's
writings: variants may be found in the *Discourse on Metaphysics*, §§8 and 9 and the Preface to the *New
Essays on Human Understanding*.

[176] Hegel, *Philosophy of Nature*, §259, Zusatz, p. 39.

the contemporaneous Classical-Romantic idiom) seems to embody so compellingly. Thus for Jean Paul, music itself seems to possess this temporally ecstatic quality: 'a note never sounds alone but always threefold, blending the Romantic quality of the future and the past with the present'.[177] And for Coleridge, too,

> the present strain still seems not only to recall, but almost to *renew*, some past movement . . . Each present movement bringing back as it were, and embodying the Sprit of some melody that had gone before, anticipates and seems trying to overtake something that is to come: and the Musician has reached the summit of his art, when having thus modified the Present by the Past, has at the same time weds the Past *in* the present to some prepared and corresponsive future.[178]

Later in the twentieth century, Victor Zuckerkandl, refracting a Bergsonian spirit through Gestalt psychology, will argue in comparable manner that

> taken by itself, the individual tone is meaningless, mere sound; it is only by entering into relation with other tones . . . that it acquires musical meaning, becomes part of the total 'melody' . . . thus past and future are given with and in the present and are experienced with and in the present; hearing a melody is hearing, having heard, and being about to hear, all at once.[179]

Despite the latter claims of such properties inhering in the musical object, the overcoming of time described in the examples above is nonetheless largely, if not solely, an ideal phenomenon, an abstract manner of thinking rather than any more concrete instance of temporal transcendence. (Given that time itself is to a considerable extent a mental construction, such a charge is not, perhaps, as debilitating as it might seem.) Yet, notwithstanding this possible reservation, Schelling has another, more tangible argument in hand for supporting music's claim to temporal transcendence: in contrast to the unity-within-multiplicity of succession (rhythm), music also demonstrates the multiplicity-within-unity of coexistence (harmony).[180]

---

[177] Jean Paul, *Kleine Nachschule zur ästhetischen Vorschule* (1825), in *Sämtliche Werke*, ed. Norbert Miller, 10 vols. (Munich: Carl Hanser Verlag, 1959–63), vol. V, p. 466. This passage is also discussed by Berthold Hoeckner in *Programming the Absolute: Nineteenth-Century German Music and the Hermeneutics of the Moment* (Princeton: Princeton University Press, 2002), p. 55.

[178] Samuel Taylor Coleridge, *The Friend* (1809), cited by Charles Rosen, *The Romantic Generation* (London: HarperCollins, 1996), p. 74.

[179] Zuckerkandl, *Sound and Symbol*, pp. 229, 235.

[180] Schelling, *Philosophy of Art*, p. 114.

This multiplicity within unity can be found on two levels, Schelling contends. First, the individual note or chord combines a number of distinct though harmonious elements into a simultaneity, either as the overtones present in the sounding of an individual pitch, or in the coexistence of pitches in a consonant chord. Hegel, Moritz Hauptmann, and a number of dialectically inclined German theorists after them, will make much out of the tonal triad's tripartite sublation of its constituent elements, whose Trinitarian implications have also not gone unnoticed.[181] Secondly, at a larger level a piece of tonal music customarily departs from and returns to its governing key, the different tonal relationships throughout its course being brought back into unity with the overarching presence of the tonic. The same idea has been seen earlier in Schopenhauer's description of the crotchety wanderings of the will away from and back to its keynote, and is indeed a commonplace in German philosophy at this time.

What appears latent in Schelling's discussion is that the second formulation may be understood as an elaborated temporal distention of the first—a composing-out of the primal chord of nature as Schenkerian ideology has it. In fact, combining this attribute with Schelling's earlier discussion of rhythm, it is implicit that melody results from the dialectical conjunction of rhythm and harmony (a point later made more explicitly by Hegel).[182] Thus music springs from the conjunction of multiplicity in unity (harmony) and unity in multiplicity (rhythm). Drastically simplifying, harmony is melody compressed into a unity, a vertical transcendence; melody is harmony distended out into time through rhythm. (This equivalency of 'musical space' need apply not only to tonal music: Schoenbergian serialism, too, makes much out of this indifference, albeit complicating the inexact notion of consonant harmony.[183]) Directly relatable to the Romantic or Idealist propensity for the systematised interrelationship between the ideal and real, the unity of rhythm is an ideal unity (in other words intentional, created in the mind), that of harmony an actual one (physically present at once).

Schelling's vision may aptly be thought of as the musical correlate to a Neoplatonic system whereby multiplicity emanates from and returns to a primal unity. Time is the medium in which this originary unity divides itself: in itself the unity is (figuratively speaking) timeless and eternal, in that its multiplicity is present at once, without qualitative before or after. In its 'divine procession' from the simultaneous unity of the tonic, the 'reversion of the end upon

[181] See Jeremy Begbie, *Theology, Music and Time* (Cambridge: Cambridge University Press, 2000), pp. 25–6.

[182] Schelling, *Philosophy of Art*, §81.

[183] On the (problematic) nature of the concept of musical space, see Robert P. Morgan, 'Musical Time/Musical Space', *Critical Inquiry*, 6 (1980), 527–38.

the beginning makes the whole order one and determinate, convergent upon itself and by its convergence revealing unity in multiplicity'.[184] Music is one of the few things that—like the supposedly transcendental ego of Kant or Husserl, only in more concrete form—seems to possess this dual quality of harmonious simultaneity and temporal successiveness in a single entity. Indeed, theorists in the early twentieth century would seize upon his bivalency. In the Schenkerian system, horizontal succession is conceived as a composing-out of a primordial vertical chord, a perfect correlate to classical ontology which sees Becoming as derivative on a primary Being. By reifying the tendency of melodic notes to move towards the ontologically primordial harmonies that govern them, musical thought will thus be led to Schenker's *Tonwille* or the melodic vitalism of Ernst Kurth, whereby harmonies contain the potential energy that are realised in the kinetic energy of melodic motion.[185]

Many of these claims, however, are not without problematic elements. The idea of a chord or pitch as being something equivalent to eternity is figurative in that even a single note has duration in time (and neither can it be sempiternal since it has a beginning and end). Admittedly a sustained note or chord may be argued to be an example of duration without change, which to this extent approximates eternity if the latter is understood as something qualitatively indivisible, present at once as a whole, a perspective that may also be maintained from a relational view of time. Like calling a quantum chronon particle 'timeless', however, the value of such a purported eternity seems distinctly pyrrhic. Rousseau was no less unhappy even if his time did consist of a string of indivisible eternities, and his life no more permanent than the final chord of his *Le Devin au Village*.[186] Furthermore, the reduction of a complex piece of music to the simple unfolding of a triad seems far from self-evident. Between a movement's opening and its final cadence a lot can happen. The harmonic progression I–V–I could be conceived as composing-out the fifth degree in the triad,

---

[184] Proclus, *Elements of Theology*, Prop. 146, trans. E.R. Dodds (Oxford: Clarendon Press, 1933), p. 129; for the relevant definitions of time and eternity see prop. 50 and 52. Schelling in particular reveals a marked affinity for Neoplatonic thought; the semi-axiomatic layout of the *Philosophy of Art* is reminiscent of something approaching Proclus refracted through a Spinozan lens.

[185] On the link between Schenker's musical metaphysics and the Kantian understanding of time see Kevin Korsyn's useful study 'Schenker and Kantian Epistemology', *Theoria*, 3 (1988), 1–58. In a related fashion, the affinities between Schenker's musical metaphysics and a Heideggerian stretching of Dasein across time have also been proposed by Harper-Scott, who notes how Ingarden's retentive/protentive model of music's supratemporality (drawn from his teacher Husserl) bears close resemblance to Heidegger's ecstatically temporal model for Dasein's authentic existence in time (also evincing evidence of their common tutelage). Harper-Scott, *Edward Elgar, Modernist*, p. 39.

[186] Aptly, Rousseau's creation does not even possess Schelling's harmonious unity in that his opera starts in D major and ends in G.

and then, in Schenkerian fashion, successive melodic diminutions might in turn create more complex temporally distended structures, but the epistemic validity of this point is still debatable. Supporting a speculative idealist metaphysics by a no-less problematic Schenkerian organicist metaphysics may not be the surest (or indeed least circular) way of grounding it. Nevertheless, irrespective of the absolute claims of such a mode of argument, we may still recognise that this line of thought has historically carried some conviction for at least a century and a half, even if its philosophic validity might now appear dubious or at best metaphorical.

One final musical element as yet unconsidered is the notion of polyphony. Extending the consideration beyond the limits provided by Schelling's rather sketchy account, such attempts at fusing the successive into a simultaneity need not be based on harmony but might relate to music's capacity for presenting several parts concurrently. A long-standing complaint about time is that its events are always divided and never wholly present. Augustine speaks of the 'limitation of being' present in time-bound existence, such as the syllables of speech 'which do not have their being at the same moment, but by passing away and by successiveness they form the whole of which they are parts'. Such sounds 'have no being, because they are fleeting and transient'. Temporal successiveness 'never has any constancy', whereas 'in the eternal, nothing is transient, but the whole is present'.[187] In contrast, the words of God, Augustine asserts, cannot be in time, because in this manner they would be divided into temporal succession, away from an immanent eternal unity.

Lamentably, normal spoken language seems not to possess the ability to present its constituent elements at the same time, as God's manner of discourse seems to. Think of the confusion arising from the game where the words from a well-known phrase are spoken by a number of voices simultaneously and listeners have to guess the original sentence. The result is almost invariably a meaningless jumble.[188] Music, however, can approach this divine ability far more convincingly, through its use of polyphony. Polyphony understood from this perspective forms a mediation between the vertical coexistence of harmony and horizontal succession of melody. In a number of pieces, moreover, music may seem bent on fusing the horizontal into the vertical: as we saw in variation 6 of Beethoven's Op. 109, what has initially been presented separated by time becomes overlaid in an 'at once'.[189] Here again, of course, music is still not

---

[187] Augustine, *The Confessions*, IV.x (15), XI.vi (8), XI.xi (13), pp. 62, 225, 228. The background to Augustine's discussion is provided in Plotinus, *The Enneads*, III.7.6 and V.3.17.24.

[188] An example given by Le Poidevin, *The Images of Time*, p. 80.

[189] One could also cite the finale of Mozart's Jupiter Symphony, Mendelssohn's Octet, Schumann's Piano Quintet, or Bruckner's Symphony No. 8.

actually an instantiation of such eternal being but merely an approximation, as it still deals with durational spans of a few notes (save in extreme cases of vertical compression). Yet even if this procedure is understood as merely a metaphor or conceptual substitute for eternity, such pieces nonetheless often result in an ecstatic sense of temporal synthesis and apparent transcendence.

The desire to find stable being that Rousseau coveted so dearly in life is matched in the modern age by the search for eternity in music. That this quest seems well-nigh impossible within our temporally bound lives explains the worth attached in this era to the concept of the transcendent 'moment'—be it the Faustian *Augenblick* in Goethe, Kierkegaard's moment of choice in which time intersects with eternity, or a Heideggerian ecstasis of past, present, and future. Ever since the mystic visions of Plotinus such temporal epiphanies or 'chronophanies' have provided a means for the mind seemingly to stand above or outside time, however briefly this state may last. Music is no exception to this tendency, in that at least two centuries of aesthetics and criticism have sought to find ways of detemporalising music's passing and setting up, either in the perceiving mind or as actual phenomenal properties of sound, ways of conceiving enduring being without before and after in this art.

Yet what might be a more realistic conclusion is that despite its claims to constituting a supertemporal, timeless entity, what is perhaps most valuable in music is the way in which it simultaneously suggests both enduring identity and yet a constant process of change. This is after all one reason why Bergson was so taken by this medium as an illustration of the irreducibly temporal nature of real duration. An actual timeless eternity, that without before or after, seems inconceivable for us, bound as we are to the Kantian perceptual preconditions of space and time—and arguably inconceivably tedious too. Music, this fundamental art of time, could not exist under such conditions. As with Goethe's conception of *Dauer im Wechsel* or the descriptions of a variative eternity underpinned by music in the *Märchen* of Novalis, music's own type of eternity is a living, mutable one, a synthesis of temporality with supertemporality—not simply an inconceivable timelessness but a fusion of permanence with change.[190]

The conscious state described by Rousseau at the start of this chapter comes close to this sense of enduring temporality. Marshall Brown reads Rousseau's Fifth *Rêverie* as an account of pure self-consciousness, the enduring transcendental self in time, which would find artistic expression in the music of Mozart and

---

[190] See Gordon Birrell, *The Boundless Present: Space and Time in the Literary Fairy Tales of Novalis and Tieck* (Chapel Hill, NC: University of North Carolina Press, 1979), pp. 87–8; Frank, *Das Problem 'Zeit' in der deutschen Romantik*, pp. 130–232.

his nineteenth-century successors.[191] But music's time is surely more diverse and rounder than this: it suggests not Rousseau's negative tenselessness but a richer temporality that implicates the past and future as an intrinsic part of the present. While remaining temporal, at the same time it is able to suggest a supertemporal wholeness. In this ability to reveal both the transient and the abiding, music constitutes the exemplary medium of modern times, the perfect expression of Baudelaire's famous conception of modernity as 'the transitory, the fugitive, the contingent, that half of art whose other face is the eternal and the immutable'.[192]

The idea that such wholeness and temporal unity might form an idealised way of coming to an understanding of the temporality of human existence is commonplace. Both in terms of its apparent logical continuity of moments joined in an indivisible, organic thread and in its larger-scale formal sense of completion in relating end to beginning, music seems the perfect medium for reflecting the temporal flux of life and yet being able simultaneously to stand outside it. Although Carolyn Abbate claims 'when music ends, it ends absolutely, in the cessation of passing time and movement, in death', what music possesses is the promise of potential renewal.[193] By virtue of its repeatability the musical work enjoys the ability to resurrect itself, to arise phoenix-like anew from the attenuating embers of its final chords; we normally return to the same piece of music, Scott Burnham observes, not in order to discover something new but rather because we desire to hear the same, to renew the ever new.[194] Music, along with other, narrative arts (such as the novel in the nineteenth century, or film in the twentieth), enables our changing yet enduring consciousness of the world to be seen as a whole, perfect and complete. Through music the temporal span of life is viewed as an ideal object that may be lifted up from the destructive passing of the hours—that 'restless course that time doth run with calm and silent foot'—and set up as a permanent persistence.[195]

'The attainment [*Einstand*] of time as an image of the end of the transitory is the ideal of music' claims Adorno. 'Through duration, art raises objection to death'.[196] Marlowe's Faust is doomed: time is relentless. In Goethe, however, Faust is saved,

[191] Marshall Brown, 'Mozart and After: The Revolution in Musical Consciousness', *Critical Inquiry*, 7 (1981), 689–706.

[192] Charles Baudelaire, 'Le peintre de la Vie moderne', in *Œuvres complètes*, eds. Y.-G. Le Dantec and Claude Pichois (Paris: Gallimard-Pléiade, 1961), p. 1152.

[193] Carolyn Abbate, *Unsung Voices: Opera and Musical Narrative in the Nineteenth Century* (Princeton, N.J.: Princeton University Press, 1991), p. 56.

[194] Burnham, *Beethoven Hero*, p. 164.

[195] Marlowe, *Doctor Faustus* (A), 4.1, ll. 92–5.

[196] Adorno, *Der getreue Korrepetitor: Lehrschriften zur musikalischen Praxis*, in *Gesammelte Schriften*, ed. Rolf Tiedemann, 20 vols. (Frankfurt: Suhrkamp, 1997), vol. XV, p. 187; *Ästhetische Theorie*, in *Gesammelte Schriften*, vol. VII, p. 48.

through the very fact of his temporal striving—a more modern conception, argu-ably unavailable to the Renaissance. It is as if humans are rewarded for seeking to master time, despite their ultimate, inevitable failure. Nowhere is this pursuit more in evidence than in the philosophical burden placed upon music in the Romantic era. If at times the weight seems too much for such an insubstantial entity to bear one should hardly wonder—though music may yet prove surprisingly resilient.

MUSIC, LANGUAGE, AND THE APORIAS OF TIME
The Problem of Language

As the arguments presented in the previous two sections have gradually and cumulatively revealed, music has consistently been understood as a metaphor for or even stylised instantiation of this quest for understanding time and its relation-ship with our worldly existence. Yet might it furthermore hold solutions to some of the seemingly intractable problems associated with these topics? Might music not only hold up a mirror (to give an optical metaphor again) but moreover be able to provide answers to questions about the very nature of time and human consciousness that prove unreflective to other linguistic modes of inquiry?

'Supposing we succeeded in giving a perfectly accurate and complete expla-nation of music' declares Schopenhauer, 'which goes into detail, and thus a detailed repetition in concepts of what it expresses, this would also be at once a sufficient repetition and explanation of the world in concepts, or one wholly cor-responding thereto, and hence the true philosophy'.[197] Recasting a formulation of Leibniz, he concludes that 'music is an unconscious exercise in metaphys-ics in which the mind does not know that it is philosophising'.[198] Yet in reality this translation of music into discursive language and concepts is impossible, Schopenhauer holds. 'Music answers [the question, "What is life?"], more pro-foundly indeed than do all the other [arts], since in a language intelligible with absolute directness, yet not capable of translation into that faculty of reason, it expresses the innermost nature of all life and existence'.[199]

Schopenhauer's latter point rests on two related though distinct issues: the limits of linguistic meaning, and the question of musical meaning—and on the

---

[197] Schopenhauer, *The World as Will and Representation*, vol. I, p. 264.

[198] Ibid., p. 264—a parody of Leibniz's 'Musica est exercitium arithmeticae occultum nescientis se numerare animi' (Music is a hidden arithmetic exercise of the soul, which does not know that it is counting).

[199] Ibid., vol. II, p. 406; also see ch. 34.

corresponding uneasy triangulation between meaning, music, and language. While music is to all intents and purposes incapable of denotative statements, a denotative understanding of verbal meaning is itself incapable of fully expressing pre-conceptual entities such as the purported transcendental ego or being transcendentally grounded (a point post-structuralist critics have eagerly seized upon). If, conversely, linguistic meaning is considered not as being representational or propositional but more performatively, as connotative or illocutionary, then the liability of its claims for bearing meaning disappear, but only at the expense of its absolute separation from—and thus any potential claim of absolute denotational superiority over—music.[200] Clearly any unconditional separation between language and music is over-simplistic: music is in certain respects akin to language and may been argued sometimes to bear semantic content, just as language possesses an important musical component. But nevertheless, 'proximally and for the most part', music and language are two ways of communication which importantly differ in how they are understood to convey meaning, and which are therefore irreducible to each other.[201] In other words, music may conceivably be capable of communicating aspects of the human experience of temporality that language is unable to disclose (although it may not be possible literally to *say* in language *what it is* that music reveals).

Nevertheless, historically some philosophers more accustomed to language than music have misunderstood music's potential to disclose aspects of temporality in a manner distinct from verbal articulation. This underestimation afflicts two of the most significant philosophical accounts of music's importance for comprehending time. That the first of these philosophical villains is Hegel will come as little surprise. We have seen the significance of music in understanding the temporality of subjectivity and self-consciousness in Hegel's aesthetics, but Hegel does not wish to concede too much power to the philosophic other formed by music, seeking instead to keep it subservient to the lordship of the word which he wields. For 'everything that consciousness conceives and shapes

---

[200] The ideas here draw partly on the theory of speech acts set out in J.L. Austin's *How to do Things with Words* (1955); Lawrence Kramer takes up Austin's distinction as a grounding principle for his development of musical hermeneutics (see *Music as Cultural Practice*, pp. 1–20, and his more recent *Interpreting Music* [Berkeley and Los Angeles: University of California Press, 2011]). Kramer further notes that the rise of hermeneutics as a discipline significantly coincided with the development of instrumental music in Germany.

[201] Lawrence Zbikowski, for instance, argues that the kind of consciousness associated with attending to music differs from that used for language: the two use different memory systems, music one which focuses more on dynamic processes than 'lexical knowledge or relationships between events'. 'Music, language, and kinds of consciousness', in Clarke and Clarke (eds.), *Music and Consciousness*, p. 190.

spiritually within its own inner being speech alone can adopt, express, and bring before our imagination'.[202] This is true of art as it is of self-consciousness. Art is an expression of the concept, and this is fully articulated only in words,

> For however far in other arts the inner life must, and does actually, shine through its corporeal form, still the *word* is the most intelligible means of communication, the most adequate to the spirit, the one *able to grasp and declare whatever lies within consciousness* or pervades its heights and depths.[203]

If Hegel were correct, then, the meaning of music (indeed any work of art) could be expressed fully in language, at least in his higher philosophic language. It barely needs saying that most people would find this claim derisory. There is surely scarcely a single composer, musician, or listener who has ever thought that musical meaning can be entirely reduced to words, let alone those of an idealist philosopher whose linguistic expression has hardly appeared ideally transparent to his readers. Though definitions of musical meaning may appear to verge on the tautological (such as Roger Scruton's assertion that 'the mean- ing of a piece of music is what we understand when we understand it as music') it is hard to argue that what a listener understands by music is not to this extent a meaning, and such understandings are rarely felt to be satisfactorily expressed in words.[204] And just as with music, the self is also something that notoriously invariably escapes objectification. Expressly contradicting Hegel, Kierkegaard will insist upon the impossibility of adequately describing one's own self-consciousness: 'the self-consciousness that is so concrete that no author, not even the one with the greatest power of description, has ever been able to describe a single such self-consciousness, although every single human being has one'.[205]

Throughout his writings there is an assumption of the transparency and rational exhaustiveness of language by Hegel, whose philosophical depen- dence on language makes him rightly most vulnerable to deconstructive attack (although not all his contemporaries can be subsumed into this viewpoint). Perhaps Hegel's distrust of music arises from the sense that it escapes the pos- sibility of complete rational elucidation. If subjectivity is something always

---

[202] Hegel, *Aesthetics*, p. 626.

[203] Ibid., p. 997, my emphasis.

[204] Roger Scruton, *The Aesthetics of Music* (Oxford: Clarendon Press, 1997), p. 344; as Scruton points out, 'music is often meaningful, in the strong sense that there is something to be understood in it'. The later Wittgenstein would argue that neither can shades of verbal meanings be fully expressed by words without a seemingly infinite regress (see *Philosophical Investigations*, §29).

[205] Kierkegaard, *The Concept of Anxiety*, p. 143.

escaping satisfactory philosophical explanation, and music, for Hegel, is closely allied with this inner subjectivity, it is no wonder that Hegel tries to wriggle free of granting too much power to music. The fact that Hegel cannot account for musical meaning even remotely adequately suggests that there are aspects of reality that his philosophy cannot absorb and dissolve within it, that in turn the entire systematic edifice (whose circular justification relies on its ability to account for all reality) is incomplete and therefore veridically imperilled, and hence questions whether indeed his philosophy does form the highest state of *Geist*'s development. We are left with the feeling that not only does music have more to communicate than may be articulated in Hegelian philosophy but that the insightful connection Hegel makes between music and the temporal constitution of self-consciousness might furthermore be part of this non-verbal significance.

The second, rather more unlikely perpetrator, is Henri Bergson—unlikely, because Bergson readily acknowledges the limits of language, and seems sensitive enough both to art and to the complexity of empirical reality to understand this point. We recall that time's essence is 'to flow'. Now, language (and spatialised concepts sedimented within), are mainly responsible for the widespread misunderstanding of time, holds Bergson.[206] Because language (as he argues at greater length elsewhere) is based on spatial, snapshot perspectives, it is never able to express the richness of conscious states completely alongside their permeation (like the infinite number of points between two points on a line). 'There is no common measure between mind and language'.[207] Again, we read in the *Introduction to Metaphysics*: 'The inner life ... cannot be represented by images.... Still less could it be represented by concepts, that is, by abstract ideas, whether general or simple'. Instead, this inner enduring self can be grasped only by intuition; philosophy's aim is to prompt this type of reflection. 'Duration can be presented to us directly in an intuition[;] it can be suggested indirectly to us by images, but ... it cannot ... be enclosed in a conceptual representation'.[208]

Given his fixation with music as illustration of this intuition of *durée*—the only real temporal instantiation of what he elsewhere describes using spatial metaphors (such as snowballs)—one might think that art, and above all music, would be the organon of philosophic wisdom for Bergson. Some passages would certainly encourage us to read this into his philosophy. In 'The Perception of Change', for instance, Bergson argues for the importance of artists in showing us

---

[206] Bergson, *The Creative Mind*, Introduction I, pp. 12, 14.
[207] Bergson, *Time and Free Will*, pp. 164–5.
[208] Bergson, *Introduction to Metaphysics*, pp. 165, 168.

what we do not naturally perceive (a Heideggerian would similarly speak of art's 'disclosure' of reality), and goes on to add that Kant establishes that 'if metaphysics is possible, it is only through intuition'. But then, we read

> Art enables us, no doubt, to discover in things more qualities and more shades than we naturally perceive. It dilates our perception, but on the surface rather than in depth. It enriches our present, but it scarcely enables us to go beyond it. Through philosophy we can accustom ourselves never to isolate the present from the past, which it pulls along with it.[209]

The irony is astounding, given Bergson's professed understanding of the temporal richness of the present, which, in order to show the persistence of the past within, he has just illustrated by (how else?) the example of a musical melody!

This is peculiar, given how much Bergson's entire effort at explicating the reality of time, consciousness, and change, relies on analogies with music, and that he elsewhere more than readily criticises language (which, notwithstanding his elegant command of, he still relies on) for its sedimented spatiality. At the very least, Bergson's philosophy seems reliant on music to an extent which contradicts his claims for philosophic autonomy and superiority. As Susanne Langer rightly sums up, 'the demand Bergson makes upon philosophy—to set forth the dynamic forms of subjective experience—only art [more specifically, music] can fulfil'.[210]

Martin Heidegger was certainly aware of the problem of language, at least in one sense (if not in that which many of his readers wish he had). Heidegger was also on the end of a notoriously acerbic critique from his contemporary Rudolf Carnap, a logical positivist from the Vienna Circle who denounced what he saw as the wilful misuse of language and mystification in Heidegger's metaphysical speculation. In an analysis of his philosophical writing (most famously the line 'Das Nichts nichtet' [the nothing nothings] from *Was ist Metaphysik?*), Carnap concluded that Heidegger's statements, taken as logical propositions, were denotatively meaningless but might still hold some expressive worth in a vague, emotional way—their quality of *Lebensgefühl*. In this Heidegger was unintentionally emulating the mission of artists, and, especially, musicians. However, music simply did this better, in a clearer, more pleasing, and accomplished

---

[209] Bergson, 'The Perception of Change', pp. 135, 140, 157. It is possible Bergson is speaking merely of visual art here—if so then arguably rather disingenuously, given that music is the art form he most frequently calls upon for philosophic service.

[210] Langer, 'The Image of Time', p. 114.

manner. If one wanted to find harmonious unity, one could turn to Mozart, if dualism was what was desired, Beethoven expressed it better than any metaphysician. 'Metaphysicians are musicians without musical ability' Carnap famously concludes.[211]

While Carnap's polemic probably has a point, the division between scientific philosophy on the one hand and artistic metaphysics on the other is arguably overdrawn (even though Heidegger remains off-bounds for many analytic philosophers to this day). But, especially in the present context, there is surely a valid point that music might be able to communicate something about our subjective experience of time at least as succinctly as any philosophic tome in Heidegger's near-private language. Indeed, in light of Heidegger's own interest in art's ability to disclose aspects of the world through non-denotative means (such as the poetic expressivity to be found in Friedrich Hölderlin's startlingly creative use of language in his mature hymns and odes), one might think the substance of Carnap's attack would be relatively uncontentious; the analysis is broadly accurate, though his evaluation debatable.[212]

Yet Heidegger, in contrast to Bergson, barely mentions music in his writings and published lectures. This, as Andrew Bowie notes, 'is pretty baffling', given music's long history of relevance with his concerns.[213] But even Heidegger is on record for confessing music's capacity for expressing meaning in a manner that his philosophy—even given the extremes to which he took language, its purported etymology and comprehensibility—could not hope to capture. Georg Picht relates his one-time teacher, fleeing the approaching Allied army with his stepdaughter and assistant in December 1944, taking refuge with him and his wife outside Freiburg. In the evening at Heidegger's request Picht's wife, the pianist Edith Picht-Axenfeld, played Schubert's final Sonata in B♭, D. 960. As the music died away, Heidegger looked at him and said simply 'we cannot do that with philosophy'.[214]

I would like to suggest that music may at the very least offer perspectives on time and human temporality that are both deeply meaningful and irreducible to linguistic articulation: that music is an alternative form of understanding temporal existence to conceptual thought, and should be taken seriously

[211] Carnap, 'Überwindung der Metaphysik durch logische Analyse der Sprache', 240.

[212] 'In "poetical" discourse', Heidegger notes, 'the communication of the existential possibilities of one's state-of-mind can become an aim in itself, and this amounts to a disclosing of existence' (*Being and Time*, p. 205).

[213] Bowie, *Music, Philosophy, and Modernity*, p. 76. Bowie comments that Heidegger's few and musically inexpert statements on this matter appear, like Hegel, to distrust music's apparent reliance on subjective emotions (see *Aesthetics and Subjectivity*, pp. 9–10, 296–8).

[214] Georg Picht, 'Die Macht des Denkens', in Günther Neske (ed.), *Erinnerung an Martin Heidegger* (Pfullingen: Neske, 1977), p. 205.

in any philosophical account purporting to come to a closer understanding of time. It may even be suggestive to consider that, if music can do something that verbal formulations cannot, it could be taken as a higher mode of philosophic understanding than conventional language (as Schopenhauer would have readily assented). However, this latter position is more contentious and—if transcending linguistic discourse—can hardly be shown within the latter's terms to answer the question only it can pose. Furthermore, given music's cultural embeddedness as a human activity, it seems most plausible to suggest that where music may offer greatest insight is into the subjective temporality of humanity. While the temporal speculations of modern physics, for instance, are both premised upon the ungroundable inductive assumptions of empirical science and are unlikely to tell us much about the actual human experience of time, I do not mean to suggest that music, conversely, is likely to offer in its place a catholicon for the understanding of time in all its schismatic diversity.

As with the examples of Bergson and Heidegger, several prominent recent philosophers of time have not really considered music in their accounts of the subject. Paul Ricoeur, whose magnificent three-volume *Time and Narrative* is a summa and distillation of two-and-a-half millennia of Western thought on time and history, contends that what is called human time is nothing other than narrated time, and that consequently 'speculation on time is an inconclusive rumination to which narrative alone can respond'.[215] But one feature Ricoeur leaves untouched is the fact that there is another way humans construct time that offers mediation between different temporal conceptions—musical time—a time that, while in some ways similar, is not reducible to narrated time. Equally, music is seldom considered in the contemporary analytic philosophy of time, even in accounts specifically dealing with temporal representation in art where one might reasonably expect it. Given the overwhelming prevalence of music in philosophical accounts of time from the last two centuries, its status as *the* exemplary art of time, and finally its capacity to articulate non-linguistic modes of meaning that might offer paths round the impasses of verbal discourse, music surely offers one of the most promising avenues for exploration of this topic.

---

[215] Ricoeur, *Time and Narrative*, vol. I, p. 6. Ricoeur concludes that 'time becomes human to the extent that it is articulated through a narrative mode': 'there can be no thought about time without narrated time' (vol. I, p. 52; vol. III, p. 241). Suggestively, however, at the very close of his work Ricoeur does acknowledge the limitations of narrative and even suggests lyric poetry as giving 'a voice, which is also a song', to the expression of human meditation on time (vol. III, pp. 272–3). As will become evident, Ricoeur's approach has proved an inspiration and valuable starting context for my far more limited attempt here.

Music and Ricoeur's Three Temporal Aporias

At the close of *Time and Narrative*, Ricoeur returns to what he calls his three 'aporias of time', whose philosophic vicissitudes he has charted throughout the 800-odd pages of what must be considered his magnum opus. These are philosophical problems in understanding time that Ricoeur demonstrates have proved consistently insoluble for philosophers since antiquity; apparent resolutions of certain aspects only give rise to yet more intractable problems that appear to leave all hope of further passage closed. (Again, whoever first chanced upon that hydra simile for time was onto a winner.) Ricoeur's *aporiai* are, namely: 1) the relation between subjective time and objective, universal time; 2) the oneness of time, evinced by the resolution of multiple individual times and histories into a collective singular time of history; and 3) the apparent resistance of time's flux and continuity to any representation. In his study, Ricoeur shows how throughout history, verbal narrative, whether fictional or historical, has offered a means of mediating between the terms of at least the first two problems. In a complementary manner, I wish to argue here that music may be seen to address these aporias as well as—if not better than—verbal narrative.

Aporia 1: Psychological versus cosmological time, or subjective time versus the time of the world. For Ricoeur, this is a philosophical stumbling point for which literary narrative seems to give at least some mediation: it does not solve the aporia, but offers ways of articulating our understanding of the relationship between the two conceptions in meaningful ways. Music, too, offers such a reconciliation, indeed arguably an even stronger one.

Most evidently, our act of listening to music is the intersection of different times—the objective time, measurable by the clock, to which the physical sound waves belong (and which to a certain extent could be said to exist independently of aural perception since the waves may be empirically measured), and the unique subjective experience of musical time in the consciousnesses of its listeners.[216] As we saw developed in the consideration of Schelling's theories of musical rhythm and Wackenroder's imaginative treatment of such ideas, the manner in which musical content may be said to fill out an objectively presented time-frame forms a powerful intermediary between cosmic and psychological

---

[216] Clearly the scientific 'objectivity' of the sounds that constitute music still need not imply that objective time is necessarily anything other than an abstraction derived from experienced time, since empirical science is itself premised upon inductive assumptions concerning an external reality that cannot be more firmly grounded than the inductive method itself. The point above assumes a certain independent veracity of external and internal times, which could be disputed (though hardly resolved).

realms. The entire Pythagorean-Platonic premise of the music of the spheres and its sympathetic resonance in human souls was an earlier formulation of this very idea (although this theory would presumably find few proponents in our disenchanted modern age). 'At every period in which people have considered music's position in the world' Spitzer comments, 'the metaphor of rhythm has provided an interface between the patterns of stress peculiar to music and the cycles of life and the universe'.[217] Friedrich Neumann even argues that time is actualised in the dialectical meeting between inner subjective time and objective outer time—a duality bridged by music's interaction between metre and rhythm, between *Zeitmaß* and *Zeitgestalt*.[218]

As Ricoeur notes, while a narrative might appear to interweave numerous times into one, larger, narrated time, it is still hard to claim that this is actually objective, universal time but not rather a stylised conceit. Where music differs from narrative time (although admittedly not so greatly from dramatic time) is that the objective time of music really is a consequential part of its presentation and meaning (unlike the looser significance of the variable time taken to read a book): music's objective time is not mediated through the intermediary of narrative technique.[219] And the impression of subjective time created by music is likewise invariably perceived as being a more immediate, direct experience of time than even the most persuasive stream-of-consciousness technique can create via words. Both music's objective and subject times are more primordial instantiations of their respective times than can be found through narrative.

Even breaking down musical time into the interaction between two time senses is arguably overly reductive, however. An intersubjective musical time may be posited between members of an ensemble or the shared experience of an audience. Since the late nineteenth century and the development of recording technology the physical sound waves that create the musical event may be partially captured and held, enabling its exact repetition within objective time. In this narrow sense, the objective time of the musical work is repeatable, though the changeable resonance of the sound waves within their immediate environment, and the subjective time of the listeners

---

[217] Spitzer, *Metaphor and Musical Thought*, p. 212.

[218] Friedrich Neumann, *Die Zeitgestalt: Eine Lehre vom musikalischen Rhythmus*, 2 vols. (Vienna: Paul Kaltschmid, 1959), vol. I, pp. 21, 93–4.

[219] The same general argument for music could also be modified to extend to other temporal arts (such as theatre, dance, or cinema). As was argued earlier, music seems to be the musical art *par excellence* in its focus on temporal qualities largely independent of space, but the difference between music and the other temporal arts may be more a matter of degree than kind. For a critique of this issue see Philip Alperson, ' "Musical Time" and Music as an "Art of Time" ', *Journal of Aesthetics and Art Criticism*, 38 (1980), 407–17.

perceiving them, is unique. Furthermore, going momentarily beyond the bounds of the present topic, the ways in which music's times may interact with verbal narrative in its dramatic application in such media as opera can give rise to yet more complications from those usually considered in literary theory (such as the standard distinctions between the 'time of the narrative' and 'narrated time').[220]

Musical time may thus be read as the mediating point between times that can be read in these different ways. It is quite probable that time is a concept that is irreducibly pluralistic: a unitary, comprehensive definition seems apparently unattainable. Like debates between quantum and relativist physics, it might be better simply to admit the value of holding incompatible but mutually illuminating perspectives. While not perhaps offering a speculative answer, music at least provides the fullest and most developed poetic solution to bridging this aporia.

Aporia 2: The singularity of time, manifested in the subsumption of plural individual histories into one collective History. This aporia clearly grows out of the first: in a manner it is a historicised recasting of it, introduced partly in order to complement Ricoeur's interest in the process of emplotment in poetic narrative with that found within narrative history. In its specifically historical form, this point arguably holds rather less relevance for music: though Ricoeur readily admits that narrative also falls short here—'there is no plot of all plots capable of equalling the idea of one humanity and one history'—music probably offers little more on this particular point.[221] Nonetheless, musical time possesses two qualities not shared by narrative time which relate to this second aporia as much as they do to the first. The first is music's capacity for a genuinely simultaneous polyphony and resulting intersubjective temporality; the second the power of its apparent ability to open a window onto another subjective time, what we could call music's 'trans-subjectivity'.

As we saw, music has long been used as a metaphor for the harmonious integration of the individual with the collective, through its special ability to

---

[220] The familiar distinction between *Erzählzeit* and *erzählte Zeit* was developed by Günther Müller and Gérard Genette and has become a standard means to analyse the use of time within narrative arts. In dramatic media such as opera one may speak alternatively of representation (*Darstellung*) in place of narrative. Furthermore, relating to performance, one may distinguish the three historical eras of the represented story, of the work's creation, and the present-day moment of its dramatic instantiation (see Clemens Risi, '"Gefühlte Zeit": Zur Performativität von Opernaufführungen', in Christina Lechtermann, Kirsten Wagner, and Horst Wenzel (eds.), *Möglichkeitsräume: Zur Performativität von sensorischer Wahrnehmung* (Berlin: Erich Schmidt, 2007), p. 153; and for a broader background to this topic, Carl Dahlhaus, 'Zeitstrukturen in der Oper', in *Vom Musikdrama zur Literaturoper* (Munich and Salzburg: Emil Katzbichler, 1983), pp. 25–32).

[221] Ricoeur, *Time and Narrative*, vol. III, p. 259.

show the harmony of different simultaneous elements by polyphonic voices. In Wordsworth's formulation:

> *Dust as we are, the immortal spirit grows*
> *Like harmony in music; there is a dark*
> *Inscrutable workmanship that reconciles*
> *Discordant elements, makes them cling together*
> *In one society.*[222]

Again, whereas 'polyphony' in the nineteenth-century novel (just as in historical accounts of events) is never really simultaneous but the individual voices must be presented one after another in temporal sequence, in music they truly are present coetaneously.[223] Thus although both musical and literary understandings of the creation of community may be metaphorical, unlike the latter, music is an actual temporal instantiation of such temporal polyphony.

Additionally, in polyphonic music each voice may be heard to exist with its immediate past and its imminent future reflected in the present through Husserlian retention and protention—a feature which becomes especially complex in imitative music where the 'present' of one voice is already the 'past' of another. In the latter case one can argue that listeners may be able to attend to a genuine sense of multiple times ongoing simultaneously while still subsuming them into their own single time of consciousness.[224] Moreover, when a polyphonic work is practically realised in group performance the separate parts are genuinely created by individual people—a re-anthropomorphising of its musical

---

[222] Wordsworth, *The Prelude* (1850), I, ll. 340–44.

[223] This notion of novelistic polyphony was developed by Mikhail Bakhtin. Even the best and literarily most accomplished narrative account of a historical event that involves multiple actors (such as Tolstoy's of the Battle of Borodino in *War and Peace*) is subject to temporal succession in its presentation of the simultaneous. In rare cases, as Ricoeur shows, twentieth-century narrative technique may momentarily suggest the simultaneity of two subjective times (such as in Virginia Woolf's *Mrs Dalloway*).

[224] A fascinating argument along these lines has been presented by Jeremy Shapiro concerning the multiple times possessed by the aggregate of the voices within an imitative polyphonic composition, such as a fugue, taking into consideration their individual retentions and protentions ('The Fugue, Meta-time, and the Phenomenology of Internal Time Consciousness', paper presented at the Philosophy and Music Conference 'Time Theories and Music', Ionian University of Corfu, 27 April 2012). The phenomenal reality of such multiple temporalities would rest on the abilities of listeners to attend to multiple temporal levels simultaneously; a two-voice canon is more likely to be perceived as formed of two separate times than a five-part fugue, where the perceived separate times of the voices will probably blend into one collective time. The cognitive capacities of different listeners are, however, quite variable; only a God-like mind could perceive an infinite aggregation of separate times at once (as Leibniz might have said, or Borges expressed in some fantastic literary form).

voices. The single time of a choral, chamber, or orchestral piece is literally a col-lective singular of collected singular voices and their associated times.[225]

A further point that may be added here is how music may appear to com-municate a different subjective time—its trans-subjective temporality. Music, as belonging to 'objective' time, is something external to the self, but appears through its apparent subjectivity to have the capacity to disclose another consciousness. Art, as Bergson claims, seems uniquely able to break down the barriers inter-posed by time and space between different consciousnesses.[226] Of course, the subjective agency of music is a fiction, but nevertheless it is a meaningful fiction. That music *has* often been heard as an expression of the temporal flow of emo-tional states experienced by its composer is incontestable, even though the issue of exactly *how* emotional states might be communicated through music remains decidedly problematic, as does the question of whether they really belonged to the composer who wrote them.[227] But after all, the ability of the word to com-municate subjective expression in literature is no less metaphorical. The 'I' of a narrative (understood in the broadest sense) is no more a real entity than the persona speaking in music (as can be witnessed by the interchangeability of first and third person narratives), yet in both media the reader or listener comes to an understanding of gaining privileged access to another consciousness, a 'mime-sis of other minds' in Dorrit Cohn's words.[228] However, in music we experience this subjective state seemingly more unmediatedly than in words. No wonder for many eighteenth-century aestheticians (and nineteenth-century epigones like Hegel) music, not verbal discourse, is the pre-eminent language of the emotions.

Through music we seem to achieve the seemingly impossible—to feel like another human being, to share another consciousness, its subjectivity, its inner temporality. The music is external—but the experience is purely our own, inter-nal. T.S. Eliot expresses it perfectly in his famous lines on 'music heard so deeply'

> *That it is not heard at all, but you are the music*
> *While the music lasts.*[229]

[225] Referring to a distinction made by Wulf Kansteiner, 'Finding Meaning in Memory: A Methodological Critique of Collective Memory Studies', *History and Theory*, 41 (2002), 186.

[226] Bergson, *Time and Free Will*, p. 18.

[227] See for instance Aaron Ridley, *Music, Value and the Passions* (Ithaca, NY: Cornell University Press, 1995), p. 13, who terms this position 'empathetic' emotional communication.

[228] See Dorrit Cohn, *Transparent Minds: Narrative Modes for Presenting Consciousness in Fiction* (Princeton: Princeton University Press, 1978). As Roland Barthes puts it, 'language knows a "sub-ject", not a "person"' ('The Death of the Author', in *Image—Music—Text*, trans. Stephen Heath [London: Flamingo, 1977], p. 145).

[229] T.S. Eliot, 'The Dry Salvages', V, from *Four Quartets*. H.H. Eggebrecht similarly notes that the identification of the listener with the music is the sinking of the self into a type of time that seems to be constituted of the self ('Musik und Zeit', in Dahlhaus and Eggebrecht, *Was ist Musik?*, p. 184).

'Music's own multiplicity and temporal dynamism engage with the general character of consciousness itself', concludes Eric Clarke, 'with the consequence that
music provides us with a domain in which to explore and experience "what it is
like to be human" in terms that are on the one hand familiar, and on the other
transformative'.[230]

One might also note that, fictional construction though it is, such ability to
feel at home in an 'Other', the propensity for self-recognition in another (apparent) subjective consciousness, would have held high value within idealist philosophies. For Schelling, the pre-eminence of art is given by this unification of
the subjective and objective, the sense of self as both subject and object. And
in such a manner, we might come to a fuller understanding of Wackenroder's
hermit. From a Hegelian perspective the coming together of the two lovers in
the story would suggest the recognition of the self in the other through which
consciousness is saved from the bad infinity of endless repetition and gains the
true infinity of self-recognition. The music arises out of this union, and as a consequence empty time stops at the moment of realisation.

Aporia 3: The unrepresentability of the flux and continuity of time. This,
Ricoeur finds, is the most problematic of the three aporias.[231] Verbal accounts of
this feature of time rarely get beyond metaphor, and even narrative offers little
help. Perhaps the most revealing example of this failure is articulated by Husserl
in his *Phenomenology of Internal Time Consciousness*. In the latter sections of this
investigation, concerning what he calls the 'constitutive flux' of consciousness,
Husserl appears to tie himself in knots in his attempt to analyse how time, if
bound up inextricably with the subject's own consciousness, can be said to flow,
and if so, in relation to what. His usually stolid, dutiful prose becomes especially
opaque and recalcitrant as he chases his own shadow, ending up resorting to metaphors.[232] At the heart of his investigation (§36, 'The Temporally Constitutive

---

[230] Eric Clarke, 'Music Perception and Musical Consciousness', in Clarke and Clarke (eds.), *Music
and Consciousness*, p. 209. This same transformative potential has been recognised by Laird Addis in
his claim that 'music represents possible states of consciousness', with the corollary that music may
furthermore suggest deeper and richer states of mind than ordinarily revealed in everyday life (*Of
Mind and Music*, p. 78).

[231] It should be noted that for a B-Theorist in the Analytic philosophical tradition, time's 'flow'
is only a subjective illusion and does not constitute an aspect of metaphysical reality: thus Ricoeur's
third aporia, while a problem, is unimportant for an adequate account of time (indeed might only
arise from this illusory everyday conception of time). Notwithstanding this, time's apparent flow is
a genuine feature of phenomenal reality for subjective or internal time consciousness (a point few
B-theorists would dispute), and music's very perception is grounded in such subjective temporality.
Thus this aporia concerns subjective, experienced time above all else, though it may, depending on
philosophical viewpoint, implicate objective or various other types of time.

[232] Husserl, *The Phenomenology of Internal Time Consciousness*, §§35–41 and Appendix VI.
Husserl wrestled with this problem throughout his life: the later collections of notes known as the

Flux as Absolute Subjectivity') Husserl essays identifying the flux of time with consciousness, which he terms 'absolute subjectivity'. 'It is evident, then, that temporally constitutive phenomena [i.e., what belongs to consciousness] are, in principle, objectivities other than those constituted in time'.

> But is not the flux a succession? Does it not, therefore, have a now, an actual phase, and a continuity of pasts of which we are conscious in retentions? We can only say that this flux is something which we name in conformity with what is constituted, but it is nothing tempo-rally 'Objective'. *It is absolute subjectivity and has the absolute properties of something to be denoted metaphorically as 'flux', as a point of actuality, primal source-point, that from which springs the 'now', and so on. . . . For this, all names are lacking.*[233]

In other words, subjective consciousness, that which constitutes our internal time sense, seems to be both in time *and* outside time, both flows *and* is the stable point of rest, the 'now'-point past which time flows. Husserl more-or-less admits defeat in conceding that the designation 'flux' is metaphorical—and can-not come up with anything more precise. 'For this, all names are lacking'.

It is here that music really seems to offer something that is simply not available in semantic discourse. As we saw, music is the exemplary medium for philoso-phers attempting to describe time's subjective flux. From Augustine's discussion of the musicality of a Psalm's recitation to the examples in Clay, James, Bergson, and Husserl, philosophers, psychologists, and phenomenologists have continu-ally returned to music as the only apparent way to express this apparent prop-erty of time that goes beyond anything words seem able to articulate.[234] For in

'L' or 'Bernauer' writings (from 1917–18) and the 'C' writings (late 1920s to early 1930s) document his continual struggles with time. The former has only fairly recently been published (*Die Bernauer Manuskripte über das Zeitbewusstsein (1917/18), Husserliana* 33, eds. Rudolf Bernet and Dieter Lohmar [Dordrecht-Boston-London: Kluwer, 2001]), the latter is still unavailable. For an account of this C manuscript see Toine Kortooms, *Phenomenology of Time: Edmund Husserl's Analysis of Time-Consciousness* (Dordrecht: Kluwer, 2002), pp. 227–88.

[233] Ibid., §36: 'The Temporally Constitutive Flux as Absolute Subjectivity', p. 100, emphasis mine. Ricoeur provides a typically clear-headed and instructive analysis of Husserl's aporia in *Time and Narrative*, vol. III, pp. 23–44.

[234] As Augustine's example might insinuate, however, the distinction between music and spoken language is not absolute on this point; there is a temporal continuity and flow to a spo-ken sentence—its 'musicality' we could say—that is comparable to that of a musical phrase. (It should be remembered that syntactic coherence is just as culturally constructed in music as in verbal language.) To this extent music is a better instance than the spoken word due only to its concentration on temporal succession without introducing a significant semantic con-tent. However, in searching for sonic instances of 'pure change' (such could be provided by the example of glissando) the ability of music seems overwhelmingly more pertinent than speech

music we gain 'a clear perception of movement that is not attached to a mobile, of a change without anything changing'.[235] David Clarke, considering this passage from Husserl's *Phenomenology*, reasonably proposes music's potential for approaching this conceptual aporia: if we 'lack all names' for this flux of absolute subjectivity, 'we do still have another invaluable source through which to approach these problems'—music—

> a source that, like language, is implicated in signification, but that, unlike language, is concerned with something other than the conceptual; a source that, more deeply than language, traces the flowing and knowing of our being.[236]

Music is not a (mediated) metaphor for temporal flux but in fact an *instantiation* of it—'pure temporality' in Jonathan Kramer's words.[237] Kant, quite justifiably, argues that 'time cannot be perceived in itself'.[238] But music, by emptying as much as possible all tangible, visible and corporeal elements and focussing on pure succession as Bergson suggests, comes closer to the immediacy of the subjective experience of temporal flow than anything else of which we seem able to conceive.[239]

A Supplementary Aporia: Time and the Transcendental Constitution of the Self

Music's capacity to instantiate a temporal entity imbued with the properties associated with the subjective structure of time suggests a possible link with

---

(which would have to become to all intents and purposes music in order to approach music's capability here).

[235] Bergson, 'The Perception of Change', p. 147.

[236] Clarke, 'Music, phenomenology, time consciousness', p. 24.

[237] Jonathan D. Kramer, 'Studies of Time and Music: A Bibliography', *Music Theory Spectrum*, 7 (1985), 72.

[238] Immanuel Kant, *Critique of Pure Reason*, trans. and ed. Paul Guyer and Allen W. Wood (Cambridge: Cambridge University Press, 1998), A183/B226 and B233, pp. 301 and 304. A similar conclusion was made earlier by Aristoxenos, a pupil of Aristotle and the most important source for Greek music theory.

[239] See further Victor Zuckerkandl's argument in *Sound and Symbol*, where music is read quasi-mystically as an example of pure becoming. However, rather than concerning himself with a Husserlian problematic of retention and protention, Zuckerkandl actually seems to believe the apparent causal connection of successive notes is inherent objectively in music—an approach which might be questionable to many readers. By hypostatising music's Gestalt to the state where obvious motivating forces of human agency in musical time are absent, Zuckerkandl is all-too-ready to attribute the latter to time's *own* agency. In his later second volume the mystic claims are held more in check (see *Man the Musician* [*Sound and Symbol*, vol. II] [Princeton: Princeton University Press, 1973], p. 347).

another long-standing aporia, intimately connected to time though broader and even more intractable, namely the constitution of the self or in Kant's terminology the 'transcendental unity of apperception'. The virtual equivalence of subjective time and the self has already been suggested in Husserl's account of the constitutive flux of 'absolute subjectivity', while the link between music and self-consciousness has been a recurring theme throughout this chapter. The full details of the parallelism between music and Kant's transcendental unity are worth exploring here as an additional, fourth aporia to the three of Ricoeur's already given.

In Kant, the transcendental unity of apperception is the ground for everything, but itself is unknowable. This concept is defined in the 1781 *Critique of Pure Reason*:

> No cognitions can occur in us, no connection and unity among them, without that unity of consciousness that precedes all data of the intuitions, and in relation to which all representations of objects is alone possible. . . . A transcendental ground must therefore be found for the unity of the consciousness in the synthesis of the manifold of all our intuitions . . . this original and transcendental condition is nothing other than the transcendental apperception.[240]
>
> Pure apperception, i.e., the thoroughgoing identity of oneself in all possible representations, grounds empirical consciousness *a priori*. . . . This principle holds *a priori*, and can be called the transcendental principle of the unity of all the manifold of our representations.[241]
>
> The transcendental unity of apperception is related to the pure synthesis of the imagination, as an *a priori* condition of the possibly of all composition of the manifold in a cognition.[242]

But the self can only know itself through its forms of perception: 'I have no cognition of myself as I am, but only as I appear to myself' Kant argues.[243] 'The consciousness of the self . . . is merely empirical, forever variable; it can provide no standing or abiding self in this stream of inner appearances'. Therefore, too, the actual self (the transcendental unity) in Kant, is implicitly timeless, itself prior to or above time, given that time is an a priori condition for perceptions experienced by that self.[244] The self is noumenal, lying outside time and space, a correlate to the 'thing in itself' of objects as they are for themselves, ever unknowable.[245]

[240] Kant, *Critique of Pure Reason*, A106–7, p. 232.

[241] Ibid., A116, p. 237.

[242] Ibid., A118, p. 238.

[243] Ibid., B158, p. 260.

[244] Ibid., B68–9, pp. 189–90.

[245] Ibid., A250, p. 348.

For phenomenology, too, no more apodictic solution to this question is forthcoming. Husserl speaks of 'the difficulty of determining how it is possible to have knowledge of a unity of the ultimate constitutive flux of consciousness'—in other words the self, of the unity of self-consciousness or Kant's transcendental unity. 'There is no doubt there is a difficulty here', Husserl repeats, lest we had missed this detail.[246] Husserl is haunted throughout his investigation by the paradox of something moving but unmoved, by the threat of infinite regress.[247] For if this flux of consciousness is in flux, must there not be a secondary flux to ground this? Husserl sees the encroaching danger. In fact, 'the flux of consciousness constitutes its own unity'. Again, the justification is given by the example of our perception of sound, relating the unity of the duration of a sound and the unity of the consciousness of the duration of the sound: 'it is the one unique flux of consciousness in which the immanent temporal unity of the sound and also the unity of the flux of consciousness itself are constituted'.[248] Husserl's doubts surface, though, in his immediate qualification that this conclusion may appear 'startling (if not at first sight even contradictory)'.

Husserl returns to this issue in a fragment included in Appendix IV of the published form of his lectures: one cannot oneself perceive the consciousness to which temporal appearance is reduced to a flux (by pain of infinite regress). Rather like Kant, 'Subjective time is constituted in absolute, timeless consciousness, which is not an Object'. And in reflecting 'as to how this absolute consciousness attains givenness' Husserl again suggests it may be realised through the example of a melody, in what appears to be a type of structural listening:

> With a melody, for example, we can arrest a moment, as it were, and discover therein shadings of memory of the past notes. It is obvious that the same holds true for every individual note. We have, then, the immanent tonal now and the immanent tonal pasts in their series or continuity: perception of the now and memory of the past; and this entire continuity must itself be a now. In fact, in the living consciousness of an object, I look back into the past from the now-point out. On the other hand, I can grasp the entire consciousness of an object as a now and say: Now I seize the moment and grasp the entire consciousness as an all-together, as an all-at-once.[249]

[246] Husserl, *The Phenomenology of Internal Time Consciousness*, §39, pp. 105–6.
[247] See ibid., §41, p. 114, displaying Husserl's grounding of his argument in a classical ontology of Being: 'In change, and likewise with alteration, something enduring must be present—something which makes up the identity of that which is altered or undergoes a change'.
[248] Ibid., §39, p. 106.
[249] Ibid., Appendix IV, pp. 150, 151.

Once again, music is on hand to offer a lifeline to explicating that for which 'all names are lacking'—the temporal being of the self. But Husserl appears not even to have convinced himself with his conclusions. This was a major philosophical problem, as he realised, and struggled with throughout his life without ever really resolving.

Know thyself! The fact that the epistemic ground of modern philosophy seems in itself unknowable—especially if this, rather perversely, is what must by rights be considered closest to oneself, that is to say oneself—was clearly mildly galling for philosophers (even if some, like Hume, cheerfully accepted this situation and continued to repast this unknowable entity upon food and wine).[250] The problem facing attempts at explicating the self or ground of self-consciousness lies in the latter's resistance to objectification. As Aristotle had wondered long before, how can the mind become an object to itself, the same thing serve simultaneously as subject and object?[251] If the mind divides itself into a perceiving subject and a perceived object it no longer possesses the unity which was the entire goal of the exercise. (To posit a secondary level of consciousness with which to observe consciousness just leads to an infinite regress, as Husserl was well aware.) The seemingly impossible task is to grasp the unity of the 'I' without splitting it (which in this very action destroys the unity). Though philosophers have been aware of this quandary for nearly two-and-a-half millennia, it became a real problem only in post-Cartesian philosophy, since the latter finds its foundational basis in the self. Thus the central problem of modern philosophy is that of self-consciousness: how can the 'I' of Descartes, Kant, and Husserl, account for itself?

Andrew Bowie has given a persuasive account of this struggle in post-Kantian philosophy. One element proffered as solution was, as noted earlier, the temporalisation of this quest, whereby both unity and division may be predicated of the mind, but at different times: a divided state gives rise to the transcendental deduction that an undivided state must necessarily have preceded it for there to be this cognition, resulting in a return to this undivided unity (a familiar Neoplatonic tripartite movement). Closely related to this strategy, and just as potentially rewarding for music, is the aesthetic notion of feeling, whose roots Bowie contends are implicit in Kant. In his *Prolegomena to Any Future Metaphysics* Kant had remarked suggestively in a footnote that 'the representation of apperception, the "I"', is in fact 'nothing more than the feeling of an existence without the least concept and only a representation of that to which all thinking relates'.[252] Just like

---

[250] *A Treatise of Human Nature*, 1.4.7.9. 'A good composition of music and a bottle of good wine equally produce pleasure' Hume later concludes (3.1.2.4, p. 472).

[251] Aristotle, *De Anima*, III/2, 427ª2–5.

[252] Kant, *Prolegomena to Any Future Metaphysics*, §46, in *Gesammelte Schriften (Akademie-Ausgabe)*, 23 vols. (Berlin and Leipzig: de Gruyter, 1923), vol. IV, p. 334.

Rousseau lying in his boat on Lake Bienne, the pure, unmediated feeling of one-self, one's own Being, without any external perception, without any mediation through the structures of thought imposed by language, is the closest one can get to an intuition of the unanalysable transcendental unity.[253] (Compare this with Bergson's analogous claim that the perception of a melody in itself, shorn of all particulars, is the closest one can get to the feeling of duration.) This—and not the caprice of mere subjective indulgence—is one of the fundamental reasons why the concept of 'feeling' becomes so important in Romantic aesthetics.

Bowie argues that from a radical, Romantic perspective, some of Kant's remarks 'can be construed as making the "musical" into the ground of cognition'.[254] Fichte already suggests that immediate access to consciousness is only found in feeling, before verbal reflection created through conceptual thought,[255] but Friedrich Schlegel is the first explicitly to link this argument with music. 'If feeling is the root of all consciousness . . . language has the essential deficit that it does not grasp and comprehend feeling deeply enough, only touches its surface'. In its stead, 'this essential imperfection must be overcome in another manner . . . through music', which is 'less a representational art than a philosophical language'.[256] Feeling relates to a pre-reflexive 'I', a unity necessarily pre-existing all reflection on it. 'In language there is reflection and therefore language cannot express the immediate' claims one of Kierkegaard's alter egos, whereas 'music always expresses the immediate in its immediacy'.[257]

Language itself is deficient in that it already reflects a divided self: understood denotatively as representing outer reality it proves to be ungroundable, leading to aporias; understood connotatively it may be legitimately seen as expressive of reality but cannot claim complete or even privileged access to it. Fairly early in *The Phenomenology of Spirit* Hegel makes a deprecating comment on the indeterminate first stage of pure consciousness as being of a lower type, like 'a musical thinking that does not get as far as the Notion, which would be the sole, immanent objective mode of thought'.[258] But this immediacy is the very virtue of music according to Hegel's contemporaries, who do not hold the same problematic belief in the ability of the word to reflect and reconstitute the entirety of reality.

---

[253] Bowie indeed proposes Kant took this 'invocation of feeling' from Rousseau's *Émile* (ibid., p. 23).

[254] Bowie, *Music, Philosophy, and Modernity*, p. 86.

[255] Fichte, *Science of Knowledge*, Pt III, §8 (Fifth Discourse), p. 260.

[256] Friedrich Schlegel, *Philosophische Vorlesungen*, bk. VII, in *Kritische Friedrich-Schlegel-Ausgabe*, vol. XIII, p. 57 [recte], cited in Bowie, *Aesthetics and Subjectivity*, p. 37.

[257] Kierkegaard (as 'A'), 'The Immediate Erotic Stages, *or* the Musical Erotic', *Either/Or*, p. 80. 'A', the pseudonymous author of this chapter, nevertheless upholds a rather old-fashioned aesthetic supporting the primacy of words in an argument highly indebted to Hegel.

[258] Hegel, *Phenomenology of Spirit*, p. 131.

Feeling is closely related to art through aesthesis or preconceptual perception. Art, as arising (in the wake of Kant's later *Critique of Judgement*) from a spontaneous, free act was seen by thinkers such as Hölderlin and Schelling as perhaps the only possible way of the self expressing this unity. Thus the author/s of the 'Oldest System-Programme of German Idealism' could proclaim that 'the aesthetic act is the highest act of reason'.[259] Schleiermacher likewise focuses on the importance of the notion of immediate self-consciousness in his *Aesthetics*. These points, when brought into conjunction with the numerous strands of earlier arguments in this chapter, reveal the way as to how music might be construed as of fundamental importance for the philosophical attempt at understanding the nature of self-consciousness.

Music as Self-Apperception

For deeper consideration of this connection between music and the constitution of self-consciousness we may return one more time to the philosophy of Schelling. As mentioned, Schelling makes fairly hyperbolic claims for art. Rather strangely, however, these are not developed extensively for music. Schelling, despite showing a greater willingness to grant art privileged status against the verbal articulation of philosophical reason than Hegel, actually appears to place music lower within his aesthetic hierarchy. It was suggested earlier that the philosophical significance of the connection of music with the self-constituting process of self-consciousness is merely implicit in the *Philosophy of Art*; one must apply the implications of Schelling's wider philosophic project to show music's enormous, though unexploited, potential within this system.

As we saw, in the *System of Transcendental Idealism* Schelling makes self-consciousness the fundamental, grounding principle of philosophy. 'Self consciousness circumscribes the entire horizon of our knowing even when extended into infinity, and that it remains in every direction the highest principle'.[260] This author certainly cannot be accused of lack of ambition: '*by achieving this task we simultaneously solve all problems whose solution has hitherto been sought in philosophy*' he exclaims.[261] We also recall that Schelling argues that self-consciousness is an activity: 'what the self is' is undemonstrable; 'one can only describe the action

---

[259] 'The Oldest System-Programme of German Idealism' is a short but key text dating from 1796 surviving in Hegel's handwriting, the content of which is presumed to be largely the intellectual work of Hölderlin or Schelling (the three being roommates at the Tübingen Theological Seminary).

[260] Schelling, *System of Transcendental Idealism*, p. 17.

[261] Ibid., p. 19.

whereby it comes about'. 'Transcendental philosophy is completed only when the self becomes an object to itself'.[262]

For Schelling, this I = I (where one side is subject and the other object, thus constituting a synthetic rather than merely analytic proposition) is only accomplished in art. 'The transcendental philosophy would be completed only if it could demonstrate this *identity . . . in its own principle* (namely the self). . . . There is but one such activity, namely the *aesthetic*'.[263] Continuing the argument seen in the *System-Programme*, art is the manner in which the self can intuit itself, a reconciling of freedom and necessity, conscious and unconscious. The work of art is an artefact stamped with our own subjectivity, a result of our free subjective creation. Hence 'it can be given to art alone to pacify our endless striving, and likewise to resolve the final and uttermost contradiction within us'. 'The work of art merely reflects to me what is otherwise not reflected by anything, namely that absolutely identical which has already divided itself even in the self'—what is otherwise inaccessible to any intuition.[264] This conclusion is repeated at the start of the *Philosophy of Art*, where it is asserted that such a philosophy of art is a necessary goal of the philosopher, 'who in art views the inner essence of his own discipline as if in a magic and symbolic mirror'.[265] And thus Schelling rounds of the *System of Transcendental Idealism* with one of the most rousing paeans to art penned by a philosopher:

> art is at once the only true and eternal organ and document of philosophy, which ever and again continues to speak to us of what philosophy cannot depict in external form [the identity of the unconscious with the conscious]. Art is paramount to the philosopher, precisely because it opens to him, as it were, the holy of holies, where burns in eternal and original unity . . . that which in nature and history is rent asunder.[266]

Accordingly, any one of the arts is already blessed with almost inestimable potential for philosophic insight into the self. But music, in particular, seems to hold out a promise here that none of the others can hope match. Remember that music is pre-eminently 'the art of reflection or of self-consciousness' and is not

[262] Ibid., p. 92.

[263] Ibid., p. 12. Quixotically, one may note that the equation I = I has a double signification in its possible senses of the self's identity with itself (as found in the 'first, absolutely unconditioned principle' of Fichte's *Wissenschaftslehre* or Schelling's 'Philosophy of Identity') and musically of the tonic returning to tonic—a parallel that we saw was eagerly taken up by Schelling, Schopenhauer and Hegel in their accounts of music's analogous temporal structure to self-consciousness. However, the symbolic identity between the Roman numeral and first-person singular is present only in English.

[264] Ibid., pp. 222, 230.

[265] Schelling, *Philosophy of Art*, p. 8.

[266] Schelling, *System of Transcendental Idealism*, p. 231.

'subjected to time but rather possesses time *within itself*.[267] All this sounds rather like the self. The self, Schelling had earlier argued, similarly constitutes time for itself, and only *is* by being a continual process.[268] In its temporal distention and imprinting of unity into multiplicity music is a mirror of self-consciousness, the originary act of the self by which the self is able to come about. Music is not a conceptual analysis of this act of self-constitution, nor a reflection of it translated into verbal terms, but *instantiates* it as a process in time, with an emotional immediacy concepts cannot compete with. As argued earlier, music provides an object which is yet felt to be like oneself. Through music the subject is able to recognise itself and feel at home in the other. And in Schelling's system, this mirroring is accorded hyperbolic worth, since it achieves something philosophy cannot hope to do.

There remains, however, one important point concerning the affiliation between music and consciousness that Schelling leaves largely unexamined, namely its non-physical substrate which supports change without movement. We saw Hegel leave some tantalising remarks on the ontological affinity between self-consciousness and music, but here we must turn to Bergson for the clearest explication of this feature. In the introduction written to the republication of a collection of his essays entitled *The Creative Mind*, Bergson reflects on his lifelong philosophical quest. His desire was to 'grasp the inner life beneath the juxtaposition of states that we effect in a spatialised time . . . in getting an idea of the substantiality of the ego, as of its duration'. This—the substantiality and duration of the ego—was, he found, the

> indivisible and indestructible continuity of a melody where the past enters into the present and forms with it an undivided whole which remains undivided and even indivisible in spite of what is added at every instant, or rather, thanks to what is added. We have the intuition of it; but as soon as we seek an intellectual representation of it we line up, one after another, states which have become distinct like the beads of a necklace and therefore require, in order to hold them together, a thread which is neither this or that, nothing that resembles beads, nothing that resembles anything whatsoever—an empty entity[.][269]

Bergson speaks of Kant's mistake, in putting the self 'outside' time, owing to Kant's assumption of time as being a homogenous, extensive medium.[270]

---

[267] Schelling, *Philosophy of Art*, pp. 162, 111.

[268] Schelling, *System of Transcendental Idealism*, p. 48.

[269] Bergson, *The Creative Mind*, Introduction II, p. 71 (these analogies are discussed at greater length in *Creative Evolution*, p. 4).

[270] Bergson, *Time and Free Will*, pp. 232–3.

Duration is pure becoming, unattached to any spatial object, and duration *is* the self. Thus Bergson insists on discarding the classical ontology that had proved so problematic for Husserl and simply accepting that the temporal being of the self is something quite unlike anything that can be derived from spatial concepts and representational language. This can be sensed through intuition, but in practice as we have seen, Bergson finds it best instantiated in music. Discussing the 'ego which endures', Bergson proposes that 'there is neither a rigid, immovable substratum nor distinct states passing over it like actors on a stage [cf. Hume]. There is simply the continuous melody of our inner life'.[271] And again, elsewhere, he speaks of the 'continuous fluidity of real time which flows along indivisible . . . as in a melody where everything is becoming *but where the becoming, being itself substantial, has no need of support*'.[272]

Thus, summing up the argument so far only implicit and drawing together all these strands: given that music provides an example of something closer to consciousness than arguably any other entity other than consciousness itself—its exemplary temporal nature as an instance of flux and continuity, its immaterial ontology, its apparent kinship with consciousness through the immediacy of its emotional suggestibility, its fusion of something that disappears as it is perceived with an apparent self-identity across time, even in some readings its purported supertemporality—might not music in fact be the best illustration we can possibly put forward for this transcendental unity? Certainly, as we have seen, philosophers of time, philosophers of mind, and psychologists alike have got little further than musical metaphors when it comes to describing the transcendental ego. If art truly is the 'organ of philosophy' as Schelling puts it, it should be capable of being used as a means to philosophic enlightenment, a tool in the pursuit of grounding truth.

But, all-too-predictably now, if trying to take this argument any further, from music as forming an analogy, metaphor, or non-linguistic mirror of consciousness to the idea that music might actually be capable of demonstrating the true nature of the transcendental unity of apperception, we run into an aporia. For music requires consciousness for its perception: our consciousness *does* this to music. All these qualities of music are intuited into sounds by the transcendental self that we are trying to obtain insight into: the argument attempted runs aground on a patent *petitio principii*. We cannot step outside our own consciousness in order to perceive music, even if we might like to think we hear another consciousness mirrored in music.

It is not clear that we can make something of this apparent aporia. A fully paid-up Hegelian might try to complete this impasse dialectically by raising it to a

---

[271] Bergson, 'The Perception of Change', p. 149.
[272] Bergson, 'Philosophical Intuition', p. 127.

higher conceptual level of thought, through the recognition of the self in the other (that is, in music's apparent mirroring of consciousness). The circularity encountered here could be passed off as hermeneutic, the result of the system providing the grounds for the opening. Like Hegelians and Heideggerians in their different ways, we simply have to jump on to this idealist carousel or ontic merry-go-round at some point and believe that where we are when the music stops was the same place where the horses had started long before we joined them in their circuit. Alternatively, it could be the case that art is able to lead us intuitively beyond the conceptual aporia, as the anti-rationalist undercurrent in Schelling, Schopenhauer, and Bergson implies. Given the limits to what may be verbally articulated on this matter, however, the best we can probably do is, rather more modestly, simply to suggest that music reflects to the presupposed transcendental self something that seems remarkably akin in temporality and ontology to itself in an immediate and pre-reflexive manner that no other art quite manages; but we cannot perceive this without a perception and therefore cannot use this to ground the self.

Carpe Diem?

Turning away momentarily from this apparently unanswerable question, perhaps in despair of ever finding a solution, a radically alternative approach suggests itself. Namely, why worry about time? Another way of understanding music's temporal condition might simply be to revel in its transitoriness. After all, the majority of listeners throughout the last two centuries have eschewed Adornian structural listening and enjoyed the succession of present moments that make no pretence to constituting an eternity.[273]

Such a viewpoint is implicitly supporting Kierkegaard's argument about music in *Either/Or*, where music's ephemerality is upheld as part of its very nature. Music is the quintessential 'aesthetic' art, existing 'only in the moment of its performance': it is 'over as soon as it stops playing and only comes back into existence when it starts again'. Thus it is perfect for expressing the aesthetic life, that which is 'the sum of mutually repellent exclusive moments that lack any coherence . . . as moment the sum of moments, as sum of moments the moment'.[274] Indeed, elsewhere we read that 'aesthetics is not much concerned about time; be it jest or earnestness, time goes just as fast for aesthetics'.[275]

---

[273] See Jerrold Levinson, *Music in the Moment* (Ithaca, NY: Cornell University Press, 1997).

[274] Kierkegaard (as 'A'), 'The Immediate Erotic Stages, *or* the Musical Erotic', *Either/Or*, pp. 79, 107–8, 102.

[275] Kierkegaard (writing as Johannes de Silentio), *Fear and Trembling*, in *Fear and Trembling/ Repetition*, trans. Howard V. and Edna H. Hong (Princeton: Princeton University Press, 1983), p. 86.

Although we noted that Kierkegaard neglects the constitutive role of memory in the mental construction of music, much passive perception of music similarly downplays the functioning of memory in processing a work's structure and its consequent potential to construct a supertemporal whole.[276]

This point might provide us with a path to a less formal aesthetic of music and time, away from the undoubted bias towards Germanic instrumental music and philosophy of the last two chapters. Such a viewpoint reinstates the centrality of the performative and improvisatory within the nineteenth century—of opera, of instrumental virtuosity, and the cult of the performer—where the composer is written in lower-case and writes for performers. After all, Rossini's operas were far more significant than Beethoven's late sonatas in their time. In Carolyn Abbate's recent formulation, this would offer a 'drastic' perspective in place of the largely 'gnostic' account presented above, away from Hanslick's intellectual or 'aesthetic' listening to what the latter calls passive or (more generously) 'pathological' perception.[277] Later, in the hands of a master, the 'formless' and fleeting can even become an entire compositional aesthetic (as found in Delius or Debussy, in so-called musical impressionism). Thus writers such as Vladimir Jankélévitch can (admittedly similarly one-sidedly) support an aesthetic that spurns eternity in favour of the moment.

In many ways this aesthetic is indeed nothing other than a logical outgrowth of Bergson's insistence on intuition, in line with the general tenor of earlier German Romantic thought. Yet to this extent, words again often seem superfluous: beyond pointing out the incompatibility of our intellectualising thought to deal with this aesthetic, analysis is largely redundant, indeed counter-productive. Certainly from a eudaemonist perspective there is no reason why we should not simply enjoy music without any further intellectualising, but replacing the apparently unanswerable nature of music's relationship with time with a different ineffability does not take us much further, although it undoubtedly simplifies the matter by cutting out vain philosophical speculation that does not and seemingly cannot ever arrive at definitive conclusions. However, as will be suggested in the

[276] The rather Hegelian views on the presumed presence of written language vis-à-vis music expressed in *Either/Or* also call out for critique (such as with Derrida's sense of Hearing-Oneself-Speak). On this problem of temporality and presence in language, see Jacques Derrida's *Speech and Phenomena and Other Essays on Husserl's Theory of Signs*, trans. David B. Allison (Evanston, IL: Northwestern University Press, 1973) and Paul De Man's 'The Rhetoric of Temporality', in *Interpretation: Theory and Practice*, ed. C.S. Singleton (Baltimore: John Hopkins Press, 1969), pp. 173–209. De Man himself turns to music as a solution to this aporia in 'The Rhetoric of Blindness: Jacques Derrida's Reading of Rousseau', in *Blindness and Insight: Essays in the Rhetoric of Contemporary Criticism* (Minneapolis: University of Minnesota Press, 1983), pp. 102–41, with mixed success.

[277] Carolyn Abbate, 'Music—Drastic or Gnostic?', *Critical Inquiry*, 30 (2004), 505–36; Eduard Hanslick, *Vom Musikalisch-Schönen*, ch. 5. Clearly the term aesthetic is being used in opposite senses by Kierkegaard and Hanslick.

conclusion to this chapter, it is strongly arguable that meaning—whether verbal or musical—is constituted from such necessarily metaphorical and imprecise discourse. And, *pace* Jankélévitch, there are not only French and Russian composers, and infinitely more richness to music than provided in such a deliberately circumscribed aesthetic.

These two contrasting aesthetics need not form a strict either/or, however. In fact one way of conceiving the problems posed by music and time is to adopt their own apparent ontological structure within the response we proffer. Rather than seeking a fixed, stable answer, perhaps the nature of our understanding of these dual transitory entities should be more conceived as the immediacy of insight that is found within a process. The meaning of time, as with music, is perhaps not something which already exists, complete and fixed, but something that itself is in flux, more a process of understanding, in the spirit of Schelling, James, or Bergson.[278] In fact, this is where Bergson's philosophy would seem finally to meet that of his antipode Plato, as outlined in his Seventh Letter. We have come—if but temporarily—full-circle.

Drawing together the strands of this lengthy account in order to offer some form of close, however provisional, we noted earlier that even without going into the seemingly insoluble problems of defining the self there appear to be aporias or lacunae in any definition of time. Many differing conceptions of time exist, and no one seems able to agree on one comprehensive definition. Moreover, there are also limits as to how far we can articulate the meaning of music through words. Art, as Kant, Schopenhauer, and Adorno all agreed, always leaves a remainder.

Such reflections cast light on the consequent insecurity in this context of any musicological enterprise. Although music, as non-verbal conveyor of meaning, may have privileged status in disclosing something about the nature of time and our temporal being, if this is the case then the extent to which we may talk about this capacity in words is also limited. In other words, music transcends verbal discourse; whether this is 'transcendent' in a higher sense is itself beyond the limits of such discourse. The apparently invidious consequence is that to the extent that music escapes verbal articulation (and therefore can be uniquely important, indeed do something that words cannot), we may not be able to

---

[278] I also think here of Sartre's apt formulation of the self: 'This effort to be to itself its own foundation, to recover and to dominate within itself its own flight, finally to *be* that flight instead of temporalizing it as the flight which is fled—this effort inevitably results in failure; and it is precisely this failure which is reflection'. Jean-Paul Sartre, *Being and Nothingness*, trans. Hazel E. Barnes (London and New York: Routledge, 2003), pp. 176–7.

formulate this adequately in words, and conversely, what we can say is to this extent trivial.

We appear to be left with the following options:

- The hermeneutic: we may continue talking about music and time in metaphors and similes, imperfectly, from a limited perspective (despite the plurality of possible approaches, none of which appear to be definitive).
- Drastically (as in early Wittgenstein), to be silent. In fact, instead of talking, we might simply compose, play, or listen to music.[279] Yet (objecting to this in the spirit of the later Wittgenstein) this misses out on the richness of the possible ways of understanding music and, furthermore, our existence in the world. After all, metaphors are an intrinsic part of language use ('meaning is difference' as Saussure held).
- The historical: historicise all verbally expressed accounts of musical temporality, with no claim to their ahistorical philosophic 'truth'. This appears a relatively safe option, but is ultimately derivative and on its own, self-defeating. If no one ventured to come up with new (if necessarily imperfect) perspectives there would be nothing to discuss; verbal meaning would dissipate along with history itself.

Predictably, throughout this book I intend to offer a mixture of the first and third approaches (although a renewed engagement with music, correlate with the second option, should never be spurned). Concerning the first category above, one can also note that while no single interpretation is likely to be uniquely valid or correct *simpliciter*, some interpretations are more obviously flawed, exaggerated, or confused than others. Careful analysis of the terminology used and the assumptions on which such claims are made is an important critical method in alleviating the worse excesses to which hermeneutics may lead. Here, too, historical critique may help us understand the cultural role of earlier theories and ground speculation in something that, if not necessarily timelessly true, at least holds meaning for a particular point in history. For just as with time, we cannot escape from history, from our own historical situation.

As we saw at the opening of this chapter, music reflects the understanding of time of a particular historical period and cultural milieu. This has clear bearing on the concerns of the present chapter, since objects or activities such as music may well be constructed to support particular, unconscious beliefs

---

[279] Mendelssohn, for instance, appears to have taken this option, as a result of his belief that words were often too unclear for music and not the other way around.

about the nature of the world around us and our mode of consciousness. The understanding of psychological time as pure flux, for instance, peaks in the late Romantic era, when music is likewise stylistically most suited to express such a conception: the notion of an absolute, ahistorical and unsullied subjectivity is questionable. In fact the very reciprocity of musical temporality and subjective consciousness, while arguably present for much of history, is a belief especially prevalent in the Romantic era in Western Europe when the metaphor of organic life becomes all-pervasive in accounts of music.[280] Both music and subjectivity are historical, albeit no less valid as such, since, as we asserted earlier, music constructs an understanding of subjectivity as much as it reflects its pre-given meaning in the world.

'By setting up music as a "working model" of time' claims Lewis Rowell, 'a culture tries to achieve a satisfactory synthesis of its conflicting understandings of time'.[281] As this chapter has suggested, it is possible that music *might* in some form solve apparent *aporiai* concerning human temporality and existence or speak to us intuitively of higher truths, but we cannot really demonstrate this. Such resolution would be necessarily untranslatable fully into language, and therefore would still not solve the philosophical problem in its own, conceptual terms. At best, we could claim that music holds out an analogical demonstration of the possibility of such resolution. This conclusion may on the face of it appear unsatisfactorily, but it should not be begrudged. As Ricoeur argues concerning the conundrums humans have encountered with time and Augustine's original overcoming of them through song, 'poetical transfiguration alone, not only of the solution but of the question itself, will free the aporia from the meaninglessness it skirts'.[282]

Music mediates between our contradictory understandings of time and our temporal existence, both reflecting a particular historical understanding of what it is to exist in time, and reciprocally constructing our cultural understanding of this. Since at least the early nineteenth century, if not indeed earlier, music's particular ability to instantiate time has been seen as holding up a mirror to the temporal constitution of the self, as able to disclose aspects of our being that words and conceptual thought could not realise. Do we ask any more, philosophically, of art? Even if some may disagree about the nature of this vision, we can probably

---

[280] This point also illustrates how much language use is already implicated in constructing musical meaning, despite the fact that musical meaning cannot be subsumed into verbal expression. Inevitably the present book is heavily involved in this relationship (a feature that will become almost paradoxical in chapter 6, which draws on literary expressions of music's capacity for transcending literary expression).

[281] Rowell, 'The Subconscious Language of Musical Time', 98.

[282] Ricoeur, *Time and Narrative*, vol. I, p. 7.

still agree with Heidegger that we are most likely to understand time 'only when this understanding culminates in the sort of reflections most suited to bringing ourselves face-to-face with our temporalness'.[283] At once unfathomably obscure and translucently clear, music forms one of the most rewarding paths towards such understanding.

---

[283] Heidegger, *The Concept of Time*, p. 71, translation slightly altered.

‖ 3 ‖

Memory and Nostalgia in Schubert's Instrumental Music

Auch ich war in Arkadien geboren,
Auch mir hat die Natur
An meiner Wiege Freude zugeschworen.
(I, too, had been born in Arcadia,
Nature, too, in my cradle,
Had promised me joy.)

       —Friedrich Schiller, 'Resignation'[1]

where art thou,
My country? On thy voiceless shore
The heroic lay is tuneless now—

       —Byron, 'The Isles of Greece'[2]

It is a veritable platitude of music history that if Beethoven was the commander of musical time, Schubert was no less the master of musical memory. Adapting Carl Dahlhaus's formulations, one looked forwards, the other back.[3] For one (according to Adorno) a fifteen-minute movement appeared to exist as a moment, for the other a beautiful moment became an eternity. Invariably, it would seem, all accounts of Schubert's instrumental music must commence with the binary opposition formed with the figure of Beethoven (this chapter is obviously no exception). And moreover, pleading for Schubert to be measured 'on his own terms', which differ from Beethoven-orientated norms, is almost as old as the comparison itself.[4]

---

[1] Friedrich Schiller, *Sämtliche Gedichte und Balladen* (Frankfurt am Main: Insel Verlag, 2004), p. 129.

[2] Byron, *Don Juan*, Canto III, LXXXVI, 5, in *The Poetical Works of Lord Byron* (London: Oxford University Press, 1909), p. 683.

[3] Carl Dahlhaus, 'Sonata Form in Schubert', in Walter Frisch (ed.), *Schubert: Critical and Analytical Studies* (Lincoln, NE: University of Nebraska Press, 1986), p. 8.

[4] Hermann Keller relates that 'already in 1920 Armin Knab had promoted ceasing viewing Schubert's sonatas as merely impeded Beethovenian sonatas; we must approach them with a completely different attitude' ('Schuberts Verhältnis zur Sonatenform', in *Musa-Mens-Musici: im Gedenken an Walther Vetter* [Leipzig: Deutscher Verlag für Musik, 1969], p. 293). Such claims are repeated by both Dahlhaus ('Sonata Form in Schubert', p. 1) and Peter Gülke ('Zum Bilde des Späten Schubert', in *Musik-Konzepte Franz Schubert*, eds. Heinz-Klaus Metzger and Rainer Riehn [Munich: Edition Text + Kritik, 1979], p. 158).

As we have seen in the first chapter, though, Beethoven's own music is already liable to collapse the all-too-ready distinctions between an 'intensive' teleological time experience and an 'extensive' or even purportedly timeless state, quite unaided by his younger Viennese colleague. It is not so much the case that the time sense suggested by Schubert's music differs from Beethoven's *simpliciter* as that both these composers, living alongside each other in 1820s Vienna, departed from the temporal qualities formed by Beethoven's 'Heroic' style some twenty years earlier. Late Beethoven is closer in musical temporality as well as historical time to Schubert than to his all-conquering heroic self.[5]

Yet there persists a sense in which, even allowing for the considerable exaggeration and crude dualisms created by music historiography, Schubert's music *is* quite distinct from Beethoven's, whether that in intensive middle-period, extensive late-middle period, or timeless late temporal mode. Playing down the distinction runs the risk of fitting one composer into the Procrustean bed of his fellow traveller. Qualities of memory, reminiscence, fatalism, wandering, circularity, or non-teleological lyricism, dwelling on the sensuous present, seem to constitute some of the most characteristic and endearing attributes that make Schubert Schubert, as reception history attests. This chapter examines how such nostalgic subjectivities are constructed in Schubert's music and the language used to describe it. It does not ultimately seek to overturn the now habitual associations between Schubert and memory, but rather to question a little more deeply how they are—or might better be—supported, how music may suggest the actions of memory and temporal consciousness. It looks principally at the String Quartet in A minor, D. 804 ('Rosamunde'), a work hitherto ceded little discussion in the discussion of Schubert and memory, though it further draws on such staples of the Schubertian memory discourse as the Quartet in G, D. 887, and Piano Sonata in B♭, D. 960.

Memorabilia: Theoretical Preliminaries

In considering the question of music and memory two fundamental factors are worth bearing in mind from the start, ideas which will reappear in different forms throughout the ensuing discussion. First, it would generally be agreed by most philosophers that memory requires both a subject and an object—that doing the remembering and that which is remembered.[6] Secondly, as Aristotle,

---

[5] As will be taken up in the subsequent chapter, the tendency to imply a single Beethovenian temporal norm based only on the intensive heroic style has misled our ability to understand the sheer variety of both the music of Beethoven and of the nineteenth century as a whole.

[6] See Paul Ricoeur, *Memory, History, Forgetting*, trans. Kathleen Blamey and David Pellauer (Chicago: Chicago University Press, 2006), pp. 3–4.

the earliest systematic examiner of the topic, states, 'memory relates to what is past'.[7] Memory involves time, specifically the relation between past and present.

How memory works—if there are not indeed multiple types and mechanisms—is still being explored and disputed, albeit nowadays more within the discipline of psychology than philosophy. How the interaction of the two factors set out above might be manifested in music is likewise open to many different permutations and interpretations. Most obviously, a human listener (the subject) may hear or recall in their head music (the object) they have heard before at some earlier point in time, and recognise that they have already heard it. This is simply memory—it is only musical in terms of the nature of the object. Memory is obviously involved in the perception of all music, indeed in all modes of understanding.[8] Towards the other end of the memory spectrum, more interestingly—and more problematic too—is the common formulation of music (as subject, having been somehow attributed agency) remembering its own earlier themes (the object of its memory). Many variations are possible between these two extremes.

Thus the remembering subject may range from the straightforward example of the present-day listener, to the composer (the biographical subject), his or her contemporary audience, the 'composer' construed as aesthetic subject (the lyric 'I'—or in collective terms, if speaking on behalf of his or her fellow people, 'we'), or even the music 'itself'. In some cases it is indeed unclear who or what is remembering. The object of memory is more consistently 'music', though even here one might speak figuratively of experiences being remembered rather than simply themes. Similarly, concerning the question of pastness, different possible types of 'memory' in music may also be briefly summarised. Music may quote or allude to past music—to a general earlier historical style, to a specific earlier historical composition, an earlier work by the same composer, or to the specific piece's own musical 'past', either at the multi-movement level (what is commonly known as cyclic form) or within a movement (which raises the question of what differentiates memory from mere formal repetition, if anything).[9] Furthermore, one might ask if there are semantic associations bound up with any of these categories above. Might the allusion involve a textual reference to something that creates a further, verbal web of memory or are we projecting a

---

[7] Aristotle, *On Memory*, 449[b]14, *The Complete Works of Aristotle*, vol. I, p. 714.

[8] Clearly there are a host of technical ways in which memory is practically involved in musical perception and performance—the role of generic expectation, the 'non-sounding' elements of music (e.g., form), motor mechanisms of performance, et cetera—which are extraneous to the more hermeneutic sense of musical memory investigated here.

[9] See Andreas Dorschel, 'Das anwesend Abwesende: Musik und Erinnerung', in Andreas Dorschel (ed.), *Resonanzen: Vom Erinnern in der Musik* (Vienna: Universal Edition, 2007), pp. 19–22.

composer's supposed state of mind, their biography, onto the music's aesthetic subject? More awkward (but also more intriguing) is the question of how music, without alluding to anything which can be shown to have been heard prior to it, may already sound like a memory.

This theme of memory easily spills over into the related idea of nostalgia. In its original, etymological meaning—as 'longing for home', whether literally or more figuratively—the concept of nostalgia implies spatial distance more immediately over any temporal loss, but obviously relies on memory and thus may easily blur with the longing not so much for a lost place but as for a lost time—the sense in which it is commonly used today. Thus nostalgia in music invokes pastness, specifically loss. It dwells on the absence or distance; it is memory with an emphasis on memory's affective modality, the emotive aspect of longing. Nostalgia has long been associated with Schubert. As Christopher Gibbs notes,

> The theme of nostalgia also has its origins in the composer's own time, which is somewhat surprising given that it would seem to require temporal mediation. . . . The air of nostalgia comes not only from verbal accounts [e.g., later reminiscences of his friends] but maybe even more strongly from visual images [e.g., posthumous paintings of the Schubert circle], from Schubert's own wistful music, and especially from later arrangements of it.[10]

This idea of nostalgia, alongside the simpler variants of musical memory involving allusion to earlier styles and works, is perhaps the most straightforward starting point for exploring the connection of memory and nostalgia with Schubert's music.

References to Earlier Music and the Broader Construction of Nostalgia

One of the most perfect and moving crystallisations of the sense of pastness, loss, and nostalgia within Schubert's oeuvre is the String Quartet in A minor, D. 804—a 'beautiful and intensely personal' work in Sir George Grove's words 'which has been not wrongly said to be the most characteristic work of any composer'.[11] Composed in February 1824, the piece was first performed soon after

[10] Christopher Gibbs, ' "Poor Schubert": Images and Legends of the Composer', in Christopher Gibbs (ed.), *The Cambridge Companion to Schubert* (Cambridge: Cambridge University Press, 1997), p. 52.

[11] Sir George Grove, *Beethoven, Schubert, Mendelssohn*, ed. Eric Blom (London: Macmillan, 1951), p. 232.

by the Schuppanzigh Quartet on 14 March and was the only one of Schubert's quartets to be published in his lifetime. Schubert's later biographer John Reed has aptly described the quartet as 'in emotional terms, a Romantic excursion to the land of lost content', a work '"about" disenchantment, and the loss of innocence'.[12]

Schubert's state of mind during the time of the quartet's conception is revealed in a letter the composer wrote to Kupelwieser on 31 March 1824, often cited in connection with this piece and the following quartet in D minor ('Death and the Maiden', written close on the heels of the A minor), both of which are referred to later in the letter:

> Think of a man whose health will never be right again, and who from despair over this always makes things worse instead of better, think of a man, I say, whose brightest hopes have come to nothing, for whom the happiness of love and friendship offer nothing but at best pain, whose ardour (at least stimulating) for beauty threatens to forsake him, and I ask you, if he is not a miserable, unhappy man?—'My peace is gone, my heart is heavy, I shall find it never, nevermore', so I may well sing this every day now, for every night, when I go to sleep, I hope to wake no more, and every morning only heralds yesterday's grief.[13]

Biographically this dejection and hopelessness is explainable in several ways, most significantly of which was the consequences of the presumed venereal infection Schubert had been diagnosed with little over a year earlier and which was incurable in his day. The early months of 1824 were spent following a Spartan dietary regime which seems to have alleviated the symptoms of syphilis somewhat, even if it did nothing for Schubert's state of mind.[14] Furthermore, the turn to chamber music initiated by this quartet was made in the wake of the failure of Schubert's concerted attempts at conquering the operatic and theatrical stage in the two preceding years, most recently with *Rosamunde*.

Maurice Brown describes Schubert's mood at this time as being one 'of aching regret for the vanished days of his youth'.[15] In his A minor Quartet a substantial

---

[12] John Reed, *Schubert (The Master Musicians)* (Oxford: Oxford University Press, 1997), pp. 105, 130.

[13] Schubert, letter to Leopold Kupelwieser, 31 March 1824, in Deutsch, *Schubert: Die Dokumente seines Lebens*, p. 234, translation modified from *Schubert: A Documentary Biography*, p. 339.

[14] Elizabeth Norman McKay (*Franz Schubert: A Biography* [Oxford: Oxford University Press, 1996], p. 164) dates the onset of syphilis as being probably in November 1822—the same time as the 'Unfinished' Symphony. It is indeed hard for listeners not to hypothesise a connection between life and art by hearing something of this sense of dread in the B minor Symphony, the contemporaneous 'Wanderer' Fantasy, or the Piano Sonata in A minor, D. 784, written the following February.

[15] Maurice J.E. Brown, *Schubert: A Critical Biography* (London: Macmillan, 1958), p. 179.

part of this sense of loss and longing for vanished innocence is embodied through the use of allusions to earlier pieces—in the sense of their status as musical memories of these previous works, the sometimes fragmentary quality of their appearance in the quartet, and last but not least in their potential semantic associations. Nicholas Rast has emphasised in this context that this 'prominent use of quotations from earlier works signif[ies] a new departure' for Schubert in his successful reengagement with chamber music that started with D. 804.[16]

Most overtly significant of these allusions for the current discussion, though not the most materially substantial, is the well-known citation in the third-movement menuetto of the haunting opening figure from Schubert's earlier 'Strophe aus Schillers *Die Götter Griechenlands*', D. 677, written in November 1819 (Ex. 3.1a & b). Schiller's poem, which might similarly be described as one of his most personal and beautiful, describes the disenchantment of the world and its present alienation from the supposed spiritual unity and wholeness of ancient Greece, a quintessential theme of both Schiller and the wider German philhellenism of which he was perhaps the most prominent advocate. (This nostalgia for what many German-speaking intellectuals perceived as Europe's spiritual homeland had been given a more recent twist by the declaration of Greek independence on 1 January 1822, precisely midway between Schubert's setting of Schiller's poem and his composition of the A minor Quartet. But as we saw, nostalgia is in practice more about longing for a lost time than a lost place.) Strophe 12, that set by Schubert, runs as follows:

Schöne Welt, wo bist du? Kehre wieder,	*Beauteous world, where art thou? Return again,*
Holdes Blütenalter der Natur!	*Sweet springtime of nature!*
Ach, nur in dem Feenland der Lieder	*Alas, only in the magic land of song*
Lebt noch deine fabelhafte Spur.	*Lives on your fabulous trace.*
Ausgestorben trauert das Gefilde,	*Deserted the plains mourn,*
Keine Gottheit zeigt sich meinem Blick,	*No god reveals himself to my view,*
Ach, von jenem lebenwarmen Bilde	*Ah, from that living picture*
Blieb der Schatten nur zurück.	*Remains behind only the shadow.*

Graham Johnson has perceptively commented on the original song's curious, if not deliberate, incompleteness: 'it is as if we are ruefully contemplating fragments of a broken Greek vase; we feel certain that we will find the missing

---

[16] Nicholas Rast, ' "Schöne Welt wo bist du?": Motive and Form in Schubert's A Minor String Quartet', in Brian Newbould (ed.), *Schubert the Progressive: History, Performance Practice, Analysis* (Aldershot: Ashgate, 2003), p. 81.

Ex. 3.1a Schubert: 'Strophe aus Schillers *Die Götter Griechenlands*', D. 677 (1819), first version, bb. 1–8

piece to render it whole once more, but this, like the belief that we can travel backwards in time, is cruel illusion'.[17] In fact the song's fragmentary quality was even more pointed in its first version, in which the questioning figure over a dominant pedal in the piano's introduction and postlude—the music cited directly in the quartet—is left open without the bass ever resolving to the tonic. Sometime later Schubert amended his manuscript in lead pencil to the present, belated resolution to a root-position A minor. Richard Kramer, for one, laments the revision: with the original 'irresolute, fundamentally dissonant' $^6_4$, Schiller's question was 'made to echo into eternity'.[18] In turn, Rast suggests that 'Schubert's recollection of this apparently fragmentary song . . . quotes only fragments'—fragments of a fragment. And as Grove describes Schubert's original song, it is a 'beautiful fragment' (one strophe) from Schiller's longer (sixteen-strophe) poem.[19]

For many commentators, this poem serves as the underlying theme of the quartet, both in expressive content and (more questionably) in musical material. Susan Wollenberg, for instance, notes how the incipit from 'Die Götter

[17] Graham Johnson, notes to Hyperion Schubert Edition, vol. 14, CDJ33014 (1992), p. 9.

[18] Richard Kramer, *Distant Cycles: Schubert and the Conceiving of Song* (Chicago: Chicago University Press, 1994), p. 53.

[19] Rast, ' "Schöne Welt wo bist du?" ', p. 86; Grove, *Beethoven, Schubert, Mendelssohn*, p. 246.

Ex. 3.1b Schubert: String Quartet in A minor ('Rosamunde'), D. 804 (1824), third movement, bb. 1–12

'Griechenlands' is inverted at the beginning of the trio and later echoed in the opening of the finale. James Sobaskie also contends that 'Die Götter Griechenlands' influences more than the third movement: the opening melodic motive of the quartet—the descending triad E-C-A in bars 3–4—may be said to be taken from the setting of '[wo] bist du?', though elsewhere the plausibility of the conjectured links is perhaps more strained.[20] More generally and probably persuasively, the major-minor interplay across the quartet, pronounced even for Schubert, seems to take its cue from the framing of the A major 'Kehre wieder . . .' by the A minor question in the song, 'Wo bist du?', especially within the first movement. Thus, for Alfred Einstein, the distinction between the Romantic lament for a lost world and the only remaining trace that survives in the 'fairyland of song' expressed in Schiller's text is symbolised in the contrast between A minor and A major which is taken up in the first movement of the quartet

---

[20] Susan Wollenberg, *Schubert's Fingerprints: Studies in the Instrumental Works* (Aldershot: Ashgate, 2011), pp. 201–2, ftn 11; James William Sobaskie, 'Tonal implication and the gestural dialectic in Schubert's A Minor Quartet', in Brian Newbould (ed.), *Schubert the Progressive: History, Performance Practice, Analysis* (Aldershot: Ashgate, 2003), pp. 53–79.

Ex. 3.2a Schubert: String Quartet in A minor, D. 804, first movement, bb. 1–6

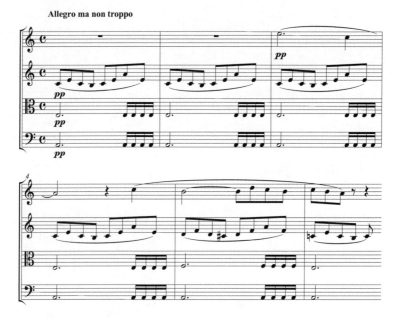

'as the basic principle governing its form and content. Thus in the instrumental work he gave expression to something he could only hint at in the song. It is not a "programme" . . . but a symbol'.[21]

The potential allusions to earlier songs do not stop here, however. Jack Westrup, picking up the suggestive allusion to 'Gretchen am Spinrade' in Schubert's letter to Kupelwieser, claims that 'something of the mood of [that] song has filtered into the first movement of the A minor quartet, particularly in the restless accompaniment which starts two bars before a melody is heard'.[22] Though hardly a direct quotation, there is nonetheless something unmistakably similar in the second violin's mesmeric, sinuous quavers weaving around degree 3̂, underpinned by the fatalistic repeated tattoo-like figure in cello and viola (Ex. 3.2a & b; the accompaniment to the first subject proper of the 'Unfinished' Symphony is similarly called to mind). The twisting line in the second violin might be thought of as further rematerialising in the constant quaver murmuring appearing in that instrument within the ensuing two movements.

Most famous, though, is the reuse of material for the second movement of the quartet, which gives rise to the subtitle affixed to Schubert's work. The second

---

[21] Alfred Einstein, *Schubert: The Man & His Music*, trans. David Ascoli (London: Cassell, 1951), p. 192.

[22] J.A. Westrup, *Schubert Chamber Music (BBC Music Guides)* (London: BBC, 1969), p. 31.

Ex. 3.2b Schubert: 'Gretchen am Spinnrade', D. 118 (1814), bb. 1–6

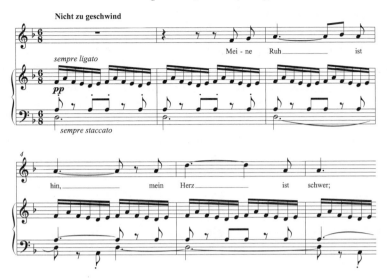

movement might seem a memory to the listener, either from the B♭ Entr'acte (andantino) from *Rosamunde*, D. 797, or in distorted form, the Impromptu in B♭, Op. 142/D. 935 No. 3 (1827). The latter was composed several years after the quartet so its status as a memory is possible only for a latter-day listener not overly concerned with compositional chronology, but the *Rosamunde* borrowing might constitute an inter-opus memory or even a projected (biographical) memory by Schubert. The staging of *Rosamunde*, as is well known, was a failure. Schubert's music itself received some praise, but the production was a flop and was taken off after only two performances. This marked the last effort on Schubert's part to attain success on the stage for some time, after two years of fruitless struggles with operatic and theatrical projects. For the composer, disillusioned by the fate of *Rosamunde*, the memory of this piece must have held connotations of disappointment. It would thus be reasonable to say, as with John Reed, that disillusion became the theme of the quartet he subsequently wrote.[23]

Despite the extensive critical attention devoted to characterising the quartet in terms of Schiller's poem, the work is commonly known as the 'Rosamunde', not the (admittedly more unwieldy) 'Gods of Greece' Quartet. Yet I would like to suggest the two titles are not as disparate as they might at first appear. This connection may be drawn out further through a hermeneutic reading stemming from both the plot of *Rosamunde* and the context of Schubert's encounter with it.

[23] Reed, *Schubert*, p. 94; also see McKay, *Franz Schubert*, pp. 171 and 188–9.

Helmina von Chézy's play *Rosamunde, Fürstin von Cypern* (*Rosamunde, Princess of Cypress*) was performed in Vienna on 20 and 21 December 1823 with incidental music provided by Schubert. The original text for the 1823 Vienna (and subsequent 1824 Munich) production is apparently lost, but there exists a fragmentary draft sketch for the first five scenes dating from the autumn of 1823 and a revised version from sometime later (the exact date is unknown), both of which have recently come to light. Both exhibit some variance in the names of minor figures and from the words used by Schubert in the extant musical numbers; the latter is also in five acts, as opposed to the four-act version advertised on the Viennese programme.[24] In effect, we are offered a tantalising glimpse of *Rosamunde* before and after Schubert's encounter with it, and are left to draw our own conclusions as to their connections with the lost version.

The first, draft conception starts with Rosamunde, on the eve of her seventeenth birthday, sitting at the spinning wheel in her adoptive mother Axa's hut by the sea, reflecting on the flight of time and the passing of her youth:

Die Flamme leuchtet mir so traulich zu,	*The flame shines on me so familiarly,*
Und sinnend, spinnend fliegen hin die Stunden,	*And musing, spinning the hours fly,*
Der kurzen Sommernacht, so bist auch Du,	*The short summer night, just as you,*
Glückselge Kindheit, wie ein Traum entschwunden![25]	*Blessed childhood, vanished like a dream!*

The scenic similarity of Chézy's Rosamunde at the spinning wheel with Goethe's Gretchen, alluded to by Schubert in his letter of March 1824, will not go unnoticed. Though the dramatic outline is similar in the second, revised version, the words of Rosamunde's opening soliloquy have been changed. In fact they seem even more familiar:

Herz, im Busen mir so schwer,	*Heart, so heavy upon my breast,*
Wird dir keine Ruhe mehr?	*Will you give no more peace?*

[24] Till Gerrit Waidelich, 'Ein fragmentarischer autographer Entwurf zur Erstfassung von Chézys Schauspiel "Rosamunde"', in *Schubert durch die Brille: Internationales Franz Schubert Institut, Mitteilungen 18* (Tutzing: Hans Schneider, 1997), 46–57; and Till Gerrit Waidelich (ed.), *Rosamunde, Drama in fünf Akten von Helmina von Chézy. Musik von Franz Schubert. Erstveröffentlichung der überarbeiteten Fassung. Mit einem Nachwort und unbekannten Quellen* (Tutzing: Hans Schneider, 1996).

[25] Chézy, *Rosamunde* (draft version), Act I, Sc. I, ll. 1–4, in Waidelich, 'Ein fragmentarischer autographer Entwurf', p. 47.

In mir war's anders, jüngst noch, wie	*In me it was so different, until of*
so wonnig	*late, blissfully*
Erglühte mir des jungen Tages Licht,	*Glowed in me the young day's light,*
Die Blum' in Thau, auf Wiesen grün	*The dewy flower, on meadows green*
und sonnig	*and sunny*
Strahlt' freudiger als meine Seele nicht.	*Beamed not more joyously than my*
	soul.
Wo bist du hin, des Lebens süße Fülle?	*Where have you gone, sweet fullness*
	of life?
Wo bist du hin, des Herzens traute	*Where have you gone, heart's*
Stille?[26]	*trusted rest?*

Compare Chézy's lines first with the opening lines of 'Gretchen am Spinrade'—
'Meine Ruh' ist hin,/Mein Herz ist schwer/Ich finde sie nimmer/Und nimmer-
mehr'—and, secondly, with the line from Schiller's 'Die Götter Griechenlands'
Schubert set at the opening of D. 677 ('Schöne Welt, wo bist du?')—the two
songs alluded to or directly cited in the first and third movements of Schubert's
quartet. To complete the analogy, the emotional content of the intervening lines
5–8 ('In mir war's anders') seem to match the lost happiness of the *Rosamunde*
borrowing in the second movement of D. 804. Indeed, in Act IV, for the words
that probably followed the B♭ Entr'acte, Rosamunde is found in a charming val-
ley in the mountains, echoing very similar sentiments:

Wie süß und hell der Morgen—wie	*How sweet and light the morning—how*
dieß Thal	*this vale*
Hat seinem Frieden traulich mich	*Has enfolded me familiarly in its peace,*
umfängt,	
Hier ist noch Alles, wie es jemals war,	*Here is everything as it yet was,*
In mir nur ist es anders—Sel'ge Ruh,	*Only in me is it different—blessed rest,*
Werd' ich Dich wiederfinden?[27]	*Shall I find you once more?*

[26] Chézy, *Rosamunde* (revised version), Act I, Sc. 1, ll. 3–10, in Waidelich, *Rosamunde, Drama in
fünf Akten von Helmina von Chézy*, p. 83.

[27] Ibid., pp. 134–5. This scene forms Act IV Sc. 4 in the revised five-act version, though contemporary accounts suggest it opened the four-act version Schubert wrote for. The plot of this act
certainly shows some variance from reports of the première (for instance, Rosamunde does not
pretend to be mad for the benefit of the tyrannical Flugentius/Fluvio in Chézy's revision). See
Franz Schubert: Dokumente 1817–1830, vol. 1: *Texte, Programme, Rezensionen, Anzeigen, Nekrologe,
Musikbeilagen und andere gedruckte Quellen* (Tutzing: Hans Schneider, 1993), pp. 173–80.

Certainly these lines seem to encapsulate perfectly the mood of the second movement within the context of the quartet.

Thus Schubert's reuse of the B♭ entr'acte from *Rosamunde* in the A minor Quartet is not merely a memory from Schubert's own recent past but carries with it further associations of a lost past happiness within the context of its use in the play—a play which appears to echo the texts associated with the musical memories found in the quartet's two surrounding movements. Perhaps D. 804 should be named the 'Rosamunde' Quartet after all. Though brought up a humble shepherdess, Schubert's Cyprian princess holds her own with the Grecian gods.

A different type of nostalgia is created in the quartet by allusion to past musical styles, most evidently in the third movement. By 1824 a minuet was certainly a little old-fashioned, and such is the pervasive air of regret with which Schubert invests the music that it readily evokes a sense of temporal distance and loss. 'Is this really a minuet, or merely a reminiscence of the genre?' asks Sobaskie, 'a nostalgic reflection, or perhaps an ironic commentary on a genre whose time has long passed?'[28] Peculiarly distinctive is the manner in which the initial questioning figure from Schubert's setting of Schiller is repeated not once but twice, heard three times in all as if the music is dwelling on the verge of remembering. The written-out pause over the fifth bar of the movement is liminal in function, the ineffable boundary between the present and the memory of the minuet that is summoned up.

If there seems something gently, almost wistfully archaic in the very use of a minuet, the musette-like drone of the trio is unmistakably Arcadian in its pastoral tone, a glimpse of a now-departed world surely too beautiful, too happy, to be true. Schubert's trio forms an idyll in the midst of a Schillerian elegy, the genres famously theorised by Schiller with respect to this same universal homesickness in *Über naïve und sentimentalische Dichtung*. In a letter written some months later, Schubert laments Schiller's same overriding theme of the mundanity of the present compared with the greatness of the past. In John Reed's paraphrase:

> The idle time, which hinders the fulfilment of all greatness, destroys me too. Even golden verse is foolishly mocked by the people, no longer attentive to its powerful message. Only by the gift of sacred art can we still image forth the strength and achievements of former times.[29]

---

[28] Sobaskie, 'Tonal implication and the gestural dialectic in Schubert's A Minor Quartet', p. 55.

[29] John Reed, *Schubert*, p. 105, a compression of Schubert's letter to Schober, 21 September 1824, in Deutsch, *Schubert: Die Dokumente seines Lebens*, pp. 258–9/*A Documentary Biography*, p. 375.

Such sentiments echo distinctly the message of *The Gods of Greece*. Only in art—more specifically, the enchanted realm of song—can one perceive the trace of this lost world of spiritual perfection. Or as Schiller expresses it in the final strophe of his poem:

Ja, sie kehrten heim, und alles Schöne,	*Yes, they returned home, and took*
Alles Hohe nahmen sie mit fort,	*All that is beautiful, highest with them,*
Alle Farben, alle Lebenstöne,	*All colours, all tones of life,*
Und uns blieb nur das	*And with us remains only*
entseelte Wort.	*the desouled word.*
Aus der Zeitflut weggerissen, schweben	*Torn from the flight of time, floating*
Sie gerettet auf des Pindus Höhn,	*They escaped to the heights of Pindus,*
Was unsterblich im Gesang soll leben,	*What should live on undying in song,*
Muß im Leben untergehn.	*Must disappear from life.*

The claim that this lost world of content and unity may survive only in song obviously has great resonance for the undisputed master of the German *Lied* and arch-lyricist among composers. In an insightful article on Schubert's lyrical sonata forms and their distinctive form of musical temporality, Su Yin Mak proposes with reference to just this poem of Schiller that 'in Schubert the cantabile style, with its long association with lyricism in music, often functions as a musical topic ... to represent the ideal of song'.[30] Though concentrating on other chamber works, most notably the Piano Trio in E♭, D. 929, Mak's argument clearly makes a valuable point in relation to D. 804. The role of *song* in the quartet, its pervasive lyricism, may hold a deeper hermeneutic meaning vis-à-vis Schiller's claim for this art. The lyricism of the A minor Quartet is pronounced even for Schubert. Westrup has commented on how the two-bar introduction for the opening movement's first subject is unusual: despite his habitual lyricism, Schubert normally refrains from starting an instrumental movement with anything sounding like a song. The second subject, moreover, starts with minimal transition, just as if it were another, different song.[31] This is perhaps the most consistently song-like sonata form Schubert ever wrote. Admittedly the second movement, taken from *Rosamunde*, is not actually a song, but its gentle lyricism is unmistakable, and while the last two movements are essentially dance-like, a lyrical quality is rarely absent.

---

[30] Su Yin Mak, 'Schubert's Sonata Forms and the Poetics of the Lyric', *Journal of Musicology*, 23 (2006), 294.

[31] Westrup, *Schubert Chamber Music*, pp. 32–3.

And what of the finale? 'Can a work with three such movements end on a gay or triumphant note in the fourth?' Einstein asks. 'It admittedly ends in the major . . . but—as a number of mysterious phrases suggest—without any real consolation, in spite of the two loud final chords'.[32] These chords themselves undermine the strength of the work's ultimate close: the weak $\hat{2}$–$\hat{1}$ cadential motion in the cello's bass line (not to mention the preceding tonic acciaccaturas) belie the very stability their fortissimo dynamic endeavours to convey. (This idea would later be taken up in even more intensified form at the close of the C major Quintet, D. 956, in the dark Neapolitan twist that spreads an uncanny shadow over the conclusion of that work.)

Earlier in D. 804, a passage in C♯ minor that functions as the movement's second subject might be thought of as forming a distant memory or echo of this tonal area which had been heard for a significant passage in the minuet's second half (Ex. 3.3). This C♯ tonality has been interpreted by Charles Fisk elsewhere as having a peculiar, fate-laden significance for Schubert—the 'Wanderer' key of the eponymous 1816 song, which crops up again in the 'Wanderer' Fantasy and for significant moments of the last piano sonatas.[33] Besides the uncanny effect of the new, insistent dotted rhythms the irreality of this passage is underscored both by the *pianissimo* marking and its apparent formal subversion. In the context of an A major movement the second theme 'should' be in the dominant, E major. It keeps on slipping there at the end of phrases, but reverts just as insistently to its relative minor. This lower ghostly presence undermines the secondary tonality, and since there is no distinct third theme in the dominant, thematically one may not speak of a normal Schubertian three-key exposition.[34] Not for nothing does Adorno label this theme in the finale a 'phantom'—'the secret that . . . runs like fine criss-crossings through Schubert's entire oeuvre, tangibly approaching and then disappearing'. It has the flavour of a native dialect or homeland, yet there is no such place: it is only a memory. 'He is never further away from that place than when he cites it'.[35]

This movement seems rather an ironic or 'failed' attempt at detachment into a more everyday, quotidian world, whose illusion is regretfully

[32] Einstein, *Schubert*, p. 285.

[33] Charles Fisk, *Returning Cycles: Contexts for the Interpretation of Schubert's Impromptus and Last Sonatas* (Berkeley and Los Angeles: University of California Press, 2001), p. 80.

[34] Though in this case the key of C♯ functions as a straightforward diatonic submediant, one is reminded of Taruskin's apt formulation that 'the flat submediant often functions in "late Schubert" as a constant shadow to the tonic, so that the music seems perpetually to hover on that "edge" of inwardness'. Richard Taruskin, *The Oxford History of Western Music*, 5 vols. (Oxford and New York: Oxford University Press, 2005), vol. III, p. 96.

[35] Theodor W. Adorno, 'Schubert (1928)', trans. Jonathan Dunsby and Beate Perrey, *19th-Century Music*, 29 (2005), 14.

Ex. 3.3 Schubert: String Quartet in A minor, D. 804, finale, bb. 67–78

signalled throughout. John Gingerich has sympathetically commented on the 'Biedermeier' aesthetic (understood non-pejoratively) of Schubert's music in relation to the heroic paradigm of middle-period Beethoven: 'For romanticism's stepchildren of Schubert's generation, the operative paradigm could no longer be heroism but had perforce become loss, and self-consciousness could no longer confidently inhabit telos but must perforce come to terms with the memories of loss. This new kind of retrospective introspection engenders a loss of epistemological innocence, of the naively unified self'.[36] The world Schubert takes us to by the end of his A minor Quartet is a resigned one, but it is one that is also more mature.

Thus we might conceive an overall temporal trajectory for the quartet, moving from the present reality and dread of the first movement ('My peace is gone'), a memory of that lost, idyllic world in the second movement ('Here is everything as it yet was'), the subsequent stage of the loss of that dream and painful longing for that world in the menuetto ('beauteous world, where art thou?') still shot through with idealised glimpses in the pastoral-like trio, followed by the last stage in the finale—a present in which we attempt to forget

[36] John M. Gingerich, 'Remembrance and Consciousness in Schubert's C-Major String Quintet, D. 956', *Musical Quarterly*, 84 (2000), 629.

this pain and move back into the world, albeit a disenchanted one. The finale, the least nostalgic movement, where memories (despite the C♯ minor apparition that flits in and out) are forgone, is hence the only one not to allude to earlier compositions.

As Schubert was to write in a letter to his brother, Ferdinand, a few months later:

> Certainly it is no longer that happy time during which each object seems to us to be surrounded with a shining youthful aura, but rather one of fateful recognition of miserable reality, which I endeavour to beautify as much as possible by my imagination (thank God). We fancy that happiness lies in places where once we were happier, whereas it is actually only in ourselves[.][37]

The Pastness of Music's Object of Memory

The A minor Quartet evokes nostalgia and memory on multiple levels, some audible, others more intellectually, abstractly constructed. It may be used to demonstrate how we can assemble a reading of nostalgia from a web of biographical, allusive, and musical details, freely mixing and combining the composer's own sense of loss, a trope taken from Schiller and the wider range of early nineteenth-century German culture with which Schubert aligns himself, his use of allusions to other pieces and styles, and not least our own disposition to nostalgia.

The question still remains, however, as to how music might be heard as itself possessing the quality of memory. How might we justify the common association between Schubert's music and memory, or at least make this connection analytically more plausible? The difficulties are not insubstantial. Beyond the fact that, as noted earlier, the ways in which the subject and object of memory may be used in conjunction with music are multifold, ranging from the literal to the purely metaphorical, a verbal account basing itself on study of the musical score risks missing a vital part of the sensuous immediacy of Schubert's music that contributes so vitally to the sense of memory.[38] Without analytical grounding, however, the discussion risks becoming amorphous, even contrived.

---

[37] Schubert, letter to Ferdinand Schubert, 16–18 July 1824, in Deutsch, *Schubert: Die Dokumente seines Lebens*, p. 250/*A Documentary Biography*, p. 363 (translation slightly modified).

[38] Dahlhaus rightly notes that 'Schubert is a composer whose musical imagination is to an exceptional degree tied to the sensuous phenomenon' ('Sonata Form in Schubert', p. 7).

A middle way, moving between phenomenological and analytical accounts of the music, appears the best way forward.

Aristotle, we recall, states that 'memory relates to what is past'. He continues 'All memory, therefore, implies a time elapsed'.[39] We might start with concentrating on the pastness of the musical object of memory. As John Daverio has noted, Schumann's influential early account of the Impromptus D. 935 hit upon 'one of the most uncanny aspects of Schubert's music: its richness in musical ideas that, even on their first appearance, are imbued with the quality of a reminiscence'.[40] How can music in itself sound past?

One potential method of temporal marking, albeit quite limited, relates to topic theory or what Kofi Agawu would call 'extroversive' musical signification. A specific musical topic such as the horncall is culturally construed as signifying distance, absence, and thus by association, memory.[41] It is arguable whether such music is heard unmediatedly as 'past', however, or is not rather understood as denoting the past symbolically. Similarly, though almost at the other extreme, a sense of nostalgia might be created simply from an overriding mood of beauty and contentment. In the Piano Sonata in G, D. 894, the limpid simplicity and purity of the opening creates a sense of wholeness and beauty, a state of grace and innocence, which somehow is too good, too pure, to be true. Like a childhood illusion or a *Märchen*, the Arcadian tone of the music is marked as distanced, past, or dreamlike—in other words, not reality.[42] Just as with the trio or second movement of the 'Rosamunde' Quartet, nostalgia seems here as appropriate a term as memory. Both these forms of signifying a quality of pastness are of some, though limited use.

A different approach would be the comparison with another communicative medium. In language, one of the most obvious ways of signalling the prior happening of events is the use of grammatical tense. They have happened. One inevitably recalls Carolyn Abbate's famous claim that 'music seems not to "have a past tense."' 'Can we conceive of some musical phenomenon that has the power of a preterite tense to represent instantaneously the already happened?' she asks. 'Does music have a *way of speaking* that enables us to hear it constituting

[39] Aristotle, *On Memory*, 449^{b}14 & 28, *The Complete Works of Aristotle*, vol. I, p. 714.

[40] John Daverio, '"One More Beautiful Memory of Schubert": Schumann's Critique of the Impromptus, D. 935', *Musical Quarterly*, 84 (2000), 610.

[41] Two classic instances in instrumental music and song respectively are Beethoven's Piano Sonata in E♭, Op. 81a (*Les Adieux* or *Lebewohl*), and Schubert's 'Der Lindenbaum' from *Winterreise*. This topic is masterfully explored by Charles Rosen in *The Romantic Generation*, pp. 116–24ff.

[42] Robert Hatten discusses this connection between Pastoral topic and temporality in 'From Topic to Premise and Mode: The Pastoral in Schubert's Piano Sonata in G Major, D. 894', in *Interpreting Musical Gestures, Topics, and Tropes: Mozart, Beethoven, Schubert* (Bloomington: Indiana University Press, 2004), pp. 53–67.

or projecting events as past?'[43] Her answer seems to be generally 'no' (although some exceptional instances when music works in conjunction with literary narrative or dramatic staging may hold out potential glimpses of this chimerical musical past tense). With regard to her first question—tense—it would be hard to disagree. One might add only that thinking in terms of grammatical tense is neither the most apposite nor the most useful means for considering temporality in instrumental music.

Posed in mildly overstated manner, does tense really exist? Or rather, is tense a fundamental part of reality? Contemporary philosophers of time dispute whether time is indeed tensed (if it even exists). Those espousing the so-called B-theory, the position that probably inspires the most consensus among current analytic philosophers of time, would say that it is not.[44] Some languages (such as Chinese), after all, have no real equivalent to the past or future tenses found in modern European languages; meaningful verbal utterances implicating the past may be made without recourse to tensed verbal conjugations.[45] Even if language and linguistic meaning were inherently tensed, as we saw in the last chapter, it is highly questionable how far one might wish to apply linguistic analogies to music. Music may justly be argued to be a pre-linguistic, precognitive mode of understanding. It is not as if verbal language possesses the capability to explain music fully or adequately, that music should be seen as derivative of language, a lesser or more basic form of it. Tense in the linguistic sense is unhelpful and clumsy here. Not only does a past tense appear not to exist in music, but the very analogy, when posed outside Abbate's immediate context of music and narrative, is moreover misconceived.

Tense seems to provide a red herring, not a thread. Abbate's second question, however, even if seemingly phrased as merely a rhetorical amplification of the preceding question, seems distinct from the first. This may be addressed by a slightly circuitous route.

A more pertinent and indeed fundamental question than that of tense is whether or not memories are actually past at all. Aristotle does not say that they

---

[43] Abbate, *Unsung Voices*, pp. 52–3.

[44] The reference is to the second of McTaggart's three series, that denoting qualities of 'earlier' and 'later' without reference to notions of past, present or future (the 'A' series).

[45] Some philosophers have sought principles for reducing all tensed statements to tenseless sentences (such as Bertrand Russell in 'On the Experience of Time', *Monist*, 25 [1915], 212–33). See further D.H. Mellor, 'The Unreality of Tense', in Robin Le Poidevin and Murray MacBeath (eds.), *The Philosophy of Time* (Oxford: Oxford University Press, 1993), pp. 47–59, and, for a general introduction to this topic, Robin Le Poidevin (ed.), *Questions of Time and Tense* (Oxford, Clarendon Press, 1998). On the complementary idea that grammatical tense might often have little to do with the experience of time see Harald Weinrich, *Tempus: Besprochene und erzählte Zeit* (Stuttgart: Kohlhammer, 1964), and Ricoeur, *Time and Narrative*, vol. II, pp. 61–77.

are past, merely that memories relate to events which are past. Similarly, that other great theorist of time, Augustine, famously held that the present consists of three times—a present of things past (memory), a present of things present (perception), and a present of things to come (expectation).[46] But, as Aristotle notes, this gives rise to a potential problem. Memory involves the paradox of the presence of absence. If the remembered object is present, it is perceived in the present and therefore is not past and cannot be a memory. If it is absent then there is no object. This is solved for him by the idea of an image (εἰκών) before the mind—the presence of a copy of the absent object of memory, which may apply for sound just as for a visual image. Thus for millennia, memory has been linked with the faculty of imagination.[47] This 'wax-imprint' model has been disputed by some theorists (most famously, perhaps, Henri Bergson), though it remains relevant to this day as a more 'primitive' model for contemporary theories of memory storage in neuroscience.

In the lectures on *The Phenomenology of Internal Time Consciousness* Edmund Husserl notes that

> Present memory is a phenomenon wholly analogous to perception. It has the appearance of the object in common with the corresponding perception. However, in the case of memory the appearance has a modified character, by virtue of which the object stands forth not as present but as having been present.[48]

If the image of the object of memory is present to the mind, perceived in the now, what then differentiates the present perception of the image of memory with reality? Philosophers in the empiricist tradition such as Berkeley and Hume have generally seen the difference between present perception and memory as being merely a matter of degree of intensity.[49] Though such accounts would probably appear inadequate now as a comprehensive definition, their point still highlights

---

[46] Augustine, *Confessions*, XI.xx (26).

[47] Aristotle, *On Memory*, 450^{b}11–451^{a}3, *The Complete Works of Aristotle*, vol. I, p. 716; the wax imprint analogy was used earlier by Plato in the *Theaetetus*, 191c. As Abbate goes on to note, citations of earlier music refer to artefacts from the past, but do not thereby create a past tense (*Unsung Voices*, p. 54).

[48] Husserl, *The Phenomenology of Internal Time Consciousness*, §28, p. 83.

[49] See George Berkeley, *A Treatise concerning the Principles of Human Knowledge*, §§30, 33, David Hume, *A Treatise of Human Nature*, Bk I, Pt I, §V 'Of the ideas of the memory and imagination'. The idea is implicit in Locke but undeveloped there. Husserl's account offers some congruence with this view (see *The Phenomenology of Internal Time Consciousness*, §21 'Levels of Clarity of Reproduction') but overall is more complex and would not translate easily for music (ibid., §§14–27, Appendix III; *Ideas: General Introduction to Pure Phenomenology*, §§99–103, 141).

an important distinction in how memory, approached phenomenologically, differs from present perception. The image, the object of memory, is part of the present, though it relates to the past. It must somehow be marked in context as being unreal, weaker, a copy—as Husserl would say, it possesses an 'as if' quality. Hence, in turn, we see why memories and dreams have long been associated.

Musical memories are therefore context dependent. (To this extent they are just like those languages without a past tense.) They must possess a past marking, a modality of pastness, whether implied gesturally, topically, or by whatever other means. They exhibit Abbate's *way of speaking* that enables us to hear [music] constituting or projecting events as past'.

This may be signed in numerous ways. Taking our cue from Berkeley and Hume, the status as memory might be indicated by a difference in intensity. Hence we find such familiar devices as music being heard more weakly through the use of a *pianissimo* dynamic, of timbral weakening (*una corda* pedal for the piano, *sul ponticello* effects), spatial distance in instrumentation (played only on the back desks of the violins or offstage), enveloped by a haze (tremolo or tonally obfuscatory harmony), or lacking the reality of true grounding (in inversion, without bass support).[50] In the A minor Quartet this might help us isolate and explain a peculiar and distinctive feature of the work: how all four movements open *pianissimo* (the middle two also end thus, with a further diminuendo). The opening of Schubert's work offers a dreamlike way into experience, the fainter echo of a beautiful world already lost. Einstein has sympathetically observed in this vein that the two bars before the entry of the melody 'consist of nothing more than harmony, resolved into quiet figuration, and rhythm, isolating the movement, setting it apart and lifting it into a dream-world'. It is as if Schubert wanted to emphasise what music meant to him: 'a moment of ordained time, wrested from eternity and projected into eternity again'.[51]

Alternatively, there may be something elusive about the musical present, a sense of stasis or at least the lack of any dynamic, forward-looking quality. Echoing criticism levelled earlier by Hans Költzsch, for Schubert the theme appears to consist as its own end, not form a means to a higher end or goal ('Selbstzweck, nicht Mittel zum Zweck').[52] Perhaps inevitably, this diagnosis is made to contrast with the temporal sense provided by middle-period Beethoven: as

[50] Similar effects may be seen in cinema (which has also been said to possess no tense): black and white or soft focus gives the stylistic impress of pastness, blurring from one scene to another the movement between different temporal levels.

[51] Einstein, *Schubert*, p. 285. Peter Pesic similarly notes the idea of D. 960's opening as dreamlike, as if the music had been ongoing for some time ('Schubert's Dream', *19th-Century Music*, 23 [1999], 138).

[52] Hans Költzsch, *Franz Schuberts Klaviersonaten* (Leipzig: Breitkopf und Härtel, 1927), p. 77.

Dahlhaus notably formulates it, 'In Schubert, unlike in Beethoven, the most last-ing impression is made by remembrance, which turns from later events back to earlier ones, and not by goal consciousness, which presses on from earlier to later'.[53] Rather than a means to attain a triumphant future, the music dwells on itself, and thus might seem loosely compatible or analogous with memory. Scott Burnham, one of the few scholars to ask in any depth how Schubert conjures up the musical sensation of memory, draws on this same orientation towards the present moment, its sensuous immediacy.[54]

This attention to the present or retention of the past at the expense of the protention of a coming future is commonly construed as resulting from Schubert's characteristic type of motivic working, repetition, and lyricism.[55] Reading a static or even retrospective quality into Schubert's music seems for many listeners inherently correct. Still, it is difficult to substantiate quite why this should be the case; the primarily synchronic, score-based analytical method, indifferent to 'tense', struggles to grapple with the diachronic, 'tensed' properties of memory.[56] If one finds close connections between themes and subtle motivic working (as one frequently will, if one looks for it, in Schubert, just as with Beethoven), what is to distinguish this between passive memory and active development? Suzannah Clark rightly questions why Schubert's motivic technique in the first movement of the G major Quartet should be interpreted by Dahlhaus backwards, nostalgically, rather than forwards (as with Beethoven). Her desultory conclusion is that at best, 'according to Dahlhaus, a moment is a memory if it can be shown in analytical terms to be non-structural'.[57] In this con-text Dahlhaus's alternative concept of 'subthematicism' seems just as pertinent to Schubert as to late Beethoven.

Yet another technique utilised by Schubert is the modified repetition of ideas in which the backdrop or emotive connotation is changed, which might

---

[53] Dahlhaus, 'Sonata Form in Schubert', p. 8. Dahlhaus does, however, make the important pro-viso that the 'teleological energy characteristic of Beethoven's contrasting derivation is surely not absent from Schubert, but is perceptibly weaker'.

[54] Scott Burnham, 'Schubert and the Sound of Memory', *Musical Quarterly*, 84 (2000), 661–3.

[55] On the relation of form, thematicism, temporality, lyricism, and logic in Schubert see further the insightful accounts given by Poundie Burstein, 'Lyricism, Structure, and Gender in Schubert's G Major String Quartet', *Musical Quarterly*, 81 (1997), 51–63, and Mak, 'Schubert's Sonata Forms and the Poetics of the Lyric'. Clemens Kühn also argues that (compared against Brahms's later practice) 'Schuberts Melodik ist für additiv und auflösend statt entwickelnd und fortströmend' ('Schuberts Zeit: Vier Versuche', in Diether de la Motte (ed.), *Zeit in der Musik—Musik in der Zeit* [Frankfurt: Peter Lang, 1997], p. 8).

[56] I am using 'tense' in a broader, non-grammatical sense here to describe the A-series qualities of temporal modality—past, present, future. As noted earlier, memory is arguably not tensed in the specific linguistic meaning of the term, but somehow still carries connotations of pastness.

[57] Suzannah Clark, *Analyzing Schubert* (Cambridge: Cambridge University Press, 2011), p. 174.

suggest the subjective, mutable quality of memory. The object stays the same, but our perspective, our interpretation of it changes. Memory here is not passive but rather constructive. Such could appear the magical shift from A minor to A major in bar 13 of the 'Rosamunde' Quartet's first movement. Edward T. Cone's celebrated remark 'formal repetitions are often best interpreted as representations of events rehearsed in memory' is onto the same point—a comment, not for nothing, made in the context of an article on Schubert.[58] A similar example is provided by Schubert's favoured technique of recasting a melodic contour of pitches in new tonal context. The opening movement of the B♭ Piano Sonata, D. 960, is a classic case in point.[59] Clark has also noted how each time a specific pitch recurs in Schubert (such as in the first movements of D. 887 or 956) it may have a different quality to it. Just as an entire melodic idea can be reclad in new harmonic surroundings, so a single pitch may be presented in different harmonic hues. 'This technique generates the sense of reminiscence, as an important pitch of the past is recast within the present harmonic context'.[60]

Possibly, as is often the case with Schubert, it is as much the way in which this 'memory' is reached that marks it out as unreal, the way in which it appears set off from the perceived temporal modality of the surrounding music.[61] As I will suggest presently, it is more the analogy with the form of remembering that is constitutive of their status as memory, not their actual content. They call upon a different level of consciousness, a different part of the brain. The effect of the stretched, elongated bar near the opening of D. 804's menuetto in moving between different temporal modalities has already been noted. A different, though related effect may be found at the close of the A major Sonata,

[58] Edward T. Cone, 'Schubert's Promissory Note: An Exercise in Musical Hermeneutics', *19th-Century Music*, 5 (1982), 240.

[59] Numerous examples of such reinterpretation of pitches and the general contours of melodic lines can be found throughout the movement, from the opening melody, its G♭ major recasting in bb. 19–23, the C♯ minor transformation initiating the development (bb. 117–21), and finally the sly sleight of hand in the recapitulation, bb. 234–42, where following the earlier duality and the famous mirage of the retransition's bb. 193–203 Schubert effects a seamless move from G♭ to A major by interchanging midphrase variants previously heard on 1̂ and 3̂. (See on this last point the brief but perceptive account in Nicholas Marston, 'Schubert's Homecoming', *Journal of the Royal Music Association*, 125 [2000], 258.)

[60] Clark, *Analyzing Schubert*, pp. 181–2. This point obviously blurs the distinction between the listener's retention of pitch—'actual' memory—and a figurative remembering of the 'musical subject'.

[61] Similarly, in the context of Beethoven's cyclic returns, Kristina Muxfeldt remarks that 'it is the staging of the return as much as the return itself that invites us to hear the passage as a memory'. ('Music Recollected in Tranquillity: Postures of Memory in Beethoven', in *Vanishing Sensibilities: Essays in Reception and Historical Restoration—Schubert, Beethoven, Schumann* [New York: Oxford University Press, 2011], p. 144.)

D. 959. The finale's rondo theme returns at the start of the coda, initially as if whole and complete, but then recurring in broken, tonally drifting fragments, punctuated by silence, as if the strength of the object of memory is dissipating. (This theme might already remind the listener of Schubert's earlier 'Im Frühling', D. 882.)[62]

Above all, Schubert achieves this detachment of the musical present from a sense of dynamic temporal flow through his famed use of harmony, found especially through his penchant for unusual harmonic slippage, or the way in which the apparition may continually slip through equal octave divisions, maximally smooth cycles, which lack an apparent grounding.[63] This may be allied with Schubert's noted propensity for large-scale sequences, whose *locus classicus* must be the development section of the E♭ Piano Trio, D. 929. The circling through parts of equal interval cycles which are themselves taken up in larger sequence provides a dizzying kaleidoscope of harmonies, a tonal weightlessness in which the underlying grounding on the simple functional progression IV–I–V is only abstractly derivable.[64] The auditory temporal experience is both static and hypnotically repetitive, dreamlike, and dissociated.

Thus we can provide some answers to Abbate's question 'Can music, though it exists always in the present moment, create the sound of pastness?'[65] In all of these instances the connection is more-or-less metaphorical. The musical procedures are obviously analogous to long-standing theories of memory, but this is not to claim the music *is* memory—merely that one can understand why it might readily be interpreted as such. In certain cases one might doubt the reality of this analogy or question its abuse by earlier writers. But nonetheless music, and Schubert's especially, is undeniably often heard as invoking memory.

---

[62] The procedure, moreover, is further reminiscent of the Rondo finale in Beethoven's Op. 31 No. 1, which as scholars such as Rosen and Cone have demonstrated was the model for Schubert's movement.

[63] Cf. Hans-Joachim Hinrichsen, 'Die Sonatenform im Spätwerk Franz Schuberts', *Archiv für Musikwissenschaft*, 45 (1988), 47–8: 'Schubert's mature sonata movements demonstrate their emancipation from their Classical models above all through their harmonic layout. Dieter de la Motte speaks appropriately in this regard of the "indifferent equilibrium" of Schubertian harmony. The hierarchical ordering of tonalities in the circle of fifths becomes broadened through the spatial and likewise paratactic assembly of distance'.

[64] In D. 929 the music works up (through alternating major and minor triads) by minor thirds built as diminished sevenths on the (non-present) functional roots IV, I, and V respectively, viz. B–D–F [on A♭]; F♯–A–C [on E♭]; D♭–E–G [on B♭]. The entire development section effectively prolongs the functional harmonic progression IV–I–V, but in a non-functional, unrecognisable manner. Neo-Riemannian analysts invariably have a field day with this movement. Also see Scott Burnham's wonderfully apposite analysis of the finale of the G major Quartet in 'Landscape as Music, Landscape as Truth: Schubert and the Burden of Repetition', *19th-Century Music*, 29 (2005), 36.

[65] Abbate, *Unsung Voices*, p. 54.

Music's Remembering Subject

As some of the preceding examples have already demonstrated, the way in which a given musical passage may be marked as being somehow unreal, set off from 'normal' musical time, and thus offer affordance with the notion of musical memory, may often be created as much through the manner in which it is reached as through its immanent qualities per se. This brings us conveniently back to the subject/object division in the perception of memory. If musical memories may often be most demonstrable through the way in which they materialise, their secret would seem to lie as much in the hypothetical perceiving subject as in the putative object of perception. It is worth broadening our inquiry now into the nature of the subject remembering.

Throughout much of the preceding discussion the nature of the subject doing the remembering has remained unstated and unexplored. Frequently a human subject has been implied, whether an average present-day listener, Schubert himself, or an ideal listener with access to a wealth of arcane contextual knowledge and occasional excess of credulity. Though the precise mechanisms by which humans remember are still being unravelled, we indubitably do have the capacity to remember (the details by which we do so being a matter more for cognitive psychology than the philosophy of music). What on the other hand remains to be developed here is the notion of music remembering, which raises the important issue of subjectivity—the regulative fiction of music as an autonomous persona.

One of the most persistent metaphors in accounts of Romantic music, we recall, is that of music speaking to us in a first person 'voice', the idea of the anthropomorphic musical subject, of music somehow exuding its own consciousness. The inclination of the A minor Quartet towards the lyric, the song-like tone of its opening, would seem only to encourage this link with subjectivity. The first violin, after waiting affectedly for two bars, steps forward to express its lyrical utterance, a speaking voice, *Stimme*. If it be granted that music may be understood as a hypothetical subject exhibiting traits of consciousness, it is obviously not such a great step further to positing that it may remember earlier events occurring within its course. The recurrence of earlier themes or events thus becomes akin to stylised memories; it is not just that we remember the themes but that the music may appear to remember its own earlier self.[66]

An obvious case in point is the recurrence of themes across a multi-movement work in pieces using cyclic form. Perhaps the clearest example of this cyclic technique in Schubert can be found in the work just discussed, the Piano Trio in E♭, where the recurrence of the second movement's mournful cello theme

---

[66] See Michael Steinberg, *Listening to Reason*, pp. 4–11, or my *Mendelssohn, Time and Memory*, p. 30.

(apparently based on a Swedish folksong) in the finale creates a moment of acute pathos, of unrelenting melancholy, the inability to escape from the past. But need this be a memory? Does this imply the music is speaking in the lyric 'I'? In some cases memory seems an appropriate analogy (Beethoven's Op. 101 or Ninth Symphony, Schubert's Violin Fantasy in C, those extraordinary early works of Mendelssohn from this same decade), but cyclic recall need not be interpreted as memory, even if one persists with the idea of musical subjectivity.[67] Just as germane for D. 929 might be the idea of fatalistic return, the folksong as something external to the musical subject's consciousness, even time as being something cyclical (see the following chapter). In many works such as the A minor Quartet, it is rather less obvious that any purported similarity or connection between movements may be heard as constituting a memory.[68] Part of this seems to lie in the question of agency, whether the musical subject appears in active or passive relation to these thematic recurrences.

One of the most characteristic forms of Schubertian cyclicism can be found in the Quartet in G, D. 887. In the second movement the outbreak of tremolos in the contrasting minor section is strongly reminiscent of the opening of the first movement, allied with its familiar unison dotted rhythms and stern minor mode following in the wake of the major. Is this merely a memory of the first movement, or may not both movements be heard, rather, as similar responses to a putative external cause? Similarly, in the third movement and near the end of the finale, the fact that the echoes or reverberations of this idea consist not of the recall of identical themes but of a similar, allusive harmonic gesture (major to minor), dotted minor arpeggiation, and a tremolo *Klang*, suggests the manifestation of similar reactions to a common deeper psychological cause, itself unstated. Somehow the actual object of memory is hidden, at a deeper, subconscious level. It is active, but unheard; the music passively absorbs its aftershocks.[69] The distorted cyclic echoes are not subjective musical memories so

[67] See Elaine Sisman, 'Memory and Invention at the Threshold of Beethoven's Late Style'; Muxfeldt, 'Music Recollected in Tranquillity: Postures of Memory in Beethoven'; or Taylor, *Mendelssohn, Time and Memory.*

[68] Cyclic works that transform material (such as the Wanderer Fantasy) are already less likely to be heard as forming memories; if anything their procedures of thematic development suggest future-orientation. There are many other examples of references, allusions, or echoes between movements in Schubert. The close of the Piano Sonata in A, D. 959, is one of the clearest, which returns in retrograde to the chord progression opening its first movement, a palindromic conception which seems rather too objective, too architectural for memory metaphors. See further Martin Chusid, 'Schubert's Cyclic Compositions of 1824', *Acta Musicologica*, 36 (1964), 37–45.

[69] The possibility of a Freudian reading—the affordance with the idea of trauma, hidden in the subconscious id—is readily suggested: the cyclic metamorphosis of material is comparable to dreamwork, Schubert tapping into a deep, subconscious psychological process in his music.

much as objective reverberations in the musical subject. The dynamic course of the music suggests a sympathetic mirror (*Abbild* Schopenhauer would say) of a deep and multileveled psychological process, the response to returning darker thoughts or situations. In other words, one might say the music mirrors the form of memory, of remembering, not its content.

This contention affords well with a perceptive and persuasive argument made by Scott Burnham, that Schubert's ability to suggest memory in music is due in part to his capacity to 'invest the surface of his music with a compellingly opaque materiality, such that we attend *to* it and not *through* it'.[70] The musical surface need not constitute a memory itself, even though the concentration on its beauty, appearing in the transient present, could give rise to the sense of nostalgia. Our perception of the music takes on an analogous form to our attending to memories—the processes are comparable. The sympathy with the dynamic process of remembering easily affords the comparison.[71]

The argument above is not an either/or, though: it is possible to posit both types of musical memory as being applicable to a composition. First, we have the more straightforward conception of music as being equivalent to a subjective persona remembering, where thematic returns or allusions are equivalent to memories; secondly, the notion that music mirrors subjectivity itself, without its content—the object of memory—being audible. This latter point seems particularly fruitful to explore at greater length.

One of the distinctive ways in which Schubert suggests this flow of consciousness in his music is in its apparent switching between different temporal levels, the interaction between different types or modalities of time. Rather like the reactive subject absorbing cyclic tremors in D. 887, in the A minor Quartet there is a peculiar quality of passivity, even fatalistic acceptance, to the temporal unfolding of the first subject. Just as in the first movement of the 'Unfinished' Symphony, the repeated figurations of the ostinato accompaniment create a sense of the inevitable occurrence of events in time—time, or its offerings, is heard as something external, implacable, probably malign, an objective, impersonal medium into which the self is thrown. This conception is not one sided: the sun may briefly shine, almost unexpectedly (the A major transformation of the

[70] Burnham, 'Schubert and the Sound of Memory', 662–3.

[71] One may note the correlation here with so-called dynamic or sympathetic theories of musical expression, which were coming to prominence within German aesthetics by the turn of the nineteenth century. Charles Rosen offers an insightful discussion of this correlation between music, time, memory, landscape, and expression, citing a review by Schiller describing how music, like landscape painting, represents feelings through their form, not (as in earlier aesthetics) through their content. Just as Hegel would later claim, for Schiller 'the entire effect of music . . . consists in accompanying and making perceptible the inner movements of the spirit analogously through outer ones' (*The Romantic Generation*, pp. 126–31, quotation from 127).

first subject, bb. 23–31)—before quickly melting away again. Yet all this happens, it seems, externally: the subject is a passive participant, who does not know and cannot control when the landscape may briefly lighten.[72] At best, we may enjoy this dream whilst we can. As Schiller writes,

Des Lebens Mai blüht einmal und nicht wieder,	Life's May blooms once and never more,
Was man von der Minute ausgeschlagen,	What one spurns from the moment,
Gibt keine Ewigkeit zurück[73]	Eternity never gives back

Within this inexorable unfolding of predetermined destiny one fitfully obtains the uncanny sense of being caught in a loop. The phrase construction of the first group is a case in point; an eight-bar antecedent (bb. 3–10) is succeeded not by the expected consequent phrase but by yet another antecedent (bb. 11–22), this time internally expanded, closing once again on an imperfect dominant. This is followed at last by the consequent phrase, but one that now, miraculously, is in the major (and thus hardly conforms to that of a normative period in A minor)—a vain hope sternly rebuked at the cadence. Somehow we have remained stuck in the first theme's ambit for longer than usual.[74] Similarly, the erstwhile transition (bb. 32ff) soon finds itself starting over again (b. 44) without having achieved the harmonic goal its transitional rhetoric would lead us to expect, and despite the greater tonal mobility of the cycle of fifths and energy-gain provided by the contrapuntal element introduced, neither does the second attempt leave A minor until the last moment (b. 54). Such repetitions might also explain how, at a larger level, the return to the first subject at the start of D. 804's development section—just as with that of the 'Unfinished' Symphony—sounds so

---

[72] This is consciously alluding to the light-shadow/major-minor analogy that threads its way throughout Schubert reception. A pertinent early example may be found in Grove: 'With Schubert the minor mode seems to be synonymous with trouble, and the major with relief; and the mere mention of the sun, or a smile, or any other emblem of gladness, is sure to make him modulate. Some such image was floating before his mind when he made the beautiful change to A major near the beginning of the A minor Quartet' (*Beethoven, Schubert, Mendelssohn*, p. 246). The image also evinces a close connection with landscape metaphors (see below).

[73] Schiller, 'Resignation', verses 2 and 18, *Sämtliche Gedichte*, pp. 129, 131.

[74] This structure is indeed normalised in the recapitulation by excising the redundant second antecedent, the result being a curiously balanced—or even dualistic—pairing of minor-major periodic subphrases. Burnham speaks of this deliberate redundancy in Schubert's music in the context of how he seems to make a virtue out of sheer length. Scott Burnham, 'The "Heavenly Length" of Schubert's Music', *Ideas*, 6/1 (1999), <http://nationalhumanitiescenter.org/ideasv61/burnham.htm>.

fate-laden in effect.[75] Generically it is hardly unusual to return to the first subject at this point. Presumably the rematerialising of those dark, insidiously repeated rhythms that had momentarily been left behind by the second theme's softer lyricism creates the feeling of inescapable destiny, the subject being enfolded in a larger loop of cyclic recurrence.

This distinctive temporal sense connects with the overriding theme of fatalistic circularity or wandering to be found within accounts of Schubert's music. In Cone's words, Schubert's music after 1822 is permeated throughout by a sense of 'desolation and dread', a feature usually interpreted as a response to the onset of syphilis in the composer and his realisation of the inevitability of an early death.[76] In technical terms this is instantiated by a particular use of repeated movement, most typically a walking or trudging figure (as in 'Gute Nacht' and 'Der Wegweiser' from *Winterreise* or the first Impromptu, Op. 90/D. 899). It gives the sense of an unrelenting movement towards a preordained goal, inevitable and implacable, eliding physical motion with a fatalistic temporal sense. In other pieces the seemingly inevitable unfolding of events withdraws into an underlying pulse or framework, such as in the first movement of the A minor Sonata, D. 784 or the present quartet. The music here is not simply an autonomous subject with agency, but may be perceived as one reacting to external events—events which are yet still 'in' the music. The musical subject thus becomes divided, simultaneously subject and object, active and reactive—rather like the divided modern self that as we saw has stalked philosophical attempts to define personal identity since Hume.

The converse seems to be those moments of subjective interiority—movements to a different, inner realm, another temporal or aesthetic level that seemingly does not have to obey external laws or temporal causality. The music exhibits a greater sense of agency here, something closely allied with subjectivity, consciousness's ability to move at will through past time, to repeat, to dream. This quality is especially characteristic of Schubert's second subjects. In the A minor Quartet the sense of relaxation from the unremitting temporal succession of the preceding music is palpable in the secondary theme beginning at bar 59. The five-bar phrase lengths lie outside the regular hypermetric divisions of clock time, and though elements of the earlier music are not entirely absent there is a new feeling of lyrical generosity that breaks free of the previous objective fatalism. The subject appears to fill-out time by its own plenitude, create it actively through its own activity, not simply exist in it passively with resigned acceptance

---

[75] Einstein helpfully avers that Schubert was 'thinking of death' here (*Schubert*, p. 285).

[76] Cone, 'Schubert's Promissory Note', 241. On this topic of wandering and fatalism see for instance William Kinderman, 'Wandering Archetypes in Schubert's Instrumental Music', *19th-Century Music*, 21 (1997), 208–22; Fisk, *Returning Cycles*, esp. ch. 3 'The Wanderer's Tracks', pp. 60–80.

of what time may bring.[77] Such qualities are even more evident in the famous secondary theme of the String Quintet's three-key exposition (an inner plateau of E♭, hovering between C and G, a 'time out of time'), the massive interior loop of D. 887's second group, or the second theme of the 'Unfinished'.[78]

That this escape from an external reality to an interior time may yet be an illusion in the quartet is projected by the continuance not only of gestures redolent of earlier material (the quavers in the viola reminiscent of the second violin's opening accompaniment, the reintroduction of triplets with imitation at the fifth in b. 69) but also by the hint of phrase circularity that has not been entirely abandoned. In effect Schubert is working with two time senses simultaneously—an external, implacable objective time and a warmer inner, subjective time—revealing how the former persists in some subtle form throughout the latter. Such an interpretation might be supported by Charles Rosen's astute analysis of Schubert's fluid movement between external time and internal memory in 'Gretchen am Spinrade'. Schubert's originality of conception is how he represents the poetry phenomenologically: 'it is not the spinning that is objectively imitated by Schubert but Gretchen's consciousness of it. . . . Schubert was able to represent a double time-scale, a relationship so crucial to Romantic poetry, both the sense of the immediate present and the power of past memory and how they interact with each other'.[79]

The implications of such shifts for understanding the temporality of Schubert's music have been emphasised by Robert Hatten. 'Tonal music has an independent capacity to cue various temporal realms by means of sharp musical oppositions, not only in mode, but in key, theme, topic, texture, meter, tempo, and style as well', he suggests. This Hatten links to different psychological states, such as the widely held belief that the opposition between major and minor in Schubert's music represents a conflict between present tragic reality and a happier past.[80] Taking up this theme, Kristina Muxfeldt has further commented on

---

[77] A Heideggerian might characterise the two temporalities as characteristic of Dasein's inauthentic and authentic Being-in-the-World respectively.

[78] Taruskin claims the latter—probably Schubert's must beloved melody—could even be excised completely from the music with no functional loss (*Oxford History of Western Music*, vol. III, p. 110).

[79] Charles Rosen, 'Schubert's Inflections of Classical Form', in Christopher Gibbs (ed.), *The Cambridge Companion to Schubert* (Cambridge: Cambridge University Press, 1997), p. 77. The 'Gretchen' parallel is apt for the A minor Quartet's opening movement, which similarly comes to a shuddering climax over a diminished seventh at its midpoint (b. 140).

[80] Hatten, 'The Pastoral in Schubert's Piano Sonata in G Major, D. 894', p. 55. One of innumerable examples is provided by Reinhold Hammerstein with specific reference to 'Die Götter Griechenlands': 'the minor normally represents grey reality, the banality of the present, pain and suffering; the major, in contradistinction, the world of beauty, of dreams, former happiness and lost love, and not least the consolation of death'. ' "Schöne Welt, wo bist du?" Schiller, Schubert und die Götter Griechenlands', in *Musik und Dichtung. Neue Forschungsbeiträge (Festschrift Viktor Pöschl zum*

Schubert's unsurpassed 'ability to represent the inner movement of experience in sound'. 'In the frequent shifts in mode in *Winterreise*, carefully calibrated to distinguish events as the wanderer's memories, fantasies, or present experiences, modulation through tonal space is used with unparalleled effect to mimic the movements of inner experience'.[81]

The secret behind this switching between different levels commonly lies in Schubert's use of transitions—or rather, his non-use of them. As noted, here in D. 804, for a long time the 'transition' actually goes nowhere. One calls it a transition only on account of its formal position and rhetoric, though it shuns fulfilling the harmonic function it seemingly promises (an even better example of this duplicity will be found in D. 960). The actual harmonic transition occupies a mere four bars of the hundred-bar exposition. Customarily Schubert will achieve this switch through his fabled love of enharmonic modulation. As Burnham says, Schubert's 'often sudden changes of key give us the sense of being instantly transported to another realm'. The new theme appears out of nowhere, approached through unusual modulation, slipped into through some magical harmonic portal.[82] Or as Taruskin puts it, 'It is like passing into another world, another quality of time, another state of consciousness'.[83]

Thus the temporal course of the music readily suggests multiple levels of time or consciousness. Rather than one, linear projection through time (time's arrow) the music may enfold upon itself, loop back, move out of one time to another. Mak's reading of parataxis on a large scale is on to this point.[84] In fact, often the conception is hardly that different from the parenthetical insertion or moments of static dreaming time commentators have read into Beethoven's late music.

Mark Evan Bonds has recently drawn attention to the historical growth of spatial representations of musical form, which depended on new conceptions of mapping time onto space. The idea of the time-line, that historical or narrative

80. Geburtstag), eds. Michael von Albrecht and Werner Schubert (Frankfurt am Main: Peter Lang, 1990), p. 314.

[81] Kristina Muxfeldt, 'Schubert's Songs: The Transformation of a Genre', in Christopher Gibbs (ed.), *The Cambridge Companion to Schubert* (Cambridge: Cambridge University Press, 1997), pp. 137, 126. On this temporal sense in Schubert's lieder, above all in *Winterreise*, see further Anthony Newcomb, 'Structure and Expression in a Schubert Song: *Noch einmal* Auf dem Flusse *zu hören*', in Walter Frisch (ed.), *Schubert: Critical and Analytical Studies* (Lincoln, NE: University of Nebraska Press, 1986), pp. 153–74, and Barbara R. Barry, ' "Sehnsucht" and Melancholy: Explorations of Time and Structure in Schubert's *Winterreise*', in *The Philosophers Stone: Essays in the Transformation of Musical Structure* (Hillsdale, N.Y.: Pendragon, 2000), esp. pp. 190–91.

[82] Scott Burnham, 'The "Heavenly Length" of Schubert's Music'. Also see Wollenberg, *Schubert's Fingerprints*, pp. 47–97, who categorises the different, often 'magical' or special ways in which Schubert gets from one place to another.

[83] Taruskin, *The Oxford History of Western Music*, vol. III, pp. 92–3.

[84] Mak, 'Schubert's Sonata Forms and the Poetics of the Lyric', 301–2.

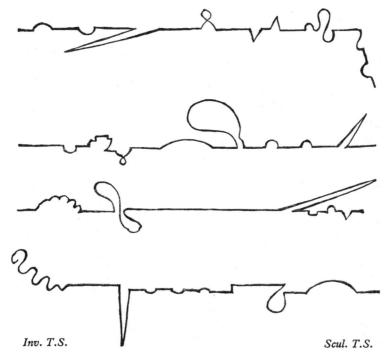

Inv. T.S.   Scul. T.S.

Fig. 3.1 Sample time-lines for his narrative drawn by Laurence Sterne in *The Life and Opinions of Tristram Shandy, Gentleman*, vol. VI, ch. XL (1762)

events in time may be represented linearly, is fairly recent in origin, dating to the mid-eighteenth century. Almost as soon as it appeared, it was lampooned by Laurence Sterne in *The Life and Opinions of Tristram Shandy*, who proposed not unreasonably that no story could really be told in linear fashion: just as no one would travel 'from *Rome* all the way to *Loretto,* without ever once turning his head aside either to the right hand or to the left', so 'a historiographer could not drive on his history' without 'fifty deviations from a straight line' (see Fig. 3.1).[85] One might say the relation between present perception and memory or between external clock time and experienced time in Schubert often follows something akin to the narrative time-lines jestingly drawn by Sterne in *Tristram Shandy*—only even more complex, as the two types of time—ontological and experienced—are in some respects incompatible. One can be represented in a Euclidean two-dimensional space, the other simply not.

[85] Laurence Sterne, *The Life and Opinions of Tristram Shandy, Gentleman*, vol. I (1759), ch. XIV (the time-lines are illustrated in a later volume); Mark Evan Bonds, 'The Spatial Representation of Musical Form', *Journal of Musicology*, 27 (2010), 281–2.

The Reciprocity of Metaphor

As the above discussion has demonstrated, accounts of memory quickly elide with ideas of temporality and these may further blur into notions of consciousness without the latter explicitly speaking of memory. Alongside these three ideas, other familiar Schubertian tropes glide in and out, such as spatially based metaphors of landscape and wandering, and the analogy of dreams. This is a motley collection of musical metaphors, a real pot-pourri of Schubertian themes; one might wonder if they are somehow connected. Are they equivalent, offering multiple ways of viewing the same musical object, or are some more appropriate than others? This fourth and final section will explore the reciprocity of memory, landscape, dreams, and consciousness as instructive metaphors for describing salient qualities of Schubert's instrumental music, touching especially on the Piano Sonata in B♭, D. 960.

The use of landscape metaphors to describe Schubert's music is well established. Grove already touches on this point in commenting that Schubert's music 'changes with the words as a landscape does when sun and clouds pass over it'.[86] This trope would be taken up even more readily by Adorno: 'when it comes to Schubert's music we speak of "landscape."'

> The ex-centric construction of that landscape, in which every point is equally close to the centre, reveals itself to the wanderer walking round it with no actual progress. . . . Those themes know of no history, but only shifts in perspective: the only way they change is through a change of light.[87]

Dahlhaus, with a nod to both Adorno and Rilke, holds that successive variations 'form a cycle insofar as they draw circles, ever expanding circles, around the theme. The variation principle as such is not goal-orientated, but rather resembles a commentary "meandering" about the theme, illuminating it from different sides'.[88] Mak finds that 'Schubert's paratactic repetitions continually revisit the same subject from different perspectives', while Burnham claims Schubert 'gives us time to take in his themes, as if they were works of visual art we could inspect at our leisure, or landscapes through which we could wander'.[89]

---

[86] Grove, *Beethoven, Schubert, Mendelssohn*, p. 241.

[87] Adorno, 'Schubert', 7, 10.

[88] Dahlhaus, 'Sonata Form in Schubert', p. 2.

[89] Mak, 'Schubert's Sonata Forms and the Poetics of the Lyric', 303; Burnham, 'The "Heavenly Length" of Schubert's Music'.

Landscape connects with a sense of spatiality derived from Schubert's use of large sequences and repetition which offers multiple perspectives of the same object, the notion of movement (or wandering) occurring within a larger objective framework, ideas of sunlight and shade resulting from the interplay of major and minor. Most particularly the sense of time suggested by landscape is different and distinctive. It might appear far slower, static, almost—but not quite—timeless. The relationship of musical form to time is seen as resembling that of moving through a landscape. Within the horizon provided by the over-all form the panorama is unchanging, though the successive viewpoints offer changing perspectives of prominent details.[90] Such is the prospect of the opening horn theme in the Great C major Symphony, when encountered again at the close of the first movement, or the craggy opening chords of D. 959, now viewed from the reverse perspective at the close of the sonata. Helpfully for Schubert, one can also look back or wander off on the wayside. Landscape is essentially space and only accidentally time. It is no wonder that, for Alfred Brendel, in Schubert's larger formal repetitions 'the listener is given the chance of wandering twice through virtually the same musical landscape'.[91] One cannot step into the same stream twice, but evidently can wander twice through the same landscape.

But the Schubertian geography is unusual. Burnham rightly comments that Schubert's music 'puts into play a different physics'.[92] The leisurely opening para-graphs of the late B♭ Sonata inhabit this peculiar space (Ex. 3.4). Opening in Tovey's words 'with a sublime theme of the utmost calmness and breadth' the famous pianissimo G♭ trill in the bass soon brings the first phrase to a tempo-rary halt.[93] Brendel sees the G♭ trill as 'the disclosure of a third dimension', and it certainly throws the expected linear course of the music onto a new plane (or plain).[94] But one could see problems besetting the music even before this rather obvious interruption. Take out the G♭, and play the resulting phrase, and it is evident that something has gone wrong with the music by the end of the sixth bar, certainly by the first beat of the seventh. The melody, initially so serene and self-assured, has come to a strange, almost aimless continuation, the

[90] See Rosen's excellent account in *The Romantic Generation*, pp. 124–204, esp. 194.

[91] Alfred Brendel, 'Schubert's Last Sonatas', p. 161. I use the singular form in place of Brendel's 'landscapes', as may be found in an earlier manifestation of the essay in *The New York Review* (2 February 1989, 33). To wander twice through two different (albeit similar) landscapes would entail four traversals. Three would be plausible, as the exposition may be repeated, but—with the exception of the beautiful opening movement of the earlier A major Sonata, D. 664—the second halves of Schubert's sonata movements are generally not (and certainly not by Brendel).

[92] Burnham, 'The "Heavenly Length" of Schubert's Music'.

[93] Donald Francis Tovey, 'Franz Schubert', in *Essays and Lectures on Music* (ed.), Hubert Foss (London: Oxford University Press, 1949), p. 119.

[94] Brendel, 'Schubert's Last Sonatas', p. 154.

harmonies returning twice to the tonic $^6_4$ at a premature stage in the harmonic phrase rhythm. The phrase structure is also disturbed, closing ineffectually on an imperfect cadence halfway through the third bar of the antecedent's continuation, with over four beats of empty metric time to fill up before the consequent phrase should start. (The unexpected materialisation of the G♭ turns this into eight—with a fermata too.) This noble, hymnlike melody has stalled. For the owner of one of the most celebrated 'melodic treasure chests' in compositional history this is not to be expected.[95] The G♭ is not simply an obtrusive external element that destroys the till-then perfect course of the music but something which has filled in and to this extent gratefully obscured a hesitancy or problem already there.[96]

The consequent phrase offers a mild improvement. This time the continuation is less belaboured; the return to the tonic is successfully effected, though occurs again in a weaker 'feminine cadence' which now pushes the continuation phrase into a fifth bar. Three bars, five bars—the continuation still is not quite there.

This time, the G♭ trill offers a way forward. Rather than recoil back in alarm, the music decides to explore this curious new realm for itself. Now the familiar melodic line is reinterpreted in this new context of G♭ rather than B♭, on $\hat{3}$ rather than $\hat{1}$, and in fact it seems to find this quite pleasing. So much so, that the continuation just grows and grows. Through repetition and sequential working the music picks up energy. Even though the music has still been unable to come up with a completely satisfactory phrase to close its periodic structure, why not leave this setback behind and push on (whilst the going is good) to the secondary theme? It is turning into a transition. Where exactly G♭ major will lead to we still do not know, but the music is going somewhere at last. An enharmonic G♭^{7} seems to herald a promising new turn of events—and all of a sudden the music tumbles back into B♭ and—even more unforeseen—the theme of the very opening.

It is as if, having finally left home after much hesitation, Schubert's wanderer has crossed the brow of the surrounding hills and is picking up speed and confidence on his travels. Earlier uncertainties and setbacks are put firmly behind him just as his home lies as he strides on. Spying a stray enharmonic entity by the wayside he turns a corner and there—suddenly—he sees his familiar village

---

[95] Adorno, 'Schubert', 10.

[96] On the trill's 'otherness' or alterity see the consideration by Charles Fisk in 'What Schubert's Last Sonata Might Hold', in Jenefer Robinson (ed.), *Music and Meaning* (Ithaca, NY: Cornell University Press, 1997), pp. 179–200. It should be noted here that the original version of the theme in Schubert's draft manuscript was actually written without the first G♭ trill (Marston, 'Schubert's Homecoming', 255).

Ex. 3.4 Schubert: Sonata in B♭ major, D. 960 (1828), first movement, bb. 1–23

lying before him once again. Although he has been travelling the whole time with the sun behind him (save perhaps for its occasional obscuring by the distant thunderclouds Tovey alludes to in bars 8 and 19) and has surely gone some distance, space has looped around on itself and he finds himself back where he was.

The topography of this landscape is non-Euclidean. Or at least it is not merely three-dimensional but belongs to a higher order (like some weird conception of Escher).[97] Such is Schubert's ability to slip into another key or realm, his harmonic sleights of hand, transitions which go nowhere, that the compositional outcome confuses our understanding of musical space and time.

Alternatively, however, if Euclidean spatiality appears insufficient to describe Schubert's music, we might be simply coming close to Bergson's argument about time being qualitatively different from space. We instinctively attempt to understand time in terms of space, but this is to simplify a heterogeneous medium into a homogenous one.[98] Here, memory may afford just as meaningful an analogy. Memory for Bergson is not actually 'in space', even though its events are all simultaneously present (which suggests the spatial metaphor); one may move at will between one memory and another.[99]

And although the distorted, unusual routes between musical events may be analysed as belonging to some curved, non-Euclidean musical space, they may just as easily be understood as constituting a dreamscape. Dreams are another class of things often associated with Schubert.[100] The blurring of familiar objects into each other, of temporal categories with space and with it the apparent suspension of normal causal relations, allies his music with a dreamlike sense (here the pictorial analogy would be with some surrealist landscape by Dalí in which solid objects melt and flow and time itself dissipates to nothing). Dreams and memory have also long been closely connected through their static quality, their lack of presentness and temporal slippage of levels. Philosophers have traditionally found the differentiation between the two hard. Not for nothing does Proust commence À la recherche du temps perdu with a description of the symbiotic blurring between sleep, dreams, and memory.

Offering a different perspective, by moving by chain of association from dreams, via the interpretation of dreams and dream-work, to psychoanalysis (or in Proust, from approximately Combray to Sodom and Gomorrah), it would easily be possible to revisit in altered light the previous descriptive analysis of the B♭ Sonata's opening using Freudian theories of the subconscious mind alongside Cone's now highly loaded description of 'vice' in Schubert. The susceptibility for

[97] See Henri Poincaré, The Foundations of Science, trans. George B. Halsted (New York: The Science Press, 1905), pp. 75–8. It is a curious coincidence that the 1820s was also the decade that non-Euclidean geometries were being developed by János Bolyai (in Vienna) and Nikolai Lobachevsky.

[98] Henri Bergson, Time and Free Will. Of course the Einsteinian conceptions of space-time alluded to slightly earlier are incompatible with Bergson's theories.

[99] Bergson, Matter and Memory, trans. N.M. Paul and W.S. Palmer (London: George Allen and Unwin, 1911).

[100] Cf. Brendel's oft-cited comparison: Schubert composes 'like a sleepwalker . . . In Beethoven's music we never lose our bearings, we always know where we are; Schubert, on the other hand, puts us into a dream' ('Form and Psychology in Beethoven's Piano Sonatas', On Music, p. 45).

corruption is present in the music even before G♭ offers its allure, but as Cone informs us, 'The first step in yielding to a temptation is to investigate it'.

> That is what happens here. One can imagine the protagonist becoming more and more fascinated by his discoveries, letting them assume control of his life as they reveal hitherto unknown and possibly forbidden sources of pleasure. When he is recalled to duty, he tries to put these experiences behind him and to sublimate the thoughts that led to them.[101]

The hammering chords of bb. 34–5 and violent, gratuitous reassertion of B♭ is the superego asserting its authority over the erring ego, led into sin (or G♭ at the very least) by that mischievous id. The F♯ minor of the 'second theme' reveals the subsequent tragic alienation of the G♭ realm, the loss of the love object or a depreciation of the self typical of melancholy, while the 'correct' F major secondary theme proffered in its stead by the superego (i.e., the third theme) is purely conventional, a tawdry filling up of the required bars in what is the socially accepted norm for a partner key, which does not begin to quell the pathos of F♯ minor. Here, unlike many other three-key expositions (e.g., D. 956), the second and third themes are not heard as existing in some dualistic though dependent relationship but rather as incompatible alternatives inhabiting different levels: the self has become split.

''Tis pity, though, in this sublime world, that/pleasure's a sin, and sometimes sin's a pleasure'. For Cone 'The past cannot remain hidden. What was repressed eventually returns and rises in the end to overwhelm him'.[102] That shunned G♭ arises suddenly, *fortissimo* (the retransition to exposition repeat). A repetition of the entire course thus far ensues (a process commonly suggestive of neurosis for Freud).[103] In the development this alienation of the self takes on new levels: a new theme, interpreted by Fisk as referring to the 1816 song 'Der Wanderer',[104]

---

[101] Cone, 'Schubert's Promissory Note', 240. Cone is describing the *Moment musical* in A♭, Op. 94 No. 6, in connection with a hypothetical real-life explanation for this 'vice' based on Schubert's contracting of syphilis. Cone's reading seems remarkably prophetic of the storm of controversy that would soon blow up following the publication of Maynard Solomon's article 'Franz Schubert and the Peacocks of Benvenuto Cellini', *19th-Century Music*, 12 (1989), 193–206. As the reader wishes, the shimmer of G♭, Taruskin's purple flat-submediant, may shine a lighter hue in the following account.

[102] Cone, 'Schubert's Promissory Note', 240.

[103] See Sigmund Freud, 'Remembering, Repeating, and Working-Through', *The Standard Edition of the Complete Psychological Works of Sigmund Freud*, trans. James Strachey, 22 vols. (London: Hogarth Press, 1953–1974), vol. XII, p. 150: 'the patient reproduces it not as a memory but as an action; he *repeats* it, without, of course, knowing that he is repeating it'.

[104] Fisk, *Returning Cycles*, pp. 78–9.

emerges, followed most tellingly by the extraordinary return to the first subject in the tonic (b. 193) which is yet heard as a mirage. The wanderer has returned home, only to find it unhomely; the alienation of the self from itself, of id from superego, is complete. And the real recapitulation? Cone continues:

> If one now apparently recovers self-control, believing that the vice has been mastered, it is often too late: either the habit returns to exert its domination in some fearful form, or the effects of the early indulgence have left their indelible and painful marks on the personality—and frequently, of course, on the body as well.[105]

Nicholas Marston has ingeniously pointed out how in b. 254 the G♭ element is not eliminated or normalised into B♭, but rather the B♭ is made to sound like its other. The subversion lies in 'that the peripheral, the deviant, might challenge and win out over the normative; indeed, that the normative might actively aspire to and attain that other realm'.[106] This wicked inclination has won out after all—at least temporarily. Some readers may well think this is all fanciful—that such broad and all-inclusive psychoanalytical concepts loosely applied to such a paradigmatic narrative archetype may explain everything and nothing—and of course it is; yet this reading fits the music about as well as memory, landscape, or dreams.

And finally, we may cross the short strait that separates psychology from psychoanalysis. Schubert's music may readily be heard as a projection of consciousness and subjectivity. Many listeners have at least felt so. 'He has strains for the most subtle thoughts and feelings', Schumann claimed, 'and innumerable as are the shades of human thought and action, so various is his music'.[107] Consciousness seems in many ways a good cover-all term for Schubertian analogical language. It may incorporate memory, the interaction of temporal levels in which memory operates, the projection of dreams, subconscious drives and psychopathology, and—even—landscape.

Maybe it is not memory as much as the shifting between different levels of consciousness that we encounter in D. 887 and D. 956. Somehow through his modulatory shifts Schubert is able to express something indescribable almost indescribably simply. It is not just the magical way in which he may move the listener into a warmer, inner dream-realm with his second subjects but also how, conversely, he is able to darken, fatalise already elegiac music. There is a moment

---

[105] Cone, 'Schubert's Promissory Note', 240.
[106] Marston, 'Schubert's Homecoming', 265.
[107] Robert Schumann, *Gesammelte Schriften über Musik und Musiker*, ed. Martin Kreisig, 2 vols. (Leipzig: Breitkopf und Härtel, 1949), vol. I, p. 206.

in the 'Menuetto' of the A minor Quartet, seemingly quite normal, in which the music moves through common-tone reinterpretation from V/A minor to C♯ minor. But this analytical description conveys nothing of the experience one obtains listening to this; by some mysterious means the bottom drops out, the despair suddenly gets even deeper. Again, there seems some connection with the movement of consciousness—a perceived psychological realism that partly explains this music's fascination. Schumann's contention of Schubert's psychologically rich and unusual connection of musical ideas surely conveys something accurate.[108]

In some ways spatial metaphors seem likewise inaccurate. As Burnham remarks on the landscapes of the Schubertian subject, 'these are not just spaces, they are subjectivized spaces, imaginary spaces'.[109] Landscape may be understood as a projection of subjectivity.[110] As noted above with regard to memory, the warped spaces of Schubert's musical landscapes suggest internal labyrinths. Schubert's music opens up the infinities of the self, the endless caverns of the ego's self-consciousness found in the idealist and Romantic philosophy of his day (or for its sceptics, their hall of mirrors).

Thus, in certain instances, speaking of this music as exploring the depths of consciousness appears at least as appropriate as the use of memory or spatial metaphors. But consciousness seems even harder to theorise—less warm and user-friendly than memory, less visualisable than landscape. Moreover, in other cases, such as those involving nostalgia and allusion to earlier music discussed at the opening of this chapter, memory would evoke a stronger sympathetic resonance. It would be fairer to conclude that Schubert's music creates a distinctive musical fabric which may easily suggest a range of interpretations revolving around memory, subjective inwardness, and the psychological chain of thoughts—analogies that can move effortlessly into each other, all of which are 'merely' metaphorical, and all of which may be revealing.

There are multiple ways of understanding how memory and nostalgia may be constructed in Schubert's music. They are irreducible to one aspect it seems—just as we have different types or mechanisms of memory, different understandings of time and consciousness. The ways in which these qualities are musically constructed are furthermore so intimately involved with other

---

[108] Robert Schumann, *Jugendbriefe*, ed. Clara Schumann (Leipzig: Breitkopf und Härtel, 1886), pp. 82–3, cited by Daverio, 'One More Beautiful Memory of Schubert', 604.

[109] Burnham, 'The "Heavenly Length" of Schubert's Music'.

[110] Burnham, 'Landscape as Music, Landscape as Truth', 36.

quintessential Schubertian compositional traits such as lyricism, his harmonic deftness and idiosyncratic formal structure, that memory might well appear to be a guiding thread to understanding Schubert's music.[111]

But memory, as we saw, is not a necessary metaphor. It may fit Schubert's music, but other, related ideas such as landscapes, dreamscapes, imaginary spaces, psychological processes, and those of subjective consciousness may have just as good an affordance. The popularity of memory metaphors in musico-logical accounts of Schubert's music, especially in the last two decades, might thus be the reflection of the greater recent propensity for memory discourse, a postmodern *malaise de mémoire*. Yet memory was an important notion for Schubert and his contemporaries, and as Gibbs says, nostalgia has been associated with Schubert since his own day. One need only think of *Winterreise* to be convinced of the importance of memory for Romantic consciousness. Not long after Schubert's untimely death, his first important critic, Robert Schumann, set the terms for the reception of Schubert's music in terms of this same theme of memory. Moreover, as is so often noted, music's own temporal qualities obviously endow it as the ideal bearer of such attributes. Modern audiences might be more susceptible to memorial language, but this quality has been intimately bound up with Schubert all along.

Memory thus provides a powerful conceptual metaphor for understanding Schubert's music, creating a richer meaning for it. To ask whether the memory metaphor is right or wrong is to ask the wrong question. His music affords the comparison, often well, sometimes more dubiously, but this analogy has been seen as significant for many people and thereby contributes towards constructing the music's meaning. And, as a temporal art, irreducible to linguistic determination, there is always the possibility that music is telling us something about memory and consciousness that other lines of scientific and philosophical inquiry are unable to disclose. As Burnham fittingly remarks,

> Schubert's achievement can now be mustered alongside some of Western modernity's other grand statements about memory, such as those of Proust or Bergson. At the very least, we seem finally ready to work from the assumption that this is not just innocently beautiful music spun out at heavenly length, but music that has as much to say about the human condition as the music of Beethoven or anyone else.[112]

---

[111] See for instance Walter Frisch's introduction to the 2000 edition of *The Musical Quarterly* devoted to Schubert and memory (84 [2000], 581).

[112] Burnham, 'Schubert and the Sound of Memory', 657.

Memory is one of the bedrocks of the human psyche and of modern subjectivity. It is arguable that this is one of the main reasons why Schubert's music fascinates so many listeners, why it inspires such feelings of affection and kinship, why we choose to wander to the tunes he makes. For in his music we recognise nothing other than ourselves.

4

Temporality in Russian Music
and the Ideology of History

I don't reproach the Russians for being what they are;
what I blame them for is their desire to appear to be what we are.
—Astolphe de Custine, *La Russie en 1839*[1]

Glinka was German. All composers are German.
—'The Stranger' (Custine), in *Russian Ark*

Alexander Sokurov's 2002 film *Russkij Kovcheg* [*Russian Ark*] has attracted considerable interest for a number of reasons—as a technical feat of cinematogra-
phy and human endurance, for its daring conceptual novelty, and not least for
its seemingly arcane commentary on the nature of history. Shot in a single take,
the film offers a tour through the Hermitage Museum in St Petersburg, interweaving scenes revealing the riches of the imperial collection with different and
non-contemporaneous strata of times witnessed by the building. From Peter the
Great to the valedictory last imperial ball before the First World War at its close,
the film spans the 300-year history of the former Winter Palace, jumping forward
intermittently to traumatic reverberations of post 1917 (Stalin's Terror; the Siege
of Leningrad 1941) and the uncertain present. A strictly unedited, unrepeatable
diachronic re-presentation of history becomes strangely dislocated chronologically. Ambling alongside the cameraman-narrator is the historical personage
of Astolphe de Custine, the nineteenth-century French aristocrat famous for
his 1839 travelogue of Russia. From the sardonic disposition adopted towards
Custine's European chauvinism by the unseen Russian narrator, the film offers
a prolonged musing on the problematic nature of Russian identity vis-à-vis the
West. And in the wilful manipulation of history and filmic discourse, it prob-
lematises the nature and our accustomed perception of historical time.

---

[1] Astolphe de Custine, *La Russie en 1839*, 2 vols. (Brussels: Wouters, 1843), vol. I, p. 166.

Suggesting to some commentators a Derridean bifurcation of signifiers (the paradox of a history experienced once—as a repetition), the film has also been rendered from the perspective of Gilles Deleuze's time-image.[2] The discontinuous or eccentric movement through time and space, the non-chronological representation of the past as a totality, functions as a direct image of time.[3] History is seen as a continued presence. As the title suggests, the past endures in an autonomous existence, floating statically in the ever re-formed present; 'we are destined to sail forever' murmurs the narrator in the film's final words. The museum becomes an ark preserving Russia's past culture and identity. After the catastrophe—the twentieth century—the clock effectively stops ticking; we are left with the shards of the past, departed and continuously reformed; there is, in short, no longer any future to await.

Whatever *Russian Ark* might be thought of saying, the implications for our understanding of time are complex and probably irreducible to a single reading. However, the particular historical moment at which this film appeared is hardy accidental. The film surely reflects a wider post-Soviet unease, even post-modern malaise, at the idea of history and straightforward chronological narratives of progress. Yet this ambiguous relationship to time and historical temporality has been present in Russian art for much longer than the immediate post-Soviet period. One might say that for several centuries Russian thought has been haunted both by its relation to the neighbouring European West and the question of its identity, and, in conjunction, by ideas of temporal lateness, afterness, or non-participation in the progressive continuum of modern Western European history.

Cinema has become a privileged medium for twentieth-century thinkers seeking to understand the notion of temporality, as Deleuze's notable example demonstrates. But another artistic medium had long existed that proved highly susceptible to such theorising in the nineteenth century—music, for many (as we have seen) the temporal art par excellence. Here, the division constructed between Western European and Russian identities, and their conceptions of temporality, was accentuated, for the relation of Russian music to the concept of temporality has traditionally been seen in the West as a problem: that of development.

---

[2] See Dragan Kujundzic, 'After "After": The *Arkive* Fever of Alexander Sokurov', *Quarterly Review of Film and Video* (2004), accessible at <http://www.artmargins.com/content/cineview/kujundzic.html>.

[3] See Gilles Deleuze, *Cinema 2: The Time-Image*, trans. Hugh Tomlinson and Robert Galeta (Minneapolis: University of Minnesota Press, 1989); further, for a good consideration of Deleuze's difficult writing on this subject, D.N. Rodowick, *Gilles Deleuze's Time Machine* (Durham, N.C., and London: Duke University Press, 1997), esp. pp. 79–128.

Russian Music, Western Historiography, and the Idea of Musical Development

The question of thematic development in nineteenth-century Russian instrumental music has long been viewed—at least from a normative Germanocentric perspective—as a deeply problematic one. Frequently Western critics have made the objection that Russian composers lack a true sense of thematic development, motivic working and teleological process requisite to a 'proper' symphonic style. Gerald Abraham, writing in 1935, in an account by no means intended to be disparaging, offers a neat résumé of the comments typically heard about Russian music:

> The Russian musical mind is 'naïve', with a love of bright colours, concern for the present moment at the expense (vis-à-vis the Germans) of the ability to think progressively, and the tendency not to conceive a work as an aesthetic whole. Russians rarely *evolve* music from material; rather, it is juxtaposed or contrasted. In opera this is manifested by a lack of dramatic interest and predilection for static, tableaux-like plots.[4]

Although written over seventy years ago, these sentiments are echoed and if anything amplified throughout the century. Carl Dahlhaus, for instance, among the most authoritative of such critical voices, has reproved Tchaikovsky's symphonic writing for its lack (by Beethovenian standards) of true development, and written elsewhere of 'those folklorish symphonies, with their ill-conceived mixture of lied-like melody and motivic fragmentation', comments aimed, surely, at the nineteenth-century Russian symphonic tradition.[5] Such objections have in fact become rather the norm, a truism of musicological criticism which would have us complicit in divorcing the evident continual popularity of the works of Tchaikovsky, Borodin, or Rimsky-Korsakov from their alleged true worth.

Yet, as is well known, many Russian composers—in particular the Nationalists, the 'Mighty Little-Heap' clustering around Mily Balakirev and Vladimir Stasov—were quite conscious in claiming to distance themselves

---

[4] Paraphrased from Gerald Abraham, 'The Essence of Russian Music', in *Studies in Russian Music* (London: William Reeves, 1935), pp. 9–12, 15. The same opinions are indeed repeated throughout this author's writings and their republication up to the 1980s.

[5] Carl Dahlhaus, *Nineteenth-Century Music*, trans. J.B. Robinson (Berkeley and Los Angeles: University of California Press, 1989), pp. 266, 158. A wider survey of the twentieth-century musicological abuse aimed at Tchaikovsky's symphonic output is provided by Richard Taruskin in *Defining Russia Musically: Historical and Hermeneutical Essays* (Princeton: Princeton University Press, 1997), pp. 253–60.

from Germanic developmental procedures. As Mussorgsky remarked, 'when a German thinks, he reasons [or waffles] his way to a conclusion. Our Russian brother, however, starts with the conclusion, and only then might amuse himself with reasoning.'[6] In its purest form, this lack of developmental principle is found in music stemming from the tradition of the 'Glinka variation'—the continual variation of a small number of themes, themselves essentially unvarying but colourfully decked out in ever-changing orchestral garb—whose *locus primus* is usually taken to be Glinka's fantasy on two Russian folk tunes, *Kamarinskaya*, of 1848. Tchaikovsky would later claim that in this work the 'whole Russian Symphonic School' was encapsulated, 'just as the entire oak is contained in the acorn.'[7] The music of Glinka, Balakirev, Rimsky-Korsakov, Borodin, even Tchaikovsky, Glazunov, Kalinnikov, and Rachmaninov, may be seen as drawing in places on this well-established technique.[8]

In this context, it hardly seems tenable to take on trust the received judgement regarding the supposed naïveté of Russian composers. Such an apparent divergence between composers' stated intentions on the one hand and their critical misconstrual on the other might raise the question of whether we have simply been evaluating these works from the wrong critical perspective. How justifiable, after all, is the criterion of development and teleological process as a prerequisite for instrumental music? If such works *are* genuinely non-developmental, what, if anything, replaces developmental working in this music, and how, as a consequence, should we listen to it? This study is a suggestion of an alternative, perhaps more illuminating, way of approaching Russian instrumental music, from the perspective of a different conception of musical and historical time.

This very idea of development, so highly prized in the music of the Austro-German symphonic tradition, is in fact premised upon a particular conception of time. To see something as developmental is to see future events as to some extent determined by and growing from the present, to view the future as being amenable to change. Put another way, the underlying conception of time here is essentially linear, teleological, and progressive. This premise may seem natural and self-evident to us since it is a belief about time that is found

---

[6] Mussorgsky, letter 15 August 1868, taken from Richard Taruskin, *Stravinsky and the Russian Tradition: A Biography of Works Though 'Mavra'*, 2 vols. (Berkeley and Los Angeles: University of California Press, 1996), vol. I, p. 127, incorporating elements of the translation offered by Marina Frolova-Walker in 'Against German Reasoning: The Search for a Russian Style of Musical Argumentation', in Harry White and Michael Murphy (eds.), *Musical Constructions of Nationalism* (Cork: Cork University Press, 2001), p. 107.

[7] Tchaikovsky, diary entry of 27 June 1888, cited in David Brown, *Mikhail Glinka: A Biographical and Critical Study* (London: Oxford University Press, 1974), p. 1.

[8] See especially here, Richard Taruskin, 'How the Acorn Took Root', *Defining Russia Musically*, pp. 113–51.

particularly strongly in the last four centuries of Western thought, but, as argued earlier in this book, this conception is in fact neither universal nor absolute. Rather, it is a belief underpinned by the rise of modernity, scientific thinking, and the Enlightenment in Western Europe, and sustained after 1800 particularly in German philosophy and aesthetics. Western Classical music has traditionally emphasised this progressive, teleological conception of time, but other forms of temporality can be found in music, such as those in non-Western cultures and experimental music in the twentieth century.[9]

Given this context, it is far from self-evident that all Russian music should have to comply with this particular model of temporality. The notion of music as developmental and goal-orientated may fit certain pieces of Beethoven—a German and exact contemporary of Hegel—extremely well, but why should it be taken as necessary for musicians of another culture who (in some cases) claimed to find the former's music anathema? In truth, just as German music—indeed Beethoven's (see chapter 1)—is far richer and more varied in its temporal attributes than the customary essentialised account allows, so the notion of temporality in nineteenth-century Russian music admits of more variety than the monolithic linear-teleological model beloved of Western critics. This chapter takes as its starting premise the idea that many pieces of Russian music may be seen to problematise aspects of the conventional 'Western' model of time. Put simply, I am concerned here with the idea that in numerous nineteenth-century Russian works musical time is not necessarily unilinear and teleological, but in fact may contain distinctively static, repetitive, cyclical, and non-progressive elements.[10]

---

[9] Kramer, 'New Temporalities in Music'.

[10] As will become apparent later, by this I am not suggesting that stasis, repetition, and lack of developmental teleology are uniquely Russian traits, nor indeed that there is necessarily something intrinsically Russian about them (they are, rather, present across virtually all cultures). It may be arguable that as David Brown claims, 'the very nature of Russian creativity' was static and 'grew most naturally through various kinds of variation method . . . [the] often prodigious ability to repeat something with ever new significances' ('Russia before the Revolution', in Robert Layton (ed.), *A Guide to the Symphony* [Oxford: Oxford University Press, 1995], p. 263), or, as Abraham puts it, that it is 'as natural for a Russian to think episodically as for a Frenchman to think logically' ('The Essence of Russian Music', p. 20). Nonetheless, however tempting it may be, essentialising national characteristics is a fraught activity in modern scholarship. My underlying justification is rather that historically, many nationally minded Russians (such as the Slavophiles and in music the *Kuchkists*) defined their purported Russianness in opposition to what they perceived as quintessentially Western (often specifically German) traits, most relevantly in music the idea of goal-orientated development, and therefore these non-developmental qualities can be found particularly prominently in many nationalist works from the *Kuchka*. On the problematic relationship between music and constructions of Russian identity see further Marina Frolova-Walker, *Russian Music and Nationalism: from Glinka to Stalin* (New Haven: Yale University Press, 2008), esp. pp. 12–21, 138–9.

I will argue that for some Russian composers—especially those of a more nationalistic disposition such as Balakirev and Mussorgsky, as well as in some compositions by Borodin and Rimsky-Korsakov—'non-Western' models of temporality, emphasising notions of repetitiveness, stasis, and circularity, and a concomitant negation of Beethovenian developmental working in favour of other modes of thematic treatment, may often be highly rewarding for understanding the dynamic of the music. Even in cases where these composers' music is not so evidently static or non-developmental, demands of goal-directed motion and organicism still often obscure characteristic aspects of the music's relationship with time. For other figures, meanwhile, more overt elements of organicism or goal-directedness may appear. This approach gives rise to the opportunity to consider more complex variations on the overly simple binary teleological/non-teleological model: some music, for instance, might reveal a highly 'organic' process of thematic-harmonic metamorphosis without achieving a progressive trajectory to a triumphant telos (Rachmaninov being a case in point), while for a cosmopolitan Russian who looked continually to the West such as Tchaikovsky, elements of temporality characterising Western modernity may be in dialogue with other, conflicting conceptions.

Such an approach also has further implications for the way in which we investigate music; it is a commonplace of recent musicological criticism that the modes of analysis, critical vocabulary, and indeed metatheoretical assumptions that are traditional in the discipline are based on a Germanic repertory and ideology, and in order to examine pieces with alternative approaches to temporality and thematic manipulation it will at times be necessary to explore new ways of understanding music. The ideas of musical unity without organic development, or organic development without progressive teleology, are cases in point. Once we open up the range of temporalities we are prepared to admit, we can perceive the variety and richness of much familiar music: paraphrasing Herder, one might even say that there are almost as many musical temporalities as there are pieces of music.[11]

Circular and Static Temporality
in Nineteenth-Century Russia

Much of Russia in the nineteenth century was outside the Western European sense of time. It was for a start lagging behind the West—by thirteen days to

[11] Herder, *Eine Metakritik zur Kritik der reinen Vernunft*, p. 68, quoted in chapter 1; also cf. David Greene's similar contention in *Temporal Processes in Beethoven's Music*, pp. vii and 6.

be exact. This was not just the inconsequential matter of observing a different calendar (it was not until 1918 that the nation moved from the Julian to the Gregorian system) but reflected the quintessential agrarian basis of life for the vast majority of the population. For a country in which well over ninety per cent of its inhabitants lived in rural areas, in an age long before industrialisation, modernisation, and the widespread use of electricity, time was still defined by the circular daily, lunar, and seasonal movement of nature. The pervasive reach of the Orthodox faith rooted life in the annual replication of the liturgical calendar, the feast days, name-days, and festivals that had been present for centuries.[12] This temporal viewpoint, once widespread in Europe but increasingly disappearing with the industrial revolution and consequent urbanisation of Western nation states, is equivalent to what the historian Reinhart Koselleck designates (from a Western European perspective) as medieval or pre-eighteenth-century time. The Russian populace was subject to 'a uniform and static experience of time' where 'the temporal situation of past history bounded a continuous space of potential experience'.[13] Precisely because history can offer nothing essentially new, the future, since immanently contained within the present, is in this sense effectively no different from the past.

For the intellectual and artistic classes, of course, this was not the only time that they experienced, but for self-proclaimed nationalists such as the *Kuchkists*, the belief (sustained by the growth of the Slavophile cause) that the world of the peasant was nearer to God than was the civilised mendacity of the West supported their desire to base art on what they saw as more quintessentially Russian models and paradigms. Russians, so it was held, possessed true, uncorrupted insights into life, and any attempt to Westernise the country consequently could not but destroy its very being. The Russian nation could only be renewed by the return to its roots and heritage that had been forcibly abandoned in the Petrine reforms of the late seventeenth century—to return to the simple Orthodox faith of the peasant and 'the black earth of Mother Russia', as Mussorgsky wrote.[14] Progress as such—when understood from a Western Enlightenment

[12] Linda J. Ivanits, *Russian Folk Belief* (Armonk, New York: M.E. Sharpe, 1989), pp. 23–4; a good survey of the prehistory of temporal conceptions in Russian folk and religious belief may also be found in Michael S. Flier, 'Till the End of Time: The Apocalypse in Russian Historical Experience Before 1500', in Valerie A. Kivelson and Robert H. Greene (eds.), *Orthodox Russia: Belief and Practice under the Tsars* (University Park, PA: Pennsylvania State University Press, 2003), pp. 127–58.

[13] Koselleck, *Futures Past*, pp. 230, 28. Also cf. pp. 22, 263–4.

[14] Mussorgsky, letter to Vladimir Stasov, 16 and 22 June 1872, given in *The Musorgsky Reader*, ed. and trans. Jay Leyda and Sergei Bertensson (New York: Da Capo, 1970), pp. 185–6. For a critical overview of this topic (especially relating to the disparity between the Slavophile intellectual elite and the common people whom it claimed to champion) see Susanna Rabow-Edling, *Slavophile Thought and the Politics of Cultural Nationalism* (New York: State University of New York Press, 2006).

perspective—was therefore a chimera, a dangerously seductive poison acting on the youth of the day.[15] The Balakirev group in particular was heavily influenced by the prominent Slavophile Ivan Kireevsky, and it is this concept of temporality suggested by Slavophile thought that is so intriguing in music of the time.[16]

One of the most significant existing scholarly accounts of circular, non-progressive time in Russian music has been made by Caryl Emerson and Richard Taruskin in relation to the operatic output of Mussorgsky. The dramaturgy of *Boris Godunov* is, as Emerson has argued, both circular and deeply pessimistic.[17] We begin and end with the coronation of one false pretender to the throne, following the death at his hands of the previous incumbent. In a sense, Mussorgsky's bleak view of Russian history is a dark, meaningless chaos where one tyrant is succeeded by another, but nothing really changes. Likewise, Emerson reads *Khovanshchina* as a philosophy of history that is 'non-progressive and enfeebling', where 'stasis and a sense of predetermination are the ruling mood'.[18] As these examples readily demonstrate, the dramaturgy of Russian operas is often characterised by a predilection for epic, tableau structures, and the resulting distance created from contemporaneous paradigms such as those of Wagner and Verdi. The magical fairy-tale plots of Rimsky-Korsakov's operas provide further examples of such non-linear temporality, demonstrating as they do a principle that is often encountered in folk belief—the notion of time as circular and essentially static.

Perhaps the most transparent illustration of this negation of goal-directed motion in instrumental music is Balakirev's symphonic poem *Rus* [*Russia*] (originally 1863). This work, at one stage entitled '1,000 Years' in commemoration of the (semi-) historical founding of the Russian nation in 862, was ostensibly a musical depiction of Russian history, from its very beginnings up to the present, formed out of the interplay of three characteristic themes that for the composer

---

[15] This theme is familiar to Western readers from the novels of Turgenev and Dostoevsky (e.g., *Fathers and Sons, The Possessed*). Tolstoy's memorable portrait of Platon Karataev from book XII of *War and Peace* is a notable personification of the Slavophile ideal of the uncorrupted truth of the simple peasant at one with life, nature, and the Orthodox faith, inspiring Pierre's movement away from the false Western panacea of Freemasonry towards the genuine soul of Russia.

[16] Dorothee Eberlein, *Russische Musikanschauung um 1900 von 9 russischen Komponisten* (Regensburg: G. Bosse, 1978), p. 21; on Slavophilism and temporality see also Rabow-Edling, *Slavophile Thought*, esp. pp. 35–50.

[17] Caryl Emerson, 'Musorgsky's Libretti on Historical Themes: From the Two *Borises* to *Khovanshchina*', in Arthur Groos and Roger Parker (eds.), *Reading Opera* (Princeton: Princeton University Press, 1988), pp. 235–64.

[18] Emerson, 'Apocalypse Then, Now, and (For Us) Never: Reflections on Musorgsky's Other Historical Opera', *Khovanshchina (ENO Opera Guide)* (London: John Calder, 1994), p. 8. See further, Taruskin, *Musorgsky: Eight Essays and an Epilogue* (Princeton: Princeton University Press, 1993), pp. 313–24.

'characterise some of the elements that have featured in this history—the periods of Paganism, the Popular Government of the Cossacks, and the Muscovite Empire'.[19] But what is most remarkable about Balakirev's musical construction of history is that it is essentially static, circular—in fact the antithesis of historical progress. The work begins with a dark B♭ minor introduction, and, after a livelier B♭ major internal sonata structure, ends with the same music, returning to round off the work (retaining the B♭ minor key-signature to the end), with only the pianissimo d♯s in the closing bars providing a glimmer of light. After all the mosaic-like play of themes from Russia's historical past, nothing has really changed; it could almost be as if it had never happened.[20] Balakirev's tone-poem is, in short, the embodiment of Mikhail Bakhtin's formulation of epic time:

> This past is distanced, finished and closed like a circle. This does not mean, of course, that there is no movement within it. On the contrary, the relative temporal categories within it are richly and subtly worked out . . .; there is evidence of a high level of artistic technique in matters of time. But within this time, completed and locked into a circle, all points are equidistant from the real, dynamic time of the present; . . . it is not localized in an actual historical sequence; . . . it contains within itself, as it were, the entire fullness of time.[21]

It is something of this timeless, static, almost hypnotic quality of historical time that is captured in Sokurov's *Russian Ark*. In this film the historical scenes climax with the grand ball of 1913 featuring a performance of the Mazurka from Act II of Glinka's *Zhizn' za tsarya* [*A Life for the Tsar*] (1836)—the founding national opera by the composer understood traditionally as the father of Russian music—by the present-day Kirov Opera Orchestra under its conductor Valery Gergiev. Outside, we can see through the windows only a grey fog lying over the Neva, which envelops us in a measureless, atemporal dream-space. At the end, the unseen narrator leaves the building, which appears to be floating in a wide,

---

[19] Note added by the composer to the republication of the score in 1886. It should be acknowledged that this programme was only added long after the work's initial composition (originally entitled the more neutral 'Second Overture on Russian Themes'), by which time the composer's political views had radically changed; the relationship between the two is debatable (see Edward Garden, *Balakirev* [New York: St. Martin's Press, 1967], p. 51; Taruskin, 'How the Acorn Took Root', pp. 146–9). Yet it is still significant that a piece hardly marked by any sense of overall development or progress by was considered by Balakirev as being suitable for the commemoration of Russian history.

[20] One reason for this pessimism might be Balakirev's hostility towards the reforms of Peter the Great, increasingly pronounced with age, that is evident in his programme note.

[21] Mikhail Bakhtin, 'Epic and Novel', in *The Dialogic Imagination: Four Essays by M.M. Bakhtin*, trans. Caryl Emerson and Michael Holquist (Austin: University of Texas Press, 1981), p. 19.

empty ocean. It is as if the past is dissociated from the historical continuum and becomes a spectral aspect of the present, the two melding into each other. Time here is iconic, spatial, moving out slowly in ever-increasing rings from a still epicentre.

Temporality and Thematic Process in the Work of the *Kuchka*

Given this context, the idea of time as something rather static, cyclically repeating, and non-progressive fits in very well with the Russian variation technique, mentioned earlier. The central point of the Glinka 'background' variation is the continued identity of a theme throughout countless surface changes in its presentation. Balakirev in particular was extremely skilled at this. While Glinka's *Kamarinskaya* is normally taken as the *locus primus* of this technique,[22] Balakirev's own Overture on Three Russian Themes (1858), written in tribute to the elder composer who had died only the year before, could perhaps be considered its *locus classicus*. The exposition of the internal sonata-like structure of this work is formed almost entirely from the recycling of two similar themes in twelve-bar phrases, each of which is moreover highly repetitive internally (3 + 3; 3 + 3), a reiterative mode of thematic construction that persists throughout the course of the piece. A sense of four-squareness is nonetheless avoided through Balakirev's evasion of expositional and recapitulatory harmonic closure and his undercutting of the clear 'standing on V' articulation of the medial caesura in b. 159 by a subdominant-minor lead in to the secondary thematic area.[23] Similarly *Russia*, *Tamara* (1867–82), the Overture on Czech Themes (1867), *Islamey* (1869), and the two symphonies all illustrate these kaleidoscopic changes of colour, myriad rearrangements of what is essentially the same material, and correspondingly the rejection of fussy developmental working and any real sense of linear progression. Likewise, many works of Rimsky-Korsakov—*Antar* (1868/75), *Ispansko kaprichio* [*Capriccio Espagnol*]

---

[22] In fact, this 'changing background variation' can be found earlier in Glinka's *Ruslan and Lyudmila* and the two Spanish overtures, but *Kamarinskaya*, being based on genuine Russian folk-tunes, provided a more conveniently national model for Russian composers.

[23] There is not a single PAC in the secondary tonality of D major throughout the secondary thematic area in the exposition (the music bypassing any harmonic expositional close and moving directly to a caesura on V/B♭ in preparation for the development section, b. 235), and only a very weak one mid-phrase (b. 407) in the recapitulation, which similarly dissolves into the recall of the framing introductory theme. Thus despite the extremely repetitive nature of the small- and medium-level phrase syntax there is a still a fluid continuity to the musical unfolding.

(1887), *Shekherezada* [*Scheherazade*] (1888), and the *Svetliy prazdnik* [*Russian Easter Festival*] Overture (1888), to name just a few—derive directly from this practice.

In these works there is rarely a sense of *process*; the listener is not interested in what *becomes* of a theme, in the much cited Beethovenian-Hegelian manner (as epitomised in the *Eroica* Symphony). In much German-orientated music criticism the concern is with linear teleology and historical progression; for Schoenberg most notably, 'Germanness' in music was synonymous with 'development'.[24] The idea has become a pervasive truism of musicological criticism, freely applied by non-German scholars to non-German music as a more-or-less normative demand. It is not the theme itself (which can often be quite plain, even banal) that matters but the actual process it undergoes. As Dahlhaus puts it, 'the whole significance of the musical instant, unimportant in itself, is that it points the way forward to something greater'.[25] The idea *is* the process—the destiny, coming to self-development of the theme—an entire conception that must necessarily be predicated upon the notion of a 'future' and the ability to change the course of and control one's own destiny.[26] For certain Russians of a nationalist mindset (as indeed with many disillusioned Romantics across Europe), this very conception was false.

Running throughout what is probably the most celebrated Russian novel ever written is an extended (and notorious) meditation on history, that calls upon the very same historical figure—Napoleon—as the Beethoven 'Eroica' paradigm, but to radically different conclusions. Tolstoy's *War and Peace* pits Napoleon against the Russian general Kutuzov, or rather the belief that any individual can control his own destiny against the inscrutable might of providence. Generals, holds Tolstoy, do not make but are 'the blind tools of history'; what occurs in history 'depends on the coincidence of the wills of all who take part in the events, and that a Napoleon's influence on the course of these events is purely external and fictitious'.[27]

---

[24] Arnold Schoenberg, 'Italian National Music' (1927), in *Style and Idea* (London: Faber & Faber, 1975), p. 175.

[25] Carl Dahlhaus, 'Issues in Composition', in *Between Romanticism and Modernism*, trans. Mary Whittall (Berkeley and Los Angeles: University of California Press, 1980), p. 49. It is worth noting that the syntactical structure of the German language seems itself to implicate such a teleological conception of time: the listener often has to wait until the end of a sentence for the appearance of the decisive second verb or separable prefix, thus postponing semantic determination and creating a tension which lasts until the very end of the utterance.

[26] See, amongst others, Dahlhaus, *Ludwig van Beethoven*, pp. 116–8 and 169–71; Burnham, *Beethoven Hero*; Brinkmann, 'In the Times(s) of the "Eroica"'.

[27] Leo Tolstoy, *War and Peace*, trans. Louise and Aylmer Maude (London: Macmillan & Co., 1959), X/xix, p. 834; X/xxviii, p. 867.

In historic events the so-called great men are labels giving names to events, and like labels they have but the smallest connexion with the event itself. Every act of theirs, which appears to them an act of their own will, is in a historical sense involuntary, and is related to the whole course of history and predestined from eternity.[28]

Opposing the view of historians who believed in the power a great figure such as Napoleon (Hegel's 'World Spirit on horseback')[29] could wield, Kutuzov emerges as an unlikely hero owing to his understanding of the powers—far greater than any individual—that move history. He does nothing; he tries not to change, make, or alter history. He knows this is out of any man's control. Instead he is content to let events unfold as they inevitably must—a perspective far removed from the self-making destiny of Beethoven's heroic subject. In such a world, moreover, it is impossible, believes Tolstoy, to arrive at a standpoint from which we can assert the reality of that 'certain kind of European culture called "progress"'.[30]

Even for a prominent Russian socialist such as Alexander Herzen, to postpone the aim of human existence to the unknown (and probably unrealisable) future is to misunderstand life:

What is the purpose of the song the singer sings? . . . If you look beyond your pleasure in it for something else, for some other goal, the moment will come when the singer stops and then you will only have memories and vain regrets . . . because, instead of listening, you were waiting for something else . . . I would rather think of life, and therefore of history, as a goal attained, not as a means to something else.[31]

---

[28] Ibid., IX/I, p. 667.

[29] The expression is actually a paraphrase of Hegel's account of seeing Napoleon enter Jena in letter to his friend Friedrich Immanuel Niethammer, 13 October 1806. Hegel's own views on the relationship between the world-historical individual and underlying *Weltgeist* are admittedly more nuanced than is often thought; the great individual typically acts unconsciously in furthering the inscrutable aims of history (see the *Lectures on the Philosophy of History*, pp. 29–33).

[30] Tolstoy, *War and Peace*, Ep. I/i, p. 1247. Tolstoy's theoretical views are of course not always as respected as his genius as a writer of fiction and moreover are made even more difficult to pin down owing to his problematic later 'conversion'. See Isaiah Berlin's famous essay, 'The Hedgehog and the Fox', reprinted in *Russian Thinkers* (Harmondsworth: Penguin, 1978), pp. 22–81.

[31] Alexander Herzen, 'From the Other Shore', quoted in Berlin, *Russian Thinkers*, p. 196; also see Berlin's introduction to Alexander Herzen, *My Past and Thoughts*, trans. Constance Garnett (London: Chatto & Windus, 1968). Herzen himself is notable in this context as a socialist thinker who nevertheless denied the totalising master-narratives and subsumption of the individual into historical process entertained by many other intellectuals on the left. Marxism, need it be said, is Western and strongly teleological—a delightful irony of history.

In contrast, this music simply 'is'. Nietzsche is onto this distinction between these two contrasting approaches to temporality when he famously remarks that 'we Germans would have been Hegelians even if Hegel had never existed, insofar as we place a deeper significance and more value on what is evolving, still becoming, than to that which 'is', in contradistinction to the Latinate [or, one might say, Slavic] races'.[32] The Russian pieces named above articulate more a sense of temporal *Being*.

The interest in such music is the moment-to-moment quality of the theme itself, decked out in ever-changing garb. Therefore, it needs good melodies and a virtuoso command of instrumentation to sustain continual interest. Hence we have one of the fundamental reasons why so much Russian music has proved so popular with audiences: it depends upon attractive themes—good tunes—and colourful, inventive orchestration. This emphasis on theme goes hand-in-hand with a downplaying of connective, 'athematic' transitional passages or melodically less-strongly characterised developmental passages of melodic fragmentation and working-out.[33] When everything is theme (and its continual variation), there are no 'boring' parts, while the skill and mastery of orchestration ensures continual surface contrast and an everchanging play of colours and interest. Indeed, we might say that a formerly peripheral element (the orchestration) has now become foregrounded—like, perhaps, by analogy, Russia itself and its position within European music. As Rimsky-Korsakov famously described his *Capriccio Espagnole*, the felicities of instrumentation 'represent the *essence* of the composition and not its garb, that is, not merely its orchestration'—a reversing of ornamentation and essence.[34]

---

[32] Nietzsche, *The Gay Science*, §357. Also note the same figure's portrayal of *Carmen* at the expense of Wagnerian *unendliche Melodie*: Bizet's music 'builds, organises and finishes', in contrast to Wagner's, which, like Germany, 'belongs to the day before yesterday and the day after tomorrow—*but yet has no today*' (*The Case of Wagner*, §1; *Beyond Good and Evil*, §240). As already borne out in chapters 1 and 3, the depiction of a characteristic 'German' approach to temporality as marked by progress and goal-directedness is obviously an oversimplification of the diversity of nineteenth-century German thought and art (Nietzsche himself is one of the most prominent counterexamples). However, as the example of musicology throughout the last century demonstrates, values drawn from these assumptions as to how we (and how music should) exist in time have attained widespread currency.

[33] Cf. Henry Zajaczkowski, *Tchaikovsky's Musical Style* (Ann Arbor: UMI Research Press, 1987), p. 2. One of the best examples of this conscious shunning of Germanic motivic-developmental working by a Russian composer is provided by Tchaikovsky's impassioned criticism of Brahms's music: Brahms 'never expresses anything, or if he does, he fails to do it fully. His music is made up of little fragments of something or other, artfully glued together' (letter, 18 February/1 March 1880, quoted by Taruskin in *Defining Russia Musically*, p. 254).

[34] Rimsky-Korsakov, *My Musical Life*, trans. J.A. Joffe (New York: Alfred A. Knopf, 1947), p. 254. This aesthetic foreshadows a tradition of French music associated with Debussy, in which the play of momentary colours and textures, non-schematic form and concentration on musical 'surface' create an aesthetic paradigm far removed from Germanic ideas of instrumental form and thematic development. The connection between the nineteenth-century Russian repertoire and the twentieth-century

As a result of these qualities, though, such works might not always prove especially amenable to analytical criticism of the type routinely visited on the Austro-German mainstream. To appreciate this music one requires awareness of its melodic quality and orchestral colour—aspects that can readily be obtained by any listener, but are not so conducive to musicological analysis, at least with the techniques currently devised (largely, it must be admitted, from German music to deal with its own particular qualities). There is simply less to say from the perspective of motivic working and thematic process. This is not *prima facie* so much a problem with the music as it is with the capacity of analysis, but one should note that it would be unjustified to extrapolate from this that Russian music has 'less worth' on some imagined technical level. The respective criteria are incompatible. There is no absolute yardstick to tell us that the aesthetic plea-sure derived from an exemplary analytical demonstration of certain technical aspects is greater or more real than that stemming from a (perhaps untutored) listener's direct experience of different features of such music.[35] ('Technical anal-ysis', Vladimir Jankélévitch pointedly remarks, 'is a means of refusing to abandon oneself spontaneously to grace'.[36])

Despite these features, it would be quite wrong to believe that there is no unity or coherence in such Russian works. There is often a sophisticated manip-ulation of thematic material in pieces from this tradition, manifested through the 'invented' connection between seemingly opposing themes. Glinka's *Kamarinskaya* again is a paradigm, where two apparently distinct folk-like themes are gradually revealed to possess latent affinities with each other through the honing in and concentration on one motivic figure that seems common to both.[37] Balakirev's Overture on Three Russian Themes similarly demonstrates this principle (Ex. 4.1); the two folksongs that go to make up the central sonata section of this work are associated through their common diastematic contour (an opening descent from $\hat{5}$ to $\hat{1}$) and by their nearly identical rhythmic profiles.

French tradition through Diaghilev's operatic and ballet stagings also demonstrates how this music's colourful pictorial-visual aspect was able to be further emphasised in audiences' minds (see Frolova-Walker, *Russian Music and Nationalism*, pp. 46–9).

[35] This claim also tacitly takes issue with the influential Germanic ideology of listening raised at the end of chapter 2 familiar from Hanslick's division into 'aesthetic' and 'pathological' hearing and later codified in Adorno's concept of 'structural listening'—a dichotomy further associated with a national distinction between an Austro-German repertoire (primarily instrumental) and non-German music (primarily operatic). Obviously most audiences respond readily to the immediate emotional engage-ment of much Russian music—for which Adorno explicitly censures Tchaikovsky ('The Radio Symphony', p. 266).

[36] Jankélévitch, *Music and the Ineffable*, trans. Carolyn Abbate (Princeton: Princeton University Press, 2003), p. 102.

[37] See Taruskin's analysis in 'How the Acorn Took Root', pp. 115–23.

Ex. 4.1 Balakirev: Overture on Three Russian Themes (1858)

Introduction / frame: 'Chto ne belaja bereza' ['This is not a white birch']

First sonata theme: 'Vo pole bereza stojala' ['In the field stood a birch tree']

Second sonata theme: 'Ia vechor mlada' ['I was at the party last night']

Already within the exposition a statement of the first theme, still in B minor, is able to be inserted unobtrusively within the D major second thematic group (b. 195), while a major-key transformation opening the development increases the first theme's similarity with the second still further.[38] At the retransition (bb. 321–39), the two temporarily reach near-identity, as the head-motives of both are heard in immediate juxtaposition and contrapuntal, quasi-imitative conjunction.

In a similar fashion, Rimsky-Korsakov's Fantasia on Serbian Themes, Op. 6 (1867), modelled after both *Kamarinskaya* and Balakirev's own overture, alternates between B minor *Andantino* and D major *Vivo* sections, incorporating the horns' opening Andantino motive into the final *Vivo* and thus stitching the two sections together (Ex. 4.2).

One would hesitate to call this technique 'organic'—in the sense of the much-fêted (and now similarly reviled) Anglo-German theory—as there is little sense in which a theme continuously evolves, mutates, and grows 'as if of its own accord' into another. Rather, it is a case of elective affinities, fleeting associations, being formed between essentially disparate entities. (Wittgenstein's oft-cited notion of 'family resemblances' might seem an appropriate model to describe this technique.[39]) On a hermeneutic level, such a procedure might suggest an urge to find—or invent—a common national identity for Russia out of a disparate ethnic body, not organically seeking (temporal) growth

---

[38] The latter transformation also points up the affinity of the two themes to the overture's opening gesture—a unison major-key descent $\hat{5}$–$\hat{4}$–$\hat{3}$–$\hat{2}$—which to this extent becomes a common denominator between the two internal sonata-form themes.

[39] Wittgenstein, *Philosophical Investigations*, §§66–71.

Ex. 4.2 Rimsky-Korsakov: Fantasia on Serbian Themes, Op. 6 (1867), *Andantino* and *Vivo* themes

from a single common source but rather unifying (spatially) a vast and hetero-geneous nation.[40]

One of the most notable examples of this associative technique is Borodin's *V sredney Azil* [*In Central Asia*] (1880), where the two themes heard in close proximity at the start are contrapuntally overlaid at the work's reprise (Ex. 4.3). Again, it is not the case here that either has really developed or evolved into something higher, more that both are found to be able to coexist. Time, again, becomes spatialised, through a vertical overlayering. This work likewise illus-trates another prominent feature of this style: the use of a frame. Though this design was popular in music of the later nineteenth century, a remarkable num-ber of works by Russian composers utilise this idea.[41] Technically or phenom-enally, such a design obviously imparts a clear sense of unity, a way of closing the

[40] Glinka's original idea for employing *tableaux vivants* for the end of *Ruslan* suggests a compa-rable urge to unify different geographical locations into the simultaneity of a larger, imperialist Russia (Frolova-Walker, *Russian Music and Nationalism*, p. 112); Dorothea Redepenning reads the alter-nation and final synthesis of Russian folksong and exotic orientalist themes in Borodin's *Steppes of Central Asia* along similar lines (*Geschichte der russischen und der sowjetischen Musik*, vol. I: *Das 19. Jahrhundert* [Laaber: Laaber-Verlag, 1994], pp. 272–3).

[41] Balakirev's *Overture on Three Russian Themes, Russia, Tamara*, Rimsky-Korsakov's own *Overture on Russian Themes, Scheherazade* (in its entirety), this work of Borodin, the second movement of Tchaikovsky's First Symphony and the first movements of the Second Symphony and Third Quartet, the opening movements of Glazunov's Second and Fourth, all spring to mind.

Ex. 4.3 Borodin: *In Central Asia* (1880)

ongoing, otherwise almost ceaseless variation. The first movement of Balakirev's Symphony No. 2 (1900–08), for instance, would hardly seem able to close if it were not for the return of the peremptory chords heard at the opening to round off the movement 'from the outside'. Furthermore, as part of an expressive, temporal conception, such a design is literally circular. Ultimately, there has been no progression, as we observed in *Russia*: time is palindromical, returning to the original, to nothing. The arch-like form of a work such as Borodin's *In Central Asia* solicits a quasi-spatial representation: we picture the caravan moving slowly across the plain and disappearing again, retreating back into silence and the vast, endless reaches of the Russian Steppe.

As found within some Western European examples, this design also offers the possibility of being heard as a narrative frame, as if the interposed movement is merely a story given in inverted commas, conforming to a separate level of reality.[42] This can give rise to a fairy-tale, wistful quality, of which *Scheherazade* is one of the most prominent instances. The entire story told by the music is merely a myth, a beautiful 'might have been'—perhaps, in the 'world theatre' tradition, like life, an illusion, a fiction, the stuff of dreams—ultimately ephemeral, like the sounding substance of music itself. In the famous Heraclitean formulation, everything passes; for this music, in contradistinction, everything—if it ever existed—is already past.[43]

---

[42] Mendelssohn's Overture to Shakespeare's *A Midsummer Night's Dream* is one of the earliest and most ingenious examples of this technique. See James Hepokoski and Warren Darcy, *Elements of Sonata Theory: Norms, Types, and Deformations in the Late-Eighteenth-Century Sonata* (New York: Oxford University Press, 2006), pp. 304–5.

[43] A related topic stemming from this frame idea is the role of the slow introduction in Russian music, especially concerning the frequent relationship (found in much Romantic music) between the

The iconic, quasi-liturgical aspect of these works (which the critic Boris Asafiev perceived in Glinka's *Ruslan and Ludmilla*) is intrinsically related to such circularity.[44] The first movement of Glazunov's Second Symphony (1886), for instance, circles round the liturgical theme that frames it, its alpha and omega as it were—a conception which is iconic, offering us kaleidoscopic perspectives of the same object, spiralling round a timeless, ineffable centre. (Glazunov dedicated his work to Liszt, and the manner here in which a thematic idea retains its diastematic identity unwaveringly through surface changes in its presentation certainly points up the intimate connection between the Glinka variation and the thematic transformation of Schubert, Berlioz, Schumann, and Liszt—a process which is quite distinct in both technique and effect from the seemingly organic processuality of the motivic working that typifies the works of Haydn, Beethoven, and Mendelssohn, or Brahmsian developing variation.) Icons, like the symbols found in folklore and myth, evince a process of growth and change that is not materially developmental. While our perspective on and understanding of their meaning may be modified in time, the object (itself standing for the unrepresentable and timeless) does not.[45]

Mussorgsky's 'Bogatyrskiye vorota (V stolnom gorode Kiyeve)' [the 'Bogatyr Gate at Kiev'] from *Pictures at an Exhibition* (1874) seems to capture the immanent circularity of this religious experience of time. The musical process of Mussorgsky's composition is striking in its simplicity, twice alternating a triumphant main theme with a contrasting liturgical-sounding section, calling forth the telos—the main theme again in apocalyptic dressing. The non-developmental teleology of this conception thus conforms closely to Koselleck's formulation of the medieval-Christian experience of time. We are in St Augustine's sixth age, awaiting the future divine eschaton that is both immanent and imminent; before then nothing really new can happen: 'As long as the Christian doctrine of the

slow introduction and the ensuing Allegro sonata movement (e.g., the first symphonies of Borodin and Balakirev or Rimsky Korsakov's Third). Hepokoski and Darcy have read this technique in the 'nationalist' symphony as an analogy of the idea of growth of nationhood from the earth/people into fully formed being, the organic (re)generation of the nation from its very essence (*Elements of Sonata Theory*, p. 304). This is an attractive idea, relating closely to Slavophile notions of return and renewal and the hope placed on the nation's youth (though one should note that this entire theory is a German idea—as indeed is the musical source). The implications for the music's temporality here are intriguing: implicitly the main sonata section is all written in an indeterminate 'future', itself barely temporally distinguishable internally. Like the past, this hypothetical future ultimately lacks the dynamic A-series sense of future events passing through the present into the past, a full reality or presence within time's flow, thus emphasising the fictional story-like status.

[44] Boris Asafiev, 'A Slavonic Liturgy to Eros', in *Symphonic Etudes: Portraits of Russian Operas and Ballets*, trans. David Edwin Haas (Lanham, MD: Scarecrow Press, 2007), pp. 1–25.

[45] On these themes of Orthodox iconography and temporality see Konstantinos Kalokyris, 'Byzantine Iconography and "Liturgical Time"', *Eastern Churches Review*, 1 (1966), 359–63; and Clemena Antonova's *Space, Time, and Presence in the Icon: Seeing the World with the Eyes of God* (Farnham: Ashgate, 2010), esp. pp. 103–52.

Final Days set an immovable limit to the horizon of expectation . . . the future remained bound to the past'.[46] The final apotheosis is promised and contained in all that precedes it; history is no more than a circling through time until this moment finally arrives. Inspired by Victor Hartmann's design for a gate 'in the ancient Russian style' to commemorate the escape of Tsar Alexander II from a failed assassination attempt, the work simultaneously celebrates the unity of a glorious heroic past, the present emperor, and an exultant future—a future that ironically never arrived, since Hartman's designs all came to naught when the building of the planned gate was scrapped by the authorities.[47]

Compositional Technique and Temporal Conception in Balakirev's Symphony No. 1

Most of the examples given above relate to pieces using the Glinka variation technique, stemming principally from the nationalist tradition. Predominantly, again, they consist of overtures, fantasias, or other single-movement forms. Such a model applies very well to Balakirev (conveniently the most unremit-tingly nationalist, politically as well as musically, of all these figures) and some works of Rimsky-Korsakov, Borodin, and Mussorgsky. Of course, many Russian compositions are not as extreme in their avoidance of Germanic developmental procedures or negation of a sense of progressive temporality; the range of tem-poral qualities in Russian music is clearly more varied than the binary opposi-tion developed so far suggests. Many pieces may not readily suggest a distinctive temporal profile (much of César Cui's piano music springs to mind), and in oth-ers there may be a contrast or interplay between different temporal paradigms and modes of thematic working. Nevertheless, criticism against a normative model of teleological progress obscures much that is characteristic and aestheti-cally valuable in this repertoire.

The opening movement of Balakirev's First Symphony (1864–97) presents a particularly complex conception of musical temporality touching on several of the issues raised earlier, which is deserving of more extended consideration.

---

[46] Koselleck, *Futures Past*, p. 264; St Augustine, *City of God*, XXII/30. Of course for Augustine—and Christianity—time in the broadest sense is teleological, uncyclical, and unrepeat-able, being closer to a single, progressive loop of a spiral; within such an eschatology, though, every-day human experience of time since the coming of Christ may become essentially static, cyclical, and repetitive. On this point see also the account of Balakirev's First Symphony below.

[47] Account given by Vladimir Stasov; see Alfred Frankenstein, 'Victor Hartmann and Modeste Mussorgsky', *Musical Quarterly*, 25 (1939), 268–91. Hartmann's plan incorporates both Orthodox religious icons and imagery and the bells heard in Mussorgsky's version that summon forth the climax.

This work also shows how, notwithstanding many important differences, even the most 'nationalist' Russian repertoire still uses or modifies compositional techniques associated with the Austro-German mainstream, collapsing over-schematic generalisations of West and East.

Balakirev's Largo introduction sets out two significant melodic figures that will go on to form the first and second subjects respectively of the ensuing sonata exposition (*x* and *y*, Ex. 4.4a & 4.4b). The motives are similar in their largely conjunct motion around the Symphony's pitch centre of C and in their touching

Ex. 4.4a Balakirev: Symphony No. 1 in C (1864–97), first movement, motives *x* & *y*

Ex. 4.4b Balakirev: Symphony No. 1, first movement, bb. 1–7

Ex. 4.4c Balakirev: Symphony No. 1, first movement, motivic rearrangement in first and second subjects

on the submediant degree, which corresponds to the fluid blurring of tonic and modal relative that is found throughout the symphony (and indeed in much Russian 'nationalist' music). Motive *y* in fact leads to a cadence on A, and its later appearance as second subject will be in this relative minor context. Slightly fancifully, one might demonstrate in proto-Schoenbergian fashion that the core of *y* is an ornamented retrograde of *x*, though since Balakirev does not make anything out of this connection its explanatory use is limited.

The use of familiar organic metaphors such as germ or embryo would be inappropriate here, as the motives do not so much grow into the material of the exposition as recur unchanged (save obvious rhythmic techniques of diminution). Already the kinship with the 'iconic' transformational technique described in Glazunov's Second Symphony is apparent, a quality that is underscored by the liturgical-sounding nature of the ideas and their presentation. Motive *x* is initially intoned in unison, followed by its sequential reuse with 'walking' staccato quavers in species counterpoint underneath (not dissimilar to the opening of *Boris Godunov*) that leads to a quasi-modal cadence in which *y* enters subtly in violas and flute as an expressive polyphonic voice decorating the cadence (bb. 5–6). The two ideas are thus presented side-by-side in the same opening thematic complex, but neither is expressly derived from the other.

Despite the presence of qualities that have long been constructed (problematically) as denoting 'Russianness'—the archaic tone, chant-like motivic ideas, modal harmonic touches, the unison presentation followed by polyphony—the actual harmonic course of the introduction is entirely conventional. The A major cadence in b. 7 leads via D to a restatement of the opening in the dominant G (b. 9), and after a flat-side digression in the woodwind, the same cycle of fifths progression (albeit with the pre-dominant stage being now chromatically inflected) sets up a dominant pedal that leads through rhythmic acceleration into the sonata exposition. As the exposition will demonstrate, this paradigm is indeed typical of much of Balakirev's work: the repetitive motivic syntax and local orchestral and harmonic colour overlay and to an extent mask the continued indebtedness to underlying harmonic and formal templates drawn from the Austro-German instrumental repertoire.

As with the earlier Overture on Three Russian Themes, the exposition is constructed from the continued recycling of melodic phrases (here in more regular eight-bar units that split into two matching halves) that remain fundamentally intact in terms of their contour, despite changes in harmony and orchestral presentation. Quite ingenious is the way in which Balakirev forms the first theme simply out of two statements of motive *x* enclosing a scalar transposition of the initial part of *y* in the centre; the second subject is merely *y*, but with an accented second beat that adds considerable rhythmic interest (Ex. 4.4c). Although the motivic repetition is all-pervasive, there is a skilful use of harmony and phrase syntax that, alongside Balakirev's retention of sonata form's customary tonal course, serves to articulate a familiar expositional trajectory. For instance, the second subject, entering as an interrupted cadence from V/V (and thus emphasising the submediant quality of motive *y* implicit in the introduction), consists entirely of paired repetitions of the same four-bar theme through fresh harmonic or timbral contexts without once really changing its diastematic content. Yet a myriad of techniques—the build-up over a dominant pedal in b. 86, the ensuing acceleration of phrase rhythm through the contraction of phrase lengths into 3 + 3-bar units at b. 94, the undercutting of the apparent point of tonic arrival in b. 106 by use of a first inversion, the heightening stretto effect from b. 112, the generic harmonic excursion at b. 118, the reuse of motive *x* from the first theme in a closing capacity at b. 124 and this motive's subsequent 'liquidation' through sequential repetition at the exposition's close—serve to create and then dissipate tension in a thoroughly conventional Austro-German manner.

There is thus a curious sense of continual reiteration, the music constantly looping back motivically at small- and medium-scale levels as if treading water, conjoined with a skilful use of other musical parameters which together create a certain dynamism and satisfying control of tension.[48] Balakirev's music is constantly in motion and yet simultaneously repetitive to the point of stasis— a characteristic temporal state that can be found in many other nineteenth-century Russian pieces.[49] One is reminded of Tovey's criticism of the finale of Tchaikovsky's Fifth Symphony—'of running faster and faster while remaining

[48] A related point is made by Gerald Abraham, who observes that in Beethoven and Brahms the forward impulse comes from the 'logic' of the music, whereas with Borodin and his Russian colleagues rhythmic propulsion is the sole means used to give a sense of musical progress ('Borodin as Symphonist', *Studies in Russian Music*, p. 111). Even if too reductive, Abraham's comment is evidently illustrative of how much a sense of development is traditionally bound up with music's thematic aspect, at the expense of other parameters.

[49] The first movement of *Scheherazade* is for instance a good example. One might also recall here Adorno's polemic against Stravinsky, where he accuses the Russian composer, in such works as *Le Sacre du Printemps*, of freezing and spatialising musical time. Stravinsky's obsessive repetition of small melodic fragments is for Adorno the 'antithesis of Bergsonianism' (Adorno, *Philosophy of Modern*

rooted to the spot'—though unlike Tovey we need not view this quality as an example of musical 'impotence'.[50]

The quality of stasis in this music, then, appears to be derived primarily from maintaining a motive's identity without change throughout constant repetitions. Although the obsessive reiteration of a short motivic cell is characteristic of the symphonic style of Beethoven (the first movement of the Fifth Symphony is the most famous instance), the difference in Balakirev and in Russian music generally is that the motive used is not so pliable. The melodic idea is rarely altered diastematically and certainly does not appear to grow 'organically', as if of its own accord, into more developed forms that in turn give rise to further progeny; rather, it is reshuffled intact through changing harmonic and timbral chromata. This creates the vast difference in temporal profile between the teleological, intensive symphonic time of Beethoven and the kaleidoscopic play of stasis and motion in Balakirev. Everything can change around it, but the musical subject itself does not. This motivic and rhythmic obsessiveness is far more akin to Schumann's instrumental style, which alongside Glinka's background variation and the principle of thematic transformation is the probable source for this procedure.[51]

The apparent development section that follows Balakirev's exposition is surprisingly short, being little more than a lead-back into the reprise of the exposition's material, a third of which is taken up by a retransition over a dominant pedal that unmistakably alludes to the introduction's lead into the exposition. This extremely precipitous rehearing of the exposition's opening back in C major and the unusual preceding retraversal of the introduction merely increases the movement's sense of circularity and reiterative stasis at a higher formal level.

Music, trans. Anne Mitchell and Wesley Blomster [New York: Seabury Press, 1973], p. 193). What for Adorno—the German cultural chauvinist, critic yet upholder of the Enlightenment, Marxist, dialectician to a fault—was a reprehensible, barbarous quality, is a distinctive aesthetic state achieved long before in Russian music.

[50] Donald Tovey, Essays in Musical Analysis, 6 vols. (London: Oxford University Press, 1935–9), vol. VI, p. 60.

[51] See on this point Dahlhaus's comparable observation concerning Schumann's symphonic practice as evidenced in the First Symphony, Nineteenth-Century Music, pp. 158–60. As noted, this retention of diastematic identity also recalls the techniques of thematic transformation found in Schubert, Berlioz, Schumann, and Liszt in their quite different ways. The example of Liszt's Les Préludes, for instance, seems to be a presence behind the openings of Balakirev's Russia and First Symphony, in terms of soundworld as well as motivic manipulation. This compositional feature also connects to a famous argument advanced by Dahlhaus concerning the premium placed on the originality of musical material in the later nineteenth century and the resulting tendency to reuse small characteristic motivic building-blocks, as manifested either as developing variation (à la Brahms) or as sequential repetition in the manner of Liszt and Wagner ('Issues in Composition'). Most Russian composers clearly took the second line, though in a distinctive way.

Indeed, it almost paradoxically results in greater tension, a sense of waiting for some decisive event to change the music's course—a demand that will soon be met. For this erstwhile recapitulation is shattered by two moments of break-through: a fortissimo statement of the first subject in A♭ at b. 239 and the even greater outburst of the second theme triple *forte* at b. 247, which drastically alter the subsequent form of the work.

These irruptions split Balakirev's movement into two halves of virtually equal length. The remainder of the movement follows no clear form and is consider-ably more loosely structured internally. Centred now around the tonally distant B major and starting out with new material—an idea in the cellos (b. 271) that bears close relation to motive *x*, followed by a rather naïve lilting theme in the clarinet (b. 291) that seems to have far less connection with any preceding music—themes from the first half return at stages throughout its course and the movement closes with a long coda in C major. Yet it is hard to relate this section to any prior formal model; there has been a qualitative change in the musical organisation.

Given that the recapitulation had reached the second subject in its thematic cycle of events and that previous themes from the first half return in the sec-ond part, the movement's larger structure could be read as forming some type of three-part rotational design, where the two cycles of the exposition and reca-pitulation are followed by a far looser culminatory rotation that freely modifies their material. Since there was no extensive development section within the sonata half, the third rotation thus might become a displaced functional substi-tute for this writ large.[52] This might sound redolent of the technique of teleologi-cal genesis familiar a few years later in the works of Sibelius, but the important difference here is that there is no real sense of organic creation and growth.[53] The breakthrough is unexpected, a *deus ex machina* erupting from nowhere that is not subsequently explained, and neither is the final rotation particularly devel-opmental. If anything, Balakirev's design is the inverse of Sibelius's, a large-scale movement from a state of greater to lesser organisation, a kind of entropy.

It is as if we have gone from a circular, repetitive, but highly organised mode of construction to one of complete freedom. Multiple interpretations might be given to this process, such as Balakirev figuratively shaking off the fetters of Germanic instrumental form, a Hegelian process of the coming to self-consciousness of the notion of freedom, or, in A.B. Marx's formulation, the

---

[52] See for instance Francis Maes's slightly different interpretation in *A History of Russian Music: From Kamarinskaya to Babi Yar*, trans. Arnold J. Pomerans and Erica Pomerans (Berkeley, Los Angeles and London: University of California Press, 2002), p. 68.

[53] The term 'teleological genesis', as with 'rotational', stems from the work of Hepokoski (see *Sibelius: Symphony No. 5* [Cambridge: Cambridge University Press, 1993], pp. 23–7).

Ex. 4.5 Balakirev: Symphony No. 1, third movement, growth of first theme into second subject

composer-genius gaining formal freedom as the culmination of his *Formenlehre*. Though the compositional genesis of the symphony was protracted and, as we saw, the composer altered his political and ideological views several times in later life, it seems Balakirev at some point in the 1860s conceived the break-through in distinctly religious terms as the descent of the Holy Spirit.[54] This reading may be of insight for understanding the overall temporality of the movement as reflecting the religious experience of time described earlier. Balakirev's movement moves from a repetitive, circular, pre-modern religious time to a more unmeasured, freer state almost constituting timelessness. Yet the transition is not effected immanently but imposed transcendently on the music from the outside; at no stage is there a sense of the modern progressive time of Western Enlightenment.

While formally more conventional, the Scherzo and Finale of Balakirev's symphony are no more developmental than the opening movement. In fact the movement displaying the most 'organic' manipulation of thematic material is the Andante—a languorous, quasi-orientalist movement in sonata form, featur-ing the sensuous permeation of material between subject groups. A contrasting idea within the first subject-group (b. 16) seems to grow out of the opening clarinet melody; its two parts rearranged so that it now climbs before falling back, it becomes the second subject (b. 48) (Ex. 4.5).

Here there is far more fluidity to the musical structure and thematic manipula-tion than in the other movements, yet still a sense of circularity, of expressive deep-ening and thickening rather than movement towards a goal. Notwithstanding the flexibility of thematic working there is an overall lack of tonal resolution, the second theme still not being brought under the tonic's control by the end of the movement.

---

[54] See Frolova-Walker, 'Against German Reasoning', p. 113. On the previous point Frolova-Walker notes that it is, however, unlikely that Balakirev was acquainted with A.B. Marx's writings at the time of conceiving this movement.

Temporal Complexity in the Broader
Nineteenth-Century Russian Repertory

The qualities highlighted in this account of Balakirev's symphony may frequently be reencountered in the music of his contemporaries. A comparable example of the conjunction of Germanic and Kuchkist techniques can be found, for instance, in Borodin's symphonies and string quartets. Though co-opted as a member of the *Kuchka*, Borodin never sought to hide his regard for the music of Beethoven, Mendelssohn, and Schumann, and this is especially apparent in his efforts in the classical instrumental forms. To call much of Borodin's music simply static would be inaccurate—there is often an infectious rhythmic drive to his scherzos and finales—and the techniques of thematic manipulation, whilst not conventionally developmental in a Germanic sense, are made with considerable skill. Nevertheless, to expect the music to move dynamically in time towards a culminating *telos* in the manner of middle-period Beethoven is liable to result in disappointment. A case in point is the slow movement of the First String Quartet (1875–7), where the music, seemingly loosing itself in introspective meditation, might again suggest more germane metaphors of deepening and enriching, an intensification of thought rather than spatial motion. Even in the quicker movements such as the finale of the First Symphony (1862–7) the insistent rhythmic repetition and syncopation (again indebted to Schumann's example) create a sense of motoric energy without necessarily implying any purposive movement towards a goal. Here different models than goal-directed motion through time are needed.

Overt use of melodic repetition and the Glinka variation may also frequently be found alongside more conventional Austro-German techniques of development and fragmentation within the same work, especially in music from composers located on the periphery of the *Kuchka* group, such as Tchaikovsky, Kalinnikov, or Arensky.[55] A good example is Kalinnikov's Symphony No. 1 (1895), whose lyrical second theme consists essentially of a single eight-bar melodic phrase that moves to an imperfect close on scale degree $\hat{5}$ (Ex. 4.6). All Kalinnikov does is repeat this theme, not just once, but *three* more times, increasing the orchestration for the second pair.[56] As an exposition repeat is marked, and the passage is given a regular

---

[55] In Glazunov's case Germanic thematic development surely takes priority over 'Russian' variation (the first movement of his Symphony No. 6 [1896] is a fine example of organic development), though the latter variation technique is still a likely source of inspiration behind more relaxed passages of contrasting orchestral colour, such as that often found in his trio sections or in the second movement of the Sixth Symphony. As noted, the intensive thematic transformation of the Symphony No. 2 probably owes as much to Liszt as to Glinka/Balakirev.

[56] The closing harmony for the second of each pair is altered from an imperfect ['half'] cadence on C♯ (V/F♯m) to an IAC on F♯ minor, and the melodic line in the preceding sixth bar very slightly

Ex. 4.6 Kalinnikov: Symphony No. 1 in G minor (1895), first movement, second theme
(rehearsal C)

recapitulation (although again varied in orchestration), this phrase is heard no
fewer than twelve times in barely modified form within the movement. Although
this procedure would hardly impress a critic of Germanic aesthetic disposition, a
process of fragmentation and development could not if truth be told add anything
to this simple (and rather appealing) theme here. Nonetheless, later in the development section Kalinnikov will in contrast utilise more conventional procedures
of melodic fragmentation and sequential repetition of his primary theme. This
melding of techniques may also be seen in the finales of Tchaikovsky's Symphony
No. 2 (1872) and Rubinstein's Symphony No. 6 (1886), which offer large-scale
manifestations of the Glinka variation.

varied, but essentially Kalinnikov is repeating the same melodic idea unchanged. The flexible harmonic design of the exposition is noteworthy too: this lyrical idea at rehearsal C sounds like a second
subject in terms of rhetoric, but harmonically extends the prolongation of C♯ and F♯ areas at odds
with the overall G minor tonality. The more expected secondary key of B♭ is attained later at rehearsal
F but is thematically and cadentially under-articulated, the exposition dissolving back to G minor,
which is heard alternating with its German sixth, scored to emphasise this tritonal pole C♯ in the bass.

Ex. 4.6 Continued

At a formal level, too, as demonstrated with the example of Balakirev, the designs of most nineteenth-century Russian instrumental works are normally indebted to Western models such as sonata form, though the dynamic that results may reveal the strong infiltration of static or repetitive elements characterising the Glinka variation. A notable example is Rimsky-Korsakov's *Russian Easter Festival* Overture, which through its omnipresent repetition of motives drawn from liturgical themes distils a potent sense of concentricity or iconicism, conveying the religious experience of time mentioned above in connection with Mussorgsky's 'Bogatyr Gate' and Balakirev's First Symphony.[57] This distinctive pageant of sounds and colours is nevertheless fused with elements of sonata form, culminating with the overlayering of the bell-like material used in the first subject group with the liturgical second theme. Conversely, the overture to *Tsarskaya nevesta* [*The Tsar's Bride*] (1898), an opera held up since Rimsky's own day as a rejection of the Russian nationalist style formerly associated with

---

[57] Marina Frolova-Walker aptly comments that 'Of all the works in the Kuchka canon, it is the Easter Overture that most consistently enters the soundworld of Russian Orthodoxy'. *Russian Music and Nationalism*, p. 182.

the Five, is (notwithstanding its transparent sonata design) nevertheless highly typical of the changing background variation technique in its continual recycling of first and second themes with varied orchestral dressing.

On a broader conceptual level, more complex permutations of the variables of movement/stasis, organicism, and development may also be observed in the nineteenth-century Russian repertoire. For instance, just as it is possible to have thematic unity without organic development, so it is possible to have thematic organicism without ultimate progress—an idea echoed in the thought of some of the Slavophiles. For this outlook, history could be susceptible to transformation and change, but this could only occur through the organic growth of the nation from its soil and individual character, not by importing foreign elements or trying to ape the West.[58] Yet this organicism is nonetheless problematised from a strictly progressive perspective as potentially cyclical and therefore non-teleological. The most famous propounder of these theories was Vasily Danilevsky. In *Rossiya i Evropa* [*Russia and Europe*] (1869), Danilevsky argues for the cyclical nature of world history, which embodies an organic process of growth and decay in which successive civilisations go through the same limited life-cycles. Where this differs from earlier theories of world history such as those of Hegel is that the movement here is not culminative but reiterative; at the largest level, therefore, there is no such concept as progress.[59]

A musical parallel for this conception might be found a few years later in the figure of Rachmaninov, whose music often exhibits a highly sophisticated growth and manipulation of thematic material alongside a more equivocal relationship with the customary triumphant expressive trajectory of much classical-Romantic music. Hence, while development and metamorphosis is possible, the end finally attained is no more than the beginning—a concept encapsulated in the pessimistic, arch-like design of his tone-poem *Ostrov myortvykh* [*The Isle of the Dead*] (1909), or the fateful cyclical recurrence in the Second Piano Trio (1893) and First Symphony (1895). Even in works that pay lip-service to the customary triumphant ending, the essential quality of Rachmaninov's writing appears to lie as much in the richness and profligacy of the foregoing journey. His Symphony No. 2 in E minor (1907) is a wonderfully

---

[58] Ironically, of course, such nationalism reveals the decisive influence of German theorists, most notably Herder, Schelling, and the Romantics.

[59] See Hans Kohn, *Pan-Slavism: Its History and Ideology* (Notre Dame, IN: University of Notre Dame Press, 1953), p. 153. Danilevsky's ideas (admired by both Tolstoy and Dostoevsky) were continued by Konstantin Leontyev's *The East, Russia, and Slavdom* (1886) and were later taken up in the West by thinkers such as Oswald Spengler and Arnold Toynbee. A useful source providing an overview of the thought of the Russian intelligentsia may be found in William Leatherbarrow and Derek Offord (eds.), *A History of Russian Thought* (Cambridge: Cambridge University Press, 2010).

ripe example of the continual metamorphosis of a group of cyclic themes across a work. The pervasive elegiac character of the work's first three movements is dependent upon the complex and multifarious cyclical metamorphosis of material both within and across movements, which yet in itself does not create any real progressive course but weaves a rich tapestry of thematic strands. For a restless, somewhat morbid spirit, uprooted later in life from the stability of a fulfilled present, Rachmaninov's music perfectly bears out Alexander Herzen's negative take on Aristotelian entelechy (the identifying of the end of an organism's development with its state of greatest perfection), as embodied in Herzen's claim, 'If we merely look to the end of the process, the purpose of all life is death'.[60]

Even for a more 'European', cosmopolitan figure such as Tchaikovsky, an analysis of this music from the perspective of its temporality can still offer much insight. As the most popular Russian composer of all, Tchaikovsky has long been associated in the West with musical 'Russianness', though in truth he was a conservatory-trained, highly cosmopolitan figure whose aesthetics were distanced from those of his nationalist colleagues. Yet his music has often attracted similar criticism in the West for its shunning of certain 'Germanic' techniques (an avoidance that in many cases was undoubtedly intentional, given Tchaikovsky's dislike of Brahms, much Wagner, and Bruckner), and his music is therefore well worth consideration from this perspective.

The emphasis in Tchaikovsky's music is typically on melody, which obviously suited his remarkable gift in this area. A concern with fastidious motivic working-out would normally be ill-suited to such a style, inhibiting a free rein at melodic creation. Instead, the individual melodies are more likely to be repeated or amplified, going on to construct larger melodic units, which in turn are succeeded by new ideas. Despite their typical lack of small-level motivic growth and recombination, these melodic units are still likely to be connected to one another through a technique of shared affinities that we have already noted in the Glinka-Balakirev tradition.

The opening movement of the Fifth Symphony (1888) is a revealing example of this technique of Tchaikovsky's at its best (Ex. 4.7). The lugubrious E minor introduction, which serves as a motto-theme to the symphony as a whole, discloses three characteristic elements that will go to make up the material of the subsequent exposition. The melody, low in the chalumeau register of the clarinet, is closely related to that of the first subject of the *Allegro con anima*

---

[60] Herzen, 'From the Other Shore', in Isaiah Berlin, *Russian Thinkers*, p. 196. This quality of Rachmaninov's music has also been astutely read by Stephen Downes as belonging to a pan-European aesthetic of 'decadence', emphasising the over-ripeness and decay that is the corollary of organic growth (*Music and Decadence in European Modernism: The Case of Central and Eastern Europe* [Cambridge: Cambridge University Press, 2010], pp. 97–101).

Ex. 4.7 Tchaikovsky: Symphony No. 5 in E minor, Op. 64 (1888), first movement, thematic interconnections

(b. 41, again in the clarinet), outlining the third E–G (1̂–3̂) with movement through the upper-auxiliary A (4̂). Even more transparently, the repeating plagal chord progression i–iv–i heard in the accompaniment is retained in the strings across the two sections, linking them across the formal join. Most important of all, however, is the figure beginning in b. 5—a thematic complex consisting of two voices moving scalicly in contrary motion. Labelled Tchaikovsky's 'Fate' theme by David Brown (a descending scale, as heard now in the upper voice),

Ex. 4.7 Continued

this thematic model will become the most significant common binding agent in the following movements.[61]

The opening melody of the exposition might, even initially, seem to owe something to this model in its scalic rise and fall, and such expectations are confirmed by the following variant in b. 68, in which the rise and fall of the upper voice is reflected in mirror-image in the bass. (Strictly speaking, only these last four notes relate directly to the model of bb. 5–6, but the more abstract idea of the pattern of rising and falling contrary-motion links the two passages indisputably.) The transitional theme on V/v (2.1, b. 116) clearly takes up this contrary-motion model and extends it further, and the strings' reply to the chirruping bird-like calls in the wind (2.2, b. 154) transforms this idea in a new, more optimistic context. Finally, the lyrical second theme (2.3, b. 170) returns to the idea as originally heard in the introduction, inverting the treble and bass lines from the previous examples so that the upper voice now falls against the bass's ascent. A further group of connections is suggested by the pounding (ii $\frac{3}{4}$ –i) antiphonal exchange of b. 96—itself revealing something of a kinship both in gesture and harmony to the oscillating i–iv harmonies of the opening—that is

[61] David Brown, *Tchaikovsky: A Biographical and Critical Study*, 4 vols. (London: Victor Gollancz, 1992), vol. IV: *The Final Years (1885–1893)*, p. 148; also see pp. 449–58 (on the *Pathétique*) and vol. II: *The Crisis Years (1874–1878)*, pp. 199–209 (on *Eugene Onegin*).

potentially alluded to in the sequential falling fifths heard in the horns at b. 140 and subsequently taken up by the woodwind in b. 154.

Despite, then, a lack of the style of motivic development typifying, say, the music of Brahms, there is a clear sense of logic and coherence between the various themes of this exposition.[62] In the revealed connections between essentially lyrical phrases in Tchaikovsky's exposition one may discern something of the influence of Mendelssohn (especially, for example, in the idea of simultaneously hearing in an accompanimental line something that will function elsewhere as melody)—though where Tchaikovsky perhaps differs is in his relative distance from the more 'Beethovenian' process of continual motivic growth still seen in the earlier composer.[63] Tchaikovsky's music reveals rather the spreading out of more general, gestural connections across a more 'spatial' musical conception (a technique admittedly not unlike that sometimes found in Schubert).

The opening movement of the string sextet *Vospominanie o Florencii* [*Souvenir de Florence*] (1890) provides a further example of this composer's skilful control of musical elements, demonstrating how an extremely repetitive phrase-syntax can be kept harmonically open across large musical expanses, thus sustaining an expressive tension that belies the relatively simple, reiterative nature of the thematic writing. The sextet's opening eight-bar unit moves from an initial dissonant first-inversion V^9 in b. 1 to a root-position tonic in b. 2, immediately causing a subtle hypermetric ambiguity between phrasal and harmonic accents,[64] and returns to the dominant at its end, setting up another recycling of this phrase, which leads without resolution to new Neapolitan harmony (Ex. 4.8a). Following the introduction of more fragmentary (though related) motivic ideas and further metrical disturbance, this whole thematic block returns again (b. 41).

The secondary theme (b. 92), a close relation of the first, is if anything even more repetitive, continuously circling around the same eight-bar thematic unit and persistently returning to the dominant harmony that both begins and ends it (Ex. 4.8b). Despite his use of highly repetitive thematic blocks, Tchaikovsky manages to maintain a constant tension through his hypermetric ambiguity and insistence on the unresolved dominant quality of both themes. (Here, a modified Schenkerian harmonic reduction of the middleground, with its relative insensitivity to the 'problematic' thematic, phrasal and gestural syntax, might reveal an important aspect of this music.) The influence of Schumann

---

[62] The development section itself is actually less developmental than the exposition, dutifully repeating thematic blocks in sequence in a manner typical of Tchaikovsky's writing for this part of sonata form (see Zajaczkowski, *Tchaikovsky's Musical Style*, pp. 25–47).

[63] See Taylor, *Mendelssohn, Time and Memory*, pp. 234–48.

[64] To emphasise this point the phrase could be renotated and rebarred in $\begin{smallmatrix}6\\8\end{smallmatrix}$, two old bars equalling one new bar, starting on a half-bar anacrusis.

Ex. 4.8a Tchaikovsky: *Souvenir de Florence*, Sextet in D minor, Op. 70 (1890), first movement, first subject, bb. 1–18

(a particular love of Tchaikovsky's), both in terms of the use of repetitive, quadratic thematic phrases and of the prolonged harmonic dissonance of the opening, is especially apparent.[65]

With Tchaikovsky, we could further view an expressive dimension of his music as stemming from the very opposition and clash between two different temporal conceptions. Such is manifestly the case in the first movement of the Fourth Symphony (1878), in which the gradual evolution of the music

[65] Compare, respectively, the opening movement of the First Symphony or numerous of Schumann's finales; and the large-scale opening dominant prolongations of the *Fantasie* in C, Op. 17, or (in a more intimate context) 'Mondnacht', Op. 39 No. 5.

Ex. 4.8a Continued

is constantly thwarted by the inevitable, ever more triumphant, returns of the 'fate' motto-theme, which appears at the formal junctures of the movement.[66] The actual process of growth *within* formal sections is impressively controlled, tonally as well as thematically, from the limping waltz of the first group to the impassioned striving of its cousin in the closing group, allied through their persistent dance-rhythms.[67] It is only at the juncture of each 'fold' in the form that this progression is rent in two by the fearful recurrence of the opening motto.

Carl Dahlhaus's criticism of this movement—which was mentioned at the start of this chapter—is undoubtedly perceptive in its harsh, though sharp, analysis, yet almost wilfully ignores the evident expressive richness of Tchaikovsky's conception. It is true that merely restating an earlier theme with increased orchestral dressing is hardly a sophisticated means of obtaining a musical climax, but surely—if we choose to give credence to the composer's retrospective interpretation of the work—this is the whole point of implacable fate. The subject (aesthetic protagonist) is not ultimately free to develop but is in thrall to forces beyond his or her control. Destiny is predetermined; we are but the playthings of the gods. This conforms exactly to the individual in Bahktin's analysis of the tragic chronotope: 'outside his destiny, the epic and tragic hero is nothing; he is,

[66] Referring to Tchaikovsky's interpretation of the motive disclosed to his patroness Nadezhda von Meck (cited in Brown, *Tchaikovsky*, vol. II, pp. 163–7). The extent to which the composer's programmatic interpretation of the symphony should be taken literally has been debated, but the connection of the opening theme with some notion of fate is rarely doubted.

[67] For illustration, harmonically the exposition is characterised by its three-stage enharmonic minor-third progression f–a♭–B♮ leading to a 'delusional' tritone relation only emphasising the unreality of the projected expositional goal; thematically by a sophisticated *Fortspinnung* technique (seen especially in the first subject).

Ex. 4.8b Tchaikovsky: *Souvenir de Florence*, first movement, second subject, bb. 92–128

therefore, a function of the plot fate assigns him'.[68] The struggle here is between the brave, though ultimately futile, attempts of the music to develop and progress towards a brighter prospect and the pessimistic recycling of inevitable fate—between, if you like, Western Enlightenment and an older, more primeval cyclical conception of time. And here it is the latter that triumphs—within the first movement at least.[69]

---

[68] Bakhtin, 'Epic and Novel', *The Dialogic Imagination*, p. 36.

[69] At the level of the four-movement work, 'fate' is brushed off (as indeed it is in the following Fifth Symphony); seen within the trajectory of Tchaikovsky's symphonic oeuvre as a whole—that is viewing it as a speculative 'metawork'—fate appears to have the last word (see Timothy Jackson, *Tchaikovsky Symphony No. 6 (Pathétique)* [Cambridge: Cambridge University Press, 1999], pp. 11, 29ff). One could also relate this temporal analysis to Richard Taruskin's politicised reading of the conflict between respective Polonaise (aristocratic) and Waltz (bourgeois) dance rhythms (*Defining*

Ex. 4.8b Continued

Musical Time: Betwixt
and Between East and West

Appropriately for such a discussion, there is no particular *telos* or conclusion to the argument pursued here—such an idea would, after all, be grievously teleological—but rather a restatement and amplification of my basic idea. This is, namely, that the alleged lack of development in much nineteenth-century Russian music may often not only be deliberate but may also contribute to an

Russia Musically, pp. 297–304), thus viewing Tchaikovsky's symphony as articulating a struggle between the hopes of organic growth, progress or political reform dreamt by the middle-classes of the day and the stubborn obstinacy and compromised interests of the upper classes continually frustrating such endeavours (a sentiment that finds literary expression in Dostoevsky's *The Idiot*).

Ex. 4.8b Continued

aesthetic state that goes against the linear, teleological notions of temporality conventionally associated with the Austro-German symphonic tradition; and that such uses of musical time may instead suggest a mode of temporal *Being*, stasis, or timelessness, which reveals an affinity with certain aspects of contemporary Russian thought.

And as a final consideration, one might further reflect on the extent to which the Russian tradition really differs so completely from the music of the Austro-German canon, and the validity of customary paradigms of goal-directed motion in music as an unstated norm. Though the examples drawn from Balakirev and Borodin are far removed from customary paradigms derived from the music of Beethoven or Brahms, not only is the nineteenth-century Russian repertoire marked by an extremely diverse range of temporal approaches but, as illustrated earlier, German music itself is actually far richer and more varied in temporalities than this essentialised teleological model suggests. Recent scholars have argued that the notion of a divide between Russian and Western European music is to a considerable extent an ideological construct that grew up in the nineteenth century through the proselytising efforts of Stasov and Balakirev, and was willingly perpetuated by critics in both Russia and the West in the following century.[70] The influence shown here of Mendelssohn, Schumann, and Liszt on Russian composers already points to a partial blurring of this supposed separation. More careful examination of the work of such composers as Schubert, Mendelssohn, Schumann, Wagner, Bruckner, and Mahler certainly suggests that the temporality of nineteenth-century Austro-German music is more complex than has generally been acknowledged. (As we saw in the first chapter, it is hardly the case that all of Beethoven's music follows the unrelentingly teleological paradigm customarily attributed to it, and recent scholarly accounts of nostalgia, memory and allusion in the music of Brahms has similarly complicated the picture of this composer's relationship to temporality.[71])

Though this chapter has worked with—and tried to revalue—existing binary oppositions created between the 'West' and 'Russia', it is not just nineteenth-century Russian music that may emphasise notions of stasis, cyclical recurrence, and timelessness over teleological progress and goal-directed motion but in fact a far wider range of art and philosophical thought, from ancient civilisations and non-Western cultures to twentieth-century art. A critical model drawn from a few notable examples by Beethoven and Brahms, supported perhaps by a particular interpretation of classical dramaturgical aesthetics and a monolithic reading of scientifically driven modernity, has painted a pervasive representation of how it is thought music *ought* to behave in time, which is only really applicable to a small number of pieces.[72] Indeed, given the longer provenance of non-teleological conceptions of time, one could go so far as to claim that in fact the ('German') teleological model of musical temporality is actually 'marked' with respect to a wider norm, but a bias in musicology towards this particular repertoire has been responsible for making this progressive conception appear normative.

At the very least, the investigation of nineteenth-century Russian music from the context of its temporality offers us new insight into this ever-popular tradition; a tradition that, like Sokurov's Hermitage Museum, is still floating with us on the ocean of time, and will continue to do so for the foreseeable future.

---

[70] For example Richard Taruskin, Caryl Emerson, Malcolm Brown, and Marina Frolova-Walker.

[71] See for example Reinhold Brinkmann's *Late Idyll: The Second Symphony of Johannes Brahms*, trans. Peter Palmer (Cambridge, MA: Harvard University Press, 1995); Marjorie Hirsch, 'The Spiral Journey Back Home: Brahms's "Heimweh" Lieder', *Journal of Musicology*, 22 (2005), 454–89; and the work of Daniel Beller-McKenna and Paul Berry.

[72] It is still worthwhile to consider not just *how* but *why* this teleological model has been so pervasive, as argued persuasively by Scott Burnham in *Beethoven Hero*.

5

La Sonate Cyclique and the Structures of Time

Time is not a line, but a network of intentionalities
—Maurice Merleau-Ponty, *The Phenomenology of Perception*[1]

The past is never dead. It's not even past.
—William Faulkner, *Requiem for a Nun*[2]

On the first evening of his return to the town of Balbec on the Normandy coast, the narrator of Marcel Proust's *À la recherche du temps perdu* undergoes an unnerving experience. Reaching down painfully to take off his shoes in his hotel room, he is unaccountably 'filled with an unknown, a divine presence'. More than a year after her death, he has suddenly been overcome by the memory of 'the tender, preoccupied, disappointed face' of his grandmother as he had seen her the first evening of his arrival at the Grand Hotel several years before. Having inadvertently experienced the identical sensations of an earlier moment, he had 'recaptured the living reality' of the past 'in a complete and involuntary recollection.'[3]

For Proust, such shortcuts in temporal chronology point both to the unruliness of our feelings—the 'intermittencies of the heart' that owe to 'the anachronism which so often prevents the calendar of facts from corresponding to the calendar of feelings'—and, arguably even more significantly, to the complex nature of human temporality. 'Inasmuch as the self that I had just suddenly become once again had not existed since that evening long ago . . . it was quite naturally, not at the end of the day that had just passed, of which the self knew nothing, but . . . immediately after the first evening in Balbec'. It is 'as though Time

[1] Merleau-Ponty, *The Phenomenology of Perception*, p. 484.
[2] William Faulkner, *Requiem for a Nun*, Act I (New York: Vintage, 2011), p. 73.
[3] Proust, *Cities of the Plain*, in *Remembrance of Things Past*, vol. II, p. 783.

were to consist of a series of different and parallel lines', Proust concludes, 'without solution of continuity'.[4]

Such reflections point forward to the revelation, finally attained over a thousand pages later near the end of *Time Regained*, of the supra-temporal nature of the self persisting throughout the passing of time. Memory's ability to introduce 'the past, unmodified, into the present—just as it was at the moment when it was itself the present—suppresses the mighty dimension of Time which is the dimension in which life is lived'.[5] It now also dawns on Proust's narrator that the creation of a work of art—in his case the very novel we have been reading—presents a means for overcoming time, in which the events of his life recaptured through memory are made permanent in a form that reflects the vast structure of time and workings of memory that underpins it. But he realises that such a task is not straightforward. Time, he had earlier cautioned, has its own multi-dimensional complexity that transcends the simple linear dimensionality normally attributed to it. 'Souls move in time as bodies in space. As there is a geometry in space, so there is a psychology in time, in which the calculations of a plane psychology would no longer be accurate', because we should not be taking account of time and its twin processes of involuntary memory and forgetting which introduce a higher dimensional order to its human manifestation.[6] Thus the author realises that his story will need an added, 'third-dimensional psychology' to reflect the way in which time is disposed by the different intersecting planes of individuals, each of whom is a measure of duration.[7]

What Proust is elucidating here is a particular understanding of the philosophical problem of the structure of time. It is customarily assumed that time is most akin in shape to a straight line, existing in one dimension—the 'standard topology' as W.H. Newton-Smith terms it.[8] Were we to try to conceptualise time visually, we would most likely draw a single line, running from the past to the future, upon which the present forms a constantly moving point. The model holds irrespective of whether time is conceived as infinite in duration—without beginning or end—or bounded—with a finite starting point, a moment of creation, and a possible ultimate end. Time 'has only one dimension: different times are not simultaneous, but successive', and thus 'only parts of one and the same time' held Kant, and such classical formulations have underpinned our modern

---

[4] Ibid., p. 784.

[5] Proust, *Time Regained*, in *Remembrance of Things Past*, vol. III, p. 1087. Proust's conception of (involuntary) memory here is close to a position now termed 'direct realist', a viewpoint which has recently enjoyed renewed popularity in cognitive psychology and the philosophy of mind.

[6] Proust, *The Fugitive*, in *Remembrance of Things Past*, vol. III, p. 568.

[7] Proust, *Time Regained*, in *Remembrance of Things Past*, vol. III, p. 1087.

[8] W.H. Newton-Smith, *The Structure of Time* (London: Routledge and Kegan Paul, 1980), p. 51.

understanding of time.[9] Yet as seen repeatedly throughout this book, both the linearity and the singularity of time have proved open to question, regardless of whether the time at issue is objective or subjective, whether examined from philosophical or psychological, physical or anthropological, historical or even musical perspectives.

As is well known, the invariant universal time of Newton's classical mechanics is undermined in extreme cases by both the theories of Special Relativity and Quantum mechanics. Since the development of non-Euclidian geometries in the nineteenth century Kant's claims for a single Euclidian space and the correlate 'apodictic certainty' of the propositions of geometry have been disputed, and a parallel problem might thus be directed against his argument for time (especially if, after Einstein, time and space are interrelated).[10] Though in modern analytic philosophy the linear model for time still seems generally preferred, other possible topological structures—circular, branching, one- or two-dimensional—have also been posited.[11] Even within the disciplines of cognitive psychology and the philosophy of mind, there is a growing body of evidence in recent decades to support the idea that 'consciousness quite often involves an experience of temporality that is not properly ordered to objective sequence'.[12] Moreover, as we saw in previous chapters, from an anthropological and historical perspective a more cyclical view of history has been present in many cultures and periods, while the supposed connection between the multiplicity of subjective times and a single 'time of the world' has led to a philosophical aporia that remains to this day. Obviously for our day-to-day social interactions and understanding of the physical world we inhabit the construct of a collective singular, linear, and homogenous time has numerous advantages. Kant's positing of an absolute time as 'not an object of perception' but rather 'a rule of the understanding, through

---

[9] Kant, *Critique of Pure Reason*, p. 179.

[10] Ibid., p. 170. It is still debated whether this undermines Kant's transcendental analytic; certainly, it is still hard for humans to perceive the world in anything other than Euclidian space. However, elsewhere (e.g., p. 191) Kant does imply a greater remit to his claims. Furthermore, this argument would suggest that even if Kant's singular time is valid apodictically for the sensory forms of our experience, other spaces and times are metaphysically possible (see Poincaré, *The Foundations of Science*, p. 65). Merleau-Ponty likewise criticises Kant from a phenomenological perspective: 'the idea of a single space and a single time, being grounded upon that of a summation of being, which is precisely what Kant subjected to criticism in the Transcendental Dialectic, needs in particular to be bracketed and to produce its genealogy from the starting point of our actual experience' (*The Phenomenology of Perception*, p. 256). And our actual experience, as argued below, is often not linear.

[11] For some debates on the possible topologies of time see Newton-Smith, *The Structure of Time*, pp. 48–95, and the studies in Le Poidevin and MacBeath, *The Philosophy of Time*, part IV, 'The Topology of Time', pp. 149–220.

[12] Shaun Gallagher, *The Inordinance of Time* (Evanston, IL: Northwestern University Press, 1998), p. 3.

which alone the existence of appearances can acquire synthetic unity in tempo-ral relations' is entirely credible as a regulative construct, but there are other, less orderly times too.[13]

Above all, for our subjective experience of time, linearity is quite inade-quate to understand the complex and ever-changing interaction of past mem-ory, habit, forgetting, and expectation, as Proust so persuasively demonstrates throughout his enormous novel. As Suzanne Langer puts it:

> clock-time is homogenous and simple and may be treated as one-dimensional. But the experience of time is anything but simple. . . . life is always a dense fabric of concurrent tensions, and as each of them is a measure of time, the measurements themselves do not coincide. This causes our temporal experience to fall apart into incommensurate elements.[14]

The very precondition for our ability to conceive of time is our capacity for memory, which inevitably brings the human subject into playing an inextricable part in the constitution of time. In Merleau-Ponty's words, 'there is no natural time, if we understand thereby a time of things without subjectivity', for without a subjectivity, 'the past in itself [would be] no longer and the future in itself . . . not yet'.[15] 'The past, therefore, is not past, nor the future future' he concludes. 'It exists only when a subjectivity is there to disrupt the plenitude of being in itself, to adumbrate a perspective, and introduce non-being into it'.[16]

If (at least epistemologically speaking) the past is only present through memory, what is there to demonstrate that this is necessarily arranged in linear order, that the experienced past should be seen forming a linear continuum rather than, as Proust has it, a multiplicity of strands which may fitfully rise to the surface? In fact there is considerable debate within contemporary philoso-phy and psychology 'as to whether there are any substantive grounds for saying that memory itself is chronologically organized'.[17] In other words, many disci-plines provide evidence that both our cognition of the present and our mem-ory of the past may substantially involve temporal non-linearity: that while our intersocial existence is on the one hand regulated by the reassuring chronology

[13] Kant, *Critique of Pure Reason*, p. 320.

[14] Langer, 'The Image of Time', pp. 112–13.

[15] Merleau-Ponty, *The Phenomenology of Perception*, pp. 526, 280.

[16] Ibid., p. 489. Merleau-Ponty's phenomenological insights have been applied to music with con-siderable relevance for the present chapter by Thomas Clifton in *Music as Heard: A Study in Applied Phenomenology* (New Haven: Yale University Press, 1983), esp. pp. 51–65 and 81–131.

[17] Christoph Hoerl and Teresa McCormack (eds.), introduction to *Time and Memory: Issues in Philosophy and Psychology* (Oxford: Oxford University Press, 2001), p. 6.

of clock time, our apprehension of time is built upon many more complex and intricate processes.

These arguments for the complexity of temporal experience obviously have much relevance for music—unremarkably perhaps, given the importance of music throughout Proust's novel. As I explicated in chapter two, music has been viewed since the early nineteenth century as being in a particularly privileged position to express this sense of the subjective flux of time, the thickness of the past, its constitution through memory and corresponding reincorporation into the present. Since as argued there our own perception of time is intimately bound up with events occurring within time, there is a long-standing argument that music, to this extent, creates its own time. In no musical repertoire are these points more pertinent than for the cyclic instrumental works of late nineteenth-century French composers long associated with Proust and his memorable descriptions of the music of the fictional composer Vinteuil. As Proust's novel demonstrates, this repertoire was heard as expressing the richness and multiplicity of human temporality in an unsurpassed way. For the narrator of *À la recherche*, music seems 'something truer than all known books': its 'sounds seem to follow the very movement of our being' as its themes return in different and unexpected guises, 'the same and yet something else, as things recur in life', casting unexpected light on the nature of our existence within the dimension of time.[18]

To this end, the present chapter investigates instrumental works by three composers working in France in the late nineteenth century—Camille Saint-Saëns, César Franck, and Vincent d'Indy—all of whom were bound up with Proust's world and have been frequently cited as possible models for Vinteuil's music. Formed from a series of case studies dealing with works in three representative genres—the Violin Sonata, String Quartet, and Symphony—it makes

---

[18] Proust, *The Captive*, in *Remembrance of Things Past*, vol. III, pp. 381, 261. One other significant musical repertoire for Proust which might impinge on the discussion of music and temporality and is mentioned throughout *À la recherche* is that of Wagner. However, concerning the specific question of music and time, Wagner actually serves little explicit function in Proust's work, notwithstanding future reception of the *Leitmotiv* and temporality. (The use of recurring motives or reminiscence themes in opera is anyway common long before Wagner—indeed probably a French innovation.) Moreover, it is arguable that Proust's interest in the composer was created as much by the cultural context of contemporary French *wagnérisme* as by Wagner's actual music: Cormac Newark and Ingrid Wassenaar comment that 'in common with practically all *fin-de-siècle* French Wagnerians, Proust had little experience of Wagnerian opera'. Literary reception of Wagner in *A la recherche* is 'the reception of ideas about Wagner', and thus 'the music is represented only at one remove or more, if at all' ('Proust and Music: The Anxiety of Competence', *Cambridge Opera Journal*, 9 [1997], 178–9, 165). Therefore, while noting this qualification, the non-dramatic, non-verbal context of instrumental music is of greater bearing for my current investigation than Wagnerian music drama, historically influential though the latter was.

a concession to habitual chronology in charting a historical sequence from
Saint-Saëns's First Violin Sonata of 1885 via Franck's String Quartet of 1890 to
d'Indy's later codification of the cyclic principle, focussing on his own Symphony
No. 2 (1902–3). Yet despite this straightforward music-historical chronology,
the temporal qualities suggested by these three pieces are quite distinct.

Each work suggests a subtly different relationship with time, whether in
appearing to question the apparent relation between anticipation and fulfilment
and the role of causality in time's directional asymmetry between the concepts
of earlier and later; in the presence or absence of McTaggart's three temporal
series and their unlikely interaction whereby distinctions between past, present,
and future, or earlier and later, may become dissociated from seriality; in implying the paradoxical simultaneity of incompatible tenses or states of tenselessness. The central theme of this chapter is that music—even that stemming from
a particular era and culture—brings diverse insights into the apparent properties and topologies of time. In doing so, it reengages with questions of musical
non-linearity and multiple time raised in the opening two chapters, the issue of
musical tense familiar from chapter three, and forms an important stage in the
network of strands that run throughout this book which will culminate in the
final chapter's investigation of music as the spirit of time.

The Promise of Happiness: Saint-Saëns's Violin Sonata No. 1 in D minor

Cyclic form, though associated with the late-nineteenth-century French school,
and with César Franck and his pupils and in particular, actually has a much longer history. Though after the master's death the most prominent spokesman
among Franck's circle, Vincent d'Indy, went to unscrupulous lengths to create
the notion that Franck had developed the idea directly from late Beethoven,
in truth many more prominent composers were using the idea even before
Franck's early essay in the form, his Piano Trio in F♯ minor, Op. 1 No. 1 (1840).[19]
Moreover, Franck was not to make any significant further contribution to this

---

[19] See Vincent d'Indy, *Cours de Composition Musicale*, ed. Auguste Sérieyx, 3 vols. (Paris: A.
Durand, 1903–50), vol. II/i (1909), 'La Sonate Cyclique', pp. 375–433, and numerous subsequent references to the form in the volume's second part (published posthumously in 1933). Of
canonical figures, Schubert, Mendelssohn, Berlioz and Schumann all created important examples of
cyclic instrumental works between the 1820s and early 1840s, besides a host of now lesser-known
composers. See further my *Mendelssohn, Time and Memory*, esp. pp. 6–41, or, on the pre-history
to Franck's development of the technique, Christiane Strucken-Paland, *Zyklische Prinzipien in den
Instrumentalwerken César Francks* (Kassel: Bosse, 2009), pp. 31–69.

technique until the late 1870s with the Piano Quintet, by which point the idea had become widespread among composers, and his most important and influential works in the style—the Violin Sonata, Symphony in D minor, and String Quartet—all date from the later 1880s.

Between Franck's Op. 1 and the cyclic masterpieces of his last decade the younger figure of Saint-Saëns produced numerous examples of works in the cyclic idiom. The First Violin Sonata in D minor, Op. 75 (1885), was far from the first of these pieces (the composer was already essaying the form as far back as the 1850s), but it is one that is significant for two reasons here. First is that this sonata and the related cyclic Third Symphony in C minor ('Organ') that followed a year later predate by a very short period the famous cyclic works of Franck in these genres, and thus in a chronological survey form a useful (if unexpected) starting point for discussing this French tradition. Second is the fact that this work was actually the original source for the famous *petite phrase* of Vinteuil's Violin Sonata. While not known as widely as it might be, this Proustian connection is nonetheless no secret, though rarely has the value of the link between Proust and Saint-Saëns's work been appreciated. This fact is attributable in part to the snobbery directed against this composer (one which Proust himself to some extent subscribed to later in life)[20] and in part to the fact that investigations of Proust and music have traditionally sought to identify exact musical correlates for the fictional works described—invariably a futile endeavour—rather than asking a more important question: how might what Proust actually heard in music be insightful for understanding musical temporality more deeply? For a more considered analysis of Saint-Saëns's Sonata shows that Proust certainly heard more than just a little phrase of it.

What is most distinctive about Saint-Saëns's First Sonata is the way in which the F major second subject—Proust's original *petite phrase*—is heard in the first movement's recapitulation in such a manner as to make itself felt as paradoxically absent even while it is being stated. Unconvincingly reprised here in the flat supertonic E♭, it is only in the latter stages of the finale that the theme is suddenly reencountered and at long last tonally resolved into the sonata's home key of D. The subtlety of the music's suggestion of presence and absence, of expectations left unsatisfied and finally fulfilled when almost forgotten and no longer sought, is fully worthy of the Proustian context that it unknowingly helped create.

---

[20] Proust later confessed to Jacques de Lacretelle in 1918 that the little phrase of the Sonata was 'the charming but ultimately mediocre phrase of a violin sonata by Saint-Saëns, a musician I do not like' ('Dedicace a Monsieur Jacques de Lacretelle', in the Pléiade Edition *Contre Sainte-Beuve précédé de Pastiches et mélanges et suivi de Essais et articles*, ed. Pierre Clarac and Yves Sandre [Paris: Gallimard, 1971], p. 565).

Opening with a shadowy oscillating figure that draws much of its ambiguous effect from the syncopations between the near-heterophonic violin and piano parts and the subtle metrical interchange of $\frac{6}{8}$ and $\frac{9}{8}$, the first theme of the sonata gradually grows from the stepwise ascent of the bass to prolong a more turbulent pre-dominant harmonic area (b. 13), giving rise to a provisional arrival point on the dominant where the violin imposes itself over bubbling arpeggios in the accompaniment (b. 27). The emphasis on subdominant and Neapolitan areas within these early stages will become increasingly significant as the work progresses. For the restatement of the theme at b. 34 the violin takes up its partner's original line under a newly liquid, diaphanous texture high in the piano. It is hard not to think here that something distinctly remains from the Saint-Saëns model in Proust's description of the solitary movement from the Vinteuil Sonata Swann first hears while at the Verdurins':

> At first he had appreciated only the material quality of the sounds which those instruments secreted. And it had been a source of keen pleasure when, below the delicate line of the violin-part, slender but robust, compact and commanding, he had suddenly become aware of the mass of the piano-part beginning to emerge in a sort of liquid rippling of sound, multiform but indivisible, smooth yet restless, like the deep blue tumult of the sea, silvered and charmed into a minor key by the moonlight.[21]

Naturally such are the variety of different, often contradictory attributes given to the imaginary sonata that one cannot obtain a one-to-one match with any piece of music. Just as the Narrator's loves in À la recherche are each created from multiple real figures in Proust's life, so both the Vinteuil Sonata and Septet are a composite of numerous real pieces.[22] Nonetheless, several of Proust's

---

[21] Proust, Swann's Way, in Remembrance of Things Past, vol. I, p. 227.

[22] George Painter notes that 'Proust took a sly pleasure in multiplying the minor origins of the Sonata', mentioning the Act I Prelude to Lohengrin, the Good Friday music from Parsifal, Fauré's Ballade, and 'something by Schubert' to friends as pieces which had contributed some quality (George D. Painter, Marcel Proust: A Biography, 2 vols. [Harmondsworth: Penguin, 1977], vol. II, p. 240). The description of the Marquise de Cambremer's rapturous reaction to the sonata was further taken from an incident a real life performance of Fauré's Violin Sonata No. 1 (vol. II, p. 79). Nevertheless, to the extent that real pieces may be found, the Saint-Saëns First and Franck Violin Sonatas appear almost invariably to commentators to be the most significant models. For other accounts following the sources for the little phrase see Georges Piroué, Proust e la musique du devenir (Paris: Editions Denoël, 1960), pp. 173–90; Jean-Michel Nectoux, 'Proust et Fauré', Bulletin de la Société des amis de Marcel Proust, 21 (1971), 1101–20; Jean-Jacques Nattiez, Proust as Musician, trans. Derrick Puffett (Cambridge: Cambridge University Press, 1989), pp. 3–5.

Ex. 5.1 Saint-Saëns: Violin Sonata No. 1 in D minor, Op. 75 (1885), first movement, second subject, bb. 76–91

descriptions characterise the original model, the Saint-Saëns D minor Sonata, extremely well, and even more rewardingly are of fundamental insight for understanding the broader aesthetic qualities of the piece.[23]

In place of the Neapolitan harmonies of b. 12, the consequent statement moves to F⁷ and dissolves into transitional figuration drawn from the latter part of the first subject in the unlikely tritonal key of A♭. After leading round to the less unusual submediant B♭, the transition material breaks off on diminished seventh harmonies. Without any discernable mediation there now appears the movement's second subject entering over a second-inversion F major chord (b. 76: Ex. 5.1). Famously, this is the original inspiration for the *petite phrase*.

---

[23] I thus cannot bring myself to agree with Nattiez's assertion 'From *Jean Santueil* to *A la recherché* . . . *nothing* in the text makes us think of Saint-Saëns' (*Proust as Musician*, p. 7, emphasis in original).

Around 1894, when Proust was in the midst of his relationship with Reynaldo Hahn (a composition pupil of Saint-Saëns's), he got to know the sonata and would ask his companion 'Play me that bit I like, Reynaldo—you know, the "little phrase"', which, as with Swann and Odette, soon became the 'national anthem of their love'.[24] This real-life inspiration became transported into 'The Sonata' of Proust's first novel, *Jean Santeuil* (1896–9)—'He had recognised that phrase from the Saint-Saëns Sonata, which almost every evening in the heyday of their happiness he had asked for, and she had played endlessly for him'—and is still named in drafts for *Swann's Way* from 1910 as the sonata Swann hears, before Proust finally changed Saint-Saëns into the fictional Vinteuil.[25]

Essentially consisting of a simple, eight-bar phrase that is subject first to repetition and then to gentle elaboration, the theme outlines a graceful arc down from its initial c^3 that is filled out with alternating thirds and seconds, over a prolonged dominant pedal. Quadruplets in the penultimate bar add a touch of rhythmic interest, while a subtle reverberation of voices is created through the violin's interplay with the piano, whose arpeggios pick out the pitches of the melodic line on the final semiquaver of each half-bar. What is particularly significant about this idea is, as we shall see, its blend of simplicity that makes it easily apprehended with a certain open-endedness which invites continuation through reiteration. Indeed, in place of any new, more conclusive gesture, a pendant idea is formed from the clear rhythmic variation of this theme syncopated across hands in the piano (b. 108). Again, however, no tonal closure is forthcoming. The theme gradually dissipates without any structural cadence marking the end of the exposition and the music dissolves back into the tonic minor and with it the return of the first subject (b. 132).

This point marks in formal terms the start of the development section, though the tonic minor opening might suggest the generic vestiges of an exposition repeat, a notion that is gently dispelled by the newly rippling piano accompaniment. While its structural divisions are in one sense clear, the movement nonetheless takes on an increasing formal ambiguity in that the development starts from the first subject in the tonic and features the most extensive statement of the second theme, while the recapitulation takes on coda-like characteristics and brings back the second theme in a tonally even more remote key. Saint-Saëns's movement may aptly be read as a rotational structure where the circular recurrence of thematic ideas plays out in opposition to an evolving tonal process that leads to the breakdown of the movement. A notable result of this strategy is the

[24] Painter, *Marcel Proust*, vol. I, pp. 163–4.

[25] Proust, *Jean Santeuil*, trans. Gerard Hopkins (Harmondsworth: Penguin Books, 1985), p. 660. For the text of the 1910 version of *Swann's Way* see the Pléiade edition of *À la recherche du temps perdu*, ed. Jean-Yves Tadié, 4 vols. (Paris: Gallimard, 1987–9), vol. I, pp. 909, 911, 913, 918, 935, 941.

interaction between a cyclic time sense reliant on the large-scale formal repetitions and their corresponding sense of spatial symmetry and a linear, irreversible time operating across these rotations.

Following this tonic restatement of the first theme, the development's central core is provided by a fugato on the second theme in the subdominant G minor (b. 152). Changed into the minor mode and rhythmically altered from its original straight duple values to a lilting crotchet-quaver pattern, this note-for-note thematic transformation has the effect of bringing the theme into the darker ambit of the first subject. The second theme soon re-emerges in its original major-key lustre, shining out in G major over the piano arpeggiations, but darkens again to the minor, and a more subdued, albeit major-key statement of the syncopated pendant phrase ushers in the retransition. As if influenced by the prevalent subdominant emphasis of the development, the recapitulation is approached unexpectedly from this region: a melodic fragment of the second subject vacillates between G minor and the $B\flat\substack{6\\3}$ harmony beneath it, resulting in a tonal blurring that undermines the strength of the eventual materialisation of the first subject at b. 248.

Now in the reprise, the first theme reflects the subdominant and submediant tendencies of the foregoing music through the piano's discreet replacement of the pitch a with b♭, resulting in a harmonic recontextualisation of the opening bar as $B\flat\substack{6\\3}$, in place of the previous root-position tonic. The recapitulation appears to function as a consequence of the harmonic process of the movement. Aided by Saint-Saëns's tonal undercutting of major structural points of articulation throughout the movement, the result is a highly continuous design that leads to the apparent *telos* of this return.[26] But such is the cumulative rhetorical force of the music that the movement's continuity rapidly breaks down, the first-theme recapitulation coming to a decisive halt on a D major $\substack{6\\4}$ chord (b. 286). Its momentum petering out, the music darkens to the minor before moving to A♭ minor (revisiting the parallel stage in the exposition's transition), used now as part of a subdominant progression to the Neapolitan degree of E♭, where finally the little phrase might be heard again (b. 306). Yet now, even while its pitches are faintly discernable submerged within the piano's soft arpeggiations (Ex. 5.2), it is somehow not there. It has gone.

As the dynamic gradually decreases to *ppp* and the texture thins out, the hopeful suggestion of the missing second-subject theme dissipates into nothing. The brief remainder of the movement is little more than a transition to the second movement that follows without break in this same Neapolitan key

---

[26] There is no medial caesura, no EEC, and no dominant preceding the recapitulation; neither will there be any tonal resolution of the secondary theme or an ESC.

Ex. 5.2 Saint-Saëns: Violin Sonata No. 1, first movement, failed recapitulation of second subject, bb. 302–15

of E♭.[27] In one sense this drastically curtailed opening movement feels like it has already effectively ended before this shortened, etiolated reprise of the second theme in the distant realm of ♭II. The disintegration of its projected sonata design stems from the process whereby the little phrase has become composed out of the tonal structure. It is notable that while the first subject has remained implacably in the tonic D minor throughout the movement, the second theme that so beguiled the young Proust, rather than resolving, has become increasingly estranged, following a more subdominant harmonic trajectory III→iv–IV→♭II.

In many ways this passage has all the musical markings of memory explored in chapter three. Beyond the remote key, the soft dynamic and veiled textural presentation contribute an elusive quality to the present perception, as the

---

[27] This type of cyclic sonata design in which the opening movement breaks down at the expected second subject recapitulation and elides instead with the slow movement is familiar from several other nineteenth-century works, such as Liszt's B minor Piano Sonata (a work Saint-Saëns admired) and Saint-Saëns's own Organ Symphony a year later (also charting a Neapolitan relationship, C minor to D♭ major).

turning to the minor mode at b. 314 likewise suggests the waning vivacity of the remembered image. Particularly in the manner that the melodic line creeps in amongst the ripple of semiquavers in the piano while the violin sustains its high b♭² for five bars before belatedly joining its accompanist for the phrase's final segment, the music conjures up the sensation of the theme as having been lost to the soloist-protagonist and only recalled fragmentarily after its subconscious materialisation. Yet what seems just as important here is not so much the pastness but rather the absence of the object in question, signalled by its expression as a memory. Memory, after all, is the presence of absence—or, to turn this around, the absence of presence. If the original presentation suggested the reciprocation or echo of the violin's melodic voice within the accompanying piano arpeggios, now for the greater part of the theme we hear only the latter; an echo without the presence of the original object, an almost tangible sense of absence. It is as if Saint-Saëns is conjuring up this theme only in order to suggest that it is not actually there, that its tones are an illusion, its utter removal from the world of the music's experience. The paradox here is how the music accomplishes the seemingly impossible for a medium in which signifier and signified are normally intrinsically the same, by suggesting the theme enough for its absence at this very moment to be felt.

For the trained analytical listener there is a formal need for the second subject to be resolved into the tonic by the end of the movement that has remained unfulfilled, indeed whose realisation looks farther away than ever. But even for the untutored hearer (Swann, perhaps, or the real-life Proust), the way in which the recapitulation has suggested enough of the theme to stimulate the want for its (generically obligatory) reappearance, and yet has presented this in such a way as paradoxically to show its non-appearance, there is an undeniable feeling of disappointment, a desire for the repossession of the *petite phrase* that, while perhaps inchoate, still holds out at some subliminal level the yearning for fulfilment.

Hence we can see how powerfully and yet subtly Saint-Saëns has set up a subconscious wish for the return of the theme, a deed that will be accomplished much later near the end of the sonata's finale. I think here of a passage from 'Swann in Love' where Proust, through the medium of Charles Swann, expressed this feeling so well:

> Then [the little phrase] vanished. He hoped, with a passionate longing, that he might find it again, a third time. And reappear it did, though without speaking to him more clearly, bringing him, indeed, a pleasure less profound. But when he returned home he felt the need of it: he was like a man into whose life a woman he has seen for a moment passing by has brought the image of a new beauty which deepens his own

sensibility, although he does not even know her name or whether he will ever see her again.[28]

As is typical of Proust's method, the exact details seem blurred when applied to real-life examples. The reapparition of the phrase that came 'without speaking to him more clearly' could well refer to the underwhelming third appearance of the second subject in the first movement recapitulation (as befitting the fact that at this stage only the one movement of the sonata has been heard by Swann), or allude to the eventual return of the phrase in the finale; or (what is more typically Proustian) be formed of some amalgamation between the two.[29] But in any case, the passionate longing awakened by the music, and the obscure way in which this is brought about, are the same peculiar and distinctive aesthetic properties of Proust's original model, the Saint-Saëns Sonata. It is as if, whether consciously or not, this key moment in the opening movement's failed recapitulation, as the little phrase returns only in order to show the melancholy reality of its absence, was the passage that Proust's imagination was set off by. Proust may have heard Saint-Saëns's Violin Sonata imprecisely and have successively mixed and multiplied his sources for Vinteuil's sonata, but his initial emotional impressions of this music, his broader aesthetic discernment, speak more powerfully than any inexactness of detail or the failings of the snobbery he developed later in life against this composer.

Though not manifesting clear thematic connections with the preceding music, both central movements continue to explore the subdominant and Neapolitan realms opened up within the course of the first movement by the straying second subject. Although the four standard movements of this sonata are arranged into two parts in the score, with opening and closing pair running on without clear break, the thematic links between the outer two and inverted harmonic symmetry of the central pair creates a chiastic design that breaks across the formal dualism. The E♭ Adagio that follows from the dissolution of the first movement's recapitulation interposes within its ternary design a central section that moves from G♭ to G and D before returning to E♭, while the Allegretto moderato third movement frames a chorale-like E♭ major episode within its skittish G minor

---

[28] Proust, *Swann's Way*, in *Remembrance of Things Past*, vol. I, p. 229.

[29] Similarly, another example that chimes with the Saint-Saëns Sonata, though inexactly, is Swann's chance re-encounter with the Vinteuil sonata and his beloved *petite phrase* at the later performance at the Verdurin's, where 'after a high note sustained through two whole bars, Swann sensed its approach, stealing forth from beneath that long-drawn sonority' (ibid., p. 230). Though the piano is not silent for as long as two bars in Saint-Saëns, this could still easily recall its entry with a version of the *petite phrase* under the violin's high sustained dominant pedal in either b. 108 or 216 from the exposition and development, or (especially) the elusive second subject recapitulation at b. 306.

outer section, only for the E♭ passage to return, abbreviated, at the close, as the music leads into the *moto perpetuo* finale.

'The phrase had disappeared. Swann knew that it would come again at the end of the last movement, after a long passage which Mme Verdurin's pianist always "skipped".[30] Here Proust's account of the Vinteuil sonata matches its model to the letter. Throughout the greater portion of this D major finale the *petite phrase* is absent from the musical surface, yet in retrospect has been silently waiting within it, dormant, 'hidden somewhere outside the realm, beyond the reach of intellect'.[31] A bravura first subject played *spiccato* in semiquavers, whose bassline is, without perhaps our noticing it, distantly reminiscent of the little phrase in its looping, contour, and construction from alternating seconds and thirds, is contrasted with a more aspirant second subject on the dominant at b. 45. A brief return of the first subject's semiquavers serves in lieu of a development section (bb. 88–106), the music moving continuously forwards without resting point into the recapitulation. It is after the reprise of the second theme here that the latent affinities with the first subject's bass line are finally realised by the unexpected, but no less moving, return of the little phrase from the first movement (b. 145).

There is a sense here that the return of the first movement's theme is not marked as 'past', as reminiscent or nostalgic in its expressive affect, but rather as encountering it again in the present, something that was almost unknowingly desired. It appears as if a chance reencounter, whose inner logical necessity has been hidden to us. It is like re-meeting a long-forgotten friend, who, perhaps without our realising it, we have missed. And indeed this is how Proust describes the theme's return. 'Swann felt as though he had met, in a friend's drawing room, a woman whom he had seen and admired in the street and had despaired of ever seeing again'.[32] Appearing first in B♭, a submediant to counterbalance the first movement exposition's mediant F, the theme is re-engaged within the extended coda that starts soon after at b. 177, being integrated into the finale's material and at long last affirmed in the work's home tonality of D major. Already before this, the phrase had been combined with the running semiquavers of the finale's first subject (b. 161), the undulating bassline of the latter being replaced by the earlier theme with which it shared a close kinship. Now at b. 195 the listener might begin to realise that the emphatic downbeat in octaves low in the piano which initiated the finale's second subject is extremely similar to that from the pendant

---

[30] Proust, *Swann's Way*, in *Remembrance of Things Past*, vol. I, p. 382.

[31] Ibid., pp. 47–8.

[32] Ibid., p. 231. Proust is returning to the motive of the 'fugitive beauty' glimpsed by the Narrator (or Swann) in passing (a trope familiar from Baudelaire's 'À une passante'), which runs throughout the earlier volumes of *À la recherche*.

form of the first movement's own second theme, and as if to underscore this parallel the music leads from the former to the return of the latter over a tonic $^6_4$ at b. 201. At b. 209 these clangourous downbeats change to ♭7̂, signalling the movement's imminent cadential closure while transformed suggestively into the pealing of bells. The way in which the little phrase, once so hesitant, now rings out above these makes it irresistible to recall Swann's description of the theme as 'the national anthem' of his love for Odette.[33] Virtuoso passagework in the violin takes us to the sonata's close.

On one level, Saint-Saëns's work conveys a clear sense of the causal relation of events in time. The generic demand of the sonata principle is satisfied as the first movement's second subject, lacking its expected tonal resolution in that movement's recapitulation, is finally brought back in the tonic key in the finale. Its realisation may be delayed, but it is no less certainly accomplished by the end of the piece. What happens later in the finale is consequent upon the events of the opening movement; it may be seen as a formal necessity. Moreover, through the initial frustration of this desire, its suggestion, denial, and ultimate fulfilment, a more powerful expressive trajectory is set up.

Such a reading might suggest the Saint-Saëns Sonata as forming a fitting illustration of a temporal form exhibiting a causal relationship between events in time. Philosophers seeking an explanation for the apparent asymmetry of time—the fact that it appears to 'flow' from the future to the past, that we remember the past but do not appear to have the same privileged access to the future—have fastened onto this issue of causality. Those who believe that the properties of past, present, and future that McTaggart described with his A series are merely perspectival properties of the human subject and not metaphysically real predicates of time are especially interested in the possibility that 'the direction of time is not definable as the direction from *past* to *future*, but rather as the direction from *cause* to *effect*'.[34]

It is arguable that both A-series properties of past, present, and future and B-series properties of earlier and later may be plausibly predicated of musical time (that is, the intentional temporality of the musical work, a hermeneutic construct), depending on the perceived qualities of the particular piece involved. Here, briefly, I would argue that A-series qualities are less applicable, that the musical discourse of the sonata appears relatively tenseless, while a broadly linear temporal sense of progression from earlier to later is found. The listener encountering the work diachronically in performance certainly has his or her

---

[33] Proust, *Swann's Way*, in *Remembrance of Things Past*, vol. I, p. 238.

[34] Robin Le Poidevin, 'Music without the Flow of Time', *Proceedings of the Philosophy and Music Conference 'Time Theories and Music'*, Ionian University of Corfu, 28 April 2012, <http://conferences.ionio.gr/ccpm12/download.php?f=ccpm12_ks_poidevin.pdf>, p. 8.

own constantly moving present, but this is one of many possible perspectives, not a privileged position on the musical work *qua* aesthetic object, and it is less meaningful here than in many other pieces to say that a particular passage is past or future—that is marked as possessing an inherent tense.[35] However, it is at least conceivable that a statement that the finale is later than the first movement has greater purchase on the work than one proposing that the finale is in the future, or the derivative notion that when the finale is present, the first movement is past (A-series terms which collapse trivially into properties of the B series). A clearer way of saying this is simply that in Saint-Saëns's piece the notions of past, present, and future appear less relevant to the experience of the music than the sense of causality conveyed through the successive appearances of Proust's little phrase. The sonata might hence be used as an aesthetic illustration of a temporal object for which the apparent direction of time from earlier to later is grounded in causal relationship rather than temporal passage.[36]

Yet this sense of musical causality—in any event an 'as if', a regulative fiction which we buy into—is a capricious one. It might also be argued that to read the music against such rigidly determinate conditions of rule-adherence misses the point of aesthetic works (their 'freedom' as post-Kantians would have it). The return of the *petite phrase* in the finale might never have happened. Its effect, as noted, is of pleasant surprise, an unexpected fulfilment—unexpected as the theme would not have been consciously missed had it not materialised.[37] Rather than a logical necessity this is merely the unexpected corollary of an apparently unrealised expectation of a likely future, or even less, an inchoate hope—a peculiar quality created through the first movement's playing with the listener's subconscious expectations. (To this extent, too, tense, and the contingency of the future, does seem to play an important part in the meaning of this piece.) Is this

---

[35] Many of these debates have been rehearsed in discussion of time and tense in fictional literature. See for example McTaggart, 'The Unreality of Time', 465, Gregory Currie, 'Tense and Egocentricity in Fiction', in Robin Le Poidevin (ed.), *Questions of Time and Tense* (Oxford, Clarendon Press, 1998), pp. 265–83, or Le Poidevin, *The Images of Time*, pp. 141–75.

[36] I am not entirely convinced by this argument, however. Though corresponding with a favoured B-Theorist perspective in the contemporary philosophy of time, the hermeneutic lengths resorted to seem to make any phenomenal reality for such claims tenuous. One may view the sonata synchronically as a tenseless ordered totality of B-series (or better, C-series) relations, but it is at least debatable that by doing so we have taken time out of it—that is, as it were, thrown the baby out with the bathwater. Or that the musical work thus conceived is only temporal *in potentia* and not, as when performed, *in esse*. It should be noted here that such qualities may also be projected onto most music.

[37] More cynically, it might be held (in line with Proust's rather Schopenhauerian outlook) that by the time it does return, all those bars later, it is no longer really missed. Our desires, if eventually attained, are not as glorious as we believed when we most sought them. However, I feel there is still a sense of idealised, aestheticised fulfilment in the Saint-Saëns's work that (perhaps in contradistinction to life), grants us its promise of fugitive happiness by the end.

really causality? Just as in life, tokens of future happiness may sometimes turn out after all, but often not as or exactly when expected.

Related to this is another point that has remained under-examined so far: the actual quality of this second subject. For what was it that so captivated the young Proust about this celebrated melodic entity? On the face of it there is nothing so remarkable about the second subject; indeed, both Proust's biographer George D. Painter and Saint-Saëns's, Brian Rees, are less than charitable about the real-life *petite phrase*.[38] And while a degree of unconscious residual snobbery or defensiveness may explain such responses, the innocent listener versed in Proustian poetics is likely to be mildly disappointed when first encountering the theme that inspired such panegyrics. *Is that all?* Certainly it is pleasant on the ear, agreeably balanced, containing perhaps a hidden luminosity that grows on repeated acquaintance, although so are many other 'little phrases' from less distinguished composers. But to understand this theme's effect one must understand it not in itself, outside the context of its temporal manifestation, but rather as it appears in time.

Most characteristic of the phrase was, as we saw, its open-endedness. The theme enters over a dominant pedal on $^6_4$ harmony and lets off on V. Even at the end of the second subject's first half (b. 107), it closes inconclusively on the local relative minor (A), and is followed by the return of the dominant-functioning $^6_4$, having prolonged this C throughout. Nowhere in the piece, even in its regaining within the finale, does the phrase cadence to the tonic it continually holds out the promise of. It is never closed, completed, but every time it reappears it renews such hope. It is seemingly always pointing to something more than itself, betokening an elusive realm of happiness.

No wonder Swann sees in this theme the promise of happiness, of love or future beauty. 'It had at once suggested to him a world of inexpressible delights' as 'it floated by, so near and yet so infinitely remote'.[39] Saint-Saëns's modest little phrase possesses the sense of being concrete enough to seem eminently graspable and yet is harmonically open so as to postpone perpetually any conclusion or sense of completion. Hence for Swann the phrase suggests a multiplicity of meanings, an indexical openness, a difficulty of signification that confuses him. At first the melody awakens merely an indistinct longing, it enchants and beguiles him. But it seems to point to more than this. Soon its hopes get transferred onto his still innocent love for Odette, and the phrase becomes 'the national anthem of their love'.[40] He starts believing that the anthropomorphised

---

[38] Painter, *Marcel Proust*, vol. I, p. 163; Brian Rees, *Camille Saint-Saëns: A Life* (London: Chatto & Windus, 1999), p. 257. Rees even misidentifies the theme.

[39] Proust, *Swann's Way*, in *Remembrance of Things Past*, vol. I, pp. 228, 238.

[40] Ibid., p. 238.

phrase feels and shares his joys and sufferings.[41] Later he will associate it with memories of moonlight in the Bois de Boulogne.[42] All these are too concrete; as he grows dissatisfied with the music's resistance to any ultimate and abiding signification, such beliefs will become subject to absurd trivialisation. At an earlier time in typical Platonic-Schopenhauerian fashion he had 'regarded musical motifs as actual ideas, of another world'. Finally, however, they are but a memory of 'old Verdurin in his frock coat in the palmhouse'.[43]

Swann tries to fix the phrase's meaning. But music continually escapes such definiteness of linguistic signification. As Merleau-Ponty so aptly characterises this art (and Proust's *petite phrase* in particular), 'Each time we want to get at it immediately, or lay hands on it, or circumscribe it, or see it unveiled, we do in fact feel that the attempt is misconceived, that it retreats in the measure that we approach'.[44] After multiple attempts Swann gives up, falling short of obtaining any artistic vision. His failure, however, is the catalyst to set the Narrator on the correct way of understanding such aesthetic experience. That meaning, he comes to realise, is bound up with extratemporality. Even early on, when Odette, now Mme Swann, plays him the Vinteuil phrase the Narrator realises 'I never possessed it in its entirety: it was like life itself'.[45] But rather than being a failing, this is actually the makings of the correct path to avoiding misunderstanding of the music's message. Much later, in the revelatory coda to *Time Regained*, the Narrator realises that the key he has been searching for is the supra-temporal nature of existence. And 'thinking again of the extra-temporal joy which I had been made to feel [through involuntary memory] I said to myself: "Was this perhaps that happiness which the little phrase of the sonata promised to Swann . . . ?"'[46]

There is surely something crucial about music's fascination that Proust is on to here, and that he could have heard so well in the Saint-Saëns Sonata. It is bound up with this definiteness and yet resistance to signification, music's transience, and continued supra-temporal persistence. Describing this selfsame theme of Saint-Saëns in *Jean Santeuil*, Proust already recognises this ineffability. 'Yet in that desolating phrase which told of how all things pass, the sadness still was light and airy'. 'Everything around that music too had changed, but it had not. It had lasted longer that their love and would outspan their lives'.[47] As Saint-Saëns

[41] Ibid., p. 378.

[42] Proust, *Within a Budding Grove*, in *Remembrance of Things Past*, vol. I, p. 574.

[43] Ibid., p. 575.

[44] Merleau-Ponty, *The Visible and the Invisible*, ed. Claude Lefort, trans. Alphonso Lingis (Evanston IL: Northwestern University Press, 1968), p. 150.

[45] Proust, *Within a Budding Grove*, in *Remembrance of Things Past*, vol. I, p. 571.

[46] Proust, *Time Regained*, in *Remembrance of Things Past*, vol. III, p. 911.

[47] Proust, *Jean Santeuil*, p. 660.

so miraculously achieves in the second subject's illusory recapitulation in his sonata, music may at once suggest the paradoxical qualities of presence and absence, fulfilment and incompletion, a state of permanent deferral that is itself the most potent expression of human existence within the dimension of time.

Later in life Proust was dismissive of his former lover's composition teacher. The phrase was ultimately 'mediocre'; Saint-Saëns was a musician whom he 'did not like'.[48] Yet perhaps by this stage the author was beginning to commit the same error as Swann in the volume of his novel published in the autumn of the year he made these remarks. The *petite phrase* may not be spectacular, but it points to more than it may ever be restricted to. It may even have pointed to the epiphany of time regained, to Proust's own insight. Just before he dies, Proust's fictional writer Bergotte famously goes to see Vermeer's *A View of Delft* at an exhibition of Dutch paintings. He is struck by a seemingly trivial detail, a tiny patch of yellow on the wall.[49] In itself it is slight, 'petite', seemingly unimportant. It is not even clear to present-day viewer which patch this might have been. But this image provides him with his dying thought: the realisation that his writing had become too dry, that he has lost sight of his artistic vision. In art insignificant features may hold an unaccountable radiance. Perhaps Saint-Saëns's phrase is like the patch of yellow in Vermeer's painting.

Of the Search for Lost Time: Franck's String Quartet in D

Looking back at the Vinteuil Sonata from the perspective provided by the fictional composer's Septet in *The Captive*—a passage written later, when Saint-Saëns seems to have faded from Proust's mind—the Narrator introduces some new, quite striking attributes to this impossibly elusive piece. 'The sonata', he now decides, 'opened upon a lily-white pastoral dawn', a 'virginal, plant-strewn world'.[50] While seemingly foreign to the Saint-Saëns Sonata, such descriptions might seem to have been specifically written of Franck's Violin Sonata, composed a year after.

It was in the years immediately following the Saint-Saëns D minor Sonata that the now septuagenarian César Franck produced in quick succession the three cyclic works that he is now most famous for. The first of these and most prominent of all French works in this particular genre is his Violin Sonata in A (1886), famously described by the ever-supportive d'Indy as 'the first and

---

[48] Proust, 'Dedicace a Monsieur Jacques de Lacretelle', p. 565.
[49] Proust, *The Captive*, in *Remembrance of Things Past*, vol. III, pp. 185–6.
[50] Ibid., pp. 251, 252.

the purest model of the sonata employing cyclic themes'.[51] Heedless of the long and extensive precedent for this principle, d'Indy would still have us believe that 'from this moment cyclical form, the basis of modern symphonic art, was created and consecrated'.[52] This sonata is a sophisticated example of a cyclic work where the process of thematic development, recall, and anticipation may form a persuasive analogy for a psychological process akin to the flow of consciousness.[53] Moreover, Franck's work, often presupposed by listeners to be the 'real' Vinteuil sonata, has a slight but definite Proustian connection.[54]

The sonata charts an overall progression from the dream-like poise of its opening movement—a state of innocence, a youthful vision of the hawthorns at Combray perhaps—through darker, more spiritually turbulent regions in the second and third movements, to a song-like finale where the opening theme of the first movement is transformed into a beguilingly melodious idea that miraculously appears to work in canon, an inspiration that Proust found 'angelic'.[55] What in the first movement had appeared in faltering trochaic rhythm, arpeggiating a half-diminished seventh over a suspended dominant-ninth, is transformed into the tonic harmony, gentle conjunct motion and flowing crotchets of the finale's theme. Notable too is that at almost no point in the first movement the violin and piano play the same material: the first theme, albeit emergent from the piano's accompanying harmonies, was restricted to the violin, while conversely the second theme is only ever heard in the piano.[56] At last in the finale the two are

---

[51] D'Indy, *Cours de Composition Musicale*, vol. II/i, p. 423.

[52] D'Indy, *César Franck*, trans. Rosa Newmarch (London: John Lane Bodley Head, 1909), p. 171.

[53] The implications Franck's use of cyclic form hold for conveying a sense of psychological journey and narrative plot have been explicated in this work by Gregory Karl in 'Music as Plot: A Study in Cyclic Forms' (PhD diss., University of Cincinnati, 1993), pp. 176–204.

[54] Proust was certainly a great admirer of the work. The one direct connection between Franck's Sonata and that of Vinteuil is found in a passage added at a late stage to *Swann's Way*, which echoes Proust's description of a performance by Enescu of the Franck contained in a letter to Antoine Bibesco of 19 April 1913: 'At first the piano complained alone, like a bird deserted by its mate; the violin heard and answered it, as from a neighbouring tree. It was as at the beginning of the world, as if there were as yet only the two of them on the earth' (*Swann's Way*, in *Remembrance of Things Past*, vol. I, p. 382). The passage seems to refer to the finale of Vinteuil's sonata, but even here, however, it is unclear as to which movement of the Franck Proust is referring (commentators seem often to assume the finale). On the possible links between the two, see Jöel-Marie Fauquet, *César Franck* (Paris: Fayard, 1999), pp. 631–3; and Franz Michael Maier, 'Prousts Franck: Form und Semantik in einer Sonate und einem Roman des 20. Jahrhunderts', in Christiane Strucken-Paland and Ralph Paland (eds.), *César Franck im Kontext: Epoche, Werk und Wirkung* (Cologne: Dohr, 2009), pp. 175–91.

[55] Proust, letter to Bibesco, 19 April 1913, in *Correspondance*, ed. Philip Kolb, 21 vols. (Paris: Plon, 1970–93), vol. XII, p. 148.

[56] The one exception is found at bb. 47–50 in the development section, where the piano echoes the violin's invocation of the opening motive by a bar, thus strongly prefiguring the canon of the finale.

heard in counterpoint—a coming together which has suggestive implications for understanding the sonata's temporal progression.

Within this journey, the music is shot through with glimpses of its lost ideal and foreshadowings of the future. Throughout the two inner movements distorted memories of the opening return, while two themes that emerge in the later stages of the *Recitativo-Fantasia* correspondingly offer a foretaste of the finale's contrasting idea and central climax. Yet at no other stage is a theme recalled literally: there are few actual quotations in the sonata as opposed to the continuous development of material or its revisiting in new contexts. In the Violin Sonata Franck demonstrates how the cyclic technique may be used to suggest the manifold richness of subjective consciousness. But for the even more extreme implications cyclic form may hold for musical temporality's complex interaction of past, present, and future, even the ultimate overcoming of tense, we might look to Franck's last major work and his crowning achievement in the style, the String Quartet in D (1890).

The most notable characteristic of Franck's Quartet is the coexistence of multiple musical and temporal layers that run alongside each other throughout the piece, a design which culminates in the finale with the convergence of these strands as the music becomes overwhelmed with themes from earlier movements. All four movements are closely related thematically through a mixture of underlying subthematic derivation and a more apprehensible onward process of thematic transformation. Placed in this context, the finale's overt recall of earlier themes has the effect of blending the musical past into the present. The result is an extraordinary temporal state in which not only distinctions between earlier and later become muddled, but by the end even the qualities of past, present, and future appear suspended.[57]

Franck's work opens with a D major Poco lento whose initial theme, bold, songful, and hymnic at once, forms a type of motto for the quartet (Ex. 5.3). D'Indy's term, *theme generatrice*, is an apt description, as this idea serves as the source for much—some scholars claim all—of the ensuing piece.[58] In fact even

---

[57] Two earlier studies have pointed to some of the same qualities. In an article whose parallel concerns are pertinent for the present account, Wolfgang Rathert has noted how Franck's quartet is impressed by the 'retrospective moment' or 'colour of the past'. Its structure 'stands in the context of a radically subjectivised time-conception' in which 'the past emerges as the goal of the temporal process and thereby sublates it' ('Form und Zeit im Streichquartett César Francks', in Joseph Kukkerts (ed.), *Neue Musik und Tradition: Festschrift Rudolf Stephan zum 65. Geburtstag* [Laaber: Laaber, 1990], p. 314–15). A valuable account of the quartet touching on its temporal implications has been given more recently by Strucken-Paland in *Zyklische Prinzipien*, esp. pp. 138–47, 355–77, 477–84.

[58] D'Indy, *César Franck*, p. 190 ('germinative theme' in the English translation); his influential account of the quartet may be found at pp. 182–97 and in the *Cours de Composition Musicale*, vol. II/ii, pp. 259–66. Several subsequent studies have explicated the quartet's motivic working, harmonic language and cyclic interconnections at a level which is beyond the bounds of the current chapter.

Ex. 5.3 Franck: String Quartet in D (1890), opening theme, *Poco lento*, bb. 1–12

within the theme itself, an intricate process somewhat akin to developing variation is at work, providing important shapes that will appear later in the quartet.
Harmonically too, the internal chromatic neighbour-note motion of the opening bars sets up many salient motivic aspects of the quartet's language, implications that are seen already in the early root movement to the major Neapolitan
E♭ in b. 7.

    This opening Lento is formed from two themes, a contrasting (though
motivically derivable) idea heard in the dominant at b. 27 being reprised in the
tonic after the return of the A section, thus creating a miniature abridged-sonata
design.

Section	A	B	A'	B' →	coda
Key	D	A/a	D	D/d	D
Bars	1	27	41	57	72

See Bernd Wegener, 'César Francks Harmonik dargestellt am Streichquartett D-Dur', *Revue Belge de Musicologie*, 45 (1991), 109–26; Rathert, 'Form und Zeit im Streichquartett César Francks'; Katrin Eich, *Die Kammermusik von César Franck* (Kassel: Bärenreiter, 2002), pp. 108–43; Hans-Joachim Hinrichsen, 'Individuelles Spätwerk und epochaler Spätstil: Zur harmonischen Konstruktion der "Sonate Cyclique" in César Francks Streichquartett', in Peter Jost (ed.), *César Franck: Werk und Rezeption* (Stuttgart: Steiner Verlag, 2004), pp. 88–111; and Strucken-Paland, *Zyklische Prinzipien*, pp. 138–47, 155–7, 198–9, 264–86, 307–21, and 355–77.

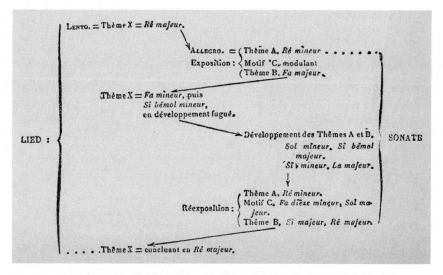

Fig. 5.1 Vincent d'Indy's representation of the intercutting design of Franck's String Quartet, first movement (D'Indy, *César Franck*, p. 192)

So extensive is the design that commentators have questioned whether the Lento section forms an introduction, in the conventional sense, or does not rather have a more autonomous status.[59] Though much of the material of the ensuing D minor Allegro (b. 81) is motivically related to ideas exposited in the Lento, the fact that not only does the Lento itself return at the close of the Allegro sonata movement but reappears too in fugal form in a clearly demarcated episode at the start of its development section suggests that it possesses an importance comparable to the interposed allegro. D'Indy notably held that this movement in fact consisted of two concurrent movements: the 'Lied form' of the D major Introduction and a D minor Sonata: 'Its form, which is essentially new and original, consists of two musical ideas, each living its own life and possessing its own complete organism, which interpenetrate without becoming merged in each other' (Fig. 5.1).[60]

Such procedures had been essayed by Franck before, such as the fusion of slow movement and scherzo in the central movement of the recent Symphony in D minor (1888) and the resultant intercutting and eventual

[59] The movement may quite plausibly be understood as concerned with the problem of mediating slow introduction and sonata form, viewed in the context of the designs encountered in late Beethoven and the structure of the opening movement of Franck's own Symphony in D minor. See Guy Ropartz, 'Le Quatuor en ré majeur de César Franck', *Revue Internationale de Musique* (1 August 1898), 564; Rathert, 'Form und Zeit im Streichquartett César Francks', p. 319; and Eich, *Die Kammermusik von César Franck*, pp. 139–42.

[60] D'Indy, *César Franck*, p. 189.

synthesis of themes from the earlier two movements in the work's finale, but he had not so far attempted this conceit at the start of a piece.[61] This purported dual-movement structure of Franck's first movement may be interpreted as a particularly intriguing case of temporal intercut, in which the musical form is divided into two streams that while running parallel, remain largely distinct.

Scholars such as Jonathan D. Kramer and Thomas Clifton have written pertinently on the temporality of such designs in music.[62] We recall from the opening chapter Kramer's notion of non-linear time in the context of the structures found in late Beethoven. Such conceptions of non-linear and multiple time are given a deeper grounding by Clifton, who argues after Merleau-Ponty for a phenomenological understanding of time in which temporal qualities are 'intentional' properties of the perceiving subject. From this perspective,

> the presumed unidirectionality and irreversibility of time is neutralised and replaced by directional 'rays' of consciousness which relate past, present, and future to each other, as well as different but simultaneous presents, interrupted times, parenthetical times, and other time relations which consciousness is capable of forming.[63]

As music has the capacity for evoking its own sense of time—the idea that music is not just 'in time' but there is another time contained intentionally 'in' music, that 'a new or different activity bears a new time within it'—time may be manifested in musical experience such that one might speak of the interruption, interpolation, or alternation of different time spans within one another, or musical situations where beginnings and endings are presented in reverse order.[64] Particularly significant here is Clifton's notion of 'Temporal Intercut', whose definition we may extend to include situations when two or more musical materials or processes are understood as continuing without break across their

---

[61] For Maier, in Franck's Violin Sonata 'the idea of the simultaneous presence of different levels' is already 'concretely represented through the diverse interconnections that run concurrently throughout' ('Prousts Franck', 188).

[62] Kramer, 'Multiple and Non-Linear Time in Beethoven's opus 135' and 'New Temporalities in Music'; Clifton, *Music as Heard*, pp. 81–131. A variant of this well-established idea is Kinderman's formulation of parenthetical enclosure noted in chapter 1.

[63] Clifton, *Music as Heard*, p. 56. Building on a revised Husserlian basis that complements Clifton's phenomenological recourse to Merleau-Ponty, Shaun Gallagher also argues for the idea that the 'past' in art need not be a real [*reel*] past located in objective time, so much as an intentional one (*The Inordinance of Time*, p. 95); also see Mikel Dufrenne, *The Phenomenology of Aesthetic Experience*, trans. Edward S. Casey (Evanston, IL: Northwestern University Press, 1973), pp. 239–73.

[64] Clifton, *Music as Heard*, pp. 114, 58–9.

diachronically gapped presentation.[65] This is evidently what d'Indy had in mind in his analysis of Franck's quartet.[66]

The D major Lento and D minor Allegro appear to form parallel musical strands that intercut one another without really merging. As stated, the Allegro movement derives its themes from the opening Lento. This is accomplished in such a way, however, as for the affinities rarely to register to the listener: the connections, rather, are largely subthematic, arising from Franck's intricate motivic working.[67] Thus the two sections form analogous structures, motivically interlinked yet differentiated on the surface. Moreover, in their modal duality they form opposite faces or poles of the governing pitch D. D'Indy perceptively fastened onto this feature in his contention that 'D (major and minor) constitutes the *tonique commune* of the two movements'.[68] Indeed just as the D minor sonata moves to the secondary area of F major, so the subsequent reintroduction of the Lento theme now appears in F minor (b. 173).

To this extent, though, there appears to be a strange osmosis between the two strands. While the two interposed structures seemingly pursue their own independent (albeit analogous) course, there is a sense in which the darkened, F minor fugal form in which the Lento recurs at the start of the Allegro's development section reflects the emotional tone of the preceding sonata exposition. Thus the two intercutting time-series, inhabiting seemingly parallel universes, nevertheless share some points of contact. They form an example of coetaneous strands that while not intersecting, have a mysterious, though indirect, influence on each other. Showing the interaction between such levels and their eventual melding will be the task of the finale.

Noteworthy, too, in this context is a further point relating to the larger structure of the Lento material. While d'Indy saw the Lento as being in 'Lied' form, other scholars have tended to see the opening section as in itself forming a sonata design.[69] Building on this idea, Hans-Joachim Hinrichsen argued for a

[65] Ibid., pp. 110–24. The notion of 'Time Strata' that Clifton goes on to develop provides useful theoretical support for the discussion in chapter 1 of temporal overlaying in the finales of Beethoven's Opp. 109 and 111.

[66] In one sense it is still hard to believe that the three non-contiguous parts of the Lento would ever actually form an independent movement. In contrast, Franck's sonata movement is perfectly conceivable as subsisting without the Poco lento. This notwithstanding, the musical fabric is perceptibly divided into two quite distinct strata throughout the movement.

[67] The first subject, for instance, prepared in the preceding bars, elaborates the scalic descent ($\hat{3}$–$\hat{2}$–$\hat{1}$) of b. 2 with the intermediary third-second variant of b. 5; a second idea (b. 105), transitional in nature, is derived from the first by rearranging its constituents (the prominent rising fifth from b. 82, the dotted figure inverted from b. 81). A theme used to propel the music into its unstable secondary thematic area (b. 127) closely relates to the corresponding B theme from the Lento (b. 27).

[68] D'Indy, *Cours de Composition Musicale*, vol. II/ii, p. 262.

[69] D'Indy, *César Franck*, p. 189; see also *Cours de Composition Musicale*, vol. II/ii, p. 260, and Robert Jardillier, *La musique de chambre de César Franck: Étude et analyse* (Paris: Mellottée, 1930), p. 187. For

larger sonata structure formed by this Lento material across the first movement, where the introduction's 'missing' development is displaced to the middle of the movement (its fugato appearance, b. 173), and the return of the theme at the movement's close forms a 'second recapitulation'.[70] If considered plausible, such formal permutation would imply an intriguing de-serialising of temporal events taking place already within the opening movement. The fugal development, in its 'designative' time-series anterior to a recapitulation, is presented after it.[71] In such a context, we may appreciate Kramer's contention, cited in chapter one, that 'Music makes the past-present-future exist on a plane other than that of the earlier-simultaneous-later. . . . It allows a future event to be earlier than a past event, a past event to be later than a present event'.[72] This feature will become increasingly important through the course of Franck's quartet, but arguably may be glimpsed already within the first movement.

The temporal composition of Franck's opening movement distinctly recalls Proust's description in 'The Intermittencies of the Heart' of time as consisting 'of a series of different and parallel lines'.[73] This idea was not confined to Proust. In 1893, three years after Franck's quartet, the Oxford philosopher F.H. Bradley argued in his seminal work *Appearance and Reality* that 'there is no valid objection to the existence of any number of independent time-series'.[74] Sadly, however, he admitted that neither could he offer any evidence to demonstrate their existence, starting a philosophical problem that has persisted to this day.[75] Franck's piece, of course, does not in any way demonstrate the reality of such multiple series (after all, beyond the inescapably hermeneutic nature of such accounts of music, the twin temporal series posited here are necessarily perceived from the single time of the listener), but his music may nevertheless be understood as project-ing a powerful aesthetic similitude of such a topology. In Franck's Quartet, the existence of parallel time series are 'fictionally true', to make a distinction com-mon in the philosophy of time.[76] Since some philosophers have argued that such

---

the sonata form reading see Dahlhaus, *Nineteenth-Century Music*, p. 292; Eich, *Die Kammermusik von César Franck*, p. 108; Hinrichsen, 'Individuelles Spätwerk und epochaler Spätstil', pp. 90–91.

[70] Ibid., pp. 90–91; also see Strucken-Paland, *Zyklische Prinzipien*, p. 317. D'Indy's association of the Lied form with a tripartite structure suggests the greater flexibility of his terminology in its application to this movement.

[71] On the notion of 'designated' or 'evoked' time see Clifton, *Music as Heard*, pp. 81–3.

[72] Kramer, 'Multiple and Non-Linear Time in Beethoven's opus 135', 134.

[73] Proust, *Cities of the Plain*, in *Remembrance of Things Past*, vol. II, p. 784.

[74] F.H. Bradley, *Appearance and Reality* (London: George Allen & Unwin, 1916), p. 211.

[75] See Newton-Smith, *The Structure of Time*, pp. 79–95; Le Poidevin, *The Images of Time*, pp. 162–75.

[76] The concept has been productively applied to time in other art forms such as literature and cinema by Gregory Currie amongst others.

disunified time is metaphysically possible, and given that the metaphysically possible is *a fortiori* the fictionally possible, Franck's music might well offer a fruitful analogy for this peculiar temporal structure.[77]

The subsequent Vivace movement is a dark scherzo in F♯ minor, opening with hints of octatonicism and exploring both minor and major third cycles relatable to the larger harmonic tendencies of the quartet, namely its semitonal ambivalence between third types and major/minor mode. A D major trio offers both contrast and more evident thematic connection with the first movement, relating initially to the second theme of the first subject (b. 105) and then more clearly to the Lento's contrasting idea and the related themes from the second-subject group (bb. 127 and 158). Near the end of its central section the Lento's *theme generatrice* returns triple *piano*, as if a distant reminder of the continued existence of this thematic strand, a deeper dimension persisting behind the present events.

This motto theme is absent from the ensuing B major Larghetto, which eschews overt citation in favour of the subtle motivic reconstitution of the D minor sonata theme, thus forming a stage in the 'redemption' of this material. The primary theme of the ABACA design is constructed from the re-ordered motivic constituents of the first movement's first subject, while the contrasting theme (B) at bb. 33–4 relates again to the secondary ideas of Lento and sonata exposition. At the height of the C section (b. 103) the three-note descent (3̂–2̂–1̂) of the head motive is emphasised so as to suggest a kinship with the identical figure in b. 2 of the Lento; it is followed, moreover, by a downward triadic arpeggiation reminiscent of the quartet's very opening motive (especially on its version heard in the introduction's closing section, b. 72) and that will, in fact, be heard alongside this Lento material as a countermelody in the finale's introduction (b. 53) and main theme (bb. 61–2). In its role of mediating between minor and major modes and continuous lyrical *melos* this movement may justly be considered the expressive heart of the piece.[78]

A vigorous crotchet figure played in octaves opens the finale, a motive which will become a recurring feature of the movement (following d'Indy, termed here the 'refrain').[79] Chromatic in melodic construction and unstable in harmonic implication, the idea is new but bears close resemblance in harmonic basis with the scherzo theme and is not unrelated to the head-motives of Larghetto and first movement. Through its open-ended sequential construction and instability, its function throughout the movement will be continually to propel the music onward, evincing an orientation towards the future that counterbalances, even

[77] See Le Poidevin, *The Images of Time*, p. 174.

[78] Some commentators have considered it to have been the first movement written: see Jardillier, *La musique de chambre de César Franck*, p. 184; Fauquet, *César Franck*, p. 661.

[79] D'Indy, *Cours de Composition Musicale*, vol. II/ii, p. 264.

contradicts, the retrogressive nature of much of the rest of the finale. Building on the opening movement's sense of multiple musical layers and temporal intercut, Franck's finale will bring back earlier themes in a vertiginous display of thematic recollection that Strucken-Paland aptly describes as 'a maelstrom of the past'.[80] First the cyclic procedures of the finale will confuse the B-series terms of 'earlier' and 'later', then, following this process, the coda will break up any sense of A-series distinctions between past, present, and future.

The opening fifty-eight bars form what d'Indy aptly terms an 'introduction récapitulative', a section in which themes from the previous three movements are summoned up between linking statements of the refrain figure, marked as 'memories' through their pianissimo dynamic and the frequent pauses that create a fragmentary quality.[81] The obvious connection with Beethoven's Ninth Symphony has been noted by all; Franck himself commented on the crucial difference, however. 'As in the Ninth, I begin by initially recalling the ideas of the earlier movements, but rather than giving them up, I make use of them'.[82] A further important distinction is that Franck's musical memories move back chronologically from the third movement, via the scherzo and trio, to the opening of the first, the reverse of Beethoven's procedure. Significantly, it appears as if the music, still bound to serial order, is searching ever further back into the past, in order to arrive at something lost but yet necessary for its successful continuance.[83] The desired goal seems to have been found in the opening Lento theme. Though strangely subdued (altered harmonically from its appearance in the work's opening bars, and presented in heterophony with an augmented version in the first violin redolent of the climax of the Larghetto), the theme will grow directly into the main theme of the finale's sonata form (b. 59) through a fairly straightforward instance of thematic transformation. Here the Lento theme is simply given in quicker tempo in the viola surrounded by a texture which to some extent obfuscates the audible relationship with the first movement; there has been a qualitative transformation in affect, but the diastematic content is virtually unaltered.[84]

---

[80] Strucken-Paland, *Zyklische Prinzipien*, p. 371.

[81] D'Indy, *Cours de Composition Musicale*, vol. II/ii, p. 264; cf. d'Indy's account of Beethoven's Symphony No. 9, p. 146.

[82] Pierre de Bréville, 'César Franck (1822–1890)', *Encyclopédie de la musique et dictionnaire du Conservatoire*, ed. Albert Lavignac and Lionel de la Laurencie (Paris: Delagrave, 1925), vol. I, p. 179.

[83] Proust notes that 'our memory does not as a rule present things to us in their chronological sequence but as it were by a reflection in which the order of the parts is reversed'. *Within a Budding Grove*, in *Remembrance of Things Past*, vol. I, p. 622.

[84] The melodic profile and texture is reminiscent of the finale to Beethoven's Op. 127, one of Franck's known models for his quartet (the respective openings of the first movement and finale also reward comparison).

Though much of the finale's material is derived from earlier motives, there is a distinction between what appears in fresh transformation and what, conversely, seems marked as a reminiscence. A curious case is the almost immediate return of the bustling refrain figure from the introduction at b. 83: even though unstably pressing forwards and thus evincing a future orientation, it had formed part of the 'extraneous' introduction and therefore, at least initially, carries a retrospective quality. By returning to an important motive from the movement's introduction, Franck furthermore creates a close parallelism with the first movement's structure. Indeed, from this point on the music will be overtaken by ideas increasingly revealing their affinity to the work's past.[85] The theme at b. 113 corresponds closely to the analogous second theme of the first movement's first-subject group, its rhythm and mode now altered, and when converted back into the minor at b. 137 the connection proves unmistakable. This latest passage is highly significant in the context of the movement: the augmented note values, *pochissimo più lento* tempo marking and *ppp* dynamic instil a mysterious, recollective quality, as if the finale is on the verge of something of great moment, while its appearance also darkens the music, transporting it from tonic major to dominant minor where the exposition will eventually, rather unsatisfactorily, end. For now, the recall of the refrain figure at b. 165 abruptly returns the movement to present business and drives it into the exposition's second subject group.

Hence already within its exposition, Franck's finale is marked by the interpolation of themes manifesting close ties to earlier movements and a switching between temporal levels that throws the musical discourse into distinct layers, underlining the parallelism with the intercutting structure of the opening movement. The development section (bb. 282–505) intensifies such procedures, intermixing and combining themes in a kaleidoscope of temporal intentionalities that clouds the listener's sense of past and present, earlier and later. In Rathert's apt phrase, here 'time itself becomes an object for development'.[86] Opening with a transformation of the refrain figure, heard now in augmented note values as if a genuine lyrical utterance, the primary and secondary themes of the first subject, second-subject ideas, and refrain in its original quicker values

[85] For all the reception of Franck's music in terms of late Beethoven, it is truly striking here how similar the structure and wider temporal conception of Franck's finale is to Mendelssohn's early Quartet in A minor, Op. 13. Franck is known to have held in high regard various cyclic instrumental works of this composer, including the Piano Quartet Op. 3, Cello Sonata Op. 45, and Symphony No. 3, but it is unclear how well he was acquainted with this particular quartet (see César Franck, *Correspondance*, ed. Jöel-Marie Fauquet [Liège: Mardaga, 1999], pp. 44, 49; and Fauquet, *César Franck*, pp. 208–10). For a complementary account of Mendelssohn's work also very much involving a Proustian perspective see my *Mendelssohn, Time and Memory*, ch. 4.

[86] Rathert, 'Form und Zeit im Streichquartett César Francks', p. 327.

return in numerous permutations, breaking any sense of their original serial order and increasingly contrapuntally combined. Though such techniques are certainly typical of development sections, the extent to which Franck intermixes these themes, allied with their varying 'tensed' implications and relation to earlier movements, seems the musical exemplification of Proust's claim that our life is often 'so careless of chronology'.[87] In common with the second subject themes, the refrain is still strongly oriented towards a future prospect, but its transformed version exists more in a lyrical present, while the augmented, chorale-like theme from b. 137 still evokes a retrospective quality.

What the end of the development seems set on is the regaining of the Lento motto theme, not clouded as in the memory of the introduction to the finale or transformed into the present as in its main theme, but as it originally was at the quartet's very opening. A series of repeated block chords (bb. 476–80) appears to signal the imminent arrival of the theme, inferred through the voicing of its triadic head motive over a dominant ninth. This signal gesture already possesses a history within the movement, having been heard towards the end of the second subject area (bb. 234–7) after a long passage of trills that would seem through their generic cadential connotations to herald an imminent arrival. In both cases the gesture seems strongly marked as anticipatory, an indicator of something momentous about to occur, yet both times this expectation is frustrated. Once again the Lento's head-motive dissipates, slipping chromatically downwards and linking motivically into the finale's main theme in its recapitulation. The vision of the Lento theme leads not into the projected inter-movement past but into the reprise of the finale's own exposition. The attempt is precipitous, premature; this vision will not yet be realised. Instead, a further rotation of the finale's materials will be gone through before this motto theme can return.

Just as the exposition had failed to achieve a satisfactory close but ended in the dominant minor, so the recapitulation closes in the tonic D minor, the key of the first movement's internal allegro. In both instances the final cadence is notably underscored by a variant of the repeated chord gesture that had appeared set to signal the regaining of the motto theme. By continuing now into the lyrical refrain theme Franck initially implies the coda (bb. 705ff) will form a matching rotation of the development. Instead, the music peters out and brings back the Scherzo citation from the movement's introduction, newly integrated into the note-values of the finale—to be met by an even more forceful rejection from the repeated chord gesture, now in F minor. Again the attempt is made, and this time leads into the work's culminating section, a coda formed through

[87] Proust, *Within a Budding Grove*, in *Remembrance of Things Past*, vol. I, p. 691.

the corresponding procedures of temporal synthesis followed by an even more astonishing dissolution of tense.

Over an ostinato combining the scherzo motive in the viola with a figure in the cello redolent of the trio theme or even the finale's refrain, the finale's main theme—a transformation of the Lento—returns in the violins. The music gradually builds momentum until it reaches a temporary harmonic impasse on an augmented triad.[88] For five bars the harmony remains suspended on this chord, until, with a wonderful sense of release, it breaks through into the Larghetto theme so far missing from the coda's recall of themes (b. 584⁴). This is the defining moment of the quartet. Three themes from the past have been combined into the musical present, and yet the driving quavers in the inner parts compel the music continually forward into the future. The recall of the Larghetto is the past, yet one recaptured and made present, at last fully realised in the tonic, D major.[89] And yet somehow this passage points continually forwards towards a yet unknown future. It is a melding of past, present, and future, a temporal 'ecstasis' in Heidegger's sense, transcending the division of time into tense. It is hard to convey the effect of this passage. It is an indescribable state between pained, continued searching and fulfilment, journeying, and arrival at the same time, as if riding the crest of a wave, about to break through to the attainment of some epiphanic state—the past, or possibly even something above time.

Now at last the repeated gesture signalling the motto returns (b. 836; Ex. 5.4). After synthesising the main themes from scherzo, slow movement, and finale, having reached through time and tense a state above them both, the music may regain the assurance of the opening Lento theme, just as it had managed at the close of the first movement.

And just as had happened at the end of the development, this vision falls away. The theme's promise dissipates before our ears. Again, the triadic head motive slips down chromatically, broken off by the ralentando markings and self-conscious, recitative-like questioning by the first violin. In a string of generic descending arpeggios the motivic substance of the theme is liquidated, as is the associated chromatic neighbour-note harmony (bb. 860–67). For one final time the finale's refrain interposes itself, rushing headlong into two final tonic chords. Yet there is no perfect cadence anywhere in this final section. The dominant ninth of the signal phrase leads to the final unison D through downward chromatic dissolution, attained finally by reiterations of the chromatic refrain motive

---

[88] The importance of this harmony throughout the piece is highlighted in Hinrichsen, 'Individuelles Spätwerk und epochaler Spätstil', p. 100.

[89] The statement of the Larghetto theme in the finale's 'introduction récapitulative' is admittedly in D major, but is strongly marked through its fermatas as yet unreal, a memory. Here in the coda the past seems to have been made fully present.

Ex. 5.4 Franck: String Quartet in D, finale, bb. 835–81, dissolution of themes at end of coda

moving through the Neapolitan e♮. The quartet ends, and yet remains open to a non-existent future.

One may speak of temporal dissolution here, a collapsing of distinctions between past, present, and future. After their threefold unity in the passage starting at b. 749 each temporal modality or tense conveyed by the music becomes

Ex. 5.4 Continued

dissociated from its meaning in A-series terms. The past of the Lento theme dissolves in the anonymous present of b. 860. The future loses any sense as the refrain, seemingly ever-orientated towards what is to come, leads to nothing. This final, fragmentary dissolution of tense is the other side of its ecstatic melding in the Larghetto's reattainment. The coda of Franck's String Quartet takes us from the simultaneous fusion of tenses to tenselessness. Time is not regained so much as collapsed.

For Rathert, 'it remains inexplicable why Franck ends the quartet in the anti-climax provided by a string of tonally directionless fragments of the central theme'.[90] It certainly appears that despite the continual attempts at recapturing it and indeed its virtual promised arrival towards end, the motto is never actually attained at the close. The past refuses to come back as it was, complete and

---

[90] Rathert, 'Form und Zeit im Streichquartett César Francks', p. 327.

whole. Through a working-through and transcendence of the themes from earlier movements the music reaches some raised state, but the opening's untrou-
bled lyricism does not itself become regained. Yet the most paradoxical quality
of this conclusion is that it sounds in no way a disappointment; in fact, somehow, it is deeply satisfying.

Expressively, it seems that the ecstatic melding of previous movements earlier
in the coda is still directed at some further goal. But this might be a reflection of
the ineliminable nature of temporal existence. All these times, time itself, exists
only in a state of becoming. The motto can no longer be fixed, as a stable object.
In a phrase of Merleau-Ponty that could apply to the Saint-Saëns and Franck
equally, 'A present without a future, or an eternal present, is precisely the definition of death . . . It is thus of the essence of the thing and of the world to present
themselves as "open", to send us beyond their determinate manifestations, to
promise us always "something else to see".'[91] Or to quote Bradley, 'by its incon-
sistency time directs us beyond itself'.[92]

In the finale Franck's music seems always on the verge of articulating something, perhaps something inarticulable—the actual past. We have glimpsed
some parallel world where the past lives on, as the quartet has managed to convey
through its multilayered complexity, its suggestion of another temporal dimension lying behind the present-world perception. Somehow this past is always
there. Yet despite memory's extra-temporality, its capacity to stand above time,
we can never fully inhabit the past. Just as for Proust's Narrator, the contemplation of such 'fragments of existence withdrawn from Time . . . had been fugitive'.
'This species of optical illusion, which placed before me a moment of the past
that is incompatible with the present, could not last for long'.[93] At best, both we
and the intentional temporal structure of music are limited to brief moments of
temporal epiphany.

Perhaps this insight alone—of 'something that, common both to the
past and to the present, is much more essential than either of them'—is the
cause of the satisfaction felt at the end of Franck's quartet, a quality that
Vinteuil's Septet had also seemed to suggest for Proust's Narrator.[94] Having
been granted glimpses of this extra-temporal state, this 'minute freed from
the order of time', there is no longer any need to strive effortfully towards a
further goal.[95] Rather: now to work!—the dwelling on the past is brushed
away by the finale's refrain and the music moves into an open future. In a

[91] Merleau-Ponty, *The Phenomenology of Perception*, p. 388.

[92] Bradley, *Appearance and Reality*, p. 207.

[93] Proust, *Time Regained*, in *Remembrance of Things Past*, vol. III, pp. 908, 906.

[94] Ibid., pp. 905, 910.

[95] Ibid., p. 906.

long-established interpretation of *À la recherche du temps perdu*, the insight of extra-temporality attained through involuntary memory forms the stimulus to recapturing time by writing the book we have been reading—or the quartet we have just heard.

Proust loved Franck's Quartet, as numerous accounts attest.[96] Franck's work also has a history as a favoured model (as much as there is one) for the Vinteuil Septet (a piece which, not coincidentally, started out life as a quartet).[97] Some Proustians have even tried to find an analogy between the musical structure of Franck's Quartet and Proust's novel.[98] The attempt is seldom entirely persuasive, for the usual reasons that the purported commonalities are drawn so generally between the two art-forms. But there is one famous act of Proust's that, while no doubt entirely fortuitous, is nonetheless irresistible to mention in this context. When Proust summoned the Poulet Quartet at midnight to his cork-lined apartment on the Boulevard Haussmann to play Franck's work, the author lay down and listened to the quartet with rapt attention. And on the finale's conclusion—after nearly fifty minutes of music—he happened to ask them whether they would do 'the immense kindness of playing the whole work again'.[99]

Franck's Quartet conveys an inimitable state, one suggestive of the collapse of tense, of temporal order into earlier and later, past and future. By disrupting seriality in this manner, Franck's finale achieves what could be termed after Shaun Gallagher a condition of 'inordinate' time. In *The Inordinance of Time* Gallagher discusses art's ability to disrupt temporal seriality through its 'intertwining of temporalities that escapes the order of Husserl's time-consciousness'.[100] Gallagher sees this process at work in James Joyce's *Ulysses*, but holds that perhaps even more so, music forms one of the best illustrations of the inordinate reality of experienced time. 'Musical experience transcends seriality', he contends. 'It is irreducible to a collection of objectively successive points'.[101] Gallagher terms such an understanding of consciousness a 'Joycean theory'. One might equally call it Proustian.

[96] See Painter, *Marcel Proust*, vol. II, pp. 237–43; Jean-Yves Tadié, 'L'univers musical de Marcel Proust', *Revue de littérature comparée*, 67 (1993), 500–502.

[97] Proust informed Lacretelle in his dedication of *Contre Sainte-Beuve* that 'César Franck's quartet will appear in one of the later volumes' (Painter, *Marcel Proust*, vol. II, p. 241). Like Vinteuil's imaginary chamber work, Franck's Quartet is a 'late' piece, his last major composition. On the multiple sources for the Septet see Kazuyoshi Yoshikawa, 'Vinteuil ou la genèse du septuor', *Ètudes proustiennes III* (Paris: Gallimard, 1979), pp. 289–347.

[98] J.M. Cocking, 'Proust and Music', in *Proust: Collected Essays on the Writer and his Art* (Cambridge: Cambridge University Press, 1982), pp. 109–29.

[99] Painter, *Marcel Proust*, vol. II, p. 238; the story is related by the Quartet's violist, Amable Massis.

[100] Gallagher, *The Inordinance of Time*, p. 96.

[101] Ibid., p. 97. Gallagher's point intersects with Clarke's argument against Husserl in 'Music, phenomenology, time consciousness', an issue discussed in chapter 2.

The Order of Time: Vincent d'Indy and Cyclic Form as Ideology

If Franck takes us from temporal complexity to tenselessness by the end of his Quartet, d'Indy's music rarely leaves the latter state. Though d'Indy quickly made himself the perpetuator of Franck's legacy, the temporal quality of his music is generally worlds apart from that of his teacher. Cruelly for a creative artist, d'Indy has survived in musical consciousness almost entirely by virtue of his theorising of cyclic form and sometimes unsavoury politics rather than for his actual music—the early *Symphonie sur un chant montagnard français* (*Symphonie cévenole*, 1886) forming the one real exception. And indeed there is often a degree of objectivity, even impersonality, to d'Indy's music that would seem to fit the stereotypical picture of him as a stiff military type, a dry theorist possessing more technique than inspiration. Such views, while not entirely fair, contain a degree of truth in that some of his music does seem bent on turning a flexible principle that had existed for many decades into a personal ideology, conscripted into a crusade for the glory of both Franck and France. Yet d'Indy's music is not only significant historically as the non-plus-ultra of a particular understanding of motivic cyclicism but reflects a quite distinct conception of the structure of time. Moreover, his best music contains a vigour, concentration, and even whimsy that makes it worth revisiting.

It is on the face of it strange that the music of a figure as devoted to Franck and the cyclic principle should differ so radically from that of his idol, but on reflection there are good reasons why this should be so. The cyclic principle may convey a rich sense of subjective temporality through its complex network of premonitions and recollections, but conversely a work's motivic interconnections may also function more as an abstract system of interrelationships which do not appear to implicate time except accidentally as the medium in which they are realised. This is often (though not always) the effect of d'Indy's music. Most evident is what we could term its distinct lack of subjectivity, of a lyric 'I' or protagonist. One fundamental reason for this appears to be the composer's decided preference for the ongoing modification of his thematic material, whether through development or transformation, in place of any more literal recall of themes. Such thematic affinities function not as subjective memories but objective transformations, made according to the generic character befitting their place within the four-movement cycle *Sonate, Lent* (*Lied*), *Modérés* (*Menuet* or *Scherzo*), and *Rapid* (*Rondeau*).[102] When d'Indy does recall the musical past,

---

[102] See for instance d'Indy, *Cours de Composition Musicale*, vol. II/i, p. 154, vol. II/ii, pp. 104–5. D'Indy famously starts his definition of the cyclic sonata with the description of its construction

this is often in the Beethovenian form of the 'introduction récapitulative' before the finale, conveying a rhetorical quality of summing up and offering a formal symmetry with the introduction to the first movement rather than necessarily instigating a sense of nostalgia in the listener.[103] Likewise, restatements of cyclic motto themes throughout a piece usually possess a tenseless quality, as if forming an objective disclosure of the fundamental musical reality that underpins them. Even here d'Indy is quite adamant, at least in his theoretical formulation, that apart from the generically acceptable (i.e., Beethovenian) points of thematic reprise, motives should by-and-large be transformed across movements, not simply recalled.[104] As much as it does imply time, this is an ordinate and serially well-behaved form, where 'later' will always come after 'before'.

Other plausible reasons for this qualitative difference result from d'Indy's understanding of cyclic form inferred from his theoretical formulation in the *Cours de Composition Musicale*.[105] In the well-known chapter on *La sonate cyclique* d'Indy sets out two important metaphors for the design, the *thème-personnage*—that the cyclic theme or themes and their development are akin to the characters of a novel—and the architectural metaphor of the *cathédrale sonore*.[106] Though the reference to the novel might seem to suggest a personal quality to the musical speaking 'voice', the impression of d'Indy's music, alongside his reference to potential multiple characters, is suggestive more of an impersonal narrator. It is as if much Romantic music speaks in the first person, whereas d'Indy's is uttered in the third person. In this feature lies its comparative lack of subjectivity judged against the music of Franck, let alone a fellow student such as Ernest Chausson. If according to Merleau-Ponty time only becomes time through a subjectivity to introduce perspective, d'Indy is

being 'subordinated' to 'certains thèmes spéciaux' (ibid., vol. II/i, p. 375), but it would appear that these cyclic subjects are in fact more often disciplined by the generic demands of the sonata. The similarities with the composer's political and religious views are revealing.

[103] See Stefan Keym, 'Der Rahmen als Zentrum: Zur Bedeutung von Langsamer Einleitung und Coda in Vincent d'Indys Instrumentalmusik', in Manuela Schwartz and Stefan Keym (eds.), *Pluralismus wider Willen? Stilistische Tendenzen in der Musik Vincent d'Indys* (Hildesheim: Olms, 2002), pp. 114–59.

[104] This is evidenced by d'Indy's criticism of the circular design of Grieg's G minor String Quartet, *Cours de Composition Musicale*, vol. II/ii, p. 421. Predictably, d'Indy is hardly objective in discussing the earlier cyclic works of non-Franckophile composers.

[105] As several commentators have argued, however, d'Indy is not always as rigid in his compositional adherence to his theoretical formulation as might be thought. See for instance Renata Suchowiejko, 'Auf der Suche nach dem Ideal: Vincent d'Indys zyklisches Prinzip zwischen Theorie und Praxis', in Manuela Schwartz and Stefan Keym (eds.), *Pluralismus wider Willen? Stilistische Tendenzen in der Musik Vincent d'Indys* (Hildesheim: Olms, 2002), pp. 160–75.

[106] D'Indy, *Cours de Composition Musicale*, vol. II/i, pp. 376–8. Strucken-Paland rightly questions the mutual coherence of d'Indy's choice metaphors in her summary of his theorising of the concept (*Zyklische Prinzipien*, pp. 93–107).

apparently little concerned to bring musical perfection down to the level of humanity's temporality. From the perspective of an omniscient narrator, the time of fiction looses its subjective A-series qualities and becomes merely a B-series succession of earlier and later. The metaphor of the *cathédrale sonore*, meanwhile, implies a spatial, objective quality, emphasising geometric symmetry and balance in music. (D'Indy could well be seen as paving the way, albeit distantly, for the twentieth century, the *temps espace* or *ontologique* of neoclassicism that would become debated in France during the last decade of his life.) The musical work becomes a static construction, a system of thematic interrelationships, in extreme cases a succession of permutations of cyclic paradigms on paper conceivable simply as a C series.[107]

In fact, the very density of d'Indy's cyclic working, his desire to squeeze every possible combination and transformation from his material, may detract from the ability to apprehend its temporal attributes.[108] In works such as the first two string quartets (1891 and 1897, respectively), the single-minded application of the cyclic technique can create rather an austere, impersonal effect, as is arguably the case with the less intense Violin Sonata, Op. 59 (1904).[109] Such is the intricacy of the cyclic interconnectivity in the Piano Sonata, Op. 63 (1907), meanwhile, that the whole piece suggests a massive variation on a set of variations. In this context it is no wonder that the temporal quality of the music is unclear. D'Indy is more accessible in a less severe work such as the early *Symphonie cévenole* where the cyclic transformations straightforwardly match the generic characters of movements, the mild folk note adding an appealing national-exotic flavour to proceedings. Later in life, too, the octogenarian relaxed the strictness of his recourse to this principle. Gone is the strenuous neo-Beethovenian intent and interminable rehearings of the same tiny motivic cell. A work such as the String Quartet No. 3 (1929) possesses a charm and understated nostalgia arising from d'Indy's discreet handling of the cyclic method.

---

[107] 'This other series', McTaggart explains, 'is not temporal for it involves no change, but only an order' ('The Unreality of Time', 461–2). McTaggart goes on to posit that while the A and B series may be unreal, the C series might possibly reflect reality (473–4).

[108] In a discussion of music's connection with Bergson's theory of duration, the philosopher Gabriel Marcel similarly notes how remarkable it is that 'voluntary concentration is by no means enough to give us the feeling of depth', citing d'Indy's string quartets as a perfect case in point, where the self-conscious working out of musical relationships is taken to an extreme ('Bergsonism and Music', in Susanne K. Langer [ed.], *Reflections on Art* [London: Oxford University Press, 1958], p. 150). Concerning this issue of comprehension and its possible contradiction with d'Indy's aesthetic of cyclic perceptibility see also Stefan Keym, ' "L'unité dans la variété": Vincent d'Indy und das zyklische Prinzip', *Musiktheorie*, 13 (1998), 236–8.

[109] On this cyclic concentration see further Herbert Schneider, 'Das Streichquartett op. 45 von Vincent d'Indy als Exemplum der zyklischen Sonate', in Annegrit Laubenthal (ed.), *Studien zur Musikgeschichte: Ein Festschrift für Ludwig Finscher* (Kassel: Bärenreiter, 1995), 655–67.

D'Indy's music is, in short, that of a B-Theorist. His cyclic manipulations can imply a sense of earlier and later, but only rarely one of tense, of the presence of musical agency or subjectivity. Even d'Indy's customary slow introductions seem only objective stages in the material's development, suggesting in appropriate Aristotelian terms a movement from potential to actual, as if time is accidental to the process, the medium in which such musical entelechy takes place. The future goal is always latent in the opening. The manner in which the four-note motive underpinning the String Quartet No. 2 is exposed on the dominant at its opening to be intoned conclusively in the tonic at the work's close has the irrefutable assurance of a Scholastic syllogism whereby the conclusion follows inevitably from the succession of major and minor premise. The entire edifice has been constructed to confirm a truth which was present throughout, and never seriously in doubt. And just as its early modern critics protested, one sometimes cannot help feel that as properly as the logic has been applied, the purchase the original propositions had on reality is what is really open to question, and what for all their technical artifice the Schoolmen have not even considered.[110]

One piece that does undoubtedly merit the *cathédrale sonore* epithet is the Symphony No. 2 in B♭, Op. 57 (1902–3), a work that shows the composer's cyclic style at its most imposing, described later by d'Indy's former student Albert Roussel as 'the most characteristic and undoubtedly the most perfect expression of cyclic form in its logical and ordered complexities'.[111] According to another of his pupils, d'Indy described the symphony in the following terms:

> This work places an evil and adversarial idea, which proceeds by major thirds and whole tones, in opposition to a loftier idea, an idea of goodness. After an ardent struggle this latter theme descends from heaven in

[110] The contemporary reception of d'Indy's music underscores how strongly music could be felt at this time as delivering some metaphysical message—the 'In Tune with the Infinite' that Proust ridicules through Swann (*Within a Budding Grove*, in *Remembrance of Things Past*, vol. I, p. 575). See further Brian Hart, 'Wagner and the franckiste "Message-Symphony" in Early Twentieth-Century France', in Annegret Fauser and Manuela Schwartz (eds.), *Von Wagner zum 'wagnérisme': Musik, Literatur, Kunst, Politik* (Leipzig: Universitätsverlag, 1999), pp. 315–37. D'Indy's favoured use of angular three- or four-note cells in the manner of Beethoven's 'Muss es sein?' from Op. 135 seem deliberately designed to be susceptible to such readings.

[111] Albert Roussel, 'La Symphonie en si bémol de Vincent d'Indy', *Latinité: Revue des pays d'occident*, 3 (1930), cited in Brian Hart, 'Vincent D'Indy and the Development of the French Symphony', *Music & Letters*, 87 (2006), 256. A useful discussion of d'Indy's work has also been given by Andrew Deruchie, *The French Symphony at the Fin de Siècle: Style, Culture, and the Symphonic Tradition* (Rochester, NY: University of Rochester Press, 2013), pp. 185–226, which appeared after the present study was written. Deruchie pertinently touches on the static quality of the symphony's approach to temporality with its relative preponderance of architecture over narrative (pp. 193–5).

Ex. 5.5 D'Indy: Symphony No. 2 in B♭, Op. 57 (1902–3), first movement introduction, motives *x* & *y*

the finale and triumphs over the evil idea, which in the end is pacified and subjected to discipline.[112]

These two ideas, termed *x* and *y* respectively in the *Cours de composition*, appear in germinal form right at the start of the slow introduction, and variants are used to generate much of the material of the symphony's first three movements (Ex. 5.5).[113] The first movement derives its first and second subject themes from variants of *y*, while *x* appears in transitional figuration, at first in pentatonic then in destabilising whole-tone forms. Though contrapuntally combined with the first subject's head motive (drawn from *y*) in the movement's coda, this motive will return intermittently throughout the central movements casting a baleful reminder of its purportedly malign presence.

There is unquestionably a sense that the cyclic procedure of the symphony does involve the listener in an awareness of temporal qualities. A case in point is the slow movement, whose initial section builds on variants of *y* exposed in the latter stages of the first movement's second-subject group (I: rehearsal 10, b. 6 [hereafter 10:6]) and within a contrasting episode adds this new form to *x* in an oboe line (II: rehearsal 37). For the listener who already knows the piece this passage unmistakably foreshadows *in embryo* the fugal theme of the finale, a crucial stage in the symphony's progress from disorder to light. Yet, in contrast to Franck, such memories and anticipations seem clearly part of the listener's own apprehension when confronted with objective qualities of the work's structure, not posited as (fictional) properties of the music arising from its own sense of subjective agency. The music does not remember, but the listener must in order to comprehend the complex network of thematic strands and their evolution. Nonetheless, the music's temporality may be adequately expressed using objective B-series properties, namely in terms of the progression from earlier to later, from potentiality to actuality. Subjective or perspectival A-series expressions seem extraneous.

The crowning stage of the cyclic design is as expected the finale, an extended recapitulative structure that draws the earlier strands of the

[112] Alice Gabeau, *Auprès du maître Vincent d'Indy: Souvenirs des cours de composition* (Paris: Éditions de la Schola Cantorum, 1933), p. 26, cited in Hart, 'Vincent D'Indy', 250.

[113] D'Indy, *Cours de Composition Musicale*, vol. II/ii, p. 175.

Ex. 5.6a D'Indy: Symphony No. 2, finale, fugato theme, rehearsal 63:11

symphony together. This movement is the epitome of the synthetic cyclic finale, in fact being built entirely from earlier material. A corollary of this conceit is a rather unusual formal design that continually postpones arrival until the very end.[114] Starting with the now familiar recapitulative preamble where themes from all three earlier movements are brought back in disconnected succession, the ensuing fugato (rehearsal 63:11) builds up austerely, imposingly, in B♭ minor. Its melodic line retraverses and fuses motive *x* and versions of *y* from the first movement's second subject and second movement, melding the directionless fragments of the introduction into the continuous line that had been presaged in the oboe in the second movement (Ex. 5.6a). This fugal section itself functions as if another introduction to the main body of the movement (rehearsal 67:10), whose rotational structure three times brings back in successive waves of motion a refrain-like idea (consisting of a driving ostinato formed of permutations of *y* with a theme derived from the second subject's closing idea in the first movement) between more episodic sections recalling earlier themes.

What contributes towards making this movement one of d'Indy's most exhilarating achievements is that there is a genuine sense of dynamism here to the finale. Although it was observed that this composer's music does not as a rule appear highly tensed, the finale of the Second Symphony does nonetheless seem very future-orientated in places. This is not just a result of the propulsive ostinati of the refrain and its asymmetrical $\frac{5}{4}$ metre, though this certainly contributes much to the surface effect of the music. At a larger formal level, the surfeit of passages with an introductory function—the succession of sections which are heard every time as structural upbeats to the ensuing music—project a future by continually postponing any sense of arrival to a later stage in the design.[115] In fact there appears to be a steady temporal progression from the retrospective inclination of the introduction, the expository fugal section that painfully works the past into the present, and the successive rotations of the main rondeau design which takes up and drives this earlier material forward

[114] See on this point Keym, 'Der Rahmen als Zentrum', pp. 142–5.

[115] On the importance of such structural features for creating a sense of music's temporality see especially the studies of Greene, *Temporal Processes in Beethoven's Music* and *Mahler, Consciousness and Temporality*; and Hasty, *Meter as Rhythm*.

Ex. 5.6b D'Indy: Symphony No. 2, finale, closing chorale theme, rehearsal 87:2–90:7

into the symphony's culminating stages. In an exultant apotheosis (rehearsal 87; Ex. 5.6b), themes from the symphony's earlier stages—motive *y* presented over *x*, the third and second movements—are thundered out as a chorale, its responsorial phrases interjected by the clamour of bells. It is as if this is the eternal present of the symphony, its revealed temporal unity. The listener is led by d'Indy from the past, through the present and future to a timeless state. Even after the *très vif* stretto (rehearsal 90:7) the movement will return *extremement lent* for the final word to motive *y*—the 'idea of goodness', the symphony's timeless truth and centre.

But before the triumphant coda can obtain its victory, there is an event that seems to stand outside the rest of the immediate music: the visionary episode that twice breaks in to the latter stages of the rondeau (rehearsal 83, 84). This is undoubtedly d'Indy's 'descent from heaven' of motive *y*, which prefigures the revelation of the very last bars. Heard high in solo violin and then piccolo over a *pianissimo* tremolo in the strings, it is marked by the shimmering, unworldly sonorities that so often designate the transcendent ideal in late-Romantic music. Though this motive has been heard in different forms throughout the symphony since the second bar, it is at least arguable that here the passage denotes a vision of the ultimate end of its spiritual journey, a Dantean vision of Beatrice in *Paradiso*.

Much of d'Indy's finale has been orientated towards the future, both in the additive succession of passages of formal arsis that postpone any structural downbeat and in the dynamic instability of the rondeau refrain. In both, the present moment seems to be pointing through its incompletion to a future consequence. But can we speak more strongly of a passage that itself implies its events will happen in the future, of prolepsis or of a future tense in music?[116] It was noted in chapter three how music has the capacity to suggest a modality of pastness through its marking as unreal or distant, thus implying a distinction from the self-presence of present perception. But as already argued concerning the recapitulation of Saint-Saëns's violin sonata, often the implication of spatial distance or absence might seem just as pertinent to such passages. And if neither the past nor the future is (in the commonly understood sense) present, why should such markings of temporal absence not equally imply the future?

One evident reason is simply the perceptual asymmetry of time (its 'anisotropy'); we remember the past and not the future, whose anticipation is at best inexact. But in a work of music whose perception and meaning is often derived from repeated listenings, where the A-series sense of a present moment is far looser and subject to multiple interpretations if not indeed sometimes discardable, there is less reason to privilege quotidian temporal contingency. Thus in music some of the same markers of pastness may equally be held to imply physical absence, unreality, dream or fantasy, transcendence, or the future. Much depends on connotative context and perceived expressive quality; the task is necessarily hermeneutic. Here in d'Indy's finale, the passage may be equally signed as a transcendent vision of the beyond or of the future, even of both.

D'Indy's biographer Andrew Thomson relates that as a youth 'the future symphonist found enormous sustenance in contemplating Dante's spiritual journey through the work's great structures and symmetries: the circles of Hell, the corniced mountain of Purgatory, and the Neoplatonic hierarchy of Heaven', and indeed he even contemplated writing a symphony on *Purgatorio*.[117] Certainly there is something of a Dantean vision realised in the course of the Second Symphony, a comparison we can be sure d'Indy would have loved, being enamoured of the *Commedia*, Catholicism, and manifest order. Within the cyclic course of the symphony the finale acts as its radial centre, the point towards which all the thematic strands spiral. And within the finale itself, the manner in which the successive cycles of thematic presentation concentrates, overlays, and concatenates the work's motivic ideas, creates a further heightening of the music's spiritual journey which culminates in the Empyrean vision of the close. The topology suggested by d'Indy's symphony is akin to a temporal progression moving through concentric circles, though here inward, towards the

---

[116] Again, I emphasise that tense is being used here in the wider philosophical sense of A-series qualities of past, present, and future, and not in the more specialised linguistic meaning of grammatical inflection. Music's capacity to convey tensed qualities is less definite and more open to interpretation (and hence disagreement) than linguistic tense, though it should be noted that both are merely cultural conventions.

[117] Andrew Thomson, *Vincent D'Indy and his World* (Oxford: Clarendon Press, 1996), p. 12; also cf. pp. 119–20, where d'Indy conceives historical time and the development of art as a spiral journey.

centre.[118] Time is not an ever-rolling stream but an ever-contracting ripple moving towards a timeless focal point.[119]

Even less than the other two composers considered in this chapter, the music of d'Indy is rarely a close match for Proust's imaginative accounts of Vinteuil's music.[120] There is simply not the same poetry, the mysterious charm, or expressive beauty. Yet in one respect the correspondence is unerringly apt. Already in the finale of the Vinteuil Sonata the cyclic interweaving of themes is related in terms distinctly more akin to d'Indy's practice in this symphony than that of Saint-Saëns or even Franck: 'all the scattered themes', Swann found, 'would enter into the composition of the phrase, as its premises enter into the inevitable conclusion of a syllogism.'[121] Later, this tendency would become even more discernable for the Narrator in the Septet. Here, in a phrase that d'Indy could easily have chosen to describe his symphony, 'the different elements presented themselves one after another to combine at the close,' forming 'a wrestling match of disembodied energies'. And 'in the end the joyous motif was left triumphant; it was no longer an almost anxious appeal addressed to an empty sky, it was an ineffable joy which seemed to come from paradise'.[122]

Both Vinteuil's Violin Sonata and Septet are true musical chimeras, impossible entities whose sheer variety of attributes quickly become contradictory. So too, it has often seemed, is time—that similarly impossible being once aptly characterised by Arthur Prior as a 'monstrous object'.[123] This irreducible, irreconcilable

---

[118] In Dante the Empyrean lies beyond the outer circle of Heaven; thus a journey inward through contracting circles is actually more reminiscent of the design of Purgatory—or indeed Hell.

[119] To allude to the famous formulation of Isaac Watts and Murray Macbeath's apt reworking ('Time's Square', p. 199). *Istar*, Op. 42 (1896), a reverse series of symphonic variations where the actual theme appears in all its naked glory only at the end, ideally illustrates this principle (albeit in a manner more sensual and exoticist than pious). Given d'Indy's orientation towards the orderly structures of medieval Catholicism it is worth noting here that the topographical depiction of the relation of time to eternity as comparable to that between the circumference and the centre of a circle was used earlier by Aquinas in *Summa contra Gentiles* (Pt I, ch. 66.7).

[120] It is quite plausible that any influence d'Indy might have had on Proust would have been as much through his proselytising for Franck and the idea of cyclic form as his actual music. The two figures were never close and indeed occupied opposite positions on the political spectrum. D'Indy is only mentioned twice by Proust in *À la recherche*, both times (in *Cities of the Plain*) in passing, the first merely noting his anti-Dreyfusard position. His 'quartets' are mentioned in *Jean Santeuil*, though in a passage which unpromisingly refers to further quartets (in the plural) by Franck, casting some doubt on whether the young Proust was really cognisant of this repertoire at the time or not merely citing names that were then fashionable in highbrow circles.

[121] Proust, *Swann's Way*, in *Remembrance of Things Past*, vol. I, p. 382.

[122] Proust, *Time Regained*, in *Remembrance of Things Past*, vol. III, pp. 253, 262.

[123] A.N. Prior, *Past, Present, and Future* (Oxford: Clarendon Press, 1967), p. 75.

plurality of qualities is reflected in the multiplicity of ways cyclic music may convey aspects of temporality, even when originating from the same period and culture, from composers closely associated with each other. For at the time that philosophers, artists, and thinkers were moving towards suggesting that time and human temporality was thicker and richer, more complex and unruly than the standard topographical model, these three composers were writing music which helped perceiving the sheer complexity and heterogeneity of temporal experience, its interfusion of memory and expectation, of causality and change. The reception of the French cyclic sonata—in particular its use by Marcel Proust throughout his writings—makes a persuasive case for music's central position in constructing modern subjectivity. Here we have a form, arguably more powerful and immediate than literature, through which composers, musicians, and their listeners have received meaningful articulations of temporality, what it is to exist in time.

In the last two chapters we have observed how music is not only capable of conveying a culture's understanding of history but also of problematising the very idea of a single understanding of time within a given society. Indeed, this preceding chapter has suggested that the collective singular of historical time might better be thought of as a collected singular of multiple temporal strands, returning to the aporia outlined in chapter two in offering two distinct sides of the dichotomy between intersocial and subjective times. Music appears especially suited to conveying such temporal polyphony, providing the most potent instantiation of temporal unity in multiplicity and the ideal medium for literary attempts at explicating the intricacies of time. This use of music as the exemplary model of temporality will find its ultimate form in the notion of music as the manifestation of the spirit of time in human history, an idea we turn to now in this book's final chapter.

6

Elgar's *The Music Makers* and the Spirit of Time

And thou art wrapp'd and swathed around in dreams,
Dreams that are true, yet enigmatical
 —John Henry Newman, *The Dream of Gerontius*[1]

Pues así llegué a saber
que toda la dicha humana
en fin pasa como sueño
(For I came thus to learn
that all of human happiness
passes in the end like a dream)
 —Calderón, *La vida es sueño*, Act III[2]

The Music Makers occupies an unusual position within Elgar's musical oeuvre and the affections of Elgarians. A setting of Arthur O'Shaughnessy's opening 'Ode' from the evocatively entitled collection *Music and Moonlight* of 1874, Elgar's piece for contralto soloist, chorus, and orchestra was premièred in 1912 towards the end of over a decade of creative inspiration that had produced his most famous and highly regarded music. Elgar himself considered it one of his major works, on a par with the familiar masterpieces of the Violin Concerto and Second Symphony—a piece in which 'I have written out my soul . . . I have shewn myself'[3]—and its peculiarly personal nature and significance have long been recognised. Byron Adams accurately describes it in quasi-paradoxical terms as 'the most nakedly autobiographical and most private of his scores', and other commentators have readily voiced approval and regard for Elgar's conception.

---

[1] John Henry Newman, *Verses on Various Occasions* (London: Longmans, Green & Co., 1903), p. 350.

[2] Pedro Calderón de la Barca, *La vida es sueño*, Act III, ll. 3312–14.

[3] Letter to Alice Stuart-Wortley, 29 August 1912, in Jerrold Northrop Moore, *Edward Elgar: The Windflower Letters* (Oxford: Clarendon Press, 1989), p. 107.

Michael Kennedy judges it 'one of Elgar's most endearing and unjustly under-
rated works', Percy Young as being to some listeners 'Elgar's finest choral work
excepting *Gerontius*', and Julian Rushton classifies it simply as a 'masterpiece'.[4] In
the past, however, this piece had received more than its share of critical oppro-
brium, and even recently within the new, revisionist wave of Elgar scholarship it
has still garnered the sobriquet of 'problematic'.[5]

   In the only article devoted to the work so far, Aidan Thomson outlines two
major stumbling points critics have found with the music.[6] First is the apparent
hubris of O'Shaughnessy's and Elgar's arrogation of the artist's calling to direct
world events—the fault, that, as Charles Maclean put it, 'The poem consists of
a sustained boast that poets, and not the men of action, create the world's living and practical history; though it is generally supposed that exactly the opposite happens, and that the men of action act first and the poets sing afterwards'.[7]
Second is the significant role played within the piece by quotations from other
works of Elgar. This use of allusions to earlier, normally more celebrated compositions has been interpreted as at best the sign of declining creativity and at worst
a tasteless example of artistic egotism. Yet, when reconsidered from a broader
perspective, these two points may be mutually supportive of a far more positive
reading of Elgar's work, one which makes sense of the composer's high regard
for the piece. We might start by posing a seemingly obvious question: who are
the music makers?

Arthur O'Shaughnessy, 'Ode', from *Music and Moonlight* (1874)[8]

   I
   We are the music makers,
   And we are the dreamers of dreams,
   Wandering by lone sea-breakers,

   [4] Byron Adams, Introduction to *Elgar and His World* (Princeton: Princeton University Press,
2007), p. xvi; Michael Kennedy, *Portrait of Elgar*, rev. ed. (Oxford: Oxford University Press, 1982),
p. 254; Percy M. Young, *Elgar O.M.: A Study of a Musician* (London: Collins, 1955), p. 302.
   [5] Daniel Grimley and Julian Rushton, Introduction to *The Cambridge Companion to Elgar*
(Cambridge: Cambridge University Press, 2004), p. 11.
   [6] Aidan Thomson, 'Unmaking the Music Makers', in Julian Rushton and J.P.E. Harper-Scott
(eds.), *Elgar Studies* (Cambridge: Cambridge University Press, 2007), pp. 99–105. A further significant point in negative appraisals of the work, though not directly related to Elgar's music, is the quality of O'Shaughnessy's verse.
   [7] Charles Maclean, 'London Notes', *Zeitschrift der internationalen Musikgesellschaft*, 14 (1912), 79,
cited by Thomson, 'Unmaking the Music Makers', p. 100.
   [8] Arthur O'Shaughnessy, *Music and Moonlight: Poems and Songs* (London: Chatto and Windus,
1874), pp. 1–5.

And sitting by desolate streams;—
World-losers and world-forsakers,
On whom the pale moon gleams:
Yet we are the movers and shakers
Of the world for ever, it seems.
II
With wonderful deathless ditties
We build up the world's great cities,
And out of a fabulous story
We fashion an empire's glory:
One man with a dream, at pleasure,
Shall go forth and conquer a crown;
And three with a new song's measure
Can trample a kingdom down.
III
We, in the ages lying
In the buried past of the earth,
Built Nineveh with our sighing,
And Babel itself in our mirth;
And o'erthrew them with prophesying
To the old of the new world's worth;
For each age is a dream that is dying,
Or one that is coming to birth.
IV
A breath of our inspiration
Is the life of each generation;
A wondrous thing of our dreaming
Unearthly, impossible seeming—
The soldier, the king, and the peasant
Are working together in one,
Till our dream shall become their present,
And their work in the world be done.
V
They had no vision amazing
Of the goodly house they are raising;
They had no divine foreshowing
Of the land to which they are going:
But on one man's soul it hath broken,
A light that doth not depart;
And his look, or a word he hath spoken,
Wrought flame in another man's heart.

VI

And therefore to-day is thrilling
With a past day's late fulfilling;
And the multitudes are enlisted
In the faith that their fathers resisted,
And, scorning the dream of to-morrow,
Are bringing to pass, as they may,
In the world, for its joy or its sorrow,
The dream that was scorned yesterday.

VII

But we, with our dreaming and singing,
Ceaseless and sorrowless we!
The glory about us clinging
Of the glorious futures we see,
Our souls with high music ringing:
O men! it must ever be
That we dwell, in our dreaming and singing,
A little apart from ye.

VIII

For we are afar with the dawning
And the suns that are not yet high,
And out of the infinite morning
Intrepid you hear us cry—
How, spite of your human scorning,
Once more God's future draws nigh,
And already goes forth the warning
That ye of the past must die.

IX

Great hail! we cry to the comers
From the dazzling unknown shore;
Bring us hither your sun and your summers;
And renew our world as of yore;
You shall teach us your song's new numbers,
And things that we dreamed not before:
Yea, in spite of a dreamer who slumbers,
And a singer who sings no more.

It has generally been assumed in the work's reception that the composer is referencing himself, not unnaturally, as one of the 'Music Makers'—one of the 'movers and shakers' of world history—hence the use of self-quotation, which signifies his own identification with the subjects of O'Shaughnessy's ode (an act perilously close to hubris). The artist is given privileged status as a visionary who directs the course of history. Contemporary critics understood the piece as meaning broadly this, and Elgar himself undoubtedly saw his work as being to some extent about artistic 'continuity' and 'never-ceasing change', the artist, whose 'duty . . . is to see that this inevitable change is progress', and their inevitable loneliness.[9] But when viewed within the context of Elgar's aesthetics of music and a broader trope with which O'Shaughnessy's poem and Elgar's setting align themselves, a milder version of this reading becomes apparent, one that is both more palatable to critics of Elgar's apparent self-aggrandising and philosophically richer. This reading sees the music makers as the voice of time, the spirit behind history, guiding and leading humanity on; the artist is one of those few who can hear these deeper voices behind worldly events. Ultimately the work sustains two readings—a stronger, more egotistical personal identification of Elgar with the music makers, and a softer reading of the latter as something spiritual, mystical, who sometimes speak to those who can hear.

The Spirit of History and the Music of Time

Behind *The Music Makers* lie two themes that to a certain extent may be found throughout history, but are particularly prevalent in O'Shaughnessy's and Elgar's age: that there is a spirit moving history, and that this intangible spirit of time may be understood or conveyed by recourse to musical metaphor, the idea of a secret music that resounds behind time, audible to a select few. The first idea, that of the spirit of history or a desacralised providence, is especially characteristic of Western Europe since the Enlightenment (familiar versions include the so-called Whig view of history and the historical vision of Hegel and Marx). In Kant's *Idea for a Universal History with a Cosmopolitan Intent* (1784), for instance, the terms are set out for the discussion of a progressive history which would continue through the nineteenth century. For Kant, there is a deeper purpose driving the collective history of humanity:

> Each, in their own way and often in opposition to others, follows their own purpose; yet each individual and people, as if following some

---

[9] Elgar, 'introductory note' sent to Ernest Newman, 14 August 1912, in Jerrold Northrop Moore (ed.), *Edward Elgar: Letters of a Lifetime* (Oxford: Clarendon Press, 1990), pp. 248–50. See also the letter written to Alice Stuart-Wortley, 19 July 1912, in which a desolate Elgar, relating a walk on Hampstead Heath following completion of the score, speaks of his situation in terms of the music makers—'World losers & world forsakers for ever & ever' (Moore, *Edward Elgar: The Windflower Letters*, p. 103). A selection of contemporary critical reactions may be found in Moore, *Edward Elgar: A Creative Life* (Oxford: Clarendon Press, 1984), p. 639, and Thomson, 'Unmaking the Music Makers', pp. 100–103.

guiding thread, follows a natural but to each of them unknown intent; all work toward furthering it, even if they would lay but little value on it did they know it.[10]

Yet 'it will always remain strange', he continues in his Third Thesis,

> that earlier generations appear to carry out their laborious tasks only for the sake of later ones, to prepare for later generations the foundation on which they in turn could raise still higher the building that nature had in view, and yet that only the latest of the generations should have the good fortune to inhabit the edifice on which a long line of their ancestors had (evidently unintentionally) laboured without being able to share in the fortune they had prepared.[11]

(More succinct, if barely more accomplished, is O'Shaughnessy's formulation: *They had no vision amazing/Of the goodly house they are raising.*) Ultimately, in his Ninth Thesis, Kant concludes that 'even if we are too short-sighted to see the secret mechanism of its workings' one may assume that Nature 'works not without plan or purpose'. Thus in an increasingly secular or non-denominational age, such a humanist universal history provides 'a justification of Nature—or, better, of Providence', a theodicy of spirit such as would be attempted by his successor Hegel.[12]

Such sentiments become an intrinsic part of the nineteenth-century *Zeitgeist* in an age of industrial and technological development, scientific discovery, soaring populations, and colonial expansion—even if more pessimistic Romantics and conservatives still doubted the inevitability of human progress (see chapter 4). The ethos of imperialism was writ large across the age. The nineteenth century was the time of empire and empire building, the idea of providence (or the colonial euphemism 'manifest destiny') directing civilisation on a meaningful path into the future, as if the events of world history formed pages in an open-ended but well-constructed novel. 'Past and present and future are not disjoined but joined' held that apostle of affirmative humanism Walt Whitman. 'The greatest poet forms the consistence of what is to be from what has been and is'. (It seems to follow, then, that Whitman can cheerfully assert 'The

---

[10] Immanuel Kant, *Idee zu einer allgemeinen Geschichte in weltbürgerlicher Absicht*, in *Gesammelte Schriften*, vol. VIII, p. 17.

[11] Ibid., p. 20.

[12] Ibid., pp. 29–30. See especially Hegel's *Lectures on the Philosophy of History*, which is similarly permeated throughout by the notion of the unconscious fulfilment of providential design by human actors and their suffering as necessary sacrifices on the altar of world history.

United States themselves are essentially the greatest poem'.[13]) And throughout the long nineteenth century we may readily find other examples of the joyful pantheism manifested in Whitman's work, be it Goethean Spinozism, the New England Transcendentalists, Nietzsche's conversion to life-affirming Zarathustranism, or Henri Bergson's *Élan vital*. The latter Victorian and Edwardian eras were, in short, a time when grand narratives were still believable, when liberal humanism still largely held sway. 'Is the goal so far away?' asked Victorian Britain's Poet Laureate, Alfred Tennyson. 'Far, how far no tongue can say,/Let us dream our dream to-day' came his immediate response.[14]

This sense of an ineffable spirit behind the age often connects to the age-old notion of a music behind time—a deeper note heard within time that seems somehow to transcend time and its passing, which discloses another level of reality, connecting the scattered elements of the universe together into a whole. A pertinent and quite beautiful example of this trope may be found in Canto III of Byron's *Childe Harold*:

> *All heaven and earth are still—though not in sleep,*
> *But breathless, as we grow when feeling most;*
> *And silent, as we stand in thoughts too deep:—*
> *All heaven and earth are still: from the high host*
> *Of stars, to the lulled lake and mountain-coast,*
> *All is concentred in a life intense,*
> *Where not a beam, nor air, nor leaf is lost,*
> *But hath a part of being, and a sense*
> *Of that which is of all Creator and defence.*
>
> *Then stirs the feeling infinite, so felt*
> *In solitude, where we are least alone;*
> *A truth, which through our being then doth melt,*
> *And purifies from self: it is a tone,*
> *The soul and source of music, which makes known*
> *Eternal harmony, and sheds a charm,*
> *Like to the fabled Cytherea's zone,*
> *Binding all things with beauty;—'twould disarm*
> *The spectre Death, had he substantial power to harm.*[15]

[13] Whitman, 'Preface', *Leaves of Grass* (1855), in Walt Whitman, *Poetry and Prose* (New York: Library of America, 1996), pp. 13, 5.

[14] Alfred Lord Tennyson, 'Ode Sung at the Opening of the International Exhibition', IV, ll. 29–31, in *Poems and Plays* (London: Oxford University Press, 1968), p. 207.

[15] Byron, *Childe Harold's Pilgrimage*, Canto III, LXXXIX–XC, in *Poetical Works*, p. 215.

Byron's formulation recalls St Augustine's account many centuries before of the inner note he would hear in a state of communion with God: 'my soul is bathed in light that is not bound by space and where resounds a sound that rapacious time cannot steal'.[16] The idea evidently has a long history, from the Pythagorean undergirding of the universe by music, the celestial whirl of the spheres that mundane ears are deaf to in Book X of Plato's *Republic*, and the mystical state of oneness in Neoplatonism, to which Augustine clearly alludes. In the nineteenth and early twentieth centuries, however, the idea often takes on a more explicitly temporalised form. A case in point is Byron's friend Percy Bysshe Shelley, who frequently calls upon the idea of the 'song of the world' in his poetry. One of many such examples may be found in his 'Ode to Intellectual Beauty', a work already cited by Matthew Riley in connection with the lines of this same poet's 'Song' that inspired Elgar's Symphony No. 2 ('Rarely, rarely, comest thou, Spirit of Delight!').[17] Especially interesting, as we shall see, is Shelley's equation of this spirit with the *memory* of music, with the past.

> *The awful shadow of some unseen Power*
> *Floats though unseen among us,—visiting*
> *This various world with as inconstant wing*
> *As summer winds that creep from flower to flower.—*
> *Like moonbeams that behind some piny mountain shower,*
> *It visits with inconstant glance*
> *Each human heart and countenance;*
> *Like hues and harmonies of evening,—*
> *Like clouds in starlight widely spread,—*
> *Like memory of music fled,—*
> *Like aught that for its grace may be*
> *Dear, and yet dearer for its mystery.*[18]

One might hear variants of this theme resounding stilly in the unheard melodies of Keats's Grecian Urn, or throughout the colour-bedecked dream of Friedrich Schlegel's Romantic vision:

Durch alle Töne tönet	*Through all the notes that resound*
Im bunten Erdentraum	*Within Earth's many-coloured dream*

[16] Augustine, *Confessions*, 10.6. As Canto I of *Don Juan* demonstrates, Byron was well aware of St Augustine's memoir.

[17] Matthew Riley, *Edward Elgar and the Nostalgic Imagination* (Cambridge: Cambridge University Press, 2007), pp. 43–4.

[18] Percy Bysshe Shelley, 'Ode to Intellectual Beauty', I, ll. 1–12, in *Poetical Works* (London: Oxford University Press, 1970), p. 530.

E i n leiser Ton gezogen   One *softer note is drawn*
Für den, der heimlich lauschet.   *For him, who secretly listens.*[19]

Likewise, a few decades later in Tennyson's 'Ode to Memory', the passing of
time is once again connected to a cosmic music ('nigher to heaven's spheres,/
Listening the lordly music flowing from/The illimitable years'), updating for the
nineteenth century this idea's Platonic origins.[20]

As implicit in the examples from Byron and Shelley, especially beloved
of the Romantics is the idea of a music emanating from nature, a pantheistic
world-vision found frequently in the Lake Poets. In his famous 'Lines written
a few miles above Tintern Abbey', Wordsworth tells of how he has 'learned/To
look on nature',

> *hearing oftentimes*
> *The still, sad music of humanity*
> . . .
>
> *A presence that disturbs me with the joy*
> *Of elevated thoughts; a sense sublime*
> *Of something far more deeply interfused,*
> *Whose dwelling is the light of setting suns,*
> *And the round ocean, and the living air,*
> *And the blue sky, and in the mind of man,*
> *A motion and a spirit, that impels*
> *All thinking things, all objects of all thought,*
> *And rolls through all things.*[21]

For the young Coleridge, meanwhile, the Aeolian harp would serve the quintessential symbol of the oneness of nature, its permeation by a common animating
spirit made audible through music:

> *O! the one Life within us and abroad,*
> *Which meets all motion and becomes its soul,*
> *A light in sound, a sound-like power in light,*
> *Rhythm in all thought, and joyance every where—*

[19] Schlegel, 'Die Gebüsche', in *Kritische Friedrich-Schlegel-Ausgabe*, vol. V, pp. 190–91. Franz
Schubert composed a setting of this poem in 1819 (D. 646); the passage is also famous from its use
by Robert Schumann as an epigram to the *Fantasie* in C, Op. 17.

[20] Tennyson, 'Ode to Memory', III, ll. 40–42, in *Poems and Plays*, p. 11.

[21] Wordsworth, 'Lines written a few miles above Tintern Abbey', ll. 88–91, 94–102, in *The Poetical
Works*, ed. Ernest De Selincourt and Helen Darbishire, 5 vols. (Oxford: Clarendon Press, 1940–49),
vol. II, pp. 261–2.

> *Methinks, it should have been impossible*
> *Not to love all things in a world so fill'd;*
> *Where the breeze warbles, and the mute still air*
> *Is Music slumbering on her instrument.*[22]

This idea of nature speaking through a veiled music becomes particularly prevalent in poetry at the turn of the century, just as Elgar was coming to prominence. W.B. Yeats's 'The Everlasting Voices' (*The Wind among the Reeds*, 1899) and Walter de la Mere's 'Voices' (*Poems*, 1906) are two of numerous examples.[23] Riley has also called attention to the resonance with Elgar of Kenneth Grahame's descriptions of a secret music heard by the riverbank, the rural Pan 'piping the low, sweet strain that reaches only the ears of a chosen few'.[24] Grahame's conception is reminiscent of the stories of Elgar's own *Wand of Youth* or *The Starlight Express* later—the division of existence into two worlds, one of which (the enchanted one) was accessible only to a select few (the children) able to perceive this deeper state of being.

In the last decade of Elgar's life the idea of a hidden stream of music, equatable with the ontical nature of time itself, would be taken up masterfully by Virginia Woolf in her frequent allusions to a music ongoing behind the passing of human time. Woolf's work forms one of the most persuasive existential attempts to explicate the enigmas of time and being. In *To the Lighthouse* (1927), a book in which nostalgia for Woolf's own Edwardian childhood plays a key role, music functions as a medium for expressing the intangible existence of time, especially in the second section of the novel, 'Time Passes', an extraordinary evocation of being and passing within time that functions as an interlude or *entr'acte* between the two main parts of the narrative:

> And now as if the cleaning and the scrubbing and the scything and the mowing had drowned it there rose that half-heard melody, that intermittent music which the ear half catches but lets fall [. . .]; which the ear strains to bring together and is always on the verge of harmonising, but they are never quite heard, never fully harmonised.[25]

[22] Samuel Taylor Coleridge, 'The Eolian Harp', ll. 26–33, in *Poetical Works* (London: Oxford University Press, 1967), p. 101.

[23] 'That you call in birds,/in wind on the hill,/In shaken boughs, in tide on the shore' (Yeats). 'Who is it calling o'er the darkened river/In music, "Come!"?' (de la Mere). Also note the reappearance of Pan in the opening two poems of de la Mere's collection, 'They told me' and 'Sorcery': 'They told me Pan was dead, but I/Oft marvelled who it was that sang/Down the green valleys languidly/Where the grey elder-thickets hang'.

[24] Kenneth Grahame, 'The Rural Pan', from *Pagan Papers* (1893), cited by Riley, *Edward Elgar and the Nostalgic Imagination*, pp. 88–9.

[25] Virginia Woolf, *To the Lighthouse*, II:9 (Oxford: Oxford University Press, 2008), pp. 115–16.

Through the open window the voice of the beauty of the world came murmuring, too softly to hear exactly what it said . . . entreating the sleepers . . ., if they would not actually come down to the beach itself at least to lift the blind and look out. . . . And if they still faltered [. . .], if they still said no [. . .], gently then without complaint, or argument, the voice would sing its song.[26]

This idea is taken up even more explicitly in Woolf's last, posthumously published novel, *Between the Acts* (1941). Music is most evidently provided in the story by a gramophone record played as background music to a pageant put on outside for the annual village fete; its status as real (acousmatic) music or an imaginary presence is often blurred, combining as it does with the sonic backdrop provided by the sounds of nature and a seemingly omnipotent and omnipresent voice that speaks of a deeper cosmic unity. This mutable conception of music is also problematised through the sense of ironic detachment into the often whimsical thoughts and individual consciousnesses of Woolf's characters. Here again we find music as the symbol and promise of a familiar Platonic/Romantic pantheism:

The inner voice, the other voice was saying: How can we deny that this brave music, wafted from the bushes, is expressive of some inner harmony? . . . For I hear music, they were saying. Music wakes us. Music makes us see the hidden, join the broken.[27]

As the instantiation of temporal distention and flux and of the polyphony of such elements—the idea of time as turning somehow from the multiple times of multiple voices into a collective singular (what Ricoeur refers to as the second of his three aporias of time):

Like quicksilver sliding, filings magnetized, the distracted united. The tune began; the first note meant a second; the second a third. Then down beneath a force was born in opposition; then another. On different levels they diverged. On different levels ourselves went forward; flower gathering some on the surface; others descending to wrestle with the meaning; but all comprehending; all enlisted. The whole population of the mind's immeasurable profundity came flocking; from the unprotected, the unskinned; and dawn rose; and azure; from chaos and cacophony measure; but not the melody of surface sound alone controlled it; but also the warring battle-plumed warriors straining

[26] Ibid., II:10, p. 116.
[27] Virginia Woolf, *Between the Acts* (Oxford: Oxford University Press, 2008), p. 107.

asunder: To part? No. Compelled from the ends of the horizon; recalled from the edge of appalling crevasses; they crashed; solved; united. . . .

　　Was that voice ourselves? Scraps, orts and fragments, are we, also, that? The voice died away.[28]

And as the unifying element in a 'theodicy of spirit':

> Sheep, cows, grass, trees, ourselves—all are one. If discordant, producing harmony—if not to us, to a gigantic ear attached to a gigantic head. And thus—she was smiling benignly—the agony of the particular sheep, cow, or human being is necessary; and so—she was beaming seraphically at the gilt vane in the distance—we reach the conclusion that ALL is harmony, could we hear it. And we shall.[29]

Summing up the day's events, the Rev. G.W. Streatfield lastly offers a pantheistic effusion over what he takes to be the message of the historical pageant put before the villagers (an evident example of literary meta-narrative). 'Each is part of the whole. . . . Dare we, I asked myself, limit life to ourselves? May we not hold that there is a spirit that inspires, pervades . . .'[30] Ironically his sentimental deliberations are undercut by gestures of impending war, Woolf's benign swallows replaced by twelve aeroplanes in formation. This, it seems, is the music.

　　Perhaps most formative for Elgar's generation, however, is Walt Whitman, for the Edwardian era was the age of Whitman—at least for English composers. Unlike his compatriots Delius and Vaughan Williams it is not clear how much Elgar responded to the humanist optimism of the older poet (it has been suggested he might have grown more in sympathy through his loss of religious faith in the decade preceding *The Music Makers*), though certainly he knew enough to quote *Leaves of Grass* in a Christmas card from 1929.[31] In Whitman we encounter all the familiar themes rehearsed above—the mystery of hearing a secret, inner music:

> *That music always round me, unceasing, unbeginning, yet long untaught*
> 　*I did not hear,*
> *But now the chorus I hear and am elated.*[32]

---

[28] Ibid., pp. 169–70. Cf. Ricoeur, *Time and Narrative*, vol. III, pp. 242–3, and my larger discussion in chapter 2.

[29] Woolf, *Between the Acts*, p. 157.

[30] Ibid., p. 173.

[31] Moore, *Letters of a Lifetime*, p. 422. The rather provocative quotation is from 'Song of Myself', 32.

[32] Whitman, 'That music always round me', *Leaves of Grass* (1891–2), in *Poetry and Prose*, pp. 563–4.

—the music of time, of the successive ages, the moving reverberation of still eternity:

> *Or, from that Sea of Time,*
> *Spray, blown by the wind . . .*
> *Murmurs and echoes still bring up—Eternity's music, faint and far,*
> *. . . joyously sounding*
> *Your tidings old, yet ever new and untranslatable*[33]

—and exactly like O'Shaughnessy's and Elgar's music makers, the poet privy to hearing the stream of music that is human history takes part and directs this further:

> *Strains musical flowing through ages, now reaching hither,*
> *I take to your reckless and composite chords, add to them, and cheerfully pass*
> *them forward.*[34]

In the examples cited above we encounter subtly different formulations, but all are on to the idea of music as being somehow analogous or expressive of the mystery of being and persistence within time's passing, whether this music is conceived as being behind or above time as in the earlier examples, or an instantiation of time in its purest, most essential state. Clearly this may be allied with the idea of historical providence, of music being an expression of the spirit of time. Both are onto the same thing, using music in order to describe this intangible sense of guiding spirit, a way of making sense of the world and history, of human existence in time. It is this notion that supports a revised understanding of *The Music Makers*.

This latter reading of the Music Makers is implicit in O'Shaughnessy's text but is made explicit by Elgar's musical setting. It is realised above all through Elgar's use of self-quotation—the very point that had been a cause of the work's disparagement for some critics.

'Music Is in the Air, Music All around Us': Elgar's Creative Aesthetics

The starting point for a good defence of Elgar's citational practice in *The Music Makers* has been suggested along the lines of a consideration of his compositional

---

[33] Whitman, 'Or from that Sea of Time' (1876), Supplementary Poems to *Leaves of Grass*, in *Poetry and Prose*, p. 695.

[34] Whitman, 'Starting from Paumanok', 10, *Leaves of Grass* (1891–2), in *Poetry and Prose*, p. 182.

process by Percy Young. As Young explains, 'In his youth an ardent Wagnerian, Elgar was a motivic composer. His sketch books are filled with isolated germinal ideas . . . which were finally moulded and unified under the compulsion of a commission'. The difference between *The Music Makers* and most other pieces by Elgar is simply that 'many of the pre-existing ideas had been previously used in published works'.[35]

Elgar's ideas on creative inspiration from nature fit perfectly the understanding of an underlying stream of music we saw in Wordsworth, Whitman, and Woolf, and which is explicitly thematicised in the text of *The Music Makers*. 'Music is in the air, music all around us, the world is full of it and . . . you—simply—simply—take as much of it as you require', he famously claimed.[36] As a child Elgar apparently could be found by the riverbank 'trying to write down what the reeds were singing'.[37] At the time of composing *Gerontius* he wrote to Jaeger quoting the Woodland Interlude from the earlier *Caractacus*: 'This is what I hear all day—the trees are singing my music—or have I sung theirs? I suppose I have'.[38] More literally, W.H. Reed leaves an account of an Aeolian Harp owned by Elgar in 1904, noting passages supposedly inspired by the naturally produced sound of this instrument in *Sea Pictures*, the *Introduction and Allegro for Strings, Gerontius*, and the Violin Sonata.[39] Not dissimilarly, a theme from the *Introduction and Allegro* was said by Elgar to have been inspired by the sound of distant singing borne to him through the air while on holiday in Wales.[40] Accounts attest to the composer's sudden, seemingly unaccountable bursts of inspiration, especially when surrounded by nature, such as the furious creativity that overtook him on first setting eyes on Lake Windermere in 1883.[41] 'I can only write when the spirit moves me' he claimed. 'I take no credit for the inspiration

[35] Percy M. Young, sleeve notes to Elgar, *The Music Makers*, LPO, Janet Baker/Sir Adrian Boult, HMV ALP 2311, 1967. Also see Young, *Elgar*, p. 303. As noted below, however, *The Music Makers* is not unique in Elgar's oeuvre in using material common to another work.

[36] R.J. Buckley, *Sir Edward Elgar* (London: John Lane, 1912), p. 32, relating a conversation in 1896.

[37] Robert Buckley, cited in Basil Maine, *Elgar, His Life and Works*, 2 vols. (London: G. Bell and Sons, 1933), vol. I, p. 7.

[38] Letter to Jaeger, 11 July 1900, in Jerrold Northrop Moore, *Elgar and his Publishers: Letters of a Creative Life*, 2 vols. (Oxford: Clarendon Press, 1987), vol. I, p. 212.

[39] W.H. Reed, *Elgar As I Knew Him* (London: Victor Gollancz, 1936), pp. 147–9; see further Riley, *Edward Elgar and the Nostalgic Imagination*, pp. 101–10.

[40] Programme note by Edgar F. Jacques and F. Gilbert Webb, cited in Daniel M. Grimley, '"A smiling with a sigh": the chamber music and works for strings', in Daniel Grimley and Julian Rushton (eds.), *The Cambridge Companion to Elgar* (Cambridge: Cambridge University Press, 2004), pp. 124–5.

[41] Charles Buck, interview in *Yorkshire Weekly Post*, July 1912, quoted in Moore, *A Creative Life*, p. 101.

that people may discover in my music, I cannot tell you how it comes to me.'[42] Thus for Elgar, the composer is more a listener, one attuned to the secret voice singing within nature, a transcriber of music emanating from some apparently transcendent source. Elgar would doubtlessly have agreed with Whitman: 'All music is what awakens from you when you are reminded by the instruments . . . It is nearer and farther than they.'[43]

As we can see then, inspiration seemingly came 'naturally' to Elgar, from sources unknown. The actual business of composing—putting motivic scraps and ideas together, weaving them or setting them against each other in mosaic-like fashion into an apparently organic whole—would be done in a more workman-like manner. Elgar developed a compositional method of working up sketches across a long period of time, waiting for the right form for their eventual appearance. Certain themes would coalesce when needed into a finished work, though this was only their final and most publicly visible appearance. Thus 'recycling and revising materials became a lifelong habit.'[44]

Sketches for *The Music Makers* had been accumulating over the years, as was Elgar's normal practice. Elgar had first thought of setting the ode around 1903 (the *Daily News* announced in March 1904 that he was at work on a setting), and following a request in September of the previous year obtained permission from O'Shaughnessy's executor in 1908. In other words, the charge of self-imitation is already problematised by the fact that while the completed composition appears to quote a number of his earlier works, several of these (such as the two symphonies and Violin Concerto) were completed only after Elgar had devoted serious thought to setting O'Shaughnessy's text—the works share the same gestation as well as motives. Moreover, as Diana McVeagh shows, several ideas also came, as was typical, from projected but unfinished or discarded sketches for earlier pieces.[45] Thus both the general nature of Elgar's compositional process and the specific genesis of *The Music Makers* would imply that the question of self-imitation in this work is not as straightforward as it might initially appear.

[42] Jerrold Northrop Moore, *Elgar on Record: The Composer and the Gramophone* (Oxford: Oxford University Press, 1974), p. 208; Maine, *Elgar*, vol. I, p. 77.

[43] Whitman, *Leaves of Grass* (1855), slightly modified ['awakes'] in 'A Song for Occupations', *Leaves of Grass* (1891–2), in *Poetry and Prose*, p. 94/359.

[44] Christopher Kent, 'Magic by mosaic: some aspects of Elgar's compositional methods', in Daniel Grimley and Julian Rushton (eds.), *The Cambridge Companion to Elgar* (Cambridge: Cambridge University Press, 2004), p. 39.

[45] Diana McVeagh, 'The shorter instrumental works', in Daniel Grimley and Julian Rushton (eds.), *The Cambridge Companion to Elgar* (Cambridge: Cambridge University Press, 2004), p. 61. For further details on the work's genesis see Robert Anderson and Jerrold Northrop Moore, 'Foreword' to *The Music Makers; The Spirit of England*, Elgar Complete Edition, vol. 10 (London: Novello, 1986), pp. v–vi.

The very nature of Elgar's creative beliefs further suggests that the musical material he used could, in some manner, be said to transcend its use in a finished work.
A completed piece of music was a pragmatic form for housing Elgar's ideas, a necessary medium for their public manifestation, but the ideological bias towards the
work-concept in the last two centuries has dulled us to the idea that the original
inspiration, a theme or motivic fragment, might still have had an independent aesthetic reality for him. Such a view ties in with the composer's particularly Romantic,
almost Platonist aesthetics—the idea of these melodies floating around, somewhere, in the ether, independently of their eventual materialisation. For Elgar a
motive or idea could still hold a distinctive association, quite independent of its final
use in a completed work.

This is borne out by the correspondence between the semantic meaning
of motives in earlier pieces and the new textual contexts in which they may
be found in *The Music Makers*. Instances of this practice in the piece have been
well-charted—the appearance of 'dreams' in the first stanza being underpinned by
the opening of *The Dream of Gerontius* and the words 'sea-breakers' by reference to
Sea Pictures; the allusion to August Jaeger by his 'Nimrod' theme; the aspiration of
stanza eight to the 'Ideal call' and 'massive hope' of the First Symphony; the final
'singer who sings no more' to the death of Gerontius (Table. 6.1). Thus in re-using
ideas in *The Music Makers* one could claim that Elgar is not so much quoting his earlier work as referencing the same emotive and connotative meaning.[46] The *paroles*
are the same because they come from a deeper Elgarian *langue* that pre-exists the
completed compositions. Both works involved are merely manifestations of something more elusive, deeper: temporal incarnations of the supratemporal spirit that
had been glimpsed by Elgar.

These points certainly offer a plausible justification for Elgar's practice in *The
Music Makers*, but they still do not explain why this one piece in particular should
be so filled with quotations. After all, this is not the only piece in which Elgar
reused material, but the extent to which such material infiltrates the work's musical
fabric significantly exceeds Elgar's other instances of self-borrowing.[47] Defenders
of this work have previously pointed to the fact that the quotations or allusions to
other pieces have been given critical attention far out of proportion to the actual

---

[46] As Kennedy remarks apropos of the earlier *Coronation Ode* (which reused the famous trio melody from the first Pomp and Circumstance March), self quotation is 'most natural in a composer, to
whom music is a language': 'desiring to say exactly the same thing again, one has no choice but to say
it in the same notes'. *Portrait of Elgar*, p. 171.

[47] Earlier instances of thematic borrowing may be found in *The Apostles*, which draws on *The
Light of Life*, the *Coronation Ode* that uses 'Land of Hope and Glory', and the finale to the *Enigma
Variations*, which prefigures the First Symphony. Later in life the practice became even more preva-
lent in Elgar's music (*The Starlight Express* borrows from *The Wand of Youth*, the *Nursery Suite* from the
Violin Sonata, and the Third Symphony would have drawn on several works, projected or complete).

Table 6.1 **Elgar's self-quotations within *The Music Makers*[a]**

Stanza	Bar	Work	Incipit
	55	*Enigma* Variations: Theme	
1	112	*The Dream of Gerontius*: Judgement motive	'dreams'
1	115	*Sea Pictures*: 'Sea Slumber Song'	'sea breakers'
1	117	*Enigma* Variations: Theme	'desolate streams'
5	467	*Enigma* Variations: 'Nimrod'	'But on one man's soul'
5	486	Symphony No. 2: IV	'And his look'
7	651	*Enigma* Variations: Theme	'futures we see'
7	559	Violin Concerto: I	'in our dreaming'
7	663	*Enigma* Variations: Theme	'apart from ye'
7	666	Violin Concerto: II	'in our dreaming'
7	667	*The Apostles*: Pt IV	'singing'
8	676	Symphony No. 1: motto	'infinite morning'
9	878	*The Dream of Gerontius*: 'Novissima hora'	'a singer who sings no more'

[a] The table above draws on that appended by Elgar to his 'introductory note', reproduced Anderson and Moore, 'Foreword', p. viii, and consequently those provided by Michael Kennedy in his Appendix II to *Portrait of Elgar*, p. 359, and Aidan Thomson in 'Unmaking the Music Makers', p. 102.

space they occupy within the piece. Yet while this is undoubtedly true in terms of quantity, nevertheless with regard to the peculiar quality they impart, these citations are one of the most noticeable, if not the most noticeable, properties of the work. Evidently this must have been a conscious aesthetic choice by Elgar. As far back as 1938 Thomas Dunhill had queried whether a special point might have been missed by critics concerning Elgar's use of quotations, his 'reasons for invoking the memories which are so frequently brought to consciousness in the course of this ode'.[48] To solve the question posed by Dunhill is, arguably, to understand *The Music Makers*.

For the listener, the distinctive aesthetic character of *The Music Makers* is created by this use of quotations and apparent allusions. The music suddenly slips back into what seems a memory of another piece, with magical expressive effect. Another level of time or aesthetic presence is opened up. Within the musical fabric of *The Music Makers'* normal mode of musical discourse the listener encounters these passages emanating from another realm, apparitions that provoke a flash of

[48] Thomas F. Dunhill, *Sir Edward Elgar* (London: Blackie, 1938), pp. 119–20.

recognition, a breath of inspiration that wafts its familiar perfume over the music. Just as in other works of Elgar's—the 'Welsh tune' caught fleetingly, borne in the breeze in the *Introduction and Allegro*, the motto that had been 'unfolding its long phrases and stately tread for ever' behind the Symphony No. 1, the 'spirit of delight' flitting fitfully through the lengthening evening shadows of the Symphony No. 2—we hear the separate, underlying music 'behind' the phenomenal music.[49] But in *The Music Makers* everything is raised to a meta-level: we hear the broader music behind Elgar's life.

The correspondence with Elgar's creative aesthetic and compositional process is remarkable. The effect is of this other music floating around somewhere, in the air, by desolate streams, waiting to be captured. One can imagine how the idea of the Ode had been gestating alongside the two symphonies and violin concerto. And finally, of course, all this is the very message of *The Music Makers*.

Hence, not only does knowledge of Elgar's working methods and creative aesthetics offer a defence of his decision to allude to music heard in previously published compositions in this piece, but such understanding further reveals how wonderfully apt this procedure is for treating the subject thematicised in O'Shaughnessy's ode. Both for the listener intermittently encountering apparent memories of other pieces and, at a more intellectual level, for those cognisant of these ideas' status within Elgar's own compositional process, Elgar's musical conception turns a musical setting of a text describing the music behind time into an instantiation of this very theme. The music transcends the text describing this musical transcendence.[50]

---

[49] Citing Riley, *Edward Elgar and the Nostalgic Imagination*, p. 26. Insightful accounts of multiple aesthetic/temporal levels in these pieces have been provided by James Hepokoski ('Gaudery, romance, and the "Welsh tune": *Introduction and Allegro*, op. 47', in Julian Rushton and J.P.E. Harper-Scott (eds.), *Elgar Studies* [Cambridge: Cambridge University Press, 2007], pp. 135–71, and 'Elgar', in *The Nineteenth-Century Symphony*, ed. D. Kern Holoman [New York: Schirmer, 1996], pp. 327–44), Riley (above), and Harper-Scott ('Elgar's deconstruction of the belle époque: Interlace structures and the Second Symphony', in Julian Rushton and J.P.E. Harper-Scott (eds.), *Elgar Studies* [Cambridge: Cambridge University Press, 2007], pp. 172–219). Elgar's Four Choral Songs, Op. 53, also make a fascinating comparison, especially the first, 'There is Sweet Music' (a setting of the Choric Song from Tennyson's *The Lotus Eaters*), the chorus being divided into two groups singing simultaneously in keys a semitone apart (G, A♭). The text of the third, taken from Shelley's 'Ode to the West Wind', also explicitly refers back to Elgar's favoured notion of music in nature.

[50] To this extent the 'symphonic' quality that commentators have read into the work seems justified in its implication that the music supersedes the text—as the 'absolutist' music aesthetic Elgar professed in his 1905 Birmingham Lectures might suggest (see Edward Elgar, *A Future for English Music and Other Lectures*, ed. Percy Young [London: Dobson, 1968]). Percy Young remarks on Elgar's relative indifference in the work to accentuation and text-setting, 'preferring to use the voice as a musical instrument and to translate the poet's vision directly into terms of music', and goes on to speak of the 'symphonic quality present', contending that the opening themes of the orchestra and of the voices 'run throughout, binding more technically what is already imaginatively united by the allusions' (*Elgar*, pp. 303, 305). Elgar even considered calling his ode 'Symphony' (the MS was originally entitled '? Symphony/(for solo chorus & orchestra)', later crossed through; the page is reproduced in

Undoubtedly there is a further autobiographical theme present—the 'memories' of earlier music being self-referential, a self-historicising aspect to the work—though this fits the reading proposed as well as it supports the harder notion of self-aggrandisement.[51] The reference to August Jaeger and his 'Nimrod' in Stanza V, for instance—*But on one man's soul it hath broken,/A light that doth not depart;/And his look, or a word he hath spoken,/Wrought flame in another man's heart*—is a tribute to someone who had also heard these deeper voices and recognised them in Elgar's music.[52] As in his own 'EDU' variation at the culmination of the *Enigma* Variations, Elgar referencing 'Nimrod', 'C.A.E.' and the original 'Enigma' theme, the current work functions on an autobiographical level to show how these themes are not only interwoven throughout the passing of time but have also more specifically woven their way in and around his life. As McVeagh puts it, 'the quotations turn this music from being a setting of O'Shaughnessy's Ode into what amounts to Elgar's musical and spiritual autobiography'.[53] It is as if *The Music Makers* is the metawork of Elgar's life: not peripheral, but central, essential.

It is noteworthy in this context that the reference early on to the *Enigma* Variations following the line 'sitting by desolate streams' (b. 117) is to the original 'Enigma' theme, not to Elgar's self-portrait, 'EDU'. Elgar commented in 1912 that the reminiscence signified the loneliness of the artist, as he had felt this back in 1898, before the creation of the Variations and his ensuing success.[54] If the composer had been wanting to refer explicitly to himself he could have cited his own musical portrait, just as he had quoted Jaeger's 'Nimrod' variation to refer to his departed friend. Instead, he speaks in general of the artist—one who hears the music resounding in nature—and cites the theme that underlay his earlier orchestral work in a manner rather akin to the secret stream of music behind *The Music Makers*.

As noted back in the opening chapter, the very idea of the theme and variation set seems to play with Platonist notions of the essence behind changing surface

---

the Elgar Complete Edition full score, p. xiii). See also Thomson, 'Unmaking the Music Makers', who, in a more detailed consideration of the work's structure, revises Young's rather general formal outline.

[51] As Elgar wrote to Ernest Newman, 'after all art must be the man, & all true art is, to a great extent egotism & I have written several things which are still alive' (letter, 14 August 1912, in Moore, *Letters of a Lifetime*, p. 248). Critics have pointed to Richard Strauss's *Ein Heldenleben* as a model in this respect, though an earlier example of culminating self-citation is provided by Anton Rubinstein's Third Violin Sonata in B minor, whose opening references its two predecessors before moving forward into original material. Elgar had played Rubinstein's sonatas in his youth; W.H. Reed mentions playing the First Sonata in G, Op. 13, later in life with the composer accompanying (*Elgar As I Knew Him*, p. 72).

[52] See Elgar's 'Introductory Note', in Moore, *A Creative Life*, p. 636.

[53] McVeagh, 'The shorter instrumental works', p. 62.

[54] Elgar, introductory note, in Moore, *Letters of a Lifetime*, p. 249.

appearances. Elgar's Op. 36 Variations literally personifies this process: we see the various manifestations of the opening G minor theme embodied in differing characters, though the identity of this underlying theme is left unstated. In the subject matter of *The Music Makers*—a work 'so intimately connected' with the *Enigma* Variations—this paradigm is now raised to a more explicit hermeneutic level.[55]

For what is this enigmatic essence lying behind the Variations if not something akin to the music makers, the guiding spirit behind time? Is not the subject of *The Music Makers* the key to the *Enigma* Variations itself? The spirit of time—the underlying motivation and presence behind history and all our days—this is the Enigma and an enigma. 'Through and over the whole set another and larger theme "goes", but is not played' Elgar mysteriously informed his first audience.[56] Ever since that day in 1899 writers have busied themselves with Enigma hunting. Solutions range from the musical ('Auld lang syne' or 'God save the King') to the more broadly abstract (friendship, Britain, even Elgar himself). Some critics even suggest the whole enigma is a 'jape' on Elgar's part.[57] I do not mean to solve the puzzle here, if indeed there is one, but Elgar's procedure in the Variations, in *The Music Makers*, and throughout his comments on music, might indicate to us that time, or more specifically our human existence in time, is certainly an enigma, one which is present in comparable manner to its instantiation behind these works. As Whitman puts it, 'time . . . that mystic, baffling wonder', and 'the puzzle of puzzles . . . that we call Being'—what Woolf is searching for, what a contemporary such as Heidegger was trying, however awkwardly, to latch on to.[58]

Writing in W.H. Reed's score of *The Music Makers* Elgar inscribed the apt epigram 'Musicians thinke our soules are harmonies'.[59] For Elgar, music was alive, a living spirit. 'My music . . . is alive . . . it has heart—I always say to my wife (over any piece or passage that pleases me): "If you cut that it would bleed!"' A satisfactory performance of *In the South* likewise elicited the characteristic comment 'I *love* it: it's alive!'[60] As we have seen throughout this book, ever since the early

---

[55] Young, *Elgar*, p. 281.

[56] Programme note by Charles Barry for the first performance, 19 June 1899, quoting Elgar's account of the work; cited in Moore, *A Creative Life*, p. 270.

[57] See Julian Rushton, *Elgar: 'Enigma' Variations (Cambridge Music Handbooks)* (Cambridge: Cambridge University Press, 1999), pp. 64–78, for an overview of proposed solutions to Elgar's riddle.

[58] Whitman, 'Song of Myself', 23 and 26, *Leaves of Grass* (1891–2), in *Poetry and Prose*, pp. 210, 215, the latter line used explicitly in the context of the idea of listening to 'the song' behind the events of the world at the start of the stanza.

[59] Reed, *Elgar As I Knew Him*, p. 154. Elgar is citing the Elizabethan writer Sir John Davies (1569–1626), a line take from the second part of *Nosce Teipsum*, 'On the Soule of Man, and the immortalitie thereof'—a familiar instance of the composer's arcane literary erudition.

[60] Letters to Jaeger, 6 August 1897 and 23 August 1904, in Moore, *Elgar and his Publishers*, vol. I, pp. 49–50 and vol. II, p. 580.

nineteenth century writers and philosophers have persistently turned to music in order to try to explicate this sense of temporal distention, the qualitative unity of conscious states, what Harper-Scott, in specific relation to Elgar's music, calls music's 'mimesis of human temporality'.[61] What better means could there be for conveying this intangible sense of guiding spirit, the ethereal spirit seemingly permeating our world, indeed of human existence in time, than music itself?

Sic transit gloria mundi

In the past, the supposed grandiloquence of *The Music Makers* posed a problem for its critics, a viewpoint premised upon a positive reading of the work's expressive content (most precisely its text). More recent accounts have tended to construct a defence of Elgar's work by suggesting, rather, that it is profoundly negative in message.[62] As is typical of Elgar, the music provides justification for both readings. Although possessing darker shadows, O'Shaughnessy's text is still predominantly optimistic in tone, qualities that are reflected in Elgar's setting. But at the same time Elgar's conception contains more pessimism and doubt alongside these affirmative elements.

Though commencing as in the First Symphony with a low tonic in timpani and lower strings, the opening theme of *The Music Makers'* introduction is more akin to the symphony's turbulent first subject than the diatonic clarity of its opening 'ideal call'. The underlying tonal prolongation is admittedly more secure—a clear F minor, moving to the dominant at the end of the antecedent-like first phrase—but the restless motivic repetition in the melodic line and chromaticism of the inner parts call up the same flux, the same expressive instability as the uncertain D minor/A minor void in the earlier work (Ex. 6.1). The rise and fall of the incessant inner chromaticism creates the melancholy ebb and flow of the larger rhythm of the phrase. We hear the breaking waves ever sucked back, their long withdrawal echoing the sea of time's slow cadence.

This brooding opening is contrasted with a more aspirational second theme—one of Elgar's most memorable inspirations, for Kennedy a conception 'unequalled in his music as an expression of yearning'.[63] Part of its effect stems from its evident kinship with the first theme, the idea growing unobtrusively out of the opening F minor from b. 23 to reach a secondary key of E♭ at b. 35, and sharing the same rhythmic reiteration, filling out the first theme's ♪♪| ♩ profile with a more even | ♩ ♩ ♪♪| ascending pattern (Ex. 6.2). Yet the sequential construction

---

[61] Harper-Scott, *Edward Elgar, Modernist*, p. 39.

[62] See especially Thomson, 'Unmaking the Music Makers'.

[63] Michael Kennedy, *The Life of Elgar* (Cambridge, Cambridge University Press, 2004), p. 134.

Ex. 6.1 Elgar: *The Music Makers*, Op. 69 (1912), introduction, first theme, bb. 1–12

Ex. 6.2 Elgar: *The Music Makers*, introduction, emergence of second theme, bb. 30–42

and fluctuating harmonies still retained ensure that the theme contains the seeds of its own dissolution within itself. As Riley observes, on its first appearance the upward sequence pauses on a diatonic half-diminished seventh (b. 30) before plunging down again: 'the heroic aspiration of the sequence thus dissolves and fades almost before it reaches fulfilment'.[64] After a passage of greater tonal and phrasal instability a lone memory of the 'Enigma' theme wanders through the texture, before the opening idea returns at b. 94 to round off the introduction, enclosing the entire section within the frame of F minor.

This opening section creates a paradigm that will be heard throughout Elgar's work—that of a glorious *nobilmente* surge of hope followed by its inevitable decay. (Equally, the model may be found in reverse form, as in Elgar's setting of

---

[64] Riley, *Edward Elgar and the Nostalgic Imagination*, p. 70.

the lines *For each age is a dream that is dying/Or one that is coming to birth* [bb. 315–48], a passage which, in its dying fall and re-crescendo to further heights, encapsulates *in nuce* the message of O'Shaughnessy's Ode.) *The Music Makers* proceeds in cycles of optimism and despondency: no sooner are positive sentiments affirmed as they are undercut, only to be renewed again, just as the F minor shadows of the opening which now returns (b. 350) will give way once more to the promise of the second theme.

The same pattern is in evidence for the moments of imperial swagger, such as the blaze of 'We fashion an empire's glory', the composer citing somewhat tongue-in-cheek two melodies certainly not by him, *Rule, Britannia* and *La Marseillaise* (bb. 165 and 172).[65] Yet this imperial pride, as with everything else in the piece, is shortlived. It dissipates almost immediately into the sinuous opening motive of the orchestral introduction. The music soon flares up again in its quest to 'conquer a crown', only to be harmonically annihilated by an even more destructive passage of whole-tone writing (bb. 241–7) that tramples this kingdom down. This distinctive whole-tone motive recurs later at comparable instances of destruction and dissolution in the text, in stanza III ('o'er threw them', b. 306) and finally, extended over three octaves, near the end of the work following the line 'ye of the past must die' (b. 705, Ex. 6.3). As in numerous earlier nineteenth-century examples—think of Thomas Cole's monumental series of paintings *The Course of Empire* (1836) or the limpid opening pages of Ruskin's *The Stones of Venice* (1851–3)—there is already a clear self-consciousness of the rise and fall of empire exhibited in O'Shaughnessy's and Elgar's work.[66] *Sic transit gloria mundi*: hubris is consciously articulated within the setting. The optimism of the text does not preclude awareness of the ultimate transience of human achievements.

As observed, Elgar's composition forms a succession of expressive rises and falls, a constant flux within which the memories or allusions to other music weave their way in and out. Yet one of the most curious aspects of *The Music Makers* is how on repeated listening it becomes increasingly hard to distinguish the citations from the original music, the old from the new Elgar. Such uncertainty is only increased by the presence of apparent near-quotations or allusions in Elgar's work, beyond the overt references tabulated earlier, which easily

[65] Elgar indeed wrote to Newman about the 'deadly sarcasm' of his use of 'the English tune—deliberately commercialising it' (14 August 1912, in Moore, *Letters of a Lifetime*, p. 248).

[66] Cole claimed that his series was inspired by lines from Byron's *Childe Harold*, Canto IV, CVIII: 'There is the moral of all human tales;/'Tis but the same rehearsal of the past./First freedom and then Glory—when that fails,/Wealth, vice, corruption—barbarism at last./And History, with all her volumes vast,/Hath but *one* page'. See Andrew Wilton and Tim Barringer, *American Sublime, Landscape Painting in the United States 1820–1880* (Princeton: Princeton University Press, 2002), p. 97.

Ex. 6.3 Elgar: *The Music Makers*, whole-tone passage, extended appearance, bb. 705–10

become elided with the notion of a general Elgarian style.[67] The language of *The Music Makers* combines seemingly naturally with that of Elgar's earlier music; the motives accommodate each other in a manner typical of his compositional mosaic procedure. Although some of the quotations such as 'Nimrod' retain their identity as separate entities, even here the way in which this particular theme's climax melds into a memorable passage from the finale of the Second Symphony seems entirely natural, as if the two had always belonged to each other.[68] At length even original parts of *The Music Makers* may begin to sound like an echo of some distant music.[69]

Characteristically Elgarian is the movement instigated by the music between two apparently different aesthetic levels, which may be articulated even without recourse to citation of previous works. A recurring motive in the piece is the emphasis on $\hat{6}$ in the melodic line over a familiar diatonically dissonant vii $^4_3$, which is lingered over in echt-Elgarian fashion at 'A breath of our inspiration' (b. 365, Ex. 6.4) and returned to in Stanza V for the line 'Of that land to which they are going' (b. 460).[70] This chord was heard in the introduction's embryonic second theme (b. 30, Ex. 6.2), where as noted, it

[67] See further Thomson, 'Unmaking the Music Makers', pp. 104–5.

[68] Ernest Newman, similarly, speaks of the two 'merging imperceptibly' (' "The Music Makers", by Edward Elgar', *The Musical Times*, 53/835 [1 September 1912], 569).

[69] As Dunhill comments, when 'some particularly Elgarian turn of phrase appears, it is difficult to avoid searching for some allusion which may not really be there at all'. Dunhill, *Sir Edward Elgar*, pp. 119–20.

[70] See Matthew Riley, 'Heroic melancholy: Elgar's inflected diatonicism', in Julian Rushton and J.P.E. Harper-Scott (eds.), *Elgar Studies* (Cambridge: Cambridge University Press, 2007), pp. 284–307, for a detailed account of the diatonic tritone and half-diminished seventh in Elgar's music.

Ex. 6.4 Elgar: *The Music Makers*, bb. 358–69, use of liminal half-diminished seventh

checked the upward aspiration of the new melodic idea. Here at b. 365, on the re-emergence of the second theme following the subdued close described above, Elgar pauses over the same moment, the music seemingly on the verge of discovering some as-yet undisclosed realm, the threshold of a deeper or more inward reality.

As Riley has noted, the diatonic half-diminished seventh in Elgar often serves a liminal function, forming the harmonic portal crossing the boundary into another world.[71] Here, as the text makes clear, the song of the music makers is crossing from the ideal to the real, from the potential to the actual, the future being glimpsed at the moment of its creation. Both O'Shaughnessy's text and Elgar's setting make explicit the etymological connection between breath and inspiration, as the deeper voices of the music makers breathe their guiding spirit into the artist. And as suggested, the boundaries between familiar and original music become furthermore blurred, as this distinctive hesitancy

[71] Ibid., p. 306, and Riley, 'Elgar the Escapist?', in Byron Adams (ed.), *Edward Elgar and His World* (Princeton: Princeton University Press, 2007), pp. 39–57, esp. 48–53.

over $\hat{6}$ in the melody and a half-diminished vii $^4_3$ harmony recalls this archetypal Elgarian fingerprint, to be heard most memorably in the climax from the Second Symphony given at bb. 486 and 490. This is the same gesture as was heard in the citation of the First Symphony's motto (b. 688[4]) where the half-diminished sonority provided the harmonic dissonance necessary to push the striving melody up from $\hat{6}$ to its glorious attainment of $\hat{8}$, and will also be found in b. 801 which echoes the finale of the Second Symphony alongside the introduction's second theme. With such examples multiplying, we might now realise that this harmonic-melodic paradigm is unmistakably redolent of a distinctive passage from b. 193 for the words 'with a dream': though heard over a straight diminished seventh there, the resemblance through the melodic prominence of $\hat{6}$ and descending sequence nonetheless clearly connects this passage with the numerous other instances in the work.[72] Thus this typically Elgarian harmonic schema becomes a unifying idea running through *The Music Makers*, binding allusions to earlier pieces and newly composed material into a potent interweaving of aesthetic levels.

Most apparent as a musical bearer of hope and positive ambition in *The Music Makers* is the 'ideal theme' that formed the motto of the Symphony No. 1, appearing to express the ever-renewed hope of a future that eternally beckons us on.

> *For we are afar with the dawning*
> *And the suns that are not yet high,*
> *And out of the infinite morning*
> *Intrepid you hear us cry*

The effect of this music within the context of the overall course of the new work and its decidedly subdued close points up the position of this earlier confidence within Elgar's life. It is not rejected so much as glimpsed as it had originally been conceived, as an optimism *in the future*, a state of delight that had once been heroically attained but which could always only be fitful. Elgar does not deny, negate, or overturn the genuineness of his earlier vision, but subsumes it into a larger, more complicated and balanced picture of human striving and its inevitable dissolution. Much like the poem as a whole—and indeed similar to the picture that has often been painted of Elgar in scholarship—the result is a rich mixture between optimism, imperial grandeur, and aspiration, and wistfulness, sadness, and doubt.

In this context one might do well to recall James Hepokoski's eloquent description of the Elgarian 'world vision', which 'ranges widely, from the expansive or

---

[72] The final appearance of this gesture (b. 810), recalling the introduction, is likewise as a simpler $\hat{6}$ appoggiatura to a first inversion tonic triad without the half-diminished seventh harmony.

boisterous to the desperately conflicted and, further, to the fully interior, intimate and private'.

> But it is touched throughout by a melancholy awareness of the dream-
> like quality and transitoriness of things: ghosts of unsustainability,
> regret, and loss of innocence lurk everywhere. In this valedictory world
> the magnificent, *fortissimo* moments of attainment and affirmation
> seem simultaneously to be melting away . . . as if he were trying to sustain
> an illusion forever slipping away from his grasp.[73]

For enclosing the whole work is the return of the chorus's soft opening phrase,
triple *piano*, 'We are the music makers,/And we are the dreamers of dreams'. The
voices trail off *pppp*, leaving a timpani roll and final bare fifth in cellos and bass
rounding off the work in resemblance to its very beginning. There is a real sense
of the piece's ultimate embeddedness within its opening F minor wastes—a
darkness at the opening and close and fitfully returning within, resounding
echoes from the ocean of eternity lapping on the shifting sands of time on the
shore. The tale of history and human endeavour is itself a dream, as insubstantial
and ethereal as the voices of the music makers who dream it.[74]

The idea of dreams is prevalent throughout Elgar's oeuvre—*The Dream of
Gerontius, Dream Children*, the 'Dream Interludes' from *Falstaff, The Starlight
Express*, even the last piece of the *Nursery Suite*, which was to be entitled
'Dreaming'. Dreams, like the inspiration of the music makers, are the conveyers
of gnostic wisdom in the Platonic tradition; yet, in the Renaissance world-theatre
of Shakespeare and Calderón, they are also a reminder of the transitoriness,
even vanity of human endeavours. The dream imagery of *The Music Makers* is
double sided. As much as dreams may embody aspiration or the disclosure of a
deeper, noumenal reality, so too may their darker connotations be found in the
far from optimistic close, encapsulated by the words 'Yea, in spite of a dreamer
who slumbers,/And a singer who sings no more'. Here sleep distinctly takes on
the spectre of death. Elgar passes quietly over O'Shaughnessy's initial affirmative 'Yea, in spite' and repeats instead, almost hypnotically, the mournful words
'no more . . . no more . . .'. We may be the dreamers of dreams—but our little
life is surrounded by a sleep. For all Shakespeare's 'pomp and circumstance' or

---

[73] James Hepokoski, 'Elgar', p. 329.

[74] This mystical, dreamlike quality is borne out by Nicholas Kilburn's conception (the work's
dedicatee), expressed in a letter to Alice Elgar, 24 December 1912: rehearsing the work he strove 'to
impress on all concerned the importance of a subdued and mystical treatment of certain parts'. 'Sing
and play . . . as though you were in *dreamland*'—specifically mentioning the choral opening and ending
of the work. Young, *Elgar*, p. 303.

Calderón's 'majestad y la pompa', we are yet the stuff dreams are made on—and dreams are merely dreams.[75]

Or even less? Elgar, as is well known, attached an inscription from Charles Lamb's *Dream Children* to his two pieces of that name from 1902: 'We are nothing; less than nothing, and dreams. *We are only what might have been*'. The full passage runs on further: 'We are only what might have been, and must wait upon the tedious shores of Lethe millions of ages before we have existence and a name'.[76] In a comparable formulation, during the conception of the *Enigma* Variations, Elgar, on being asked by his wife what the new theme he was playing was, reportedly replied 'Nothing—but something might be made of it'.[77] Like the souls of the dream children, the Orphic voices of *The Music Makers* emerge out from the primordial nothingness, pure potentiality, and sink back there at the close. Or, for the apostate composer of 1912, expressed rather more nihilistically in the words given to Judas in *The Apostles*, 'we shall be hereafter as though we had never been . . . and our life shall pass away as the trace of a cloud'.[78]

Even on a less existential note, the end may be interpreted as not just concerning the inevitability of death but more specifically as about the drying up of inspiration.[79] Written towards the end of Elgar's most creative period, the self-citations would lead earlier reviewers to claim that by repeating himself Elgar was already 'written out' as a creative force. Some more recent accounts

[75] *Othello*, Act III, Sc. 3, ll. 347–8, 353: 'O, now for ever/Farewell the tranquil mind! Farewell content! . . . Pride, pomp and circumstance of glorious war!'. Calderón, *La vida es sueño*, Act III, ll. 2310–13: '¿Otra vez queréis que vea/entre sombras y bosquejos/la majestad y la pompa/desvanecida del viento?'

[76] Charles Lamb, 'Dream Children: A Reverie', from *Essays of Elia*, in *The Prose Works of Charles Lamb*, 3 vols. (London: Edward Moxon, 1836), vol. II, pp. 235–6.

[77] Cited in Maine, *Elgar*, vol. II, p. 101. Also note the composer's comment to Dora Powell ('Dorabella') concerning the Variations, 'are you as nice as [quotes the 'Dorabella' variation], or only as unideal as [quotes the original Enigma theme]' (Mrs Richard Powell (née Dora Penny), *Edward Elgar: Memories of a Variation* [London: Oxford University Press, 1937], p. 38). I would contend that this, in conjunction with the wider argument here, points to an understanding of the 'Enigma' theme not as symbolising Elgar himself (variation XIV, 'E.D.U.' clearly has that function), but of bare potentiality, the 'nothing' from which, after waiting 'millions of ages', something might be fashioned before sinking back more into silence and oblivion, possibly (in a more Heideggerian vein) even the mystery of 'being' itself, its state of hiddenness and subsequent disclosure through the variations.

[78] *Wisdom* II:2–4; see also Byron Adams, 'Elgar's later oratorios: Roman Catholicism, decadence and the Wagnerian dialectic of shame and grace', in Daniel Grimley and Julian Rushton (eds.), *The Cambridge Companion to Elgar* (Cambridge: Cambridge University Press, 2004), p. 104. Adams notes Elgar's reported comment to Arthur Thomson, his doctor during his final illness, that he had no faith whatever in an afterlife: 'I believe there is nothing but compete oblivion' (p. 82). One might also compare this with Elgar's extraordinary partsong 'Owls: An Epitaph', Op. 53 No. 4, setting the composer's own text (which ends: 'All that could be is said./Is it . . . what? . . . Nothing').

[79] Percy Young, for instance, contends the work is about inspiration (sleeve notes to Elgar, *The Music Makers*).

have amended this reading, though only to the extent that this process is now posited as a message consciously articulated by Elgar—the composer 'falling on his own sword' as Aidan Thomson puts it, aware of the passing of his age, that 'ye of the past must die'.[80] But, no longer needing to offer an apologia for one of Elgar's finest works, it is surely possible to appreciate this theme as simply a genuine fear of every creative talent, especially one who professed that he could 'only write when the spirit moves me'.[81]

And, in a wider cultural setting, the latter-day listener might hear not only the death of the individual music-maker or the imminent onset of Elgar's compositional decline but, above and beyond this, the passing of a larger age, one which could still believe in the guiding spirit of history and human providence. *The Music Makers* is both a paean to and a requiem for the pre-war liberal *Zeitgeist* and of the spirit of time itself, understood in the strong sense. Just as the sunset glow of Elgar's Second Symphony has often been heard encapsulating Edward Grey's famous words on the eve of the First World War, 'the lamps are going out all over Europe; we shall not see them lit again in our lifetime', so *The Music Makers* is the diminished afterglow, that melancholy, doubly crepuscular moment of the Edwardian evening.[82]

Epilogue: The Dreamers of Dreams

Sing again, with your dear voice revealing
A tone
Of some world far from ours
Where music and moonlight and feeling
Are one.
—Percy Bysshe Shelley, 'An Ariette for Music'[83]

Perhaps it is not-being that is the true state, and all our dream of life is inexistence; but, if so, we feel that these phrases of music, these conceptions which exist in relation to our dream, must be nothing either. We shall perish, but we have as hostages these divine captives who will follow and share our fate. And death in their company is somehow less bitter, less inglorious, perhaps even less probable.
—Marcel Proust, *Swann's Way*[84]

[80] Thomson, 'Unmaking the Music Makers', p. 133.

[81] Moore, *Elgar on Record*, p. 208.

[82] Sir Edward Grey, Viscount of Fallodon, *Twenty-Five Years, 1892–1916*, 2 vols. (London: Hodder and Stoughton, 1925), vol. II, p. 20.

[83] Shelley, 'An Ariette for Music' ('To Jane: The keen stars were twinkling'), *Poetical Works*, p. 673. Elgar set this same text for his 1904 song 'In Moonlight', reusing the melody of the *Canto Popolare* from *In the South*. O'Shaughnessy also uses part of this passage as the epigram to his 1874 collection, directly following the 'Ode' Elgar set in *The Music Makers*.

[84] Marcel Proust, *Swann's Way*, in *Remembrance of Things Past*, vol. I, p. 381.

Nietzsche once commented on the idealism he perceived in Beethoven's music, its sincere pointing to a beautiful but illusory world lying beyond our own. This music

> often appears like a deeply moved consideration from the unexpected rehearing of a piece long believed lost, 'innocence in tones': it is music about music. . . . [His melodies] are to him transfigured memories from the 'better world': similar to how Plato thought of the ideas.[85]

Elgar scholars have recently devoted scrutiny to the strong idealist element within the composer's aesthetics and ethical worldview, what has been aptly described as his 'Romantic Platonism', his striving for the ideal and noble in art and life.[86] A phrase of Ernst Pauer, author of a treatise on aesthetics that Elgar had read as a young adult, chimes particularly true of Elgar's case: 'art has to exhibit to humanity the ideal picture of what perfect human beauty can be'.[87] Possibly, as it seems he drifted away from the tenets of his earlier Roman Catholicism towards a broader humanism and general disillusionment, he came to believe that this ideal might just have been a human invention.[88] As he grew older, Elgar came increasingly to the realisation that the ideal which he had captured in the Symphony No. 1, enshrined in the Violin Concerto, and elegised in the Symphony No. 2, was perhaps just a dream. And yet, like the drunken stupor of Falstaff, it is no less real or sincere for being only such. Many would willingly accord that in music such as the Adagio of the First Symphony, Elgar had exhibited to humanity an ideal picture of what beauty can be, in pages of the Second Symphony the true meaning of *nobilmente*. That the greatest hopes and accomplishments of the human spirit might merely be a daydream, the vain echo of a better world that in reality does not, and never did, exist, may be hard

---

[85] Nietzsche, *Menschliches Allzumenschliches*, vol. II, pt. II 'Der Wanderer und sein Schatten', §152, (*Sämtliche Werke*, ed. Giorgio Colli and Mazzino Montinari, 15 vols. (Berlin and New York: de Gruyter, 1980), vol. II, pp. 615–16).

[86] Byron Adams, 'Elgar and the Persistence of Memory', in Byron Adams (ed.), *Edward Elgar and His World* (Princeton: Princeton University Press, 2007), p. 78. See especially Brian Trowell, 'Elgar's Use of Literature', in Raymond Monk (ed.), *Edward Elgar: Music and Literature* (Aldershot: Scolar Press, 1993), pp. 182–326. Leon Botstein, speaking of Elgar's Romantic-Platonist aesthetic with reference to the influence of Ruskin's *Sesame and Lilies*, indeed implicitly calls up exactly that trope of a deeper melody running behind life explored earlier ('Transcending the Enigmas of Biography: The Cultural Context of Sir Edward Elgar's Career', in Byron Adams [ed.], *Edward Elgar and His World* [Princeton: Princeton University Press, 2007], p. 386).

[87] Ernst Pauer, *The Elements of the Beautiful in Music* (London: Novello, Ewer & Co, 1877), p. 47, cited in Adams, 'Elgar and the Persistence of Memory', p. 78.

[88] Compare the argument of J.P.E. Harper-Scott in 'Elgar's Invention of the Human: *Falstaff*, op. 68', *19th-Century Music*, 28 (2005), 230–53.

to accept, for what still can seem miraculous, inexplicable, is how beautiful the dream is.

To the extent that with the passing of time Elgar's ideal retreated into the memory of its onetime dream, the past takes on a charmed quality, a land of lost content inspired by that departed spirit, enchanted by its music. The past is the one place where this dream exists. Michael Allis has aptly commented on how in Elgar's music 'the evocation of the past represents a semantically-charged area'.[89] The fabric of *The Music Makers* is suffused with such semantically charged memories, the very stuff on which it is made. And yet in one evident sense the past is gone: it exists no more, *is* not.

That this fugitive dream is constructed with music is understandable, for as has been argued throughout this book, music is surely the perfect medium for suggesting the paradoxical presence of absence and absence of presence—a 'tone which is now forever fled', yet 'vibrates in the memory'.[90] Not for nothing did O'Shaughnessy entitle his collection 'Music and Moonlight', for just as with time and its passing, both music and moonlight are intangible. Music possesses that insubstantiality and transience which promises that 'beauty passes like a dream'. Music might be in the air—but it also melts back there, into thin air.

> *Like memory of music fled,—*
> *Like aught that for its grace may be*
> *Dear, and yet dearer for its mystery.*[91]

Music seemingly possesses the capacity to enshrine the spirit of a particular time and place—the quality which seems to seep like some enchanting effluvium over our memories of that former, now departed time. A phrase might stick in our mind, seeming to convey more powerfully than anything more tangible could the intangibility of that period, something that has been but is gone, that in a sense (like the present) scarcely ever was, but somehow, like the music, will always just about be. As soon as we try to grasp it, to fix its meaning (as Proust's Swann mistakenly attempts with his *petite phrase*), it eludes our grasp—like Goethe's comment on the aesthetician who captures and fastens down a butterfly in order to understand the grace of its flight; like time itself.[92]

---

[89] Michael Allis, 'Elgar and the art of retrospective narrative', *Journal of Musicological Research*, 19 (2000), 321.

[90] Shelley, 'Time Long Past', and 'Music, When Soft Voices Die', in *Poetical Works*, pp. 632 and 639, respectively.

[91] Shelley, 'Ode to Intellectual Beauty', in *Poetical Works*, p. 530.

[92] Goethe, letter to Hetzler the Younger, 14 July 1770 (*Goethes Werke [Weimarer Ausgabe]*, 4 parts, 133 vols. [Weimar: H. Böhlau, 1887–1919], Pt. IV [*Briefe*], vol. I, pp. 238–9).

Coming now to the end of this account of music and temporality, we might similarly reflect on the difficulties of the task and the apparent impossibility of ever arriving at a comprehensive understanding of music's relation with time. Throughout this book, the ways in which music has seemed intimately connected with time and human subjectivity have been explored with reference to a range of nineteenth-century pieces stretching from Beethoven to Elgar, chosen as representative of the most important and meaningful issues within the Romantic era. Music has variously been heard to suggest temporal transcendence and timelessness, a mimesis of human temporality disclosing the unity of subjective identity, the workings of memory and consciousness, as a cultural reflection of deeper metaphysical postulations concerning the nature of history, and as the expression of the time of the world in spirit. And growing out from the starting point given in the first two chapters, the aptitude of music to convey an understanding of temporality has been seen to expand across the previous four chapters from communicating the singular time of the individual subject to take in the collected and collective times of society and finally of human history.

It was argued far earlier that the reader should not expect a single, all-encompassing theory of musical temporality to be offered within these pages. Though this absence might be disappointing for some who have patiently followed me so far and who would desire a simple and straightforward conclusion to such a protracted discussion, I think this situation is sadly unavoidable. As befits the subject, it seems our understanding of the relation of music and time will remain in a state of flux, always incomplete: the extended set of meditations that is this book might yield our acceptance of music and time as a source of continual inspiration, ever provisional, ever open, rather than a quest for ultimate answers. But in order to offer at least some overriding idea with which to sum up the path of this book, I would venture to say (on the proviso that neither music nor time should be understood as being reified into a single, invariant entity) that there is no comprehensive perspective on time in the Romantic era, unless it be simply the idea that music itself is in the most privileged position to communicate or express the mysteries of time. As much as there is one, this is the single message of this book.

This idea has been illuminated across the various chapters from a range of musical perspectives and given greater historical and philosophical support in the second. And by the end of this final chapter, this notion of music *as* time and human history has been raised to the principle of a musical work. Time, as we saw in the second chapter, is a perplexing, polyvalent human construct; but music was seen in this era as saying something that no other art form or mode of discourse did in quite the same way or as powerfully, about many of the most important aspects of this enigmatic entity, and thus formed—and arguably still forms—an invaluable source of understanding about the world we inhabit.

Yet at the same time, few, if any, of the hypotheses advanced within these pages seem susceptible to any definitive argument: the problematic nature of certain claims for music may be questioned and critiqued, but nothing positive can be verified. That music might transcend linguistic formulations and disclose something about our existence in time that philosophy cannot dream of is possible, but this same purported transcendence at one stroke removes the matter from rational verification. Music seemingly holds forth the promise of answers to long intractable philosophical problems; yet it whispers back its reply in a language that philosophy cannot understand.

The urge to understand, to analyse our experience of music and temporality will not go away, even if the answers we may obtain with our clumsy tools are at best only partial and enigmatic, as through a glass darkly, where the image dimly perceived may merely be our own fainter reflection. Yet at least having considered the topic more critically our journey has been richer and more varied, even if any fugitive vision obtained may, in the end, just be a dream.

BIBLIOGRAPHY

Abbate, Carolyn: *Unsung Voices: Opera and Musical Narrative in the Nineteenth Century* (Princeton: Princeton University Press, 1991).
——— 'Music—Drastic or Gnostic?', *Critical Inquiry*, 30 (2004), 505–36.
Abraham, Gerald: *Studies in Russian Music* (London: William Reeves, 1935).
Abrams, M.H.: *The Mirror and the Lamp: Romantic Theory and the Critical Tradition* (Oxford: Oxford University Press, 1953).
——— *Natural Supernaturalism: Tradition and Revolution in Romantic Literature* (New York: Norton, 1971).
Adams, Byron: 'Elgar's later oratorios: Roman Catholicism, decadence and the Wagnerian dialectic of shame and grace', in Daniel Grimley and Julian Rushton (eds.), *The Cambridge Companion to Elgar* (Cambridge: Cambridge University Press, 2004), pp. 81–105.
——— 'Elgar and the Persistence of Memory', in Byron Adams (ed.), *Edward Elgar and His World* (Princeton: Princeton University Press, 2007), pp. 59–95.
——— (ed.): *Elgar and His World* (Princeton: Princeton University Press, 2007).
Addis, Laird: *Of Mind and Music* (Ithaca, NY: Cornell University Press, 1999).
Adlington, Robert: 'Musical Temporality: Perspectives from Adorno and de Man', *Repercussions*, 6 (1997), 5–60.
——— 'Moving Beyond Motion: Metaphors for Changing Sound', *Journal of the Royal Music Association*, 128 (2003), 297–318.
Adorno, Theodor W.: *Gesammelte Schriften*, ed. Rolf Tiedemann, 20 vols. (Frankfurt: Suhrkamp, 1997).
——— *Philosophy of Modern Music*, trans. Anne Mitchell and Wesley Blomster (New York: Seabury Press, 1973).
——— *Quasi una Fantasia: Essays on Modern Music*, trans. Rodney Livingstone (London: Verso, 1998).
——— *Beethoven: The Philosophy of Music*, ed. Rolf Tiedemann, trans. E. Jephcott (Cambridge: Polity Press, 1998).
——— *Essays on Music*, ed. Richard Leppert, trans. Susan H. Gillespie (Berkeley and Los Angeles: University of California Press, 2002).
——— 'Schubert (1928)', trans. Jonathan Dunsby and Beate Perrey, *19th-Century Music*, 29 (2005), 3–14.
Agawu, V. Kofi: *Playing with Signs: A Semiotic Interpretation of Classic Music* (Princeton: Princeton University Press, 1991).
Allis, Michael: 'Elgar and the art of retrospective narrative', *Journal of Musicological Research*, 19 (2000), 289–328.
Alperson, Philip: '"Musical Time" and Music as an "Art of Time"', *Journal of Aesthetics and Art Criticism*, 38 (1980), 407–17.

Andersen, Holly K. and Grush, Rick: 'A Brief History of Time-Consciousness: Historical Precursors to James and Husserl', *Journal of the History of Philosophy*, 47 (2009), 277–307.

Anderson, Robert and Moore, Jerrold Northrop: 'Foreword' to *The Music Makers; The Spirit of England*, Elgar Complete Edition, vol. 10 (London: Novello, 1986).

Antonova, Clemena: *Space, Time, and Presence in the Icon: Seeing the World with the Eyes of God* (Farnham: Ashgate, 2010).

Aquinas, Thomas: *Summa Theologica*, trans. Fathers of the English Dominican Province (London: Burns, Oates and Washbourne, 1911).

—— *Summa contra Gentiles*, trans. Anton C. Pegis, James F. Anderson, Vernon J. Bourke and Charles J. O'Neil, 5 vols. (New York: Doubleday 1955–7).

Aristotle: *The Complete Works of Aristotle*, ed. Jonathan Barnes, 2 vols. (Princeton: Princeton University Press, 1984).

Asafiev, Boris: *Symphonic Etudes: Portraits of Russian Operas and Ballets*, trans. David Edwin Haas (Lanham, MD: Scarecrow Press, 2007).

Augustine: *City of God*, trans. Henry Bettinson (Harmondsworth: Penguin, 1972).

—— *Confessions*, trans. Henry Chadwick (Oxford: Oxford University Press, 1998).

Bacht, Nikolaus: 'Music and Time in Theodor W. Adorno' (PhD diss., King's College London, 2002).

Bakhtin, Mikhail: *The Dialogic Imagination: Four Essays by M.M. Bakhtin*, trans. Caryl Emerson and Michael Holquist (Austin: University of Texas Press, 1981).

Barford, Philip: 'The Piano Music—II', in Denis Arnold and Nigel Fortune (eds.), *The Beethoven Companion* (London: Faber & Faber, 1971), pp. 126–93.

Barry, Barbara R.: *Musical Time: The Sense of Order* (Stuyvesant, NY: Pendragon Press, 1990).

—— '"Sehnsucht" and Melancholy: Explorations of Time and Structure in Schubert's *Winterreise*', in *The Philosophers Stone: Essays in the Transformation of Musical Structure* (Hillsdale, N.Y.: Pendragon, 2000), pp. 181–203.

Barthes, Roland: *Image—Music—Text*, trans. Stephen Heath (London: Flamingo, 1977).

Baudelaire, Charles: *Œuvres complètes*, ed. Y.-G. Le Dantec and Claude Pichois (Paris: Gallimard-Pléiade, 1961).

Begbie, Jeremy: *Theology, Music and Time (Cambridge Studies in Christian Doctrine)* (Cambridge: Cambridge University Press, 2000).

Behler, Constantin: *Nostalgic Teleology: Friedrich Schiller and the Schemata of Aesthetic Humanism* (Berne: Peter Lang, 1995).

Bekker, Paul: *Beethoven* (Berlin: Schuster and Loeffler, 1912).

Bender, John and Wellbery, David E. (eds.), *Chronotypes: The Construction of Time* (Stanford: Stanford University Press, 1991).

Berger, Karol: 'Beethoven and the Aesthetic State', *Beethoven Forum VII* (1999), 17–44.

—— *Bach's Cycle, Mozart's Arrow: An Essay on the Origins of Musical Modernity* (Berkeley and Los Angeles: University of California Press, 2007).

Bergson, Henri: *Time and Free Will: An Essay on the Immediate Data of Consciousness*, trans. F.L. Pogson (London: George Allen and Co., 1910).

—— *Matter and Memory*, trans. N.M. Paul and W.S. Palmer (London: George Allen and Unwin, 1911).

—— *Duration and Simultaneity*, trans. Leon Jacobson (New York: Library of Liberal Arts, 1922).

—— *The Creative Mind: An Introduction to Metaphysics*, trans. Mabelle L. Andison (New York: Philosophical Society, 1946).

Berkeley, George: *A Treatise Concerning the Principles of Human Knowledge* (Harmondsworth: Penguin, 1988).

Berlin, Isaiah: *Russian Thinkers* (Harmondsworth: Penguin, 1978).

Birrell, Gordon: *The Boundless Present: Space and Time in the Literary Fairy Tales of Novalis and Tieck* (Chapel Hill, NC: University of North Carolina Press, 1979).

Blake, William: *Complete Writings* (London: Oxford University Press, 1966).

Bloch, Ernst: *Essays on the Philosophy of Music*, trans. Peter Palmer (Cambridge: Cambridge University Press, 1985).

Boethius: *The Consolation of Philosophy*, trans. Peter Walsh (Oxford: Clarendon Press, 1999).

Bonds, Mark Evan: *Wordless Rhetoric: Musical Form and the Metaphor of the Oration* (Cambridge, MA: Harvard University Press, 1991).

―――― *Music as Thought: Listening to the Symphony in the Age of Beethoven* (Princeton: Princeton University Press, 2006).

―――― 'The Spatial Representation of Musical Form', *Journal of Musicology*, 27 (2010), 265–303.

Borges, Jorge Luis: *The Aleph and Other Stories (1933–1969)*, trans. Norman Thomas di Giovanni in collaboration with the author (London: Jonathan Cape, 1971).

Botstein, Leon: 'Transcending the Enigmas of Biography: The Cultural Context of Sir Edward Elgar's Career', in Byron Adams (ed.), *Edward Elgar and His World* (Princeton: Princeton University Press, 2007), pp. 365–405.

Bowie, Andrew: *Aesthetics and Subjectivity: From Kant to Nietzsche* (Manchester: Manchester University Press, 2003).

―――― *Music, Philosophy, and Modernity* (Cambridge: Cambridge University Press, 2007).

Bradley, F.H.: *Appearance and Reality* (London: George Allen & Unwin, 1916).

Brelet, Gisèle: *Le temps musical: Essai d'une esthétique nouvelle de la Musique*, 2 vols. (Paris: Presses Universitaires de France, 1949).

Brendel, Alfred: *On Music: Collected Essays* (London: Robson, 2007).

Bréville, Pierre de: 'César Franck (1822–1890)', *Encyclopédie de la musique et dictionnaire du Conservatoire*, ed. Albert Lavignac and Lionel de la Laurencie (Paris: Delagrave, 1925), vol. I, pp. 176–182.

Briner, Andres: *Der Wandel der Musik als Zeit-Kunst* (Vienna: Universal Edition, 1955).

Brinkmann, Reinhold: *Late Idyll: The Second Symphony of Johannes Brahms*, trans. Peter Palmer (Cambridge, MA: Harvard University Press, 1995).

―――― 'In the Times(s) of the "Eroica"', in Scott Burnham and Michael Steinberg (eds.), *Beethoven and his World* (Princeton: Princeton University Press, 2000), pp. 1–26.

Brown, David: *Tchaikovsky: A Biographical and Critical Study*, 4 vols. (London: Victor Gollancz, 1992).

―――― 'Russia before the Revolution', in Robert Layton (ed.), *A Guide to the Symphony* (Oxford: Oxford University Press, 1995), pp. 262–91.

Brown, Marshall: 'Mozart and After: The Revolution in Musical Consciousness', *Critical Inquiry*, 7 (1981), 689–706.

Brown, Maurice J.E.: *Schubert: A Critical Biography* (London: Macmillan, 1958).

Buckley, R.J.: *Sir Edward Elgar* (London: John Lane, 1912).

Burnham, Scott: *Beethoven Hero* (Princeton: Princeton University Press, 1995).

―――― 'The "Heavenly Length" of Schubert's Music', *Ideas*, 6/1 (1999), <http://nationalhuman-itiescenter org/ideasv61/burnham.htm>.

―――― 'Schubert and the Sound of Memory', *Musical Quarterly*, 84 (2000), 655–63.

―――― 'Landscape as Music, Landscape as Truth: Schubert and the Burden of Repetition', *19th-Century Music*, 29 (2005), 31–41.

Burstein, Poundie: 'Lyricism, Structure, and Gender in Schubert's G Major String Quartet', *Musical Quarterly*, 81 (1997), 51–63.

Butt, John: *Bach's Dialogue with Modernity* (Cambridge: Cambridge University Press, 2010).

Byron, George Gordon, Lord: *The Poetical Works of Lord Byron* (London: Oxford University Press, 1909).

Calderón de la Barca, Pedro: *La vida es sueño* (Madrid: Castalia, 1994).

Caplin, William E.: 'The Classical Cadence: Conceptions and Misconceptions', *Journal of the American Musicological Society*, 57 (2004), 51–117.

Carnap, Rudolf: 'Überwindung der Metaphysik durch logische Analyse der Sprache', *Erkenntnis*, 2 (1932), 219–41.

Chua, Daniel K.L.: *The 'Galitzin' Quartets of Beethoven* (Princeton: Princeton University Press, 1995).

Chusid, Martin: 'Schubert's Cyclic Compositions of 1824', *Acta Musicologica*, 36 (1964), 37–45.

Clark, Suzannah: *Analyzing Schubert* (Cambridge: Cambridge University Press, 2011).

Clarke, David: 'Music, phenomenology, time consciousness: meditations after Husserl', in David Clarke and Eric Clarke (eds.), *Music and Consciousness: Philosophical, Psychological, and Cultural Perspectives* (Oxford: Oxford University Press, 2011), pp. 1–28.

Clarke, David and Clarke, Eric (eds.): *Music and Consciousness: Philosophical, Psychological, and Cultural Perspectives* (Oxford: Oxford University Press, 2011).

Clarke, Eric: 'Music Perception and Musical Consciousness', in David Clarke and Eric Clarke (eds.), *Music and Consciousness: Philosophical, Psychological, and Cultural Perspectives* (Oxford: Oxford University Press, 2011), pp. 193–213.

[Clay, Edmund R.]: *The Alternative: A Study in Psychology* (London: Macmillan, 1882).

Clifton, Thomas: *Music as Heard: A Study in Applied Phenomenology* (New Haven: Yale University Press, 1983).

Cocking, J.M.: 'Proust and Music', in *Proust: Collected Essays on the Writer and his Art* (Cambridge: Cambridge University Press, 1982), pp. 109–29.

Cohn, Dorrit: *Transparent Minds: Narrative Modes for Presenting Consciousness in Fiction* (Princeton: Princeton University Press, 1978).

Coleridge, Samuel Taylor: *Biographia Literaria; or, Biographical Sketches of My Literary Life and Opinions*, ed. John Shawcross, 2 vols. (Oxford: Clarendon Press, 1907).

—— *Poetical Works* (London: Oxford University Press, 1967).

Cone, Edward T.: *The Composer's Voice* (Berkeley: University of California Press, 1974).

—— 'Schubert's Promissory Note: An Exercise in Musical Hermeneutics', *19th-Century Music*, 5 (1982), 233–41.

Cooke, Deryck: 'The unity of Beethoven's Late Quartets', *The Musical Review*, 24 (1963), 30–49.

Cooper, Barry: *Beethoven (The Master Musicians)* (Oxford: Oxford University Press, 2008).

Cooper, Martin: *Beethoven: The Last Decade 1817–1827* (London: Oxford University Press, 1970).

Cumming, Naomi: *The Sonic Self: Musical Subjectivity and Signification* (Bloomington and Indianapolis: Indiana University Press, 2000).

Currie, Gregory: *Image and Mind: Film, Philosophy and Cognitive Science* (Cambridge: Cambridge University Press, 1995).

—— 'Tense and Egocentricity in Fiction', in Robin Le Poidevin (ed.), *Questions of Time and Tense* (Oxford, Clarendon Press, 1998), pp. 265–83.

Custine, Astolphe Marquis de: *La Russie en 1839*, 2 vols. (Brussels: Wouters, 1843).

Dahlhaus, Carl: 'Issues in Composition', in *Between Romanticism and Modernism*, trans. Mary Whittall (Berkeley and Los Angeles: University of California Press, 1980), pp. 40–78.

—— 'Zeitstrukturen in der Oper', in *Vom Musikdrama zur Literaturoper* (Munich and Salzburg: Emil Katzbichler, 1983), pp. 25–32.

—— 'Musik und Zeit', in Carl Dahlhaus and Hans Heinrich Eggebrecht, *Was ist Musik?* (Wilhelmshaven: Florian Noetzel, 1985), pp. 174–80.

—— 'Sonata Form in Schubert', in Walter Frisch (ed.), *Schubert: Critical and Analytical Studies* (Lincoln, NE: University of Nebraska Press, 1986), pp. 1–12.

—— *Nineteenth-Century Music*, trans. J.B. Robinson (Berkeley and Los Angeles: University of California Press, 1989).

—— *Ludwig van Beethoven: Approaches to His Music*, trans. Mary Whittall (Oxford: Clarendon Press, 1991).

Daverio, John: '"One More Beautiful Memory of Schubert": Schumann's Critique of the Impromptus, D. 935', *Musical Quarterly*, 84 (2000), 604–14.

De la Mare, Walter: *Collected Poems* (London: Faber & Faber, 1979).

De Man, Paul: 'The Rhetoric of Temporality', in C.S. Singleton (ed.), *Interpretation: Theory and Practice* (Baltimore: John Hopkins Press, 1969), pp. 173–209.

—— 'The Rhetoric of Blindness: Jacques Derrida's Reading of Rousseau', in *Blindness and Insight: Essays in the Rhetoric of Contemporary Criticism* (Minneapolis: University of Minnesota Press, 1983), pp. 102–41.

Deleuze, Gilles: *Cinema 2: The Time-Image*, trans. Hugh Tomlinson and Robert Galeta (Minneapolis: University of Minnesota Press, 1989).

Deleuze, Gilles and Guattari, Félix: *A Thousand Plateaus*, trans. Brian Massumi (London: Continuum, 2004).

Derrida, Jacques: *Speech and Phenomena and Other Essays on Husserl's Theory of Signs*, trans. David B. Allison (Evanston, IL: Northwestern University Press, 1973).

Deruchie, Andrew: *The French Symphony at the Fin de Siècle: Style, Culture, and the Symphonic Tradition* (Rochester, NY: University of Rochester Press, 2013).

Descartes, René: *Compendium Musicae*, in *Oeuvres*, ed. Charles Adam and Paul Tannery, 13 vols. (Paris: L. Cerf, 1897–1913), vol. X.

Deutsch, Otto Erich: *Schubert: Die Dokumente seines Lebens* (Kassel: Bärenreiter, 1964), earlier edition trans. Eric Blom as *Schubert: A Documentary Biography* (London: Dent, 1947).

D'Indy, Vincent: *Cours de Composition Musicale*, ed. Auguste Sérieyx, 3 vols. (Paris: A. Durand, 1903–50).

——— *César Franck*, trans. Rosa Newmarch (London: John Lane Bodley Head, 1909).

Donelan, James H.: *Poetry and the Romantic Musical Aesthetic* (Cambridge: Cambridge University Press, 2008).

Dorschel, Andreas: 'Das anwesend Abwesende: Musik und Erinnerung', in Andreas Dorschel (ed.), *Resonanzen: Vom Erinnern in der Musik* (Vienna: Universal Edition, 2007), pp. 12–29.

Downes, Stephen: *Music and Decadence in European Modernism: The Case of Central and Eastern Europe* (Cambridge: Cambridge University Press, 2010).

Dreyfus, Laurence: *Bach and the Patterns of Invention* (Cambridge, MA: Harvard University Press, 1996).

Dufrenne, Mikel: *The Phenomenology of Aesthetic Experience* (1953), trans. Edward S. Casey (Evanston, IL: Northwestern University Press, 1973).

Dunhill, Thomas F.: *Sir Edward Elgar* (London: Blackie, 1938).

Eberlein, Dorothee: *Russische Musikanschauung um 1900 von 9 russischen Komponisten* (Regensburg: G. Bosse, 1978).

Eggebrecht, Hans Heinrich: 'Musik und Zeit', in Carl Dahlhaus and Hans Heinrich Eggebrecht, *Was ist Musik?* (Wilhelmshaven: Florian Noetzel, 1985), pp. 181–6.

——— *Musik als Zeit* (Wilhelmshaven: Florian Noetzel, 2001).

Eich, Katrin: *Die Kammermusik von César Franck* (Kassel: Bärenreiter, 2002).

Einstein, Alfred: *Schubert: The Man & his Music*, trans. David Ascoli (London: Cassell, 1951).

Elgar, Edward: *A Future for English Music and Other Lectures*, ed. Percy Young (London: Dobson, 1968).

Eliade, Mircea: *The Myth of the Eternal Return* (New York: Pantheon Books, 1954).

Eliot, T.S.: *Collected Poems 1909–1962* (London: Faber, 1974).

Emerson, Caryl: 'Musorgsky's Libretti on Historical Themes: From the Two *Borises* to *Khovanshchina*', in Arthur Groos and Roger Parker (eds.), *Reading Opera* (Princeton: Princeton University Press, 1988), pp. 235–67.

——— 'Apocalypse Then, Now, and (For Us) Never: Reflections on Musorgsky's Other Historical Opera', *Khovanshchina (ENO Opera Guide)* (London: John Calder, 1994), pp. 7–20.

Epstein, David: *Shaping Time: Music, the Brain, and Performance* (New York: Schirmer, 1995).

Faulkner, William: *Requiem for a Nun* (New York: Vintage, 2011).

Fauquet, Jöel-Marie: *César Franck* (Paris: Fayard, 1999).

Fichte, Johann Gottlieb: *Science of Knowledge*, trans. Peter Heath and John Lachs (Cambridge: Cambridge University Press, 1982).

Fischer, Edwin: *Ludwig van Beethovens Klaviersonaten: Ein Begleiter für Studierende und Liebhaber* (Wiesbaden: Insel-Verlag, 1956).

Fischer, Kurt von: 'Das Zeitproblem in der Musik', in Rudolf W. Meyer (ed.), *Das Zeitproblem im 20. Jahrhundert* (Bern: Francke, 1964), pp. 296–317.

Fisk, Charles: 'What Schubert's Last Sonata Might Hold', in Jenefer Robinson (ed.), *Music and Meaning* (Ithaca, NY: Cornell University Press, 1997), pp. 179–200.

——— *Returning Cycles: Contexts for the Interpretation of Schubert's Impromptus and Last Sonatas* (Berkeley and Los Angeles: University of California Press, 2001).

Flier, Michael S.: 'Till the End of Time: The Apocalypse in Russian Historical Experience Before 1500', in Valerie A. Kivelson and Robert H. Greene (eds.), *Orthodox Russia: Belief and Practice under the Tsars* (University Park, PA: Pennsylvania State University Press, 2003), pp. 127–58.

Forner, Johannes: *Ludwig van Beethoven—Die Klaviersonaten: Betrachtung zu Werk und Gestalt* (Altenburg: Kamprad, 2011).

Foucault, Michel: *The Order of Things: An Archaeology of the Human Sciences*, trans. A.M. Sheridan Smith (London: Tavistock, 1970).

Franck, César: *Correspondance*, ed. Jöel-Marie Fauquet (Liège: Mardaga, 1999).

Frank, Manfred: *Das Problem 'Zeit' in der deutschen Romantik: Zeitbewußtsein und Bewußtsein von Zeitlichkeit in der frühromantischen Philosophie und in Tiecks Dichtung* (Munich: Winkler, 1972).

Frankenstein, Alfred: 'Victor Hartmann and Modeste Mussorgsky', *Musical Quarterly*, 25 (1939), 268–91.

Freud, Sigmund: *The Standard Edition of the Complete Psychological Works of Sigmund Freud*, trans. James Strachey, 22 vols. (London: Hogarth Press, 1953–74).

Frisch, Walter: Introduction to 'Memory and Schubert's Instrumental Music', *Musical Quarterly*, 84 (2000), 581.

Frolova-Walker, Marina: 'Against German Reasoning: The Search for a Russian Style of Musical Argumentation', in Harry White and Michael Murphy (eds.), *Musical Constructions of Nationalism* (Cork: Cork University Press, 2001), pp. 104–22.

――― *Russian Music and Nationalism: from Glinka to Stalin* (New Haven: Yale University Press, 2008).

Fuß, Hans-Ulrich: 'Ein Laurence Sterne der Musik: Zur Kunst der Parenthesen im Instrumentalwerk Haydns', in Marie-Agnes Dittrich, Marin Eybl, and Reinhard Kapp (eds.), *Zyklus und Prozess: Joseph Haydn und die Zeit* (Vienna: Böhlau Verlag, 2012), pp. 197–236.

Gallagher, Shaun: *The Inordinance of Time* (Evanston, IL: Northwestern University Press, 1998).

Garden, Edward: *Balakirev* (New York: St. Martin's Press, 1967).

Gauchet, Marcel: *The Disenchantment of the World: A Political History of Religion*, trans. Oscar Burge (Princeton: Princeton University Press, 1997).

Genette, Gérard: *Narrative Discourse*, trans. Jane E. Lewin (Oxford: Blackwell, 1980).

Georgiades, Thrasybulos: *Music and Language*, trans. Marie Louise Göllner (Cambridge: Cambridge University Press, 1982).

Gibbs, Christopher: '"Poor Schubert": images and legends of the composer', in Christopher Gibbs (ed.), *The Cambridge Companion to Schubert* (Cambridge: Cambridge University Press, 1997), pp. 36–55.

Gingerich, John M.: 'Remembrance and Consciousness in Schubert's C-Major String Quintet, D. 956', *Musical Quarterly*, 84 (2000), 19–34.

Goethe, Johann Wolfgang von: *Goethes Werke (Weimarer Ausgabe)*, 4 parts, 133 vols. (Weimar: H. Böhlau, 1887–1919).

Goethe, Johann Wolfgang von and Zelter, Friedrich: *Briefwechsel zwischen Goethe und Zelter*, ed. Max Hecker, 3 vols. (Frankfurt: Insel Verlag, 1987).

Greene, David B.: *Temporal Processes in Beethoven's Music* (New York: Gordon & Breach, 1982).

――― *Mahler, Consciousness and Temporality* (New York: Gordon and Breach, 1984).

Grey, Sir Edward, Viscount of Fallodon: *Twenty-Five Years, 1892–1916*, 2 vols. (London: Hodder and Stoughton, 1925).

Grimley, Daniel M.: '"A smiling with a sigh": the chamber music and works for strings', in Daniel M. Grimley and Julian Rushton (eds.), *The Cambridge Companion to Elgar* (Cambridge: Cambridge University Press, 2004), pp. 120–38.

Grimley, Daniel M. and Rushton, Julian (eds.): *The Cambridge Companion to Elgar* (Cambridge: Cambridge University Press, 2004).

Grosche, Stefan: *'Zarten Seelen ist gar viel gegönnt': Naturwissenschaft und Kunst im Briefwechsel zwischen C.G. Carus und Goethe* (Göttingen: Wallstein, 2001).

Grove, Sir George: *Beethoven, Schubert, Mendelssohn*, ed. Eric Blom (London: Macmillan, 1951).

Gülke, Peter: 'Zum Bilde des Späten Schubert', in *Musik-Konzepte Franz Schubert*, ed. Heinz-Klaus Metzger and Rainer Riehn (Munich: Edition Text+Kritik, 1979), pp. 107–66.

Hammerstein, Reinhold: '"Schöne Welt, wo bist du?" Schiller, Schubert und die Götter Griechenlands', in Michael von Albrecht and Werner Schubert (eds.), *Musik und Dichtung. Neue Forschungsbeiträge (Festschrift Viktor Pöschl zum 80. Geburtstag)* (Frankfurt: Peter Lang, 1990), pp. 305–30.

Hanslick, Eduard: *The Beautiful in Music*, trans. Gustav Cohen (London: Novello, 1891).

Harley, John: 'The Trill in Beethoven's Later Music', *The Musical Times*, 95 (1954), 69–73.

Harper-Scott, J.P.E.: 'Elgar's Invention of the Human: *Falstaff*, op. 68', *19th-Century Music*, 28 (2005), 230–53.

――― *Edward Elgar, Modernist* (Cambridge: Cambridge University Press, 2007).

—— 'Elgar's deconstruction of the belle époque: Interlace structures and the Second Symphony', in Julian Rushton and J.P.E. Harper-Scott (eds.), *Elgar Studies* (Cambridge: Cambridge University Press, 2007), pp. 172–219.

Hart, Brian: 'Wagner and the *franckiste* "Message-Symphony" in Early Twentieth-Century France', in Annegret Fauser and Manuela Schwartz (eds.), *Von Wagner zum 'wagnérisme': Musik, Literatur, Kunst, Politik* (Leipzig: Leipzig Universitätsverlag, 1999), pp. 315–37.

Hasty, Christopher: *Meter as Rhythm* (New York: Oxford University Press, 1997).

Hatten, Robert S.: *Musical Meaning in Beethoven: Markedness, Correlation, and Interpretation* (Bloomington, IN: Indiana University Press, 1994).

—— *Interpreting Musical Gestures, Topics, and Tropes: Mozart, Beethoven, Schubert* (Bloomington: Indiana University Press, 2004).

Hegel, Georg Wilhelm Friedrich: *Phenomenology of Spirit*, trans. A.V. Miller (Oxford: Oxford University Press, 1979).

—— *Logic* (*Encyclopaedia*, Part I), trans. William Wallace (Oxford: Clarendon Press, 1975).

—— *Philosophy of Nature* (*Encyclopaedia*, Pt II), trans. A.V. Miller (Oxford: Oxford University Press, 1970).

—— *Aesthetics: Lectures on Fine Art*, trans. T.M. Knox, 2 vols. (Oxford: Clarendon Press, 1975).

—— *Lectures on The Philosophy of History*, trans. J. Sibree (New York: Dover, 1956).

Heidegger, Martin: *The Concept of Time*, trans. Ingo Farin (London: Continuum, 2011).

—— *Sein und Zeit* (Tübingen: Max Niemeyer, 1967), trans. John Macquarrie and Edward Robinson as *Being and Time* (New York: Harper and Row, 1962).

Hepokoski, James: *Sibelius: Symphony No. 5* (Cambridge: Cambridge University Press, 1993).

—— 'Elgar', in D. Kern Holoman (ed.), *The Nineteenth-Century Symphony* (New York: Schirmer, 1996), pp. 327–44.

—— 'Gaudery, romance, and the "Welsh tune": *Introduction and Allegro*, op. 47', in Julian Rushton and J.P.E. Harper-Scott (eds.), *Elgar Studies* (Cambridge: Cambridge University Press, 2007), pp. 135–71.

Hepokoski, James and Darcy, Warren: *Elements of Sonata Theory: Norms, Types, and Deformations in the Late-Eighteenth-Century Sonata* (New York: Oxford University Press, 2006).

Herder, Johann Gottlieb: *Eine Metakritik zur Kritik der reinen Vernunft*, ed. Friedrich Bassenger (Berlin: Aufbau Verlag, 1955).

Herder, Johann Gottlieb: *Werke*, ed. Martin Bollacher, 10 vols. (Frankfurt: Deutscher Klassiker Verlag, 1985–2000).

Herzen, Alexander: *My Past and Thoughts*, trans. Constance Garnett (London: Chatto & Windus, 1968).

Hesiod: *The Homeric Hymns and Homerica*, trans. Hugh G. Evelyn-White *(Loeb Classical Library)* (London: Heinemann, 1920).

Hinrichsen, Hans-Joachim: 'Die Sonatenform im Spätwerk Franz Schuberts', *Archiv für Musikwissenschaft*, 45 (1988), 16–49.

—— 'Individuelles Spätwerk und epochaler Spätstil: Zur harmonischen Konstruktion der "Sonate Cyclique" in César Francks Streichquartett', in Peter Jost (ed.), *César Franck: Werk und Rezeption* (Stuttgart: Steiner Verlag, 2004), pp. 88–111.

Hirsch, Marjorie: 'The Spiral Journey Back Home: Brahms's "Heimweh" Lieder', *Journal of Musicology*, 22 (2005), 454–89.

Hoeckner, Berthold: *Programming the Absolute: Nineteenth-Century German Music and the Hermeneutics of the Moment* (Princeton: Princeton University Press, 2002).

Hölderlin, Friedrich: *Sämtliche Werke (Große Stuttgarter Ausgabe)*, ed. Friedrich Beißner and Adolf Beck, 8 vols. (Stuttgart: Cotta, 1943–85).

Hoerl, Christoph and McCormack, Teresa (eds.): *Time and Memory: Issues in Philosophy and Psychology* (Oxford: Oxford University Press, 2001).

Hopkins, Robert G.: 'When a coda is more than a coda: Reflections on Beethoven', in Eugene Narmour and Ruth Solie (eds.), *Explorations in Music, the Arts, and Ideas: Essays in Honor of Leonard B. Meyer* (Stuyvesant, NY: Pendragon, 1988), pp. 393–410.

Hume, David: *A Treatise of Human Nature*, ed. L.A. Selby-Bigge (Oxford: Clarendon Press, 1951).

Husserl, Edmund: *The Phenomenology of Internal Time Consciousness*, trans. James Churchill (The Hague: Martinus Nijhoff, 1964).

—— *Ideas Pertaining to a Pure Phenomenology and to a Phenomenological Philosophy: General Introduction to a Pure Phenomenology*, trans. F. Kersten (The Hague: Martinus Nijhoff, 1983).

—— *Die Bernauer Manuskripte über das Zeitbewusstsein (1917/18), Husserliana 33*, ed. Rudolf Bernet and Dieter Lohmar (Dordrecht-Boston-London: Kluwer, 2001).

Ingarden, Roman: *The Musical Work and the Problem of its Identity*, trans. Adam Czerniawski (London: Macmillan, 1986).

Ivanits, Linda J.: *Russian Folk Belief* (Armonk, NY: M.E. Sharpe, 1989).

Jackson, Timothy L.: *Tchaikovsky Symphony No. 6 (Pathétique)* (Cambridge: Cambridge University Press, 1999).

James, William: *The Principles of Psychology*, 2 vols. (New York: Holt, 1890).

Jankélévitch, Vladimir: *Music and the Ineffable*, trans. Carolyn Abbate (Princeton: Princeton University Press, 2003).

Jardillier, Robert: *La musique de chamber de César Franck: Étude et analyse* (Paris: Mellottée, 1930).

Jean Paul [Richter]: *Sämtliche Werke*, ed. Norbert Miller, 10 vols. (Munich: Carl Hanser Verlag, 1959–63).

Johnson, Graham: notes to Hyperion Schubert Edition, vol. 14, CDJ33014 (1992).

Johnson, Julian M.: 'The Subjects of Music: A Theoretical and Analytical Enquiry into the Construction of Subjectivity in the Musical Structuring of Time' (DPhil diss., University of Sussex, 1994).

Johnson, Mark L. and Larson, Steve: '"Something in the Way She Moves"—Metaphors of Musical Motion', *Metaphor and Symbol*, 18 (2003), 63–84.

Jones, Sir William: *Dissertations and Miscellaneous Pieces Relating to the History and Antiquities, the Arts, Sciences, and Literature of Asia*, 2 vols. (London: G. Nicol, 1792).

Kalokyris, Konstantinos: 'Byzantine Iconography and "Liturgical Time"', *Eastern Churches Review*, 1 (1966), 359–63.

Kansteiner, Wulf: 'Finding Meaning in Memory: A Methodological Critique of Collective Memory Studies', *History and Theory*, 41 (2002), 179–97.

Kant, Immanuel: *Gesammelte Schriften (Akademie-Ausgabe)*, 23 vols. (Berlin and Leipzig: de Gruyter, 1923).

—— *Critique of Pure Reason*, trans. and ed. Paul Guyer and Allen W. Wood (Cambridge: Cambridge University Press, 1998).

Kapp, Reinhard: 'Haydns Persönliche Zeiterfahrung', in Marie-Agnes Dittrich, Marin Eybl, and Reinhard Kapp (eds.), *Zyklus und Prozess: Joseph Haydn und die Zeit* (Vienna: Böhlau Verlag, 2012), pp. 25–68.

Karl, Gregory: 'Music as Plot: A Study in Cyclic Forms' (PhD diss., University of Cincinnati, 1993).

Keller, Hermann: 'Schuberts Verhältnis zur Sonatenform', in *Musa-Mens-Musici: im Gedenken an Walther Vetter* (Leipzig: Deutscher Verlag für Musik, 1969), pp. 287–95.

Kennedy, Michael: *Portrait of Elgar*, rev. ed. (Oxford: Oxford University Press, 1982).

—— *The Life of Elgar* (Cambridge, Cambridge University Press, 2004).

Kent, Christopher: 'Magic by mosaic: some aspects of Elgar's compositional methods', in Daniel Grimley and Julian Rushton (eds.), *The Cambridge Companion to Elgar* (Cambridge: Cambridge University Press, 2004), pp. 32–49.

Kerman, Joseph: *The Beethoven Quartets* (New York: Norton, 1966).

Keym, Stefan: '"L'unité dans la variété": Vincent d'Indy und das zyklische Prinzip', *Musiktheorie*, 13 (1998), 223–41.

—— 'Der Rahmen als Zentrum: Zur Bedeutung von Langsamer Einleitung und Coda in Vincent d'Indys Instrumentalmusik', in Manuela Schwartz and Stefan Keym (eds.), *Pluralismus wider Willen? Stilistische Tendenzen in der Musik Vincent d'Indys* (Hildesheim: Olms, 2002), pp. 114–59.

Kiem, Eckehard: 'Der Blick in Abgrund: Zeitstruktur beim späten Beethoven', in Richard Klein, Eckehard Kiem and Wolfram Ette (eds.), *Musik in der Zeit: Zeit in der Musik* (Göttingen: Velbrück Wissenschaft, 2000), pp. 212–31.

Kierkegaard, Søren: *Either/Or: A Fragment of Life*, trans. Alastair Hannay (Harmondsworth: Penguin, 1992).

—— *Fear and Trembling/Repetition*, trans. Howard V. and Edna H. Hong (Princeton: Princeton University Press, 1983).

—— *The Concept of Anxiety: A Simple Psychologically Orienting Deliberation on the Dogmatic Issue of Hereditary Sin*, trans. Reidar Thomte and Albert B. Anderson (Princeton: Princeton University Press, 1981).

Kinderman, William: 'Thematic Contrast and Parenthetical Enclosure in the Piano Sonatas, Op. 109 and 111', in Harry Goldschmidt and Georg Knepler (eds.), *Zu Beethoven: Aufsätze und Dokumente* (Berlin: Neue Musik, 1988), pp. 43–59.

—— 'Integration and Narrative Design in Beethoven's Piano Sonata in A-flat Major, Opus 110', *Beethoven Forum I* (1992), 111–45.

—— *Beethoven* (Oxford: Oxford University Press, 1995).

—— 'Wandering Archetypes in Schubert's Instrumental Music', *19th-Century Music*, 21 (1997), 208–22.

Kirk, G.S., Raven, J.E., and Schofield, M.: *The Presocratic Philosophers* (Cambridge: Cambridge University Press, 1983).

Kitto, H.D.F.: *The Greeks* (Harmondsworth: Penguin, 1951).

Klein, Richard: 'Thesen zum Verhältnis von Musik und Zeit', in Richard Klein, Eckehard Kiem and Wolfram Ette (eds.), *Musik in der Zeit: Zeit in der Musik* (Göttingen: Velbrück Wissenschaft, 2000), pp. 57–107.

Knab, Armin: 'Die Einheit der Beethovenschen Klaviersonate in As-Dur, op. 110' *Zeitschrift für Musikwissenschaft*, 1 (1919), 388–99.

Koselleck, Reinhard: *Futures Past: On the Semantics of Historical Time*, trans. Keith Tribe (Cambridge, MA: MIT Press, 1985).

—— *Zeitschichten: Studien zur Historik* (Frankfurt: Suhrkamp, 2003).

Kohn, Hans: *Pan-Slavism: Its History and Ideology* (Notre Dame, IN: University of Notre Dame Press, 1953).

Költzsch, Hans: *Franz Schuberts Klaviersonaten* (Leipzig: Breitkopf und Härtel, 1927).

Korsyn, Kevin: 'Schenker and Kantian Epistemology', *Theoria*, 3 (1988), 1–58.

Kortooms, Toine: *Phenomenology of Time: Edmund Husserl's Analysis of Time-Consciousness* (Dordrecht: Kluwer, 2002).

Kramer, Jonathan D.: 'Multiple and Non-Linear Time in Beethoven's opus 135', *Perspectives on New Music*, 11 (1973), 122–45.

—— 'New Temporalities in Music', *Critical Inquiry*, 7 (1981), 539–56.

—— 'Studies of Time and Music: A Bibliography', *Music Theory Spectrum*, 7 (1985), 72–106.

—— *The Time of Music: New Meanings, New Temporalities, New Listening Strategies* (New York: Schirmer, 1988).

Kramer, Lawrence: *Music as Cultural Practice, 1800–1900* (Berkeley and Los Angeles: University of California Press, 1992).

—— *Interpreting Music* (Berkeley and Los Angeles: University of California Press, 2011).

Kramer, Richard: *Distant Cycles: Schubert and the Conceiving of Song* (Chicago: Chicago University Press, 1994).

—— *Unfinished Music* (New York: Oxford University Press, 2008).

Kühn, Clemens: 'Schuberts Zeit: Vier Versuche', in Diether de la Motte (ed.), *Zeit in der Musik—Musik in der Zeit* (Frankfurt: Peter Lang, 1997), pp. 5–14.

Kujundzic, Dragan: 'After "After": The *Arkive* Fever of Alexander Sokurov', *Quarterly Review of Film and Video* (2004), <http://www.artmargins.com/content/cineview/kujundzic.html>.

Lakoff, George and Johnson, Mark: *Metaphors We Live By* (Chicago: University of Chicago Press, 1980).

Lamb, Charles: *The Prose Works of Charles Lamb*, 3 vols. (London: Edward Moxon, 1836).

Landes, David S.: *Revolution in Time: Clocks and the Making of the Modern World* (Cambridge: Belknap Press, 1983).

Langer, Susanne K.: 'The Image of Time', in *Feeling and Form: A Theory of Art* (New York: Scribner, 1953), pp. 104–19.

Le Poidevin, Robin: *The Images of Time: An Essay in Temporal Representation* (Oxford: Oxford University Press, 2007).

—— 'Music without the Flow of Time', *Proceedings of the Philosophy and Music Conference 'Time Theories and Music'*, Ionian University of Corfu, 28 April 2012, <http://conferences.ionio.gr/ccpm12/download.php?f=ccpm12_ks_poidevin.pdf>.

—— (ed.): *Questions of Time and Tense* (Oxford, Clarendon Press, 1998).

Le Poidevin, Robin and MacBeath, Murray (eds.): *The Philosophy of Time* (Oxford: Oxford University Press, 1993).

Leatherbarrow, William and Offord, Derek (eds.): *A History of Russian Thought* (Cambridge: Cambridge University Press, 2010).

Leibniz, Gottfried Wilhelm: *Die philosophischen Schriften*, ed. C.I. Gerhardt, 7 vols. (Berlin: Weidmann, 1875–90).

Lenz, Wilhelm von: *Beethoven: Eine Kunst-Studie*, 5 vols. (Hamburg: Hoffmann und Campe, 1860).

Lepenies, Wolf: *Das Ende der Naturgeschichte: Wandel kutureller Selbstverständlichkeiten in den Wissenschaften des 18. und 19. Jahrhunderts* (Munich and Vienna: Hanser, 1976).

Lessing, Gotthold Ephraim: *Werke*, ed. Herbert G. Göpfert et al., 8 vols. (Munich: Winkler, 1970–79).

Levinson, Jerrold: *Music in the Moment* (Ithaca, NY: Cornell University Press, 1997).

Lévi-Strauss, Claude: *The Raw and the Cooked* (*Mythologiques* vol. I), trans. John and Doreen Weightman (Chicago: University of Chicago Press, 1983).

Locke, John: *An Essay Concerning Human Understanding* (Oxford: Clarendon Press, 1979).

Lockwood, Lewis: '"Eroica" Perspectives: Strategy and Design in the First Movement', in Alan Tyson (ed.), *Beethoven Studies*, vol. 3 (Cambridge: Cambridge University Press, 1982), pp. 85–106.

—— *Beethoven: The Music and the Life* (New York: Oxford University Press, 2003).

Lodes, Birgit: '"So träumte mir, ich reiste … nach Indien": Temporality and Mythology in Op. 127/I', in William Kinderman (ed.), *The String Quartets of Beethoven* (Urbana and Chicago: University of Illinois Press, 2006), pp. 168–212.

Loesche, Heinz von: 'Final gerichtete Zeit oder final gerichtete Musik?', in Diether de la Motte (ed.), *Zeit in der Musik—Musik in der Zeit* (Frankfurt: Peter Lang, 1997), pp. 69–76.

London, Justin: 'Time', *The New Grove Dictionary of Music and Musicians*, 29 vols. (London: Macmillan, 2001), vol. XXV.

Lovejoy, Arthur O.: *The Great Chain of Being: A Study of the History of an Idea* (Cambridge, MA: Harvard University Press, 1936).

Lütteken, Laurenz: *Das Monologische als Denkform in der Musik zwischen 1760 und 1785* (Tübingen: Niemeyer, 1998).

MacBeath, Murray: 'Time's Square', in Robin Le Poidevin and Murray MacBeath (eds.), *The Philosophy of Time* (Oxford: Oxford University Press, 1993), pp. 183–202.

Maes, Francis: *A History of Russian Music: From Kamarinskaya to Babi Yar*, trans. Arnold J. Pomerans and Erica Pomerans (Berkeley, Los Angeles and London: University of California Press, 2002).

Maier, Franz Michael: 'Prousts Franck: Form und Semantik in einer Sonate und einem Roman des 20. Jahrhunderts', in Christiane Strucken-Paland and Ralph Paland (eds.), *César Franck im Kontext: Epoche, Werk und Wirkung* (Cologne: Dohr, 2009), pp. 175–91.

Maine, Basil: *Elgar, His Life and Works*, 2 vols. (London: G. Bell and Sons, 1933).

Mak, Su Yin: 'Schubert's Sonata Forms and the Poetics of the Lyric', *Journal of Musicology*, 23 (2006), 263–306.

Mann, Thomas: *Doktor Faustus: Das Leben des deutschen Tonsetzers Adrian Leverkühn, erzählt von einem Freunde* (Frankfurt: Fischer Verlag, 1947).

Marcel, Gabriel: 'Bergsonism and Music', in Susanne K. Langer (ed.), *Reflections on Art* (London: Oxford University Press, 1958), pp. 142–51.

Markosian, Ned: 'Time', *The Stanford Encyclopedia of Philosophy* (rev. 2010), ed. Edward N. Zalta, <http://plato.stanford.edu/archives/win2010/entries/time/>.

Marlow, Christopher: *Doctor Faustus and Other Plays* (Oxford: Oxford University Press, 1995).

Marston, Nicholas: 'Schenker and Forte Reconsidered: Beethoven's Sketches for the Piano Sonata in E, Op. 109', *19th-Century Music*, 10 (1986), 24–42.

—— *Beethoven's Piano Sonata in E, Op. 109* (Oxford: Clarendon Press, 1995).

—— '"The sense of an ending": Goal-directedness in Beethoven's music', in Glenn Stanley (ed.), *The Cambridge Companion to Beethoven* (Cambridge: Cambridge University Press, 2000), pp. 84–101.

—— 'Schubert's Homecoming', *Journal of the Royal Music Association*, 125 (2000), 248–70.

Marx, A.B.: *Ludwig van Beethoven: Leben und Schaffen*, 2 vols. (Berlin: Janke, 1863).

Matthews, Denis: *Beethoven Piano Sonatas (BBC Music Guides)* (London: BBC Publications, 1967).

Mähl, Hans Joachim: *Die Idee des goldenen Zeitalters im Werk des Novalis* (Heidelberg: Carl Winter, 1965).

McClary, Susan: *Conventional Wisdom: The Content of Musical Form* (Berkeley and Los Angeles: University of California Press, 2000).

—— 'Temp Work: Music and the Cultural Shaping of Time', *Musicology Australia*, 23 (2000), 160–75.

McKay, Elizabeth Norman: *Franz Schubert: A Biography* (Oxford: Oxford University Press, 1996).

McTaggart, John McTaggart Ellis: 'The Unreality of Time', *Mind*, 68 (1908), 457–74.

McVeagh, Diana: 'The shorter instrumental works', in Daniel Grimley and Julian Rushton (eds.), *The Cambridge Companion to Elgar* (Cambridge: Cambridge University Press, 2004), 50–62.

Mellers, Wilfrid: *Beethoven and the Voice of God* (London: Faber & Faber, 1983).

Mellor, D.H.: 'The Unreality of Tense', in Robin Le Poidevin and Murray MacBeath (eds.), *The Philosophy of Time* (Oxford: Oxford University Press, 1993), pp. 47–59.

Meredith, William: 'The Origins of Beethoven's Op. 109', *The Musical Times*, 126 (1985), 713–16.

Merleau-Ponty, Maurice: *The Phenomenology of Perception*, trans. Colin Smith (London: Routledge, 2002).

—— *The Visible and the Invisible*, ed. Claude Lefort, trans. Alphonso Lingis (Evanston IL: Northwestern University Press, 1968).

Monelle, Raymond: *The Sense of Music: Semiotic Essays* (Princeton: Princeton University Press, 2000).

Moore, Jerrold Northrop: *Elgar on Record: The Composer and the Gramophone* (Oxford: Oxford University Press, 1974).

—— *Edward Elgar: A Creative Life* (Oxford: Clarendon Press, 1984).

—— (ed.): *Elgar and his Publishers: Letters of a Creative Life*, 2 vols. (Oxford: Clarendon Press, 1987).

—— (ed.): *Edward Elgar: The Windflower Letters* (Oxford: Clarendon Press, 1989).

—— (ed.): *Edward Elgar: Letters of a Lifetime* (Oxford: Clarendon Press, 1990).

Morgan, Robert P.: 'Musical Time/Musical Space', *Critical Inquiry*, 6 (1980), 527–38.

Motte-Haber, Helga de la: 'Historische Wandlungen musikalischer Zeitvorstellungen', in Diether de la Motte (ed.), *Neue Musik—Quo vadis? 17 Perspektiven* (Mainz: Schott, 1988), pp. 53–66.

Müller, Günther: 'Erzählzeit und erzählte Zeit', in *Morphologische Poetik* (Tübingen: Max Niemeyer, 1968), pp. 257–68.

Mussorgsky, Modest: *The Musorgsky Reader*, ed. and trans. Jay Leyda and Sergei Bertensson (New York: Da Capo, 1970).

Muxfeldt, Kristina: 'Schubert's songs: the transformation of a genre', in Christopher Gibbs (ed.), *The Cambridge Companion to Schubert* (Cambridge: Cambridge University Press, 1997), pp. 121–37.

—— 'Music Recollected in Tranquillity: Postures of Memory in Beethoven', in *Vanishing Sensibilities: Essays in Reception and Historical Restoration—Schubert, Beethoven, Schumann* (New York: Oxford University Press, 2011), pp. 118–47.

Nattiez, Jean-Jacques: *Proust as Musician*, trans. Derrick Puffett (Cambridge: Cambridge University Press, 1989).

—— *The Battle of Chronos and Orpheus*, trans. Jonathan Dunsby (Oxford: Oxford University Press, 2004).

Nectoux, Jean-Michel: 'Proust et Fauré', *Bulletin de la Société des amis de Marcel Proust*, 21 (1971), 1101–20.

Neumann, Friedrich: *Die Zeitgestalt: Eine Lehre vom musikalischen Rhythmus*, 2 vols. (Vienna: Paul Kaltschmid, 1959).

Newark, Cormac and Wassenaar, Ingrid: 'Proust and Music: The Anxiety of Competence', *Cambridge Opera Journal*, 9 (1997), 163–83.

Newcomb, Anthony: 'Structure and Expression in a Schubert Song: *Noch einmal Auf dem Flusse zu hören*', in Walter Frisch (ed.), *Schubert: Critical and Analytical Studies* (Lincoln, NE: University of Nebraska Press, 1986), pp. 153–74.

Newman, Ernest: '"The Music Makers", by Edward Elgar', *The Musical Times*, 53/835 (1 September 1912), 569.

Newton, Isaac: *The Mathematical Principles of Natural Philosophy*, trans. Andrew Motte, rev. Florian Cajori, 2 vols. (Berkeley: University of California Press, 1934).

Newton-Smith, W.H.: *The Structure of Time* (London: Routledge and Kegan Paul, 1980).

Nietzsche, Friedrich: *Sämtliche Werke*, ed. Giorgio Colli and Mazzino Montinari, 15 vols. (Berlin and New York: de Gruyter, 1980).

Novalis [Friedrich von Hardenberg], *Schriften. Die Werke Friedrich von Hardenbergs (Historische-kritische Ausgabe)*, ed. Paul Kluckhohn, Richard Samuel, Gerhard Schulz and Hans-Joachim Mähl, 6 vols. (Stuttgart: Kohlhammer, 1960–2006).

O'Shaughnessy, Arthur: *Music and Moonlight: Poems and Songs* (London: Chatto and Windus, 1874).

Painter, George D.: *Marcel Proust: A Biography*, 2 vols. (Harmondsworth: Penguin, 1977).

Pesic, Peter: 'Schubert's Dream', *19th-Century Music*, 23 (1999), 136–44.

Picht, Georg: 'Grundlinien einer Philosophie der Musik', in *Wahrheit—Vernunft—Verantwortung: Philosophische Studien* (Stuttgart: Ernst Klett, 1969), pp. 408–26.

——— 'Die Macht des Denkens', in Günther Neske (ed.), *Erinnerung an Martin Heidegger* (Pfullingen: Neske, 1977), pp. 197–205.

Piroué, Georges: *Proust e la musique du devenir* (Paris: Editions Denoël, 1960).

Plato: *Complete Works*, ed. John M. Cooper (Indianapolis: Hackett, 1997).

Plotinus: *The Enneads*, trans. Stephen MacKenna (Harmondsworth: Penguin, 1991).

Plutarch: *Essays and Miscellanies*, trans. R. Brown, ed. William W. Goodwin, 5 vols. (Boston and New York: Little, Brown and Co., 1909).

Poincaré, Henri: *The Foundations of Science*, trans. George B. Halsted (New York: The Science Press, 1905).

Poulet, Georges: *Studies in Human Time*, trans. Elliott Coleman (Baltimore: Johns Hopkins Press, 1956).

Powell, Mrs Richard (née Dora Penny): *Edward Elgar: Memories of a Variation* (London: Oxford University Press, 1937).

Prior, Arthur N.: *Past, Present, and Future* (Oxford: Clarendon Press, 1967).

Proclus: *Elements of Theology*, trans. E.R. Dodds (Oxford: Clarendon Press, 1933).

Proust, Marcel: *Correspondance*, ed. Philip Kolb, 21 vols. (Paris: Plon, 1970–93).

——— *Contre Sainte-Beuve précédé de Pastiches et mélanges et suivi de Essais et articles*, ed. Pierre Clarac and Yves Sandre (Paris: Gallimard, 1971).

——— *À la recherche du temps perdu*, ed. Jean-Yves Tadié, 4 vols. (Paris: Gallimard, 1987–9). English translation as *Remembrance of Things Past*, trans. C.K. Scott Moncrieff and Terence Kilmartin, 3 vols. (Harmondsworth: Penguin, 1981).

——— *Jean Santeuil*, trans. Gerard Hopkins (Harmondsworth: Penguin Books, 1985).

Rabow-Edling, Susanna: *Slavophile Thought and the Politics of Cultural Nationalism* (New York: State University of New York Press, 2006).

Rast, Nicholas: '"Schöne Welt wo bist du?": Motive and Form in Schubert's A Minor String Quartet', in Brian Newbould (ed.), *Schubert the Progressive: History, Performance Practice, Analysis* (Aldershot: Ashgate, 2003), pp. 81–8.

Rathert, Wolfgang: 'Ende, Abschied und Fragment: Zu Ästhetik und Geschichte einer musika-lischen Problemstellung', in Otto Kolleritsch (ed.), *Abschied in die Gegenwart: Teleologie und Zuständlichkeit in der Musik* (Vienna and Graz: Universal Edition, 1998), pp. 211–35.

——— 'Form und Zeit im Streichquartett César Francks', in Joseph Kukkerts (ed.), *Neue Musik und Tradition: Festschrift Rudolf Stephan zum 65. Geburtstag* (Laaber: Laaber, 1990), pp. 311–32.

Redepenning, Dorothea: *Geschichte der russischen und der sowjetischen Musik*, vol. I: *Das 19. Jahrhundert* (Laaber: Laaber-Verlag, 1994).

Reed, John: *Schubert (The Master Musicians)* (Oxford: Oxford University Press, 1997).

Reed, W.H.: *Elgar As I Knew Him* (London: Victor Gollancz, 1936).

Rees, Brian: *Camille Saint-Saëns: A Life* (London: Chatto & Windus, 1999).

Réti, Rudolph: *The Thematic Process in Music* (New York: Macmillan, 1951).

Ricoeur, Paul: *Time and Narrative*, trans. Kathleen Blamey and David Pellauer, 3 vols. (Chicago: University of Chicago Press, 1984–8).

——— *Memory, History, Forgetting*, trans. Kathleen Blamey and David Pellauer (Chicago: Chicago University Press, 2006).

Ridley, Aaron: *Music, Value and the Passions* (Ithaca, NY: Cornell University Press, 1995).
────── Review of Laird Addis, *Of Mind and Music, Mind,* 110 (2001), 423–7.
Riemann, Hugo: *Ludwig van Beethovens sämtliche Klavier-Solosonaten,* 3 vols. (Berlin: Max Hesses Verlag, 1919).
Riley, Matthew: *Edward Elgar and the Nostalgic Imagination* (Cambridge: Cambridge University Press, 2007).
────── 'Heroic melancholy: Elgar's inflected diatonicism', in Julian Rushton and J.P.E. Harper-Scott (eds.), *Elgar Studies* (Cambridge: Cambridge University Press, 2007), pp. 284–307.
────── 'Elgar the Escapist?', in Byron Adams (ed.), *Edward Elgar and His World* (Princeton: Princeton University Press, 2007), pp. 39–57.
Rimsky-Korsakov, Nicolai: *My Musical Life,* trans. J.A. Joffe (New York: Alfred A. Knopf, 1947).
Risi, Clemens: '"Gefühlte Zeit": Zur Performativität von Opernaufführungen', in Christina Lechtermann, Kirsten Wagner and Horst Wenzel (eds.), *Möglichkeitsräume: Zur Performativität von sensorischer Wahrnehmung* (Berlin: Erich Schmidt, 2007), pp. 153–62.
Rodowick, D.N.: *Gilles Deleuze's Time Machine* (Durham, N.C., and London: Duke University Press, 1997).
Ropartz, Guy: 'Le Quatuor en ré majeur de César Franck', *Revue Internationale de Musique* (1 August 1898), 563–70.
Rosen, Charles: *The Classical Style* (London: Faber & Faber, 1971).
────── *The Romantic Generation* (London: HarperCollins, 1996).
────── 'Schubert's inflections of Classical form', in Christopher Gibbs (ed.), *The Cambridge Companion to Schubert* (Cambridge: Cambridge University Press, 1997), pp. 72–98.
────── *Beethoven's Piano Sonatas: A Short Companion* (New Haven: Yale University Press, 2002).
Rothstein, William: 'National metrical types in music of the eighteenth and early nineteenth centuries', in Danuta Mirka and Kofi Agawu (eds.), *Communication in Eighteenth-Century Music* (Cambridge: Cambridge University Press, 2008), pp. 112–59.
Rousseau, Jean-Jacques: *Œuvres complètes de J. J. Rousseau,* ed. Victor-Donatien Musset-Pathay, 22 vols. in 8 parts (Paris: Dupont, 1824).
────── *Reveries of the Solitary Walker,* trans. Peter France (Harmondsworth: Penguin, 1979).
Rowell, Lewis: 'The Subconscious Language of Musical Time', *Music Theory Spectrum,* 1 (1979), 96–106.
────── 'The Study of Time in Music: A Quarter-Century Perspective', *Indiana Theory Review,* 17 (1996), 63–92.
Rumph, Stephen: *Beethoven After Napoleon: Political Romanticism in the Late Works* (Berkeley and Los Angeles: University of California Press, 2004).
Rushton, Julian: *Elgar: 'Enigma' Variations (Cambridge Music Handbooks)* (Cambridge: Cambridge University Press, 1999).
Russell, Bertrand: 'On the Experience of Time', *Monist,* 25 (1915), 212–33.
Sartre, Jean-Paul: *Nausea,* trans. Robert Baldick (Harmondsworth: Penguin, 1965).
────── *Being and Nothingness,* trans. Hazel E. Barnes (London and New York: Routledge, 2003).
Schelling, Friedrich Wilhelm Joseph: *System of Transcendental Idealism* (1800), trans. Peter Heath (Charlottesville, University Press of Virginia, 1978).
────── *Philosophy of Art,* trans. Douglas W. Stott (Minneapolis: University of Minnesota Press, 1989).
────── *Die Weltalter: Fragmente, in den Urfassungen von 1811 und 1813,* ed. Manfred Schröter, *Schellings Werke* (Nachlaßband) (Munich: C.H. Beck, 1946).
Schenker, Heinrich: *Beethoven: Die letzten Sonaten. Kritische Ausgabe mit Einfuhrung und Erlauterung,* ed. Oswald Jonas (Vienna: Universal Edition, 1971–2).
Schiller, Friedrich: *On the Aesthetic Education of Man,* trans. E.M. Wilkinson and L.A. Willoughby (Oxford: Clarendon Press, 1967).
────── *Sämtliche Gedichte und Balladen* (Frankfurt am Main: Insel Verlag, 2004).
Schlegel, Friedrich: *Kritische Friedrich-Schlegel-Ausgabe,* ed. Ernst Behler et al, 35 vols. (Paderborn, Munich, Vienna: Schöningh, 1958–2002).
Schleiermacher, Friedrich: *Ästhetik,* ed. Rudolf Odebrecht (Berlin: de Gruyter, 1931).
Schneider, Herbert: 'Das Streichquartett op. 45 von Vincent d'Indy als Exemplum der zyklischen Sonate', in Annegrit Laubenthal (ed.), *Studien zur Musikgeschichte: Ein Festschrift für Ludwig Finscher* (Kassel: Bärenreiter, 1995), pp. 655–67.

Schoenberg, Arnold: *Style and Idea* (London: Faber & Faber, 1975).

Schopenhauer, Arthur: *The World as Will and Representation*, trans. E.F.J. Payne, 2 vols. (New York: Dover, 1969).

—— *Parerga and Paralipomena*, trans. E.F.J. Payne, 2 vols. (Oxford: Clarendon Press, 1974).

Schubert, Franz: *Dokumente 1817–1830*, vol. 1: *Texte, Programme, Rezensionen, Anzeigen, Nekrologe, Musikbeilagen und andere gedruckte Quellen* (Tutzing: Hans Schneider, 1993).

Schumann, Robert: *Jugendbriefe von Robert Schumann*, ed. Clara Schumann (Leipzig: Breitkopf und Härtel, 1886).

—— *Gesammelte Schriften über Musik und Musiker*, ed. Martin Kreisig, 2 vols. (Leipzig: Breitkopf und Härtel, 1949).

Scruton, Roger: *The Aesthetics of Music* (Oxford: Clarendon Press, 1997).

Seidel, Wilhelm: *Über Rhythmustheorien der Neuzeit (Neue Heidelberger Studien zur Musikwissenschaft)* (Bern: Franke, 1975).

—— 'Descartes' Bemerkungen zur musikalischen Zeit', *Archiv für Musikwissenschaft*, 27 (1975), 288–303.

—— 'Division und Progression: Der Begriff der musikalischen Zeit im 18. Jahrhundert', *Il Saggiatore Musicale*, 2 (1995), 47–65.

Shapiro, Jeremy: 'The Fugue, Meta-time, and the Phenomenology of Internal Time Consciousness', paper presented at the Philosophy and Music Conference 'Time Theories and Music', Ionian University of Corfu, 27 April 2012.

Shelley, Percy Bysshe: *Poetical Works* (London: Oxford University Press, 1970).

Sisman, Elaine: 'Memory and Invention at the Threshold of Beethoven's Late Style', in Scott Burnham and Michael Steinberg (eds.), *Beethoven and his World* (Princeton: Princeton University Press, 2000), pp. 51–87.

Sobaskie, James William: 'Tonal implication and the gestural dialectic in Schubert's A Minor Quartet', in Brian Newbould (ed.), *Schubert the Progressive: History, Performance Practice, Analysis* (Aldershot: Ashgate, 2003), pp. 53–79.

Solomon, Maynard: *Beethoven Essays* (Cambridge, MA: Harvard University Press, 1988).

—— 'Franz Schubert and the Peacocks of Benvenuto Cellini', *19th-Century Music*, 12 (1989), 193–206.

—— *Late Beethoven: Music, Thought, Imagination* (Berkeley and Los Angeles: University of California Press, 2003).

Spitzer, Michael: *Metaphor and Musical Thought* (Chicago: University of Chicago Press, 2004).

—— *Music as Philosophy: Adorno and Beethoven's Late Style* (Bloomington, IN: Indiana University Press, 2006).

Stanley, Glenn: 'Voices and their Rhythms in the First Movement of Beethoven's Piano Sonata Op. 109: Some Thoughts on the Performance and Analysis of a Late-Style Work', in Scott Burnham and Michael Steinberg (eds.), *Beethoven and his World* (Princeton: Princeton University Press, 2000), pp. 88–123.

Steinberg, Michael P.: *Listening to Reason: Culture, Subjectivity, and Nineteenth-Century Music* (Princeton: Princeton University Press, 2004).

Sterne, Laurence: *The Life and Opinions of Tristram Shandy, Gentleman*, 9 vols. (London: R. & J. Dodsley and T. Becket and P. A. Dehondt, 1760–67).

Stockhorst, Stefanie: 'Zur Einführung: Von der Verzeitlichungsthese zur temporalen Diversität', *Das achtzehnte Jahrhundert*, 30 (2006), 157–64.

Stockhorst, Stefanie (ed.), 'Zeitkonzepte: Zur Pluralisierung des Zeitdiskurses im langen 18. Jahrhundert', *Das achtzehnte Jahrhundert*, 30 (2006), 157–252.

Strucken-Paland, Christiane: *Zyklische Prinzipien in den Instrumentalwerken César Francks* (Kassel: Bosse, 2009).

Suchowiejko, Renata: 'Auf der Suche nach dem Ideal: Vincent d'Indys zyklisches Prinzip zwischen Theorie und Praxis', in Manuela Schwartz and Stefan Keym (eds.), *Pluralismus wider Willen? Stilistische Tendenzen in der Musik Vincent d'Indys* (Hildesheim: Olms, 2002), pp. 160–75.

Sutcliffe, W. Dean: *The Keyboard Sonatas of Domenico Scarlatti and Eighteenth-Century Musical Style* (Cambridge: Cambridge University Press, 2004).

—— 'Temporality in Domenico Scarlatti', in Massimiliano Sala and W. Dean Sutcliffe (eds.), *Domenico Scarlatti Adventures: Essays to Commemorate the 250th Anniversary of His Death* (Bologna: Ut Orpheus, 2008), pp. 369–99.

Sulzer, Johann Georg: *Allgemeine Theorie der schönen Künste* (Leipzig: In der Weidmannschen Buchhandlung, 1792).

Tadié, Jean-Yves: 'L'univers musical de Marcel Proust', *Revue de littérature comparée*, 67 (1993), 493–503.

Taruskin, Richard: *Musorgsky: Eight Essays and an Epilogue* (Princeton: Princeton University Press, 1993).

—— *Stravinsky and the Russian Tradition: A Biography of Works Though 'Mavra'*, 2 vols. (Berkeley and Los Angeles: University of California Press, 1996).

—— *Defining Russia Musically: Historical and Hermeneutical Essays* (Princeton: Princeton University Press, 1997).

—— *The Oxford History of Western Music*, 5 vols. (Oxford and New York: Oxford University Press, 2005).

Taub, Robert: *Playing the Beethoven Piano Sonatas* (Portland, OR: Amadeus Press, 2002).

Taylor, Benedict: 'Nostalgia and Cultural Memory in Barber's *Knoxville: Summer of 1915*', *Journal of Musicology*, 25 (2008), 211–29.

—— 'On Time and Eternity in Messiaen', chapter in Judith Crispin (ed.), *Messiaen: The Centenary Papers* (Cambridge: Cambridge Scholars, 2010), pp. 222–43.

—— *Mendelssohn, Time and Memory: The Romantic Conception of Cyclic Form* (Cambridge: Cambridge University Press, 2011).

—— 'Sullivan, Scott, and *Ivanhoe*: Constructing Historical Time and National Identity in Victorian Opera', *Nineteenth-Century Music Review*, 9 (2012), 295–321.

—— 'The Triumph of Time in the Eighteenth Century: Handel's *Il trionfo del Tempo* and historical conceptions of musical temporality', *Eighteenth-Century Music*, 11 (2014), 257–81.

Tennyson, Alfred, Lord: *Poems and Plays* (London: Oxford University Press, 1968).

Thomson, Aidan: 'Unmaking the Music Makers', in Julian Rushton and J.P.E. Harper-Scott (eds.), *Elgar Studies* (Cambridge: Cambridge University Press, 2007), pp. 99–134.

Thomson, Andrew: *Vincent D'Indy and his World* (Oxford: Clarendon Press, 1996).

Tolstoy, Leo: *War and Peace*, trans. Louise and Aylmer Maude (London: Macmillan & Co., 1959).

Tovey, Donald Francis: *A Companion to Beethoven's Pianoforte Sonatas* (London: The Associated Board of the Royal Schools of Music, 1931).

—— *Essays in Musical Analysis*, 6 vols. (London: Oxford University Press, 1935–9).

—— 'Franz Schubert', in *Essays and Lectures on Music*, ed. Hubert Foss (London: Oxford University Press, 1949), pp. 103–33.

Trowell, Brian: 'Elgar's Use of Literature', in Raymond Monk (ed.), *Edward Elgar: Music and Literature* (Aldershot: Scolar Press, 1993), pp. 182–326.

Varwig, Bettina: 'Metaphors of Time and Modernity in Bach', *Journal of Musicology*, 29 (2012), 154–90.

Wackenroder, Wilhelm Heinrich: *Sämtliche Werke und Briefe: Historisch-kritische Ausgabe*, ed. Silvio Vietta and Richard Littlejohns, 2 vols. (Heidelberg: Carl Winter, 1991).

Waidelich, Till Gerrit (ed.): *Rosamunde, Drama in fünf Akten von Helmina von Chézy. Musik von Franz Schubert. Erstveröffentlichung der überarbeiteten Fassung. Mit einem Nachwort und unbekannten Quellen* (Tutzing: Hans Schneider, 1996).

Waidelich, Till Gerrit: 'Ein fragmentarischer autographer Entwurf zur Erstfassung von Chézys Schauspiel "Rosamunde"', in *Schubert durch die Brille: Internationales Franz Schubert Institut, Mitteilungen* 18 (Tutzing: Hans Schneider, 1997), 46–57.

Wald, Melanie: 'Moment Musical: Die wahrnehmbarkeit der Zeit durch Musik', *Das achtzehnte Jahrhundert*, 30 (2006), 207–20.

Wegener, Bernd: 'César Francks Harmonik dargestellt am Streichquartett D-Dur', *Revue Belge de Musicologie*, 45 (1991), 109–26.

Weinrich, Harald: *Tempus: Besprochene und erzählte Zeit* (Stuttgart: Kohlhammer, 1964).

Wendorff, Rudolf: *Zeit und Kultur: Geschichte des Zeitbewußtseins in Europa* (Opladen: Westdeutscher Verlag, 1983).

Westrup, J.A.: *Schubert Chamber Music (BBC Music Guides)* (London: BBC, 1969).

Whitman, Walt: *Poetry and Prose* (New York: Library of America, 1996).

Whitrow, G.J.: *The Natural Philosophy of Time* (Oxford: Clarendon Press, 1980).

—— *Time in History: Views of Time from Prehistory to the Present Day* (Oxford: Oxford University Press, 1988).

Will, Richard: 'Time, Morality, and Humanity in Beethoven's *Pastoral* Symphony', *Journal of the American Musicological Society*, 50 (1997), 271–329.

Wilton, Andrew and Barringer, Tim: *American Sublime, Landscape Painting in the United States 1820–1880* (Princeton: Princeton University Press, 2002).

Wintle, Christopher: 'Corelli's Tonal Models: The Trio Sonata op. 3, no. 1', in Sergio Durante and Pierluigi Petrobelli (eds.), *Nuovissimi Studi Corelliani: Atti del Terzo Congresso Internazionale Fusignano, 1980* (Florence: Olschki, 1982), 29–69.

Wiora, Walter: 'Musik als Zeitkunst', *Die Musikforschung*, 10 (1957), 15–28.

Wittgenstein, Ludwig: *Werkausgabe*, 8 vols. (Frankfurt: Suhrkamp, 2006).

Wollenberg, Susan: *Schubert's Fingerprints: Studies in the Instrumental Works* (Aldershot: Ashgate, 2011).

Woolf, Virginia: *To the Lighthouse* (Oxford: Oxford University Press, 2008).

—— *Between the Acts* (Oxford: Oxford University Press, 2008).

Wordsworth, William: *The Poetical Works*, ed. Ernest De Selincourt and Helen Darbishire, 5 vols. (Oxford: Clarendon Press, 1940–49).

Xenakis, Iannis: 'Concerning Time', *Perspectives of New Music*, 27 (1989), 84–92.

Yeats, William Butler: *Collected Poems* (London: Macmillan, 1990).

Yoshikawa, Kazuyoshi: 'Vinteuil ou la genèse du septuor', *Études proustiennes III* (Paris: Gallimard, 1979), 289–347.

Young, Percy M.: *Elgar O.M.: A Study of a Musician* (London: Collins, 1955).

—— Sleeve notes to Elgar, *The Music Makers*, LPO, Janet Baker/Sir Adrian Boult, HMV ALP 2311, 1967.

Zajaczkowski, Henry: *Tchaikovsky's Musical Style* (Ann Arbor: UMI Research Press, 1987).

Zbikowski, Lawrence M.: 'Music, language, and kinds of consciousness', in David Clarke and Eric Clarke (eds.), *Music and Consciousness: Philosophical, Psychological, and Cultural Perspectives* (Oxford: Oxford University Press, 2011), pp. 179–192.

Zuckerkandl, Victor: *Sound and Symbol: Music and the External World*, trans. Willard R. Trask (London: Routledge & Kegan Paul, 1956).

—— *Man the Musician* (*Sound and Symbol*, vol. II) (Princeton: Princeton University Press, 1973).

INDEX